Towards an Era of Development
The Globalization of Socialism and Christian Democracy
1945-1965

Cover: In this Dutch cartoon, the American and Soviet Ministers of Foreign Affairs J.F. Dulles and A.A. Gromyko are trembling with fear while they are watching the so-called Third World marching into the political arena of the United Nations.
[Fritz Behrendt in *Algemeen Handelsblad*, 20/08/1958; Amsterdam, IISG]

KADOC Studies on Religion, Culture and Society 5

Towards an Era of Development

The Globalization of Socialism and Christian Democracy

Peter Van Kemseke

1945-1965

Leuven University Press
2006

© 2006
Leuven University Press/Presses Universitaires de Louvain/Universitaire Pers Leuven
Blijde-Inkomststraat 5, B-3000 Leuven (Belgium)

ISBN 90 5867 560 2
ISBN 978 90 5867 560 6
D/2006/1869/54
NUR 697

Contents

Contents

Introduction
From Cold War to Third World

In the year 2000, at the brink of the new millennium, 189 Heads of State and Government from the North and South committed themselves to a set of eight development targets: the so-called Millennium Development Goals. If achieved, they will end extreme poverty and underdevelopment by 2015. As such, they reflect a globally shared and endorsed set of priorities, which in itself is an unprecedented achievement. Strategies to tackle the global challenge of poverty and underdevelopment, however, are nothing new. Before the Second World War - in the colonial period - ideas and theories about 'the underdeveloped' or 'backward regions' were already widespread. The attention they were given, however, grew spectacularly after the war. In the late 1940s and early 1950s, 'development theory' even became a specific academic discipline in its own right. These were the years in which global politics were indeed moving into an 'era of development'.

The growing attention to developing regions after 1945 and subsequent theories about them did not emerge outside the then geopolitically and ideologically polarized international system, which clearly helped shape them. The international context of the Cold War initially prevented the Western world from 'discovering' the Third World as a topic on its own, as a topic which could not only be reduced to the Cold War. Only when the division between East and West became somewhat less important - very gradually from the early 60s onwards - the North-South divide became clearly visible. In other words, the North-South topic was then able to set itself free from the dominant, blinding East-West issues. It is from that moment onwards that an authentic view on development, and a real development policy became possible.

This evolution occurred at several levels. It became visible in the United Nations, an organization that had an unparalleled role in development issues due to its universal membership, as this book will show. It slowly became visible in the policy of developed countries as well, which one by one started to develop their own development policies, frequently inspired by discussions that had taken place at the UN. In the same period, at the non-governmental level, a 'Third World movement' started to take shape.

The distinction between these three levels - international, national and non-governmental - is not always clear-cut. In reality, these levels are intertwined. In that process, a crucial role is played by a very specific category of actors, which so far has received relatively little attention: the large transnational political organizations such as the Socialist International, the Christian Democratic International and the Liberal International. Transnational topics - particularly transnational relations between political parties - are only marginally discussed in the literature, although fortunately there seems to be a growing interest now.

Transnational political organizations occupy a special place in the international system: their reactions to world politics can be swift and flexible, quite unlike those of some intergovernmental organizations. This characteristic makes them breeding grounds of ideas, which trickle down to their members, national political parties. In this way they can influence national politics. The growing attention to the Third World in Belgian socialism after the war, for example, can not be properly understood without taking into account the debates in the Socialist International, which became an important source of inspiration. The explicitly pro-European vision of the Austrian ÖVP in the 50s and 60s - in a neutral state - can partially be explained by its long lasting membership of the Nouvelles Équipes Internationales, a pro-European Christian Democratic 'think tank' and the predecessor of the Christian Democratic International. Thus, well-functioning 'Internationals', where national party programs confront each other, brought about an 'upgrading' of individual parties' viewpoints and policies. When the Socialist International was founded, 'modern' Scandinavian socialists explicitly stated this aim. They regarded the International as a means of modernizing the more traditional Belgian, French, and Greek socialist parties. The British Labour Party gladly took advantage of the Socialist International to make the European socialist parties accept the Marshall Plan. And the Nouvelles Équipes Internationales were, as already mentioned, a handy medium to spread the idea of a united Europe. So, by what Rosenau in 1969 called a 'penetrative process', transnational organizations could influence not only the attitude of their members, but also their frame of reference, in particular in the field of foreign policy.

Transnational political organizations occupy a special place in the international system for yet another reason. Unlike 'traditional NGOs' Internationals usually have access to international fora where the decision making processes actually take place. This creates the possibility, which traditional NGOs have to a much lesser degree, to influence international politics. The postwar Socialist International and the Nouvelles Équipes Internationales had access to the highest diplomatic circles: the Socialist International through the British Labour Party, which controlled the Foreign Office from 1945 until 1951, and the Christian Democrats through the French Christian Democratic MRP, which occupied the Quai d'Orsay from 1944 until 1954. Thanks to these contacts they were able to infiltrate into the diplomatic world They practiced a sort of semi-diplomacy.

This book will show that transnational political organizations can be an element of international transformation if they organize themselves at the right level. A good illustration of this is the history of European integration: the more the political arena shifted to the European level, the more political parties were drawn to organize themselves on that level: the European People's Party, the Party of European Socialists, and the European Liberal, Democratic and Reform Party resulted. 'Party diplomacy' gradually became an important phenomenon, and an essential factor in the decision making process. Scientific research on this 'Europeanising' of national political parties has since become a separate discipline. And so, Sigmund Neumans' 1956 statement can only be confirmed: "when the frontiers between domestic and international affairs are blurred - political parties have become international forces that must be studied".

The global level is now increasingly comparable to the European one: there is a growing tendency to have foreign (global) policy influence internal policy and vice-versa. This global dimension in politics, with its specific challenges, needs specific global strategies and ideas. The present Internationals, with their extensive web of contacts, are well placed and are used to tackle global issues. The 22nd Congress of the Socialist International, in October 2003 in Sao Paolo, was entitled "The Return of Politics: For just and responsible global governance". The 49th Congress of the Liberal International, which took place in Brussels in March 1999, set as its central theme "Globalization and the Future of the Nation-State". The final resolution underlined that "the process of economic and commercial globalization must however be accompanied by a parallel development of political democratization". Globalization and the related issue of development was also an important subject for discussion in the Christian Democratic International. Their 13th Congress, in October 2000 in Santiago de Chile, adopted a declaration of principles, which primarily dealt with the possibilities and limitations of globalization.

Scope of the Book

The current global orientation of the Internationals only emerged after a long history, and its development often only advanced with great difficulty. This book describes how two leading ideologies, social democracy and Christian Democracy - both originally Western-European - step by step left their home bases and discovered a world outside Europe, an expedition which mainly took place in the two decades after the Second World War. It all started soon after the war, when the Socialist International (SI) and their Christian Democratic counterpart the Nouvelles Equipes Internationales (NEI) were (re-)established. The NEI made their entrance into the international system in 1947 - and kept afloat until 1965, when an enduring crisis provoked a transformation and a change of name. Four years after the NEI were established, the social democratic parties revived the Socialist International, in 1951.

The choice for these two organizations in this study is self-evident. After the war, socialists and Christian Democrats were shaping the political landscape in many areas of Europe, and even outside the continent. A number of parties - the French Christian Democrats, the British Socialists - held their country's foreign offices. It was inevitable, but not obvious, that national political parties would meet each other outside their own borders. The development of those transnational contacts and structures between 1945 and 1951 will be discussed in the first part of this book.

In the next decade, the 1950s, both organizations left their European home base, each one at its own pace. That phase of globalization is the main issue of the second part of this book. Towards 1965, both political families had built bases on which their current global commitments are founded.

In the 1960s, and as a result of this expansion process, both ideologies became susceptible to the new global issues, in particular to the development issue. The globalization process of the 1950s implied, in other words, a closer contact with the world outside Europe, the underdeveloped world, which would soon be known as the 'Third World'. These contacts, and the impact on the ideological content of both social democracy and Christian Democracy is elaborated in the third and last part of this book.

The Socialist International and the Nouvelles Équipes Internationales will be consistently compared with one another in each stage of their development: their establishment, their globalization process and their discovery (or lack thereof) of the Third World. This book, an adaptation of a PhD-thesis defended at the University of Leuven (Belgium), rests on a considerable body of academic work. It is based on thorough research in the records, mainly from the archives of the Socialist International, which are stored in the Internationaal Instituut voor Sociale Geschiedenis (IISG) in Amsterdam, the Archiv für Christlich-Demokratische Politik of the Konrad Adenauer Stiftung (ACDP-KAS) in Sankt-Augustin, near Bonn, which houses the complete NEI archives, and those of their successor, the Union Européenne des Démocrates Chrétiens (UEDC). Part of those archives were also studied at the Katholiek Documentatie- en Onderzoekscentrum (KADOC) in Louvain. The 'August de Schryver'-section is especially important here as he chaired the NEI for almost the whole period covered by this book. The archives of the British Labour Party (BLP) in Manchester, and the French Mouvement Républicain Populaire (MRP) in Paris were also consulted. The archives of the MRP are the property of the Fondation Nationale des Sciences Politiques and are located in the Archives Nationales in Paris.

I would like to express my gratitude to the helpful staff members of these institutions, without whom this book would not have been written and published. The support and help of the translator, the proofreaders and the staff of the KADOC was also greatly appreciated. Special thanks go to Professor Emiel Lamberts, who has supported this project from its very conception until its final result. His expert guidance and inexhaustable patience have been very rewarding.

I
Social Democracy
and Christian Democracy
on the Eve of their Global
Expansion, 1945-1950

Social Democratic and Christian Democratic Transnationalism
A True Reflection of National Politics

Made in London: the Postwar Socialist International

There have been few other political ideologies in history which have more convincingly exhibited the internationalist character of their mission than socialism. After the First International (1864-1876) and the Second International (1889-1914), the Socialist Labour International (SLI) was established, not without difficulty, in 1923, in an attempt to carry on the illustrious 19th century tradition of Socialist Internationals.[1] However, the SLI was never to be a great success. Already by the early 1930's, the organization was leading a rather paltry existence.[2] In May 1940, when the Germans invaded Belgium and shortly thereafter plundered the Secretariat of the SLI in Brussels, all SLI activity came to a halt.

Fleeing the violence of the war, many socialists took refuge in Sweden, Switzerland and the US. Some even went so far as Mexico and Argentina. Yet, Great Britain was the chief meeting place for the exiled European social democrats. London became the pre-eminent center of social democracy. The British Labour Party (BLP) - the sole wartime socialist party able to function reasonably well and which, as a ruling party, enjoyed much prestige - became the natural leader of all social democratic activity during the war. This British dominance was an important political fact to those European socialists who in their place of exile looked to maintain cooperation between the various socialist parties, and even to the establishment of a new, postwar International.

---

1   Braunthal, *Geschichte der Internationale*; Knopp, *Die Sozialistische Internationale*.
2   Collette, *The International Faith*.

The European socialists were at the mercy of the concessions and limitations which the BLP conceded them or imposed upon them. In other words, it was the BLP and no other party which determined the rhythm of postwar transnational cooperation. This was nothing new. It was simply the continuation of a policy of consolidating power within the SLI, which the BLP had been systematically pursuing ever since 1933, the year in which National Socialism was to silence German socialism in the Reich. The war situation substantially strengthened the powerful position of the British. Thus, the party did not allow for the slightest doubt that the foundation of a "new" postwar International - an objective advanced principally by French and Belgian socialists - would only occur on its terms.

These terms were a perfect mirror image of the internal political constellation within which the British Labour Party found itself at the end of the Second World War. After the historic electoral victory in July 1945, the British socialists were seated in government.[3] The party leadership saw a double challenge here. Firstly, they had to demonstrate that the BLP was actually able to cope with the responsibilities of governing which had been entrusted to it. Secondly, but closely related, it was important for the party to throw off its radical prewar image and to mature into a very broadly based popular party. This automatically precluded any form of cooperation with the British communists, who rejected reformism and parliamentarianism. This was the intent of clause 3 of the BLP's statutes, which stipulated that party members had to strictly avoid "identifying themselves with, or promoting the interests of, any other political party".[4] This same drive towards a moderate and trustworthy image had as a consequence, however, that the BLP also became distrustful of having close ties with certain European socialist parties. The party leadership, as represented by international secretary Denis Healey, interpreted the Marxist, radical, and utopian rhetoric of some "Latin" parties as especially unproductive for parties that bore the weight of government.[5] The socialist parties from southern Europe - France, Italy and Spain - had a different ideological accent than the social democratic or workers' parties from Great Britain and Scandinavia, which due to their close ties with labour unions often had a much more pragmatic approach. In addition, it should also be mentioned that in the years immediately following the Second World War, some of the European parties, in contrast with the British, were indeed in favour of cooperation with the communists. In Great Britain such cooperation

3   Sassoon, *One Hundred Years*, 121-123.
4   Collette, *The International Faith*, 59.
5   Healey, "The International Socialist Conference", 366.

would have been impossible for the BLP, which had to face the fierce opposition of Churchill's fervently anti-communist Conservative Party.

It was owing to the continual delay tactics on the part of the British and Scandinavian socialists that the chiefly Franco-Belgian demand to reinstitute the Socialist International was only realized in 1951, six years after the end of the war. From the discussions that preceded the reinstitution, it appears that the Franco-Belgian standpoint was just as based on national interests as was that of the British.[6] Of course, other factors were also at play, such as the realization that if the socialists did not organize themselves they would be left behind by capitalism ("that imperialism of the Americans"), communism, and Catholicism ("the Vatican, yet another powerful and questionable international force") which at that moment were all organizing themselves internationally. Factors of an emotional nature also played a role. For example, there was a nostalgic longing for the tradition of socialist cooperation within which the Belgians and Austrians, among others, had always played a prominent role.

All the same, this did not diminish the importance of the constellation of national interests within which the French and the Belgian parties functioned. Unlike the Labour Party, which after the Second World War had no competition on the left of the political spectrum, the French and Belgian socialist parties indeed wrestled with strong communist parties which were aimed at precisely the same electorate. So as to prevent a large-scale defection of workers to the Communist Party, radical, internationalist discourse and radical, internationalist symbols were used. The Socialist International was probably one of the most powerful symbols that supported the claim and identity of the socialist party as the authentic workers' party. It was not in the least coincidental that declarations of love for "international socialism" were a matter of course precisely at those moments when this authenticity was put in question.

This was the case when the Belgian SP and the French SFIO, for example, decided to form their respective governments together with center-right parties, a decision which left them both vulnerable to communist criticism. In March 1947, when the future Belgian prime minister P.H. Spaak worked out a coalition agreement with the Christian Democratic CVP-PSC, he was well aware of the risk of setting sail with a conservative party while the communists would be able to offer radical opposition. He stated: "it is up to us to

---

6   As quoted by the Belgian Larock, in International Socialist Conference, Zürich, 06-09/06/1947. Minutes. IISG, SI 235.

enlighten the working classes." This was expressed in a radicalization of the discourse. It was no coincidence that on the day that the new government was announced the socialist newspaper *Le Peuple* declared: "We are, and will always be an anticlerical party, an international party and a party of social liberation, all in the most specific and radical sense."[7]

From May 1947 onwards, the French SFIO was also "condemned" to coalition governments with the Christian Democratic Mouvement Républicain Populaire (MRP) - which was to shift ever more to the right - and with smaller center-right parties. SFIO chairman Guy Mollet was an advocate of keeping to the orthodox Marxist line within the party (including the class struggle) in order to be able to "outrun" the French Communist Party "on the left". Despite the internationalist creeds which both the French and Belgians professed, they both used the International to pursue national interests.

Eventually, the Anglo-Scandinavian thesis won the day, a logical consequence of the power relationships within transnational socialism at that moment. The result was a rather loose transnational organization which left intact the autonomy of its constituent parties. Arriving at unanimity became a mandatory condition for political or politically loaded themes, and no party could be required to publish all the resolutions of the International. The secretary of the SI, the Austrian socialist Julius Braunthal, received a purely administrative position with no real political power. The proposal that party leaders or members of government had to regularly attend the meetings of the new International was rejected because resolutions endorsed by prominent party members or ministers had a more "binding" character than resolutions that were signed only by the party's international secretary.

The advocates of an energetic and efficient International were ultimately able to resign themselves to this. When in December 1950 the Belgian Larock called for the reinstitution of the International in an open letter, he took pains to ensure that his appeal was very pragmatically formulated.[8] He did not want to touch upon the concrete, "functionalist" working method, for example, without adopting resolutions that could cause embarrassment to any member party. He was realistic enough to realize that each attempt to make majority decisions binding would be seen as an unacceptable assault on the autonomy of the parties: "socialist parties which carry governmental respon-

7   Spaak, quoted in *La Libre Belgique*, 18/03/1947; *Le Peuple*, 20/03/1947; Wall, *French Communism in the Era of Stalin*.
8   *Le Peuple*, 20/12/1950.

sibilities in a complex and difficult situation, and are accountable to their electorates, [cannot] be bound by directives from outside." Larock's proposal was simple, and it strikingly illustrated the symbolic importance of the SI: the relatively non-binding meetings, which up till then took place in a framework called Committee of the International Socialist Conference (COMISCO) would from 1951 onwards take place in a framework that could be called "the International". The BLP had no objection to this. During the next general congress, at the end of June and the beginning of July 1951, in the German city of Frankfurt, the reinstitution of the International was officially and unanimously approved. Seven years after the liberation there was once again a Socialist International, although be it cut of the cloth of national interests.

Made in Europe: the Christian Democratic Nouvelles Équipes Internationales

S imilarly to the socialists, after the war the Christian Democrats also began to set up their network of transnational cooperation. In this regard, they kept a sharp eye on their socialist political rivals. It was no coincidence that the first postwar conference of European Christian Democratic parties took place in the Swiss city of Lucerne, a few weeks after the socialists had announced that their 1947 conference would be held in nearby Zurich. The fact that the Swiss Conservative People's Party (KVPZ) wanted to cover the costs of all the invitees demonstrates the amount of importance certain circles placed in the Lucerne Conference. It was important, therefore, that the convention strengthen the position of the KVPZ within Switzerland. In a country where, after World War II, the religio-political fault lines were once again clearly in the foreground, and which had as a result a predominantly bipolar political system, anti-socialism quickly became a natural element of being right-wing.[9] This was all the more so in those times of the leftist euphoria which followed the defeat of the (extreme-)right. Franz Lust, editor of Vaterland, grasped the uncertainty of many Swiss political Catholics perfectly when he wrote: "Due to Its aggressive move to the left, the future of European politics looks nothing but dim."[10]

9   Bouquet, Histoire de la Suisse; Favez, ed. Nouvelle histoire de la Suisse; Helbling et al., Handbuch der Schweizer Geschichte.
10   Vaterland, 31/10/1945.

The anti-socialism of right-wing politicians was expressed most sharply in party chairman Escher's opening address to the Lucerne conference:"We are of the opinion that our leading position entitled us to invite you all, since the leftist parties are already organizing international conferences in Switzerland and they are planning to do even more so in the future," a clear reference to the approaching socialist conference in Zurich.[11] Careful arrangements were also made to ensure that the (Catholic) newspapers provided sufficient publicity for the convention.[12]

The competition from the socialists was an important motivating factor behind the decision which the European Christian Democrats took in Lucerne to form their own transnational league of cooperation, called the Nouvelles Équipes Internationales (NEI). The debate which preceded the foundation of the NEI revealed that not all European Christian Democrats were following the Swiss line. In particular, the powerful French and Belgian Christian Democrats marched to a different beat. Just as the British and Scandinavian workers' parties had pushed to the fore their preference for a minimalist transnationalism which could function as a sort of common denominator, the most reluctant elements in Lucerne were also able to leave a deep imprint upon the form of the new organization. The advocates of a strong Christian Democratic "International", composed of Christian Democratic *parties* which both in their own countries as well as on the international level would strive for a conformity of position regarding specific problems - namely the Italians, Swiss, and Austrians - ultimately had to surrender. Instead of opting for an inter-party organization, the Christian Democrats in Lucerne chose for a loose *movement* of *groups* which could represent and propagate Christian thinking.[13] A national équipe (or group) could fall in with a party, but it would be under no obligation to do so. At any rate, the French MRP and the Belgian CVP-PSC did not join the NEI as parties, although many party members participated in the activities of their national 'équipes'. The CVP-PSC would remain unaffiliated until November 1959, and the MRP until as late as May 1964, a point in time at which the party had already de facto ceased to exist.

There is a twofold explanation for the Franco-Belgian reserve. A first explanation is that the Christian Democrats were equally as prone to let the national

11   Procès-verbal de la Conférence politique internationale de Lucerne, Berne. 27/02-02/03/1947, 2. KADOC, ADS 7.2.1. 'Our leading position' referred to the fact that after the 1943 elections the KVPZ had become the most powerful group in the important Vereinigte Bundesversammlung.
12   Ibidem.
13   Ibidem, 40-42.

political constellation determine the formation of a transnational organiza-
tion, as had already been seen in the attitudes of the Swiss KVPZ. The "modern"
Christian Democratic, non-confessional people's parties like the MRP and the
CVP-PSC - although the MRP would not immediately apply that label to the
CVP-PSC - obstinately opposed too closely affiliating with parties that had
an all too clear and, in their eyes, obsolete confessional profile. For example,
Désiré Lamalle, the secretary-general of the CVP-PSC, in his speech in Lucerne,
frequently stressed the non-confessional character of his party. Not the
Catholic Church, but rather "Christian civilization" lay at the base of CVP-PSC's
program. Lamalle distanced himself explicitly from the prewar Catholic Party
in Belgium: "the burning flame of the Catholic party went out a long time
ago."[14]

Just as the modern, reformist British and Scandinavian workers' parties feared
entanglements by having too close ties with European parties which, in their
eyes, were pursuing a backward orthodox Marxist discourse, so too the MRP
and the CVP-PSC feared, among other things, too far-reaching an association with confessional Catholic parties. The form and even the somewhat
meaningless name Nouvelles Équipes Internationales, which contained absolutely no reference to the Christian character of the movement, reflected the
dominance of the Mouvement Républicain Populaire in the first years after
the Second World War. The MRP, which had itself also removed any Christian
reference from its name, hoped in this way to avoid any association with a
"confessional International". The "right" had compromised itself in France with
"Vichy" and no longer played any meaningful political role; and the Church
hierarchy too had fallen into discredit, all of which contributed to the struggle
for a pronouncedly non-confessional arrangement within the party.

A confessional collaboration would also be diametrically at odds with the
image of the party, which clearly bore the marks of the radical-progressive
environment from which it had sprung, shortly after the liberation. The party's
slogan - "Revolution through the Law" - was in tune with the Zeitgeist and
with the attitudes then current among the electorate. MRP members André
Noël and Albert Gortais expressed it most clearly: "We cannot express our
solidarity with right-wing Christian Democratic parties, we do not agree with
their politics; it would imply losing the support of certain social classes."[15]
It would above all have laid a heavy burden on the governing coalitions in
which the MRP was involved from the liberation until 1947: coalitions with

14   Ibidem.
15   Réunion de la Commission Exécutive, 17/02/1949. AN, Archives du MRP 350 AP 71.

socialists and communists moulded "in the image of the resistance".[16] The French representative at the Lucerne conference in February 1947, for that matter, had cited this alliance as an argument to justify the reserve of his party. He suggested that the MRP considered it fundamentally, almost morally, unwarranted to break solidarity with the other parties of the resistance - the socialists and communists that sat together with the MRP in the government: "The fraternity that was born during the resistance may not be broken up".[17]

Yet, the national political context offers only a partial explanation. As the center of gravity in French politics was shifting more and more towards the right at the end of the 1940's, the party too gradually adapted its position in that direction, certainly under the pressure of De Gaulle's RPF (founded in April 1947), which exercised a great power of attraction over the members of the MRP and their electorate. Consequently, the gap between the MRP and like-minded European parties on the ideological level was continually shrinking. Nevertheless, the MRP intentionally remained on the sidelines of the NEI, just like the CVP-PSC. So a second explanatory factor is necessary, one which could be referred to as "hereditary material". To both the MRP and to its electorate the NEI held no symbolic or emotional value, nor did it offer them any additional sense of identity. For the socialists it was quite another story. The International was, despite how undermined or backward the concept might have been in practice, still laden with tradition. Internationalism, as it were, constituted part of the socialist genetic code and for a specific segment of the population it had a mobilizing and propagandistic value. Moreover, the International was the authority which could issue the "socialist" or "social democratic" label. It was a label of quality that in moments of need could be displayed to the rank and file.

The French MRP lacked such a tradition or symbolism. Their symbols - Marc Sangier, the resistance - all had a national character. Unlike the Swiss and the Austrians, the French did not attribute any identity generating role to the NEI. At no single moment could there be said to have been a correlation between the NEI and the identity and individuality of the MRP. Rather than an element of identity, the NEI was an *instrument*. The movement was seen as one of the (many) movements that had as a goal the promotion of European integration. The MRP judged this European lobby group with instrumental criteria

16   Callot, *Le Mouvement Républicain Populaire*, 253.
17   Procès-verbal de la conférence politique internationale de Lucerne, 27/02-02/03/1947. KADOC, ADS 7.2.1.

(its efficiency) rather than with emotional criteria (such as its propagandistic value for the party's base and the electorate). For this reason the members of the MRP were equally able to realize their European engagement outside of the NEI. Some joined the Socialist Mouvement for the United States of Europe.[18] Others, such as Teitgen, Coste-Floret, and de Menthon, joined the French Council for a United Europe.[19] Still others were to be found in the French Federalist Mouvement 'La Fédération'.[20] Since the party permitted its members free reign in this less "essential" field, it could of course not join the NEI, despite the fact that the Nouvelles Équipes Internationales were perhaps the natural habitat for many members of the MRP. As a consequence, the NEI, as the largest common denominator, could not be an inter-party organization.

The Legacy of Different Traditions: Continuity and Discontinuity in Transnational Cooperation

The explanation for the difference between the socialist and Christian Democratic transnational design provides yet another interesting point of distinction. While the socialists during the establishment of their International more than once referred to the First Socialist International or, to a lesser extent, to the Socialist Labour International, the Christian Democrats did not place their initiative within a larger tradition. Their tradition was in any case somewhat more limited. The first Christian Democratic transnational organization, the International Secretariat of Democratic Parties of Christian Inspiration (Secrétariat International des Partis Démocrates d'Inspiration Chrétienne, SIPDIC), which was founded in 1925, died ingloriously in the early 1930's as a result of, among other things, the collapse of the Franco-German political rapprochement. Nor did the International Christian Democratic Union (ICDU), the cooperation of Christian Democratic exiles wishing to further the work of SIPDIC in London, lead automatically to the foundation of a new postwar transnational organization. While the postwar alliance of European socialists was able to build upon the contacts that were maintained and institutionalized during the war - the re-establishment of the Socialist International was, as it were, a gradual process led and controlled

18 Réunion de la Commission Exécutive, 17/02/1949. AN, Archives du MRP 350 AP 71.
19 Notes sur les Mouvements pour l'Union Européenne. Rapport confidentiel. AN, Archives du MRP 350 AP 71.
20 Le Dohr, *Les démocrates-chrétiens français face à la construction européenne*, 187.

by the British socialists - the Christian Democratic exiles that had settled in London could not go knocking on the door of a well-structured party of intellectual allies. Their points of reference, the German Center Party and the French PDP, had both gone under during the war in the tidal wave of Nazism. Thus the ICDU - in reality not more than a "tea-party" of convinced, somewhat idealistic Christian Democrats - also failed to offer much.

If there was reference made to the SIPDIC or the ICDU after the war in Lucerne or at later conferences, then that was above all in order to point out a number of fundamental differences. The NEI had to be something new and not a rein-stitution of the ICDU, which, especially under the impulse of the Dutch profes-sor J. A. Veraart, was meant to be an embryonic "Catholic International". Veraart explicitly stated: "We want to prepare the work after the victory. We want to help to reconstitute a democratic order throughout Europe, but we want the voice of Catholics to be heard everywhere. We hail in friendship all men of good will, but we want especially the important group of Catholics to come forward in the new order, not only on the defensive, as so often in the past, but above all on the offensive." In other words, the ICDU was to prepare the way for the reinstitution of the post-liberation Catholic confessional parties.

Moreover, the center of gravity of the postwar Christian Democratic parties did not lie so much amidst the exiles, but rather with the politicians who had sat in the resistance or who had gone underground in their own countries. From this quarter, and not from London, came the dynamism that would lead to the institution of the Nouvelles Équipes Internationales after the war. Precisely because of this organizational discontinuity those who took the initiative to build up the NEI, for lack of an international precursor, fell back upon a conceptual framework in which the specific national contexts took a central place. For the socialists, on the other hand, an inter-party structure was, as it were, "implanted" beforehand and this was handed down by the BLP, thus ensuring organizational continuity. However, it would be misleading to exaggerate the differences in inherited tradition so much so as to confirm the persistent cliché that socialism in the interbellum and in the postwar period was more "international" in its essence than Christian Democracy. The German historian Alwin Hanschmidt put forward as the essential distinction between both ideologies in the interbellum that the Christian Democrats in contrast with the socialists "considered their autonomy highly important, and as a result always refused a centralized supranational leadership". This cliché is also to be found in Andreas Khol: "International cooperation between Christian Democratic parties (…) has been rather unusual until far into the second half of the 20th century." Khol further added that in the communist and socialist parties, one was certainly accustomed to such transnational cooperation, contrary to the "patriotic-nationalistic spirited" and "very provincial" Christian Democratic parties.[21]

It goes without saying that there was little space on the Christian Democratic flank for any internationalism during the interbellum. Such a weak internationalism, or even anti-internationalism, had a long history. Patrick Pasture describes the origin of the Christian workers' movement principally as a reaction against socialism, and against its internationalism, among other things. This anti-internationalism was not only a typical characteristic of the workers' movement, but also of Christian Democracy as a whole. It ultimately went back to the ancient entanglement of religion and the nation-state, as Pasture stated: "This anti-internationalism stems from an age-old association in Europe between religion and nation-states, which is partly rooted in the Christian world view itself. In the 19th century the European churches, Catholic as well as (even more) Protestant, associated themselves with national movements; often nationalism offered the churches a way to restore the privileged links with the state which they had lost in the aftermath of the French Revolution or even earlier during the Reformation (...) Christians considered the national state - and occasionally the 'region' as well - as an important focus of identification and a source of personal education, the main reason why they rejected internationalism as such."[22]

However, it has already been mentioned above that the safeguarding of the autonomy of the parties and the loyalty to the nation-state also played a dominant role in the SLI, despite rhetorical and undoubtedly often sincere declarations that must have suggested the contrary, or despite the achieved ambitions of a number of individual socialists. That was certainly the case for the parties which already bore the responsibility of government, such as the British Labour Party. In years when tensions were relatively low, internationalism flourished, perhaps more among socialists, who had a certain tradition in it, than among Catholics or Christian Democrats, for whom cross-border cooperation was relatively new and whose transnational cooperation seemed more dependent on Franco-German relations. In the 1930's, however, with growing authoritarianism and the increasing threat of war, the SLI was paralyzed by precisely those same problems which the SIPDIC had had to

---

21   Hanschmidt, "Eine christlich-demokratische 'Internationale'", 154; Khol, "Die internationale Parteienzusammenarbeit", 367.
22   Pasture and Verberckmoes, *Working-class Internationalism*, 9-10.

cope with. Although even in such circumstances individual socialists remained true to their international calling, what was dominant was the great importance which the socialists attached to their national autonomy, and the rejection of every form of supranational central authority in their cooperation. This heritage of the interbellum persevered with even more self-assuredness after the Second World War, even though the symbolic reinstitution of the SI can suggest the opposite.

Two Europes: a Social Democratic and a Christian Democratic Europe?

In order to complete the picture of both transnational social democracy and Christian Democracy on the eve of their going global, it is important to consider for a moment an aspect that likewise had its roots in the interbellum, if not earlier: the differing European orientations of both postwar transnationals.

Even if there was no organizational continuity, after its founding the Nouvelles Équipes Internationales were very quick to pick up the continental European accents of the SIPDIC, which can be reduced to its, in essence, Franco-German dimension. At its peak, besides the French PDP and the German Center Party, more than ten other parties constituted the SIPDIC, both Christian Democratic parties (Hungary, Poland, Lithuania, Czechoslovakia) and traditional Catholic parties (Austria, Switzerland, the Netherlands, Luxemburg). The Belgian Catholics were represented by members of the Belgian League of Christian Workers and Italy by the exiles Don Sturzo and F.L. Ferrari. Furthermore, there were a few other looser contacts with Spanish, Yugoslav, and Romanian groups. Yet, the French PDP and the German Center Party formed without any doubt the central axis of the organization. The absence of a British component strengthened this exclusively continental character even further. The theme of the Franco-German reconciliation ran as a leitmotif throughout the activities of the SIPDIC, even if it was never as such explicitly placed on the agenda of the yearly congresses so as not to offend public opinion.

This pro-European, continental direction of the SIPDIC was not completely foreign to the interbellum Socialist Labour International either. Just as in the SIPDIC, in the SLI as well there had long been talk of a strong Franco-German axis. At the beginning of the 1920's, so judged John Francis Wrynn in his dissertation *The Socialist International and the Politics of European Reconstruction*, Socialists from Germany and France were largely in agreement regarding the need for reparation payments, regarding the rejection of "Versailles" and regarding other related cases that could trouble relations between the two countries. Building upon these Franco-German relations, in the SLI just as in the SIPDIC, by far the majority of their attention went to European issues. From the mid-1920's onwards, the continental European orientation in various socialist parties, just as in their Christian Democratic counterparts, also led to a careful exploration of the theme of a more closely integrated Europe. This was certainly the case for the "continental core" of the SLI: the German, French and Belgian socialists.

However, the ever dominant role of the British Labour Party in the Socialist Labour International significantly slowed developments down. Between 1929 and 1931, the BLP had the Foreign Office well in hand and was extremely suspicious of Aristide Briand's European initiatives. The party could not agree with initiatives which - so ran the official position - could inflict damage upon the prestige or the authority of the League of Nations, regardless of their intention. New institutions had to be established within the framework of, and not in competition with, the League of Nations. The critique continued: "We cannot help to create any political or economic group which could in any way be regarded as hostile to the American or any other continent, or which would weaken our political cooperation with the other members of the Commonwealth (...)."[23] The British socialists, in other words, had a number of fundamental objections, which had their origin in policies favouring the British Commonwealth and good relations with the United States.

This fundamental fault line in transnational socialism would come to the surface time and time again, especially after the Second World War, when Britain was to dominate European socialism to an even greater extent than in the 1920's. It was to come up once again in the debates concerning European integration, which became relevant as of 1948. The continental parties, initially with the exception of the German SPD, conducted a very ambitious program in this field. In November 1948, for example, the "Socialist Movement for the United States of Europe" was established through the initiative of the SFIO. The British socialists (and the Scandinavian ones) were not very pleased with this. For the British socialists, next to their traditional Commonwealth

23   Woodward and Butler, *Documents on British Foreign Policy, 1919-1939*. 2/1 no.189. Memorandum, 30/05/1930.

and "Atlantic community" orientation, and their drive to preserve as much sovereignty as possible, internal political concerns also played a role. Bevin had always kept himself aloof from the European integration movement because it was strongly dominated by his political opponent Churchill.

It was a different matter for Christian Democracy: after the Second World War European integration became the main concern of the NEI, building further upon some loose foundations that had been - very thinly - laid in the SIPDIC. The dominance of Western-European Christian Democracy and the absence, for the most part, of Great Britain - which kept the pro-European course on track - meant that in practice there was a striking continuity with the heritage of the SIPDIC, at least as soon as the postwar climate made possible a restoration of the Franco-German axis. The NEI would regard that as one of its major tasks.

Social Democratic and Christian Democratic Transnationalism
A True Reflection of International Politics

The dramatic occurrences of the late 1930's and the early 1940's had in a raw manner exposed the shortcomings of an international system that was based on an uncontrolled logic of power politics. The aversion to that constituted a fruitful breeding ground for blueprints for an alternative organization of the international system. Both socialism and Christian Democracy had sufficient elements in their ideological substance for an "ideal" international form of organization that could function as an alternative to the classic politics of power. Yet, all too swiftly power politics once again became the organizational principle at the international level. The Cold War made the development, let alone the execution, of an "authentic" socialist or Christian Democratic foreign policy impossible. In the polarized climate of the Cold War only a pragmatic policy dictated by national interests was feasible. Instead of they themselves influencing the development of a postwar international system, the Socialist International and the NEI were themselves influenced to a much greater extent by that postwar international system.

The Socialist International in Search of an International Position

On the socialist side, the sense that a mouldable and impressionable international context was at hand after the Second World War stimulated the elaboration and promotion of a "socialist" international system. The Belgian socialist Victor Larock defined a just and durable peace - the ambition and goal of socialists - as a peace based on "an understanding between the working classes internationally; equal rights of all free nations who take part in an international system; collective security and mandatory arbitration procedures; the creation of an international force; a gradual and controlled reduction of national armed forces."[24] He called upon socialists to "become themselves once again", i.e. being "decisively against war, against totalitarian regimes and against nationalism", practically the core of an ideological, socialist world view.[25] In his study of the British Labour Party's foreign policy, Michael Gordon saw that (normative) world view as dependent upon four principles that were tightly woven into one another: internationalism, solidarity with workers, anticapitalism, and antimilitarism.[26]

In particular "international solidarity with workers" had a very specific meaning for certain socialists after the Second World War. It contained a benevolent bearing toward the USSR, which had paid a heavy price for its struggle against Nazism and deserved respect for this. For many the USSR was above all a natural ally who could help realize the revolution in Europe. This pro-Soviet bearing also had adherents in British socialism which at that moment held an authoritative position. Influential British socialists such as G. D. H. Cole and Harold Laski praised the merits of the USSR and had no problem with a Soviet-dominated Central and Eastern Europe. Cole even went so far as to believe that the cause of world peace would be furthered if "Germany just like Eastern Europe would be taken up in an expanded USSR".[27] One of the slogans with which the BLP marched into the July 1945 election, for that matter, was "Left understands Left": an election victory for Labour would be a guarantee for a lasting friendship between Great Britain and the Soviet Union. Thus would the basis be laid for the continuation of the wartime coalition, the basis for a postwar world order.

24   Larock, "Une Paix Juste et Durable", 17.
25   Larock, "Le Nationalisme", 17.
26   Gordon, *Conflict and Consensus*, 13-44.
27   Cole, *Europe, Russia and the Future*; Laski, *Britain and Russia*.

However, ideological (and often idealistic) axioms collided all too quickly with reality. This was certainly the case for the top leadership of the BLP, who allowed themselves to be inspired much less by principles such as internationalism and solidarity with workers.[28] They thought primarily in terms of national security, power politics and national interests. The experience of governing during the war had taught them to rethink the principles of a socialist inspired foreign policy and ultimately to subordinate them to the often much more raucous reality of international politics.

Until 1946, British interest had always dictated finding a compromise with the USSR. However, by the summer of 1946, the conflict of interest with Moscow was too big for the British Foreign Office to bridge. Molotov's demand for reparations, the situation in Poland, the regimes in Hungary, Poland, Romania, and certainly also the USSR's interest in southern Europe and the Mediterranean - a region in which Great Britain had enormous interests to protect - had already caused tensions earlier. During the Council of Foreign Ministers in Paris, in the summer of 1946, those tensions reached a climax. The talks concerning Germany and reparation payments came to a hopeless deadlock. Stalin had already made it known at Yalta that, besides capital goods, he also wanted a share of the German annual production in the form of finished products for the reconstruction of the USSR. This last demand was too much for Great Britain. After all, the British had to import raw materials and foodstuffs into their zone of occupation - the most densely populated zone with the highest industrial production. Initially, imports came from Eastern Germany, but when that region was given to Poland in March 1945, the US became the most important supplier. The British did not want to pay for their imports, including grain, with dollars, but with German export products from their own zone. If these products would go to the USSR as reparations, as Stalin demanded, this option would be considerably impeded. Herein lay a fundamental conflict between the USSR, which prioritized reparation payments, and Great Britain and the US, which opposed them. The British did not want to import raw materials whose end products would go to the USSR, while they still had to take care of the importation of foodstuffs.

The British demand in Paris that a surplus of production in any zone could not be used as reparation payments, and the Russian demand for an immediate economic unification of Germany, rendered further negotiations in Paris not very meaningful. Great Britain realized all too well that a quick economic

---

28   Gordon, *Conflict and Consensus in Labour's Foreign Policy*, 93; Schneer, *Labour's Conscience*, 59.

unification - while the USSR was busy plundering its own zone empty - would burden the Western occupation forces with an economic battlefield.[29]
The idea to first rebuild the Western zones into prosperous economic zones - independent of the USSR - became more and more attractive, even if that implied a "temporary" political division of the country. The decision taken by the British and the Americans in September 1946 to merge their occupation zones into "Bizonia" on 1 January 1947, must be seen in this light.[30]

Once London had chosen its anti-Soviet German policy, it attempted to draw the Americans into it as well. Historians such as Fraser Harbutt and Anne Deighton point out that British pressure was an important factor in the radicalization of American foreign policy. After the failure of the Council of Foreign Ministers in Paris, Bevin repeatedly pushed his American colleague Byrnes to seek out an alternative to a unified Germany and to give up all hope of a possible agreement with Stalin. Toward the end of 1946, Bevin's advances began to yield fruit.[31] Now even the Americans weakened their demand for the reunification of Germany. Shortly afterwards, with the Truman doctrine of March and the Marshall Plan of June 1947, the United States fully took up its role as leader and threw themselves, at first a bit hesitantly but then with full conviction, into the organization of a Western bloc that was necessarily directed against the USSR.

Now that close relations with the USSR - the goal in 1945, and still partially in 1946 - seemed less and less viable, the concept of a "third way" or a "third force" became more and more emphatically the basis for an alternative social-ist world view. The debate between "realists" and "idealists" was also played out within the BLP. In contrast with foreign secretary Bevin and a majority of the party leadership, the advocates of a third way did not, based on the new international context, conclude that Great Britain had to resolutely join the United States. To the contrary, according to them, Great Britain under the Labour government had to form and lead a bloc of European states: neutral, socialist, and strong enough to guarantee their own security and able to mediate between the two other blocs and in this manner prevent a third world war. The instrument chosen to realize this objective would be a re-established and empowered Socialist International. Pleas for a third force, for

---

29   Naimark, *The Russians in Germany.*
30   Alter, *The German Question and Europe*, 112-113.
31   Harbutt, *The Iron Curtain: Churchill, America and the Origins of the Cold War;* Reynolds, "Great Britain", 80; Deighton, *Impossible Peace: Britain, the division of Germany and the origins of the cold war*, 55-78.

European integration, and for the re-establishment of the International were thus very closely related. Already during the war socialists of BLP's leftist wing used to say that "if America gives us headaches, Russia gives us heartaches ... The only solution likely to lay the foundations for peace and prosperity (...) is an organic confederation of the Western European nations."[32] However, Denis Healey, the party's international secretary, silenced these idealists with his pamphlet *Cards on the Table*. He ushered in - for the time being - the beginning of the end of the third way in the BLP.

In a few other socialist parties variations on a third way were indeed successful and these influenced the bearing of the party representatives at socialist congresses. The most outspoken of these were the Belgian BSP and the French SFIO. However, they were defending a forlorn position. First the Marshall Plan and the USSR's rejection of it in July 1947, then - two months later - the founding of Cominform, and finally the Prague coup of February 1948, gave the socialist parties that dominated the Socialist International a concrete chance to realize their wishes for realpolitik.[33] On March 19 and 20th, just after the coup, the Central and Eastern European parties, which were strongly influenced by communism, were excluded from the SI. Moreover, the suspension of the membership of Pietro Nenni's "pro-communist" Partito Socialista Italiano (PSI) and the admission of the social democratic faction of Giuseppe Saragat, which had splintered from the PSI with financial support from the United States (particularly from the AFL labor union), proved inevitable.[34] By March 1948, in other words, the purging of 'dissident' members had begun in the SI, as well as in the BLP and in other socialist parties.

With the critics gone the way lay open for realizing one of the priorities of British foreign policy. The International could be an extremely suitable instrument with which to make the Marshall assistance program and the attendant bloc formation in the West acceptable, to consolidate it, and to control it. All of which was of high priority to the Labour government. Labour was in desperate need of US assistance. They wanted to keep the United States in Europe, and strove therefore to fulfill to the best of their ability the conditions

32   Bevan, as quoted in Schneer, *Labour's Conscience*, 53.
33   To avoid confusion, we are using the name "Socialist International" here, although until the reinstitution of the Socialist International in 1951 it would be more accurate to use the term COMISCO.
34   In 1947 Saragat's faction had splintered from the PSIUP, which - led by Pietro Nenni - had chosen a marxist course. The PSIUP also wanted to continue the coalition with the Italian communists and pursue a neutral foreign policy.

that the Americans had attached to their assistance. Fear of the novel, as well as tiresome criticisms of the Marshall Plan and the Western alliance, could all be taken up through the International, and there too ideological differences between socialist parties could be eliminated. In that context, a clear portrait of the enemy came in very useful: firstly, it could make the abandonment of a "bothersome" ideologically socialist policy acceptable to the outside world. Secondly, it could also help to bring the various parties and countries in Western Europe into one line. This "revisionist" interpretation of the re-establishment of the International has at least as much explanatory power as the "traditionalist" argument that the Socialist International was a defensive reaction to a communist offensive.

The BLP only wanted to support an International which could serve its foreign policy. This is why after having purged the dissidents, the decision was taken to strengthen the operation of the organization. Thus the basis was also laid at the transnational level for a "Western socialist bloc" that seamlessly followed the rhythm of international bloc formation. Nothing more stood in the way of the construction of a Western-European Socialist International which fully placed itself within the Western camp under the leadership of the United States. This implied the definitive end of the hope in an alternative socialist and ideologically inspired order of the international system that a great number of socialists had cherished during and after the Second World War.

Consequently, in the course of 1948 a strongly pronounced anti-communism became the guiding principle of international social democracy. Such anti-communism had always been a characteristic of a considerable segment within socialist parties. However, from this point in time on, it became dominant, in the measure that alternative points of view were expertly liquidated. 1948 spelled the end of all possible alternative attitudes, the death of a properly socialist foreign policy, the swan-song of a third way between the USSR and the USA. It implied a choice for the Atlantic construction which was gradually taking form and which in April 1949 was institutionalized with the establishment of NATO. An alliance of the Western world was apparently the only option during the Cold War.[35]

The impact of this international evolution on the transnational level was made clear in a report from April 1948, written by the Dutchman Bolle, who

35   *Tribune*, 26/11/1948; *Sunday Pictorial*, 25/10/1949.

was asked to define the future tasks of the SI.[36] Social democracy from that moment on had to apply itself to what Bolle put forth as its principle task: the propagation of democratic socialism in the struggle against communism.[37] The BLP immediately promised to grant the International £1000 so as to build the organization into an instrument of propaganda for socialism, in the words of Morgan Phillips, "armed for combat, for democracy and socialism".[38]

Not all socialist parties necessarily set out on an Atlantic course. The Swiss, Swedish, Austrian and the (nonetheless very anti-communist) Finnish socialists held tightly to a neutral positioning that was in harmony with and dictated by what "national interest" prescribed. Based on these very same convictions, Schumacher's fervently anti-communist SPD theoretically kept an equal distance between East and West, even if Western Germany under Adenauer indeed embarked on an Atlantic course. The SPD had hoped through a "policy of neutrality" to be able to reunite Germany in the relatively short term, but this hope would later prove illusory. Indeed, the Socialist International reflected this diversity of opinion - the differences were "tolerated" - but the Atlantic emphasis was to dominate, ever more after the outbreak of the Korean War. This illustrates just how far the international context, within which socialist cooperation took shape, was at crucial moments able to provide the content, form, and rhythm of development of the Socialist International. Stated differently, the Socialist International followed a predominantly pragmatic course defined by the beacons of interest, generally those of the British. The British Labour Party functioned thus as the medium between the international and the transnational level, which very quickly gave the International a pronounced Atlantic character.

NEI's ideal: Europe as a third force

The NEI, to the contrary, held much more tightly to the ideal of a third way in international politics. Their September 1948 congress concerning "The Organization of Europe" in The Hague is an excellent example of this. There, the NEI fully engaged themselves on behalf of a Europe defined by its autonomy with regard to both superpowers: "The NEI would like to give a voice to the representatives of all countries oppressed by dictators, be it

---

36   Sub-Committee meeting, 05/04/1948, London. Minutes. IISG, SI 349.
37   Statement on the Activities and Finance of the SILO and the Sub-Committee of COMISCO in charge of it. IISG, SI 349.
38   International Socialist Conference. Vienna, June 1948. Minutes. IISG, SI 237.

left-wing or right-wing. They should be heard in this European Assembly and in the organs that it could create. This does not just imply morally support-ing those people, but also stressing the fact that the kind of Europe that we are striving for cannot be realized if not all European nations take part in its creation. The NEI clearly state that they will never accept an artificially divided Europe, consisting of antagonistic blocs. The European nations - different as they are, though solidary on an economic level - are the representatives of a commun civilization (...). The American aid, so necessary in Europe, must main-tain the European autonomy.'[39]

This position, at that moment in time, is remarkable in comparison with the attitude of the Socialist International. It seems also not completely to conform with the situation at that time in international politics, certainly not after the Prague coup - shortly after which the Treaty of Brussels was drawn up, a step closer towards an Atlantic Europe - and at the height of the Berlin Blockade.[40]

The differing positions of Christian Democratic and socialist transnationalism in the international system can be explained by two factors. A first factor was the particular course followed by French foreign policy, which in the decade after 1945 was determined by the Mouvement Républicain Populaire. In other words, the MRP fulfilled a similar mediating role among Christian Democrats to that which the BLP fulfilled among socialists. Just as with the Labour Party immediately after the war, the MRP had French foreign policy firmly in hand, although be it as a member of a governing coalition. Except for only one month, the MRP controlled the Quai d'Orsay uninterruptedly from September 1944 until June 1954. Similar to how the British controlled the SI, the French to a large extent controlled the earliest developments in the NEI. Neverthe-less, in the area of foreign policy, the MRP was less likely to press its stamp directly on the NEI, as the BLP did upon the SI. After all, the NEI was merely one of the movements in which the MRP was active, and thus less an exten-sion of the party. Nevertheless, the prestige of the MRP as the largest party in France gave it a certain moral authority on the transnational level.

After the liberation of France the French MRP minister of foreign affairs Georges Bidault pursued a policy that closely conformed to the priorities of then government leader Charles De Gaulle. De Gaulle fought for a strong France with sufficient security guarantees against a new German invasion and able to play an independent role at the international level. That meant

39   Résolution du Congrès de La Haye. KADOC, ADS 7.2.4.3.
40   Reid, *Time of Fear and Hope*, 53.

that the revival of a strong Germany in Europe had to be curbed at all costs, and that France ought to maintain an equal distance from the United States as from the USSR.[41] The Soviet-French Friendship Treaty of December 1944, which established reciprocal aid in case of German aggression, conformed entirely with that ambition. Even after De Gaulle resigned as the head of government in January 1946, Bidault traveled the same path.[42] In this way French policy remained distinct from British.

This is illustrated by the French reaction to the failure of the Council of Foreign Ministers in Paris in the summer of 1946. This failure had convinced the British Foreign Office that an agreement with the USSR was very unlikely. In the course of 1946, both Bidault and the MRP refused to go along with this development.[43] A change of course in the Anglo-American direction would not have been able to count on much support either from the USSR or from the Parti Communiste Français, which sat in government together with the SFIO and the MRP. Above all, with the approach of parliamentary elections in September and November 1946, Bidault feared that any abandonment of De Gaulle's policy would be punished by the electorate. For this reason, immediately after the announcement of the Marshall Plan, Bidault took various measures to actively involve the Soviet Union in the discussions. This did not alter the fact that the idea of different or even opposing blocs, certainly after the Soviet rejection of the Marshall "offer", had a secure following in the MRP. But still far from everyone in the MRP saw the Marshall Plan as an instrument in the fight for freedom and democracy that had to be fought out on the side of the Americans. According to MRP chairman Schumann, the Marshall Plan would in the first place give France - without having to give up its own national sovereignty - the chance to take the lead of a unified Europe, which had to steer a third way between the two great powers. In this way, according to Schumann, a "tête à tête" which would ultimately result in a "corps à corps", could hopefully be avoided.[44] In other words, next to an Atlantic accent, clear "Gaullist" tones also rung in the discourse of the MRP.

The foreign policy of the MRP was not the only factor stimulating the NEI's preference for a third way. A second factor was the bearing of the Vatican

41   Poidevin, "La politique allemande de la France".
42   Poidevin, "France, the Marshall Plan and Germany".
43   Poidevin, "Die Französische Deutschlandpolitik", 15-17.
44   Schumann, "Hésitation au bord de la folie." In the quotes he refers to the literal meaning of the French word tête-à-tête (literally head to head). This so-called confidential conversation between the two superpowers could get out of hand and lead to a corps à corps (literally body against body), i.e. war.

and Pope Pius XII. In his Christmas message of 1947, the head of the church explicitly avoided taking up a viewpoint concerning the, at that time, very clear bloc-formation:"Our stand against the two opposing parties is free of partiality. We do not have any preference for one people or the other, for one nation or the other. We will never interfere with worldly matters."[45] Even in his less public statements, such as in his guidelines to the papal nuncios, Pius XII emphasized that "no-one should ever find a reason to accuse the Holy See of having the intention to undertake a biased crusade."[46] The Vatican's pleas in 1947 and 1948 for a "Europe of the third way" were in great measure dictated by concerns to work out a modus vivendi with the communist authorities so as to protect Catholics in the lands under communist influence.[47] However, at the same time, and this emerged from the mentioned citations, the pope wanted to convey a different perspective than that of "worldly" politics. The Vatican, certainly under Pius XII, propagated in the first place a vision that was rooted in a normative Catholic thinking concerning the international order.[48]

Right from his first encyclical *Summi Pontificatus* (1939), Pius XII consistently emphasized that natural law and Christian morality had to be the foundation of the international system. An international order that was not subject to the "rules of universal morality" could only lead to chaos and war. This also had implications for the concept of peace which Pius XII, the "architect of peace", proclaimed with great single-mindedness. According to him, peace was not merely the absence of war, which necessarily comes forth from an unstable and short lasting "balance of power"; the "peace" that diplomats generally pursued. Peace could even less be realized as a consequence of a miscellany of juridical-structural reformations alone, for example, through the rational application of the (juridical) principles of organization of the nation-state at the international level. A lasting peace arrangement had to be "animated", supported by "a set of moral principles in heart and spirit". Without this spiritual-psychological factor, he saw every juridical-organizational order as doomed to fail.

The international doctrine of Pius XII could count on a secure following among Catholic intellectuals and in the NEI. This does not alter the fact that the NEI in general attempted to maintain its autonomy with respect to the Vatican. However, an explicit statement of difference would have been a step

45   Pius XII, *Documents pontificaux*, 462.
46   *Guidelines to the nuntios, January 1948*, cited in Chenaux, *Une Europe Vaticane?*, 34.
47   Schwarte, *Gustav Gundlach*, 116.
48   See among others Riccardi, *Pio XII* and Idem, *Il potere del papa*.

too far. So discovered the Belgian co-founder Jules Soyeur, who, in 1947, in his *Preliminary Notes* (a sort of a draft charter of the NEI) had wanted to formulate this autonomy more explicitly: "The NEI have a very clear goal: to establish relations between democratic political movements and individuals who have their Christian faith in common, and in doing so to remain completely independent vis-à-vis the Church (...). The NEI will not maintain any relations with the Church on a political level."[49]

This passage would not be included in the statutes. Incidentally, in practice the inspiring influence that issued from the Vatican was clearly visible. For example, the opening address of the conference of Luxemburg, held by Reuter, the Christian Democratic prime minister of Luxemburg, gave a very complete picture of topics, inspired by Catholic social thinking, which recurred time and time again within the NEI. This justifies the length of the following citation, within which the influence of *Summi Pontificatus* and later encyclicals of Pius XII are irrefutable: "We will handle all political, social, economic and cultural problems from a perspective of integral humanism [note the influence of Maritain, pvk], in the light of the transcendence of the human being (...). It is important that the people in power accept divine law, or in other words, the categorical imperative of absolute respect for the human being, his liberty, his dignity, his primordial rights to self-fulfilment, and to personal and familial happiness. This moral conception, which the world owes to Christianity, must become visible in laws and social mores (...). On an international level it confirms the judicial equality of big and small countries; it replaces the law of the jungle with a code of justice and human solidarity; it condemns all imperialist tendencies, which often are the source of armed and bloody conflicts."[50]

Based in this conceptual framework the NEI, in its speeches and discussions, in workgroups and in resolutions, went on to tackle concrete international-political problems such as the increasing bloc-formation. This was evident, for example, in the discussions concerning the German question, which was discussed in exhaustive detail at the Luxemburg conference (29 January till 1 February 1948). In order to join the "European Community" once again, the German people themselves had to be spiritually reborn. They had to "in the first place retrieve their loyalty to the heritage of Christian civilization."[51]

---

49   Soyeur, Notes préliminaires. KADOC, ADS 7.2.1.
50   NEI Conference Luxemburg. Opening speech Reuter, 29/01/1948. KADOC, ADS 7.2.4.2.
51   Frieden, Le Problème Allemand. Session de Luxembourg, 29/01-01/02/1948. KADOC, ADS 7.2.4.2.

The resolution of the conference at The Hague ran as follows: "The crisis in Europe seems to be mainly a spiritual and moral one. Under the influence of individualism, it is materialism that has gradually substituted for this Christian basis, penetrating the European soul."[52]

The social-Catholic, strongly normative world view based on natural law forced the classical unit of analysis in international politics - the nation-state - and the (international) relations between them, into a secondary role. The subordination of the nation-state to a universal moral law was difficult to reconcile with absolute national sovereignty and the reason of State. This, however, created space for active transnational relations. Building a bridge between the two blocs would only be possible if one used as a base the people living on both sides of the iron curtain, and not the various political or social regimes. The "unity of humanity", politically translated as a "Community" (in contrast with a system) of peoples, was the natural, and thus the desirable, organizational form. A "Europe of the third way" could have been a first step towards this, a first step that the NEI attempted to promote.

Up until and including 1948, doctrinaire considerations and realpolitik largely seemed to converge in the repeated pleas of the NEI for a "Europe as a third force". It was the policy of the Vatican, inspired by a combination of Catholic interests and social-Catholic postulates. It was also the policy choice of the French Foreign Ministry, and thus of the MRP, which still played a dominant role within the NEI.

However, by the end of 1948, a change was ushered in. The intensive persecu-tion of Catholics in the Eastern Bloc caused Pius XII to take up a more militant bearing. The arrest and conviction of the Hungarian Cardinal Mindszenty, on 26 December 1948 and 8 February 1949 respectively, played a decisive role in the Vatican's change of attitude. The distinction between the Cold War as a "religious" and a "political" problem was no longer maintainable and was gradually abolished. From 1949 onwards, the head of the church seemed increasingly less embarrassed by taking up "purely" political stances. Later this was to give Pius XII the nickname "NATO's chaplain".[53]

52   Résolutions du Congrès de La Haye sur l'Organisation de l'Europe. 17-19/09/1948. KADOC, ADS 7.2.4.3.
53   Hebblethwaite, "Pope Pius XII: Chaplain of the Atlantic Alliance?", 74.

The Entry of Geopolitics in the NEI

S cenarios for a third way were ever more relegated to the margins of party activity, also in the French - and other Western European - parties. After a long period of obstinacy, France finally consented in September 1948 to participating in a future North Atlantic Treaty Organization. Already starting in the spring of 1947, France had begun - behind the scenes - to shift in an Anglo-American direction. The reason was clear: contrary to the United States and Great Britain, the USSR had rejected the Saar ambitions of Bidault during the fourth Council of Foreign Ministers in Moscow in March 1947. The increase of coal exports from the Ruhr - Paris needed them badly - that the United States and Great Britain had permitted, led to a further rapprochement with the British and the Americans. Above all, the Marshall Plan was a life buoy for the then sinking French economy. As of 1948, the rapprochement took also place in public, as evidenced by the founding of NATO on 4 April 1949.

In these developments, as before, the MRP was to follow its minister, and through the MRP this same evolution afterwards recurred in the NEI. At the NEI congress of April 1950, in the Italian city of Sorrento, the difference with the past was clear.[54] Since its founding, a fervent anti-communist conviction had had a place within the NEI, but except for a few references, the accent had continually been placed on the ideological conflict (Christian Democracy versus communism/materialism/nihilism), and not on the geopolitical conflict with the USSR. In Sorrento, however, the climate was completely different. There, the congress attendees plunged themselves completely into international *reality*. The use of language was more precise, and in terms of content was there at least one new element: an explicit condemnation of "the Bolshevik government" (in contrast with a condemnation of "communism"), coupled with a declaration of love of the United States.[55] The Italian representative Lodovico Benvenuti, for example, could not imagine a Europe that stood detached from the "important community overseas", a part of the "free world" with which Europe had traditional ties that had to be consolidated and strengthened. And he added: "The Christian Democrats thus consider the ongoing process of unification of Europe as a consolidation of

---

54   Italy was chosen as host country since 1950 was also a 'Holy Year'. Letter from Bichet to the
      NEI members. ACDP, IX-002-011/4.
55   NEI. Réunion Internationale à Sorrento, April 1950. KADOC, ADS 7.2.4.4.

the extreme oriental pillar of the free world, impregnated with christian civilization", a subtle reference to NATO.[56]

Still, the NEI apparently did not want to go so far in an Atlantic romance: not one of Benvenuti's ideas was included in the closing resolution. De Gasperi's Atlantic Europe was, indeed, not the only project. At the next conference in September 1951, in Bad Ems (Germany), Adenauer defended his (European) answer to the Soviet threat: "The German Federal Republic attaches great importance to close cooperation with other Western nations, especially with those in Western Europe (...). Carrying out the Schuman Plan, and the creation of a European Defense Community (...) according to me, are secure and unique ways of creating a United Europe, which will be the only means possible to resist Soviet pressure."[57]

However, it was clear that by 1951 the Cold War held the NEI, just as the Socialist International, tightly in its grip. The Cold War as a geopolitical and geo-strategic reality had the full attention of the NEI. It would nevertheless be an exaggeration to describe the NEI in 1951 as a "Cold War International", a term that we reserve for the Socialist International. In contrast with the SI, the NEI never saw themselves as a spearhead in the conflict between East and West, even if the Central and Eastern-European Christian Democrats in exile continually pushed them in that direction.[58] For the exiles, the anti-bolshevism of the NEI needed to become very explicit, especially in the strengthening of the organization, just as was occurring on the socialist flank. However, neither the Prague coup, nor the subsequent intensification of the Cold War, gave sufficient impetus to desire a transformation of the NEI into a kind of "Christian Cominform", as Konrad Adenauer expressed it.[59] Although it is impossible to doubt the negative attitude of Western-European Christian Democracy towards the USSR, this factor appears insufficiently decisive to

---

56   Objectifs de la Démocratie Chrétienne dans l'Europe actuelle. Rapport politique par Lodovico Benvenuti, Sorrento, 1950. KADOC, ADS 7.2.4.4.

57   Discours du Chancelier Adenauer. L'Allemagne et la Paix en Europe. Congrès des NEI Bad Ems. KADOC, ADS 7.2.4.5.

58   The Czech People's Party was the first non-Western European party attending an executive committee meeting (in February 1948). Later on, also the Christian Democratic parties in exile from the following countries were accepted as members: Poland (21/03/1948), Romania (16/09/1948), Hungary (21/11/1948), Bulgaria (15/07/1949) and Lithuania (11/02/1950). Finally, Yugoslavia followed on 13/12/1954.

59   The Tablet, 22/09/1951, 186.

initiate the step from a loose cooperative union to an instrument capable of action that could parry the propaganda of the USSR and its supporters in the West.

It was another motivation that underlay the attempts to strengthen trans-national cooperation among Christian Democrats: the perception - not completely unjust, for that matter - that the incipient process of European integration was dominated and led by European socialists. In the beginning phases of NEI's existence there was hardly any talk of a credible European engagement coming from the Christian Democratic side. At the 1947 confer-ence in Chaudfontaine, Belgium, that theme came up only briefly in the margins. In 1947 the NEI were absent when representatives of the European Union of Federalists, the United Europe Movement, the League Van Zeeland, and the French Council for a United Europe sat down round the table in order to set up an international committee to coordinate the relations between the various pro-European organizations. The NEI were involved in the orga-nization of the European congress in The Hague in May 1948, which was organized by this international committee, but their influence was minimal. The NEI limited themselves in practice to a rather contentless "policy of just being present". However, the leading role taken by their socialist rivals began to cause them more and more concern. The Christian Democrats saw this socialist dominance symbolized in the figure of the Belgian Paul-Henri Spaak. That he was the chairman of both the Assembly of the Council of Europe and the European Movement badly rankled them. This led to continually recurring irritation. At the meeting of the national committee of the MRP on 10 Febru-ary 1949, the Frenchman Bichet - based on fear that the socialist and workers' parties would gain a sizable majority in the future European Assembly - proved to be an advocate of the expansion of the NEI.[60] Two years later the competition had scarcely lost importance. In November 1951, Strauss again complained that the socialists would be able to profit from the continual inactivity of the Christian Democrats: "Look at the European Movement. It clarifies the danger by the socialists."[61]

The feeling of having been pressed into a second rate role by the socialists reached a provisional high point in 1951. In connection with the European Campaign of the European Movement, Lewandowski, in the spirit of combat, declared that if the IUSY, the youth organization of the Socialist International, was to seek out international recognition, then the Christian Democratic

60   Executive committee, 17/02/1949, 35. AP47. AN, MRP Archives.
61   Procès-verbal du Comité Exécutif, 24/11/1951. ACDP, IX-002-005/1.

youth would also do so. Indeed, it was unacceptable to Lewandowski that significant funds would be used by socialists alone. NEI Chairman August De Schryver agreed: "Catholics and Protestants usually do not play an important role in political movements. By not being interested in politics, they are consequently restricting their influence, since they are never represented according to their number and their importance. The socialists, on the other hand, only for reasons of affiliation, attend all congresses and become members of all organizations in which they can be represented. As a consequence, their representation does not reflect reality anymore, which often leads to the adoption of resolutions that are incompatible with the spirit and the goal of the organizations in question."[62]

When at the meeting of the executive committee, in January 1952, Robert Bichet proposed to establish a permanent secretariat in Strasbourg, his argument ran as follows: "The socialists have already established such a secretariat."[63] The acceleration of European integration, which was coupled with the creation of new institutions, and the alleged socialist dominance in these institutions, stimulated the NEI to engage in an ever more thorough reflection of their working method. Additionally, at that point in time there were two important developments. Firstly, the MRP by this point had expressly chosen for a European image. "Europe" was, as a counterweight against the propaganda of the French Communist Party, indeed an appropriate theme to justify the French agreement - under American pressure - to German rearmament. It was only from that point onwards (1950), that the MRP earns its characterization as a European party par excellence. The Schuman Plan and support for the Pléven Plan for a European Defense Community are two good illustrations of this. Secondly, by then Franco-German contacts within the NEI, which initially had been very difficult, had been repaired.[64] It was the congress in Bad Ems in September 1951, that sealed the reconciliation. From that moment on the NEI proved to be a fierce advocate of European integration, whereby the organization again corresponded to the continental European orientation of the SIPDIC.

62   Procès-verbal du Comité Exécutif, 24/11/1951. ACDP, IX-002-005/1.
63   Procès-verbal du Comité Exécutif, 12/01/1952. ACDP, IX-002-005/1.
64   Letter from Bichet to Dörpinghaus, 04/01/1951. ACDP, IX-002-012.

The Socialist International and the NEI in 1950: the Eve of Globalization

The acquisition of a place in the European institutions was not the only border-crossing activity that the socialist parties after the Second World War had placed on their agenda. At the same time, under the lead of the British Labour Party, they attempted to breathe new life into the International. These attempts were also followed with suspicion by the Christian Democrats. The first open expression of criticism of the poor activity of the NEI, coming principally from the Swiss and the Austrians, roughly speaking converged with the beginning of the long final sprint to re-establish the Socialist International. When the Austrian Felix Hurdes in November 1949 expressed his uneasiness concerning the progress that the socialists had made, the secretary-general of the NEI, the Frenchman Robert Bichet, could still reassuringly reply that there still was no Socialist International and that the difficulties in establishing it were immense.[65] Afterwards Bichet also provided the members of the NEI with a pamphlet from the Socialist Movement for a United Europe, in which the deep, even fundamental differences between certain continental socialist parties on the one hand, and the British and Scandinavian parties on the other, must have appeared.[66] However, starting at the end of 1950, the socialists headed full speed for the official reinstitution of their International, which was baptized at the Frankfurt conference in July 1951. Again this caused quite a bit of agitation among the Christian Democrats, which was strongly expressed at the next congress of the NEI, in September 1951, in Bad Ems, Germany - once again a beautiful example of "location imitation".

During the Bad Ems conference Konrad Adenauer, in particular, took the first step. The Christian Democrats indeed stood strong, according to Adenauer, but "the others, who are serving a cause that we consider unjust, have a great advantage over us. Their different parties are working together on an international level, in a way that makes them stronger than us. Please, consider this (…), look at the new Socialist International. I cannot but admit that our organization is not able to compete with them. Their strength and propaganda are unequalled."

The German chancellor closed his argument with a sharp call for a tighter cooperation between the various Christian Democratic parties (instead of

---

65   Procès-verbal du Comité Exécutif, 18-19/11/1949. ACDP, IX-002-002.
66   Philip, Le Socialisme et l'Unité Européenne. Letter from Bichet to the secretary-general, 13/10/1950. ACDP, IX-002-89.

between groups or 'équipes'), a demand that had already been published before the conference in part of the German press.[67] In Bad Ems the call of the Germans, Italians, Austrians, Swiss, and, to a somewhat lesser extent, also the Dutch for a "Christian Democratic International" rang louder than before. Rarely were the criticisms of inefficient cooperation so loud, and so justified. The Bad Ems congress was itself, for that matter, a model of inefficiency. Only one report, that of the Frenchman Teitgen, was distributed beforehand among the participants, because of which the retorts during the discussions necessarily were limited to mere improvisations.

This was nevertheless an old wound. The exchange of information between the various groups or parties throughout that entire period remained indeed below the desired level. The executive committee on May 1951 still complained that only the French, and to a lesser extent the Dutch, were in the habit of circulating documents.[68] The subsequent resolutions of the Bad Ems congress hardly built upon what was discussed during the conference and confirmed only a number of general principles instead of dictating real agenda items. Moreover, the resolutions were scarcely reported in the press, let alone commented upon, which displayed the weakness of the NEI in terms of propaganda. The conclusion, as formulated by one of the groups, was also harsh: there was no "team spirit"."One has the impression that the Équipes Internationales are not really alive."[69] The malaise was furthered even more by the fact that the NEI - in contrast with the SI - despite various attempts, did not succeed in producing a generally accepted platform. The extremely limited authority of the transnational organ over the individual groups and the limited latitude which the secretary-general, the chairman, and in the end also the executive committee of the NEI had at their disposal, were of course nothing unusual. It would be a while before much would change. At the end of 1955, for example, the newly elected secretary-general, Alfred Coste-Floret, wrote a crushing report on the organization which he was going to lead. There was a disconcerting lack of contact between the groups and the international secretariat, to be attributed to "the lack in discipline of the groups that do not do the tasks that are asked of them", according to Coste-Floret.

In 1951, it was clear to everyone who was directly concerned that the NEI had missed their entrance on the international stage. The movement's painful

---

67   Discours du Chancelier Adenauer. Congrès des NEI à Bad Ems, September 1951. KADOC, ADS 7.2.4.5.
68   Procès-Verbal du Comité Exécutif, 28/05/1951. ACDP, IX-002-005/1.
69   Procès-verbal du Comité Exécutif, 24/11/1951. ACDP, IX-002-005/1.

inefficiency made politicians who saw the NEI as a political instrument - a lobby group of closer European cooperation - drop out. The impossibility of arriving at a doctrinal consensus led to indifference in those who saw in the NEI an identity generating forum.

The results that the social democratic parties could put on the table in 1951, after more than five years of cooperation, were just as unspectacular. Yet, their cooperation and communication was much more efficient than that of the Christian Democrats, not least because the organization was more strictly led in a more centralized fashion by the energetic secretary-general Julius Braunthal, and the organization had more financial and logistical means at its disposal. Also important was the fact that in 1951 the social democrats could indeed show one result at the ideological level. After long discussions, they finally succeeded in defining their ideological identity in a Charter. Conse- quently, in Frankfurt, in July 1951, accompanied by the necessary aplomb and to the tune of the socialist hymn the 'International' ('So comrades, come rally / and the last fight let us face / The Internationale unites the human race'), the "International" was re-established.

By the beginning of the 1950's, social democracy and Christian Democracy each had a clear transnational structure. The Socialist International, a relative- ly centralized association that respected the autonomy of its members, was dominated by the British Labour Party, and had drafted a somewhat hybrid program statement that was acceptable to all social democrats. The SI was principally intended to be an instrument of propaganda against communism, for the Western bloc, and for the value for which that bloc stood, namely free- dom. The Nouvelles Équipes Internationales were a somewhat more loosely organized movement, which chiefly but not exclusively consisted of Christian Democratic parties. The influence of the MRP was very important in it, but not fundamental. The NEI was principally intended to be an instrument for the spreading of the Christian Democratic doctrine. More specifically, it was intended that the NEI should leave its mark on the European institutions and thereby function as a counterweight to social democracy.

In the 1950's, both transnationals would be subject to the influences of globalization, which on the international level became ever more visible. The Korean War and decolonization expanded the view of many Europeans far beyond Europe. In part two we shall investigate which of the two transna- tionals was best placed to take advantage of these new developments.

II
The Socialist International and the *Nouvelles Équipes Internationales* in the Period of their Global Expansion, 1950-1960

The two transnational political organizations which made their appearance on the international stage after the close of the Second World War owe their genesis to three unequal factors of fluctuating importance. The first factor was composed of the entirety of traditional orientations and sensitivities. We referred to this by the term "hereditary material". The second factor was the political reality at home within which each constituent party of the transnational had to function. Lastly, international events exercised a stronger influence on the form and content of the transnational level than the other way around. These three mutually influential factors gave rise to two transnational organizations which by around 1950 already fundamentally differed from one another in terms of both form and content. One was a rather centralized inter-party organization with a strongly defined ideology, while the other was more a loose association of "groups", lacking a clearly presented ideology. During the 1950's both the Socialist International and the Christian Democratic Nouvelles Équipes Internationales underwent important evolutions which allowed both of them, by about 1960, to transform themselves into globally oriented organizations. This process of globalization, however, proceeded differently in the two parties, in terms of tempo, direction and depth.

The Socialist International goes Global
British Interests, International Pressure and Missionary Zeal, 1950-1955

The Drive to Globalize

Going Global on the Ruins of the British Empire

The re-establishment of the Socialist International during the Frankfurt congress of 1951 was the end result of a complex process. As already mentioned, that congress marked the end of a long period of infighting between advocates and opponents of any form of institutionalized cooperation between socialist or social democratic parties. At the same time, this very same congress is often seen as a starting point because it was here that the International's period of global expansion seems to have its origins. Guillaume Devin noted in his study that of the 31 parties present in Frankfurt only seven came from outside of Europe. He drew the conclusion that in 1951 the International was not yet really "international".[70] By the end of the decade the membership list looked a good deal more "global". The International succeeded not only in greatly expanding its membership in Latin America and Asia, it also began to make its first tentative, exploratory ventures on the African continent.[71] Therefore, in principle, 1951 could to some extent be considered as the (symbolic) starting point of a genuine process of globalization. 1951 was, however, by no means a breaking point, since the European socialists, particularly the British, did not wait for the re-establishment of the Socialist International to begin actively recruiting followers outside of Europe.

---

70   Representatives of socialist parties from Canada, Argentina, Uruguay, India and Japan were present in Frankfurt, next to those of two different parties from the United States. Devin, *L'Internationale socialiste*, 49.
71   Secretary's Report to the Bureau of the SI. London, 06/02/1959. Circ. B.5/59. IISG, 95.

The Anglo-Indian Axis

In their recruitment campaign the socialists cast their gaze especially on South and South-East Asia - colourful exotic regions which in earlier centuries had attracted many a European adventurer, as well as a few pirates drawn to the busy trade routes of the lucrative Chinese markets. After World War II it was the socialists' turn to try their luck in Asia, where they saw much potential in its slowly developing political arena. This pronounced preference for the region was, one could say, "genetically predetermined". The Socialist International was predestined even from before its official birth, in 1951, to serve as an extension of the British Labour Party's foreign policy. This was especially so in the years leading up to 1951. As long as the "International" was unable to come up with its own fully fledged and independent organizational structure, all important (administrative) tasks were carried out by the BLP. Its *Newsletter*, for example, was published by the International Department of the BLP. The rather loose collaboration between socialist parties became somewhat better structured as of January 1948, when the "Committee of the International Socialist Conference" (COMISCO) was established. Through COMISCO other socialist parties slowly began to get a little bit of say in the leadership of the still rather primitively organized association. Yet it was not until 1950, when COMISCO appointed its own salaried secretary-general, that the organization, since 1951 called Socialist International, was able to exercise a degree of autonomy from the British Labour Party. Up until then, however, the BLP had free reign to enforce its ambitions and policy points via COMISCO.

A few of these policy points were tainted by imperialism. For the BLP transnationalism was an ideal instrument to keep the territories which had gained their independence from Great Britain in 1947 - India, Pakistan, Burma and Ceylon - within the British sphere of influence.[72] A first, somewhat cautious call to begin "canvassing" in Asia was heard in January 1947, half a year before the formal recognition of Indian Independence. A second call came in December 1948, once again at the behest of the BLP.[73] Exactly one year later COMISCO officially put "expansion into Asia" onto its agenda. From the minutes of the 14 December 1949 meeting it appears that only the Japanese Social Democratic Party (SDP) was added to COMISCO, yet the correspondence of the newly appointed secretary-general Julius Braunthal shows that

[72]   India and Pakistan had become independent on 15 August 1947, Birma on 4 January 1948 and Ceylon exactly one month later, on 4 February 1948. In 1972 Ceylon became the 'Democratic Socialist Republic of Sri Lanka'.
[73]   Fourth COMISCO-meeting, Clacton-on-Sea, 03/12/1948. Circular 121. IISG, SI 47.

the addition of Japan was only one aspect of a larger strategy. "The meeting of the Committee of the International Socialist Conference at Paris in December 1949", according to the secretary-general, "expressed the hope of seeing the Labour and Socialist Parties of the British Commonwealth and of Asia united in a great association of the Labour and Socialist Parties of the world. The meeting charged the Administrative Secretary with opening conversations with these Parties which had not so far affiliated to COMISCO."[74]

The temptation to see in the expansion of COMISCO (on a purely chronological basis) a mirror image of the patterns of the Cold War is very seductive. After all, only six weeks earlier, on 1 October 1949, Mao had proclaimed the People's Republic of China. To attribute the resolution of 14 December 1949 solely to Mao's victory would, however, be reductionistic. The increasing amount of emphasis which COMISCO was placing on Asia had its origin rather in a policy decision which had been taken years before but which had never been given its due, owing to the dramatic turn of events in Europe and the fact that COMISCO had been primarily occupied with organizational questions. The fact that in the meeting's report no explicit connection was made between the events in China and the need to become more active in Asia is of course an insufficient argument, but Braunthal's explicit referral to the "British Commonwealth", and not to Mao's taking power, indicates that a sort of "neocolonial" policy on the part of the BLP was at least partly responsible for COMISCO's heightened interest in Asia at the end of 1949.[75]

The BLP was responsible not only for urging the International to expand, they also directly moulded the expansion according to their vision. The cooperation between COMISCO and kindred spirits in Asia was born of previously existing contacts which the British Labour Party had already established with party supporters or local Asian socialists. The latter were mainly being found in India. The intense correspondence between the COMISCO mother organization in London and certain persons in India confirms the importance of the Anglo-Indian axis shortly after the Second World War.[76] In other words, India played a crucial role in the nascent global expansion of the future International.

74   Letter from Braunthal to U Ba Swe, 09/06/1950. IISG, SI 491. India had joined the
      Commonwealth in 1947, Ceylon in 1948.
75   Howe, *Anticolonialism in British politics*, 7-11.
76   Correspondence India. IISG, SI 657.

Initially, despite India's having a relatively well organized political situation, it was not entirely clear to the BLP who exactly on the Indian side of the equation they should consider as their principal interlocutor.[77] In COMISCO, this question came up as a topic of conversation in the months leading up to the Zurich congress of June 1947. The discussion had long been anticipated by the press, both internationally and in India itself. On 27 January 1947, the *Hindusthan Standard* announced that one Indian socialist party was to be invited to the Zurich congress. According to the paper, at the suggestion of the BLP's international secretary Denis Healey, the choice fell to the Congress Socialist Party (CSP). Apparently the paper was well informed. Three days earlier, during one of its first meetings, the advisory committee of COMISCO had indeed discussed the possibility of forging tighter bonds with Asian socialists. According to the meeting's (rather neutrally formulated) minutes it was decided to "encourage contact with socialist movements in Asia."[78] No party was mentioned by name, but it is highly probable that the CSP already carried Healey's approval.[79]

On an organizational level the Congress Socialist Party was a subdivision of the legendary Indian National Congress Party (INC), the party of Mohandas (Mahatma) Gandhi and Jawaharlal Nehru. Founded in 1885, the INC is generally considered to be the oldest political party on the Asian continent. From the beginning, the INC was characterized as having a pronounced pro-British orientation. The party was, incidentally, co-founded by an Englishman, Allan Octavian Hume, and various Britons had fulfilled leading roles in the party over the decades. By the beginning of the 20th century, however, the party had gradually begun to become more radical in its nationalist demands and consequently relations with the British soured. Nationalist agitation, as led by Gandhi, had in 1930 and 1932 reached a temporary high point with the mobilization of millions of Indians. It was during these turbulent years that certain young party members, desirous of giving the nationalist agenda of the party a socialist tint, decided to form their own party. Their involvement with the nationalist campaigns had landed all of them in jail, where the idea of founding a socialist party had been worked out. In this way, in 1934, the Congress Socialist Party arose as a sub-party within the much larger INC.

---

77 In the 1951-1952 elections, for instance, only 5 parties received more than 3% of the votes, the minimum to be recognized as a "national party". Hinton, *Major Governments of Asia*, 359.
78 The BLP was asked to draw up a memorandum about India. The Dutchman Thomassen was invited to do the same for Indonesia. Consultative Committee, Meeting 24/01/1947. IISG, SI 47.
79 Letter from Healey to Sander, 14/04/1947. IISG, SI 235.

Amongst those who had taken this initiative were to be found Jayaprakash Narayan, Rammanohar Lohia and Asoka Mehta, three socialists destined to play a key role in the Socialist International, and to become the natural contact persons in India for that British dominated cooperative association.[80]

In the 1930's, however, none of this was yet apparent. The opposition of the INC mother party - led by Gandhi among others - to India's taking part in the Second World War placed the British government (and the BLP, then a constituent party of that government) at direct odds with the INC. Most INC leaders sat out the entirety of the war behind bars. Narayan was once again picked up in 1939, but was soon able to escape from prison, being already familiar with the building from a previous stay. Gandhi himself was freed in 1944 for reasons of poor health.

As soon as the war was over, Great Britain was all that much more willing to show its obliging side. With the war's end the question of India's political status could no longer be postponed. In order to facilitate the transition the British considered Congress' support essential. The Congress Party played an active role both in the institutions which Labour had created to facilitate the transition, as well as in the actual negotiations of August 1947 which were to result in Indian independence. This restored British trust. The INC's decision to enter the British Commonwealth as a dominion, despite giving much surprise at home, can best be understood in the context of a marriage of convenience between the British Labour Government and the Indian National Congress.

The situation being what it was, the Congress Socialist Party didn't really feel very threatened by other Indian socialist-minded parties and was counting on a quick admission to COMISCO. Yet competition did exist and the announcement in the press of CSP's invitation to the Zurich congress incited a rival group, the Radical Democratic Party (RDP), to propose its own candidacy as COMISCO's potential representative in India. They did this in two ways. Firstly, RDP party secretary Vithal Mahadev Tarkunde contacted London directly in order to present his party and to recommend it for the congress in Zurich. Being both judge and philosopher, Tarkunde emphasized like no other the importance of international cooperation between social democratic parties: "The RDP of India believes that future progress throughout the world

---

80   When the Congress Socialist Party was founded, Narayan was appointed secretary-general. Lohia became editor in chief of the party paper *Congress Socialist*. Braunthal, *Geschichte der Internationale, 3*, 270. Nevertheless, Asoka Mehta would become the most important contact person of the Socialist International in Asia.

depends upon the growth of democratic socialism. It is of the opinion that the impending conflict between the USA and the USSR (...) can be averted, if at all, by the rapid growth of a type of social democracy, which reconciles individual liberty with socialist planning. The RDP has been striving to evolve and popularize principles in consonance with this ideal, and it would heartily welcome the chance of cooperating with other forces in the world travelling in the same direction."[81]

Secondly, the party also attempted to gain favour by means of less official channels. V.B. Karnik, one of the party leaders, approached Labour members of parliament asking them "to speak on our behalf and to do everything that may be possible for securing us recognition as a Socialist Party"[82] At least one of them, member of parliament Bottomley, who had himself spent some time in India, applied himself to his task with ardour. He informed Healey that his experience had shown to him that the RDP was an enthusiastic and energetic party with a wide following among the youth. He continued: "certainly the most powerful party in India akin to the Labour Party in this country." Moreover, he added that he was not alone in his assessment: "You will find that the Head Office of the Labour Party has actively for some years past supported the claims of the RDP."[83]

The position of the party during the war, in any regard, spoke in its favour. During the war, relations between the British government and the RDP, which fully supported the Indian government's war effort, were excellent.[84] In his correspondence with London, Tarkunde did not neglect referring to this wartime loyalty, especially in light of the Congress Party's antiwar position. In a letter dated 19 March 1947, he wrote: "I understand from news reports that your Committee (the advisory committee of COMISCO) is considering the question of whether Indian representation should be granted to the Radical Democratic Party or the Congress Socialist party. We are surprised that such an issue should have arisen. Obviously, an intensely nationalist Party like the Congress Socialist party cannot implement a socialist program. The CSP did not do so during the last war, nor is it doing so now."[85]

81   Letter from Tarkunde to Consultative Committee. SILO, 19/03/1947. IISG, SI 657.
82   Letter from Karnik to Bottomley, February 1947. IISG, SI 235.
83   Letter from Bottomley to Healey, 14/03/1947. IISG, SI 235.
84   Thanks to these excellent relations the party got financial and material aid. Letter from Bottomley to Healey, 14/03/1947. IISG, SI 235.
85   Letter from Tarkunde to Consultative Committee SILO, 19/03/1947. IISG, SI 657.

However, memories proved to be short or at least easy to outweigh with a good dose of pragmatism. Besides, the Congress Socialist Party had its own network. Jayaprakash Narayan was close friends with Fenner Brockway, who after the war played an important role in the left wing of the Labour Party.[86] In March 1947, Brockway brought Healey, among others, in contact with Anna Asafali, the wife of the Indian Ambassador to Washington and a firm supporter of the CSP. By April 1947, Healey's preference for the CSP was decided:"A choice may have to be made between the Radical Democrats and the Congress Socialist Party. From the scanty evidence in my possession I would tend to think that the Congress Socialist Party was more representa-tive of socialist opinion than the Radical Democratic Party, whose emergence to political influence during the war was due at least in part to a subsidy received from the British government while the leaders of the Congress Socialist Party were in prison."[87] Among the "scanty evidence" which Healey claimed to possess was a report from the congress which the CSP had orga-nized a month earlier in Kampur. At that congress the CSP forswore its prewar Marxist pro-soviet past and fully embraced democratic socialism, making the party ideologically perfectly acceptable to the strongly anti-communist Healey.

All the same, circumstances kept the International from making a decision. On 9 May 1947, the Western socialists decided to invite not a single Asian party to the Zurich congress and to put off the entire question until a further date. The assembly had more important things to discuss: the growing tensions between East and West, which were bringing the highly sensitive question of extending membership to the German SPD to the forefront.[88] The East-West tension was also tangible in the discussions on Bulgaria, where two parties vied for the favour of the Western socialists: Neykov's party which sat in government, and Lultchev's party in the opposition, and falling more and more the victim of state sponsored censorship of the press.

The communist-oriented Eastern European delegates in Zurich pleaded repeatedly for Neykov's group to be admitted to the International. For the Romanian delegate Radaceanu, only one socialist party existed in Bulgaria: Neykov's, which consequently deserved full membership in the International. The Hungarian delegate Ban would be satisfied with granting Neykov

---

86   Howe, *Anticolonialism in British Politics*, 169-172.
87   Letter from Healey to Sander, 14/04/1947. IISG, SI 235.
88   See Steininger, *Deutschland und die Sozialistische Internationale*, 64-79.

observer status at the congress and was fully supported in this by the Italian Nenni. Yet even this proposal could not count on backing from Great Britain, the Benelux and Scandinavia. As a compromise it was decided not to invite either of the two parties for the moment (for "lack of sufficient information") and to resume the discussion at a later date.

This decision also set the tone for the Indian question which was tabled just afterwards. Denis Healey once again spoke out in favour of the Congress Socialist Party[89], but the Pole Hochfeld blocked all decisions regarding the CSP, stating categorically that if no decision could be taken over Bulgaria "for lack of sufficient information", how is one to take a decision regarding parties from a country of which even less is known.[90] Consequently, the issue was put off till a further date. In other words the Indian question did not escape the increasing European polarization within the International, and the choice of an Indian partner was explicitly linked to the discussion of the Bulgarian partner. In Zurich it became very apparent just how much the situation in Eastern Europe continually troubled the delegates.

Hardly four months later, two invitations were sent out: one to the Radical Democratic Party and the other to the Congress Socialist Party, inviting them both to take part as observers at the next congress in Antwerp, in December 1947.[91] The double invitation was not at all well received by the Congress Socialist Party, which had been trying to put an end to the ambiguous situation. Both preceding and following the Antwerp congress, Madhu Limaye, the CSP's foreign affairs representative, made informal complaints regarding the RDP's presence in Antwerp. About one year later the CSP finally got its way when at the COMISCO meeting of 3 December 1948, it was decided to invite the CSP "as the only accredited socialist representatives from India" to the next international congress.[92]

89   In the meantime the Congress Socialist Party had changed its name to All-India Party. From March 1948 onwards they called themselves the Socialist Party of India, which - after a merger - became the Praja Socialist Party in September 1952.
90   International Socialist Conference Zürich. IISG, SI 234.
91   Letter from SILO to the secretary of the Radical Socialist Party, 03/10/1947. IISG, SI 657.
92   Circ. 121/47. Meeting of COMISCO. Clacton-on-Sea, 03/12/1948. IISG, SI 47. Letter from M.C. Bolle, secretary Sub-Committee COMISCO, to Suresh Desai, 05/01/1949. IISG, SI 657. A representative of SILO was then invited to the 7th 'Annual Conference of the Socialist Party India' in Padna, early in March 1949. For the travelling expenses would be too high, SILO decided not to participate. Initially, travelling long distances was indeed an obstacle. At the International Congress in Copenhagen (June 1950), for instance, representatives of Indian Socialism did not turn up.

Meanwhile, the situation in India had fundamentally shifted. The RDC had quickly diminished to a party of relative unimportance while the CSP had developed into a fully independent party. Not that that was by any conscious choice of its own. The gradual transformation of the Indian Congress Party after Indian independence, in August 1947, from an umbrella organization fighting for independence into a better structured ruling party meant an immediate end to "parties within the party". In March 1948, the Congress Socialist Party was forced to leave the mother party and in this way it was transformed into the Socialist Party of India, which after disappointing election results in 1951 and 1952 would in September 1952 join forces with the Kisan Mazdoor Praja Party - a socialist party with a large following among farmers. Together they would become the Praja Socialist Party (PSP). Yet, even with such prestigious party leaders as Jayaprakash Narayan and Asoka Mehta, as a party the PSP still had a good deal less political clout than the Congress Party.

For the International it seems there was never really any question of further collaboration with the Congress Party itself. In letters concerning India, from the period between 1946 and 1960, there is hardly even any mention of the Indian National Congress Party (INC). A partial explanation for this can be found by examining the course which the INC had set in the initial years after independence. In independent India's first years Nehru busied himself exclusively with questions of the integrity of the new state and he left the party in the hands of the much more conservative vice-prime minister, Vallabhbhai Patel. Patel, unlike Nehru, had little sympathy for large-scale social and economic reforms and under his watch he slowly filled important party positions with similarly minded individuals (sometimes even radical orthodox hindus).[93] Only after 1953, when Nehru took control and the party began to follow a more leftist line, did the International start to take some interest in the party.

The fact that the INC dramatically shifted to the left did not go unnoticed among Western European socialists, especially amongst the Scandinavians. In the talks which Nehru held that spring with Jayaprakash Narayan of the Praja Socialist Party he made it clear that he was interested in having closer cooperation between the two parties and potentially even a formal political alliance. In January 1955, the INC's shift to the left resulted in the "Avadi Resolution", in which the party postulated "a socialistic pattern of society". Immediately Nehru's party became the topic of a short discussion within the International. The direct cause for the discussion was a question from the Finnish socialist Ola Wikström to SI secretary-general Julius Braunthal

93   Palmer, "Political parties in India," 339.

regarding Nehru's 'socialist credentials'.[94] Braunthal's answer to Wikström indicates that the evolution within the Congress Party had indeed awakened the International's interest: "It is correct that Nehru himself has vowed to be a Socialist, and although he never was a member of a Socialist Party his sympathies undoubtedly tend towards Socialism. Moreover, he maintains close friendship with a number of leaders of the Praja Socialist Party. He has never clearly defined his conception of Socialism, but from his whole outlook it can be assumed that on the whole (...) it corresponds to the conception of Socialism of the fraternal Indian party".[95] However, the International had made its choice; it would not come to a rapprochement.

India: the Door to Asian Socialism

The detailed attention which India is receiving in this chapter is only in proportion to the importance of Indian socialism to the later global expansion of the International. Ever since its admission into the International it had been the intention of the Congress Socialist Party to become the key to the door of Asian socialism. In January 1949, Narayan received a letter welcoming his party which contained not only a sort of contract of exclusive commitment but also a specific request: "COMISCO also considered the question of getting into closer touch with socialist groups and socialist parties in Asia and expressed the hope that your Party would be able to inform us of bona fide socialist individuals or parties in Burma, China and possibly Japan, with whom we could establish contacts."[96] Somewhat later the wish list was further expanded, after Braunthal had found references to socialist parties in Egypt, Syria, Lebanon, Pakistan, East Pakistan, Ceylon and Burma in the report of the eighth congress of the Indian SP. Before that, the Socialist International had not had contact with any of these parties. It hadn't even had any knowledge of their existence.[97] The Indian socialists were given the task of forming a bridgehead for the International in Asia. A task which they were able to meet with a certain degree of success. Through the Indian party the International first came into contact with newly formed socialist parties in Japan, Burma, Ceylon and Indonesia. A short while later the socialist parties of these four countries together with India would form the nucleus of an Asian regional socialist organization.

---

94   Letter from Wikström to Braunthal, 05/01/1955. IISG, SI 657.
95   Letter from Braunthal to Wikström, 07/01/1955. IISG, SI 657.
96   Letter from Bolle, secretary Sub-Committee COMISCO to Desai, 05/01/1949. IISG, SI 657.
97   Letter from Braunthal to Desai, 28/10/1950. IISG, SI 657.

In Japan socialist ideas had been around since the turn of the century, but it wasn't until after the First World War that leftist parties effectively appeared. Various developments contributed to this evolution: the growth of large cities, the emergence of a worker's movement, the spread of more universal education, the slow democratization of the country and the granting in 1925 of suffrage to all male residents 25 years of age and above. The following elections, which took place three years later, saw the first socialists in the House of Representatives. By the end of the thirties, however, their forward march was abruptly halted by the rising tide of militarism in the country. By 1940, they had entirely disappeared from the political scene. For the Western European socialists who knew history - and the historian Julius Braunthal was certainly one of them - this was simply one more example of the golden rule that democratic political diversity was of fundamental importance for the further continuation of socialism. This was a lesson which would come in handy in their struggle against dictatorial communist regimes in Europe itself.

After the capitulation of Japan in 1945, party politics in that country would get another chance. On the social democratic side of things this resulted in the formation of the Social Democratic Party (SDP). Initially, this party achieved very good results. In the elections of 1947, it even became the largest party in the House of Representatives, which led to their sitting in a coalition government until October 1948. Good electoral results along with the fact that the Japanese SDP faced no serious rival social democratic party at home undoubtedly simplified their admittance into the International. In December 1949, the International approved the SDP as a full member, not even one year after the committee had requested its Indian "division" to contact "potential" socialists in Japan.[98] During the course of 1950 internal conflicts significantly weakened the Japanese party both in terms of position and influence. These came to a head in October 1951, and the party split in two.[99] The two new parties, both recognized by the International, continued, however, to work towards reunification into one social democratic party.

The Labour Party also showed considerable interest in the socialist experiments going on in Burma, which had gained its independence in January 1948. The contact which the SI had with the Socialist Party there, led by

---

98 Letter from Bolle, secretary Sub-Committee COMISCO to Desai, 05/01/1949; Circ. 61/49. 14/12/1949. Minutes of the meeting of COMISCO, Paris, 10-11/12/1949. IISG, SI 48.
99 The 'right-wing' Socialist Party will from now on be referred to as Japan-R, the 'left-wing' party as Japan-L. The reason for the scission was the clear pro-American safety pact that was signed with the United States in August 1952.

U Ba Swe and U Kyaw Nyein, was not established via India however. In June 1950, Julius Braunthal had received the addresses of both party leaders via the Burmese ambassador in London. A certain David Worswick functioned as a go-between and he promised Braunthal that during his next visit to Rangoon he would discuss the possible admission of the Burmese SP into the International with U Ba Swe and U Kyaw Nyein. Other go-betweens between the International and Rangoon were E. G. Farmer, Labour's Commonwealth Officer, who was close with the chairman of the socialist party in Rangoon and Michael Young, who had advised Braunthal to contact a certain Furnivall, the last Brit to still be functioning in the Burmese administration. He would most certainly have had connections in the Burmese government and was himself a member of the influential British Fabian Society. These contacts with Burma as well as with India clearly illustrate the extent to which the International was able to utilize the British colonial and post-colonial network, a subject much in need of further investigation.

At the same time, they also illustrate how much the International's global expansion was dependent upon the whims of British national politics. The existing literature on the Socialist International gives hardly any attention to this nonetheless important motivating factor behind the emerging impulse for global expansion in the direction of Asia. Rather, it lays the emphasis primarily on two other factors. First and foremost, as indicated above, the Cold War. Secondly, the fact that the International's choice to expand to Asia mainly served as a distraction manœuvre to put off the European integration agenda of some continental socialist parties. The French political expert Guillaume Devin, for example, suspected that this factor lay not only at the bottom of the International's global mission but that it was also one of the motivating factors for re-establishing the International in the first place: "The agreement of the BLP on the official reconstruction of the International partially intended to divert the pressure of the "continental socialists" (i.e. the PSB, the SFIO and the PvdA) to horizons that extended those of the European Union. It also illustrated the persistent differences of opinion. To a certain extent the International was re-established to 'forget Europe'."[100]

There can indeed be no doubt as to the deep divisions which existed within COMISCO on this subject. In almost every European-wide institution (the Council of Europe, ECSC, EDC,...) one could see socialists from Belgium, the Netherlands and to a lesser degree France continually at odds with those from Britain and Scandinavia (and from Germany at least until the end of the

100   Devin, *L'Internationale socialiste*, 251.

fifties). The British socialists feared that a supranational Europe would loosen Europe's bonds with the United States and weaken NATO. The Germans feared exactly the opposite - that the integration of Western Europe in a "Europe of the Six" would prolong the division of the German state.[101] Every time the subject of European integration was raised the International was totally paralyzed, so it is quite understandable that the subject was often kept off of the agenda. It was much easier to reach consensus on global issues.

Yet, all the same, this choice for the global over the European was not always only an "emergency exit" out of the "European" dilemma. After all, the initial drive for global expansion had already begun a few years earlier, immediately after the Second World War, and seemed to be more the result of British Commonwealth politics (which at that moment were entirely in the hands of the Labour Party) than of any British aversion for a continental European integration project. What better way to strengthen a free association of independent states, with the British crown at its heart, than to set up a Socialist International with London as its centerpiece?

Latin America: the Limits of British National Interest

The conclusion that specific national interests helped stimulate if not initiate the global expansion process may find its confirmation in COMISCO's (and later the International's) relative reserve with regard to Latin America. Just as the British socialists had worked nonstop from the outset for expansion of the International into Asia, their Spanish associates - as soon as the war was over - began to plea for expansion into Latin America. At the Vienna congress in June 1948, Llopis, the PSOE representative, made a heartfelt appeal not to abandon Latin American socialism.[102] One could hardly expect that the three or four socialist parties there would on their own initiative approach the International. The International would have to cross the ocean, according to Llopis. The Spanish exiles doubtless were motivated by something which went well beyond a mere historical, cultural or emotional affinity. After the Second World War, Franco sought to court the various Latin American states using the rather vague concept of "hispanidad". He hoped that through their support he would be able to attain the much coveted UN recognition which the first meeting of the General Assembly had denied him. Thus it was to be expected that the anti-Franco socialists in exile, just like the Spanish govern-

---

101   Newman. *Socialism and European Unity.*
102   Rodolfo Llopis Ferrándiz was the secretary of the PSOE from 1944 to 1974. He was succeeded by Felipe González Márquez.

ment in exile in Mexico, would try to thwart his attempts with active lobbying throughout the Western Hemisphere. [103]

There was, however, an important difference between the British and the Spanish socialists. Compared to their British compadres, who completely dominated the early International and who, moreover, controlled the very apparatus of government in their country, the Spanish exiles found themselves in an entirely marginal position. In addition to which they were strongly divided amongst themselves. At the gatherings of the International they split themselves into two opposing groups. One group in exile formed around Ramón Lamoneda Fernández and Rodolfo Llopis. The other group, which had remained active in Spain, formed around Rafael Sanchez. At the international socialist assemblies in both Bournemouth and Zurich both groups sought to be recognized. In March 1948, COMISCO finally took a decision and accepted Llopis' Partido Socialista Obrero Español in exile as a full member of the International.[104] The party's influence, however, was to remain limited. From their home in exile, in Toulouse, the party had access to a much more limited network in Latin America than that of the BLP in Asia.

There were other parties within the International which as governing parties, in principle, had interests to defend in Latin America. France, the Netherlands and, once again, Great Britain had territories in the Caribbean, but ethnically, linguistically and geographically these were relatively separate from Latin America. Furthermore, Latin America itself was also more or less indifferent to the existence of these Caribbean territories. Great Britain, and to a lesser degree France and Germany (who at that moment hardly played any role in the International) had economic interests in Latin America, but compared with what they were before the war, these interests were now of minor importance. Great Britain's main worry after 1945 was the Commonwealth in Asia and (of course) the reconstruction of Britain itself. From a strictly economic perspective, Latin America did have a certain importance to Western Europe, but at most it was of a secondary nature. The same was true when considered from the point of view of national security; not a single Western European nation thought Latin America to be of any importance to its own national security.[105]

103   Alba, "Spanish Diplomacy in Latin America".
104   Summarized Report of the First Meeting of COMISCO, 19-20/03/1948. IISG, SI 47.
105   Atkins, *Latin America in the International Political System*, 54.

It is therefore no great surprise, considering the relative lack of "national interest", that COMISCO was not actively recruiting in Latin America. At the moment of the re-establishment of the International in Frankfurt in June 1951, the following of the new organization in Latin America was limited to two "old line socialist" parties in Argentina and Uruguay which had already taken part in the Socialist Labour International during the interbellum.[106] In January 1950, the Socialist Party of Uruguay decided to re-establish relations with the International. José Cardoso, the party secretary delivered his party's message personally while visiting Braunthal.[107] With no prior knowledge of the party's program or political standing at home COMISCO took the party back into the fold.

Shortly afterwards, the Argentine socialists also joined rank. In 1946, the Argentines had already been invited by the BLP to participate in the conference at Clacton-on-Sea. Most probably there was a hidden political motive for this invitation. The fierce anti-Perón Argentine SP (which suffered much under Perón's regime) found some sympathy with the British when in the wake of the war Argentina became one of the principal places of exile for ex-Nazis. Yet just as with the Uruguayan socialists, here too it was a question of continuing a tradition. After the appointment of Julius Braunthal as secretary-general of the International, COMISCO began to take its expansion to Asia more seriously. Braunthal wrote to different "socialist" movements in the Americas asking for more information but it would be an exaggeration to call those requests for information a recruitment campaign such as the one which was going on in Asia.[108]

National interest was of course an important factor. Nevertheless, the global expansion process of COMISCO, and later of the Socialist International, which was initially directed at Asia, can only partially be attributed to those national interests. Very quickly a second element became much more important in the contacts between Western Europe and both Asia and Latin America: the Cold War.

---

106   The term "old-line socialist parties" was coined by the American Robert Alexander, who worked at the department of economics at Rutgers University, New Brunswick. Letter from Alexander to Braunthal, 16/02/1950. IISG, SI 699.
107   Circ. 58/50. IISG, SI 51.
108   One of Braunthals most important informants, from January 1950 onwards, was Robert Alexander. Alexander provided Braunthal with an extensive list of socialist-like movements or parties, which he commented on. IISG, SI 699.

Global Expansion to the Rhythm of the Cold War

1950: The Cold War moves to Asia

Just like its predecessor COMISCO, the Socialist International turned out to be a child of the Cold War. There are two reasons why this was so. Firstly, the organization was very quick in making it clear which side it took on the international scene dominated by the Cold War. Moreover, at the instigation of the British Labour Party, it actively chose for an anti-Soviet realpolitik, even if that choice sometimes clashed with (what some within the ranks called) "pure" socialist ideology. Secondly, the growing East-West tensions appeared to be able to significantly determine the form and composition of the International. Anti-communism became a deciding criterion in the choice of potential partner parties. Parties that were not unambiguously "pro-Atlantic" were, when possible, purged. In other words, the International expanded "to the rhythm of the Cold War." So, at the moment when socialist transnationalism was leaving its European breeding ground the Cold War became its companion de route and helped determine the path followed. This was apparent in the position which the International took up in Asia, in the first half of the 1950's.

Until the beginning of 1949, the Cold War had remained a purely European phenomenon. After the end of the Second World War and the defeat of Japan, an enormous power vacuum was left in Asia. Naturally, both superpowers realized that all events of any importance which arose in Asia would be likely to shift the delicate balance of power. Consequently, both sides paid careful attention to the other's ambitions in the region, be it without letting the situation become a matter of obsession. The internal power struggle in China, for example, between Chiang Kai-shek's nationalists and Mao Zedong's communists was closely followed but a certain sense of perspective was never lost. Recent archive research has shown that Stalin wished at all costs to avoid a conflict with the United States in East Asia. Accordingly, his support for Mao was limited and he even encouraged Mao to a certain restraint. Shortly after 1945, Stalin actually even opted for good relations with Chiang Kai-shek over supporting the communist insurgents.[109]

For his part, Truman, of course, had no desire to see the communists come to power and he was concerned by the real risk that Mao would soon become Moscow's puppet. Yet still in the late forties, Washington saw no great threat in Mao's taking power. For quite a while, the American State Department

109   Goncharov et al., *Uncertain Partners: Stalin, Mao, and the Korean War*, 69.

would hold onto the hope that Mao might become an "Asian Tito", who instead of becoming a close ally of the Soviet Union instead would become its rival.[110] Furthermore, after the war, Japan was occupied by the Americans and had become a solid "Western" bulwark in the area, which apparently put the Americans at ease. For all of these reasons it was common thought in Washington that a communist controlled China would not fundamentally disturb the balance of power in the world. The proclamation of the People's Republic of China on 1 October 1949 was therefore received with no great worry in the decision centers of Washington. This rather pragmatic reaction in the highest policy circles was rather different from the rhetorically canned message which was disseminated to the larger world. Both the press and public opinion in the US and in the whole of the Western World reacted in a much more emotional and panicked way to "the loss of China" than the policy makers in Washington.

The year 1950 saw the clear delineation of an important fault line in Asia. From that year onwards, it was no longer possible to see any event on the Asian continent outside of the light of the Cold War. The Cold War had definitively spilled over into Asia. Mao's legendary train journey to Moscow and his two month sojourn there underlined the close relations between the two communist powers. On 15 February 1950, Mao's visit was brought to a close with the signing of the Sino-Soviet pact, which made clear - if indeed any doubt had remained - that Mao was not at all to become a "new Tito", something which he was to continually remind the Soviets of. By means of this pact, the Soviet sphere of influence was instantly doubled, or this is how the pact was received at any rate.

The flash point of the Cold War, however, was not to be in the potential superpower China but rather on the Korean peninsula, which at that moment, politically, was still relatively insignificant. It is surprising how little interest the two superpowers showed in Korea during the period from 1945 until 1950. Since the collapse of the Japanese occupation regime the country had been split between the US and the Soviets at the 38th parallel.[111] The Korean peninsula was not of vital strategic interest for either side. The USSR withdrew its troops at the end of 1948. Halfway through 1949, the Americans were also to have left the peninsula. A most improbable and exceptional series

---

110   Gaddis, *The Long Peace*, 149-164. In a more recent book Gaddis suggests that the image of Mao as an 'Asian Tito' persisted until after the Sino-Soviet Pact of 1950. Idem, *We Now Know*, 62.

111   Dobbs, *The Unwanted Symbol: American Foreign Policy*; Weathersby, *Soviet Aims in Korea*.

of events, misinterpretations and miscalculations - undoubtedly a shock for adherents of game theory in the field of international relations - ensured that what was essentially a local conflict, in a very short time festered into the first open struggle in which the East (China and Russia) and the West (the United States and its allies) found themselves, to their own surprise, facing off against one another.[112]

The Korean War had important consequences. Firstly, it put an end to the withdrawal of American troops from the Asian continent. Secondly, from that moment onwards every piece of territory, no matter how peripheral, became vitally important to both camps. From the American side this was expressed in the new security doctrine, NSC 68, which was adopted shortly after the beginning of the Korean War. Henceforth, communism was seen as a "Soviet coordinated *global* movement", which had to be fought on all fronts, no matter where. The tripling of the American defense budget was one of the first measures taken in the defense campaign.

For the United States' junior partner, Great Britain, the need to maintain influence in the former colonies of South Asia immediately took on another dimension. Not only were (neo)colonial motives at play, it was now more important than ever to prevent the spread of communism and to block the USSR from gaining any influence in the region. This concern already dated from before the Korean War. In September 1947, for example, the Soviets had founded Cominform which immediately had begun infiltrating nationalist movements in the colonies in an attempt to appropriate the anti-colonial theme. The outbreak of the Korean war, however, placed (what were originally) isolated incidents into a larger context. At the Labour Party conference of October 1950, the question of Korea received much attention. It led to a more general debate on Asia as a whole. The theme of Aneurin Bevan's speech, for example, was the "underdeveloped countries", meaning principally Asia: "In such countries as India, Ceylon, and Burma, it would be hard for our comrades to obtain the principles of civilized intercourse unless we can go to their assistance early enough with the products of industrial civilization (…) If help for the so-called backward areas was not given they would become breeding grounds for war and all sorts of other horrors". Foreign secretary Ernest Bevin, who spoke directly after Bevan was in complete agreement: "Peace cannot be defended without arms - or by arms alone. We must make

112   Cumings, *The Origins of the Korean War, 1945-1947* and Idem, *The Origins of the Korean War, 1947-1950.*

resources available for increasing the wealth of the world's underdeveloped areas."[113]

On the transnational level the effects of the concern to safeguard the rest of Asia from communist influences were soon to be felt. Within the Socialist International the British Labour Party further increased its demands to let the International play an active role in Asia. Thus, in July 1951, precisely at the moment when the peace talks in Asia were reaching a faster tempo, the executive committee of the BLP worked out a proposal stating that "the Socialist International should establish a special fund outside its normal budget for the sole purpose of financing its activities in Asia."

This was consistent with the party's belief that Asia held much unrecognized potential for social democracy. They had given themselves the task of encouraging existing parties in Asia and of helping to establish new parties in countries where as yet socialism had not been organized. The British emphasized that they were in earnest - if indeed such a fund were set up the BLP was ready to come forward with a first contribution of £1,000.[114] Even before the council of the International had discussed the British fund proposal (that would only occur the following December), Braunthal had already guaranteed his Indian colleague, Asoka Mehta, that the fund was sure to be established, which indeed it eventually was.[115]

According to the International, the fund could play an efficient role "in forging closer links between the Socialist movements of the white men's Continents and the Socialist movements of their coloured brothers." At the council meeting of the International in December 1951, a second proposal from the BLP was presented, on which SI chairman Morgan Phillips spoke at length. According to the British socialist, the United Nations' technical assistance program, Truman's Point Four program, and the Colombo Plan were each in their own right very good initiatives aimed at raising the standard of living in the "underdeveloped" countries. Yet, all the same, an extra effort was needed. To that end the BLP proposed that the International, together with socialists outside of Europe, set up their own socialist initiative, a "World Plan for Mutual Aid". The necessity of such a plan was doubted by none and the Belgian socialist Larock described it most clearly: "There is the position in Asia and Africa where misery threatens to provoke revolt in many places, with

113   Circ. 189/50. 06/10/1950. IISG, SI 55.
114   Letter from Phillips to Braunthal, 28/07/1951. IISG, SI 657.
115   Circ. 1/52, 03/01/1952. IISG, SI 64.

the communists ever ready to utilize any movement of revolt, be it social or national, for their own ends."[116]

In this way, with general endorsement, a relatively new theme trickled into the International, a theme that in the years to come would change the orientation of the International itself. A committee was set up composed of representatives from Belgium, the Netherlands, France and Great Britain, four colonial powers, who in consultation with certain Asian socialists endeavored to give voice to the socialists' position with respect to the "underdeveloped" territories in a memorandum which was to be exhaustively discussed at the Milan congress in 1952.[117] The document, *Socialist Policy for the Underdeveloped Territories - A Declaration of Principles,* which was approved in Milan, gave an initial blueprint for a socialist "development policy". In sum, from the year 1951 onwards, the process of global expansion of the International moved into the fast lane, both in terms of content and in terms of organization and networking. It was certainly considerably motivated by the escalating pressures of the Cold War.

Latin America: a Continent firmly in Washington's Hands

Did the Cold War, in the early 1950's, influence the Latin American aspect of the International's global expansion process to the same extent that it influenced its expansion into Asia? It has already been mentioned that Julius Braunthal, SI's dynamic secretary-general, immediately upon being appointed in January 1950, began gathering information on like-minded parties throughout the Western Hemisphere, despite the lack of any specific national interest in that region. This initiative, which he took together with an American expert on Latin America, Robert Alexander, was not purely personal, it was also in response to a specific request from COMISCO.

We can very precisely reconstruct the details of the 1950 information gathering tour made by Braunthal in Latin America based upon the letters he wrote in that period. They give a very detailed image of the regional party landscape in the year 1950. In Chile, there were two rival parties: the relatively small Partido Socialista de Chile under the leadership of Bernardo Ibañez and the

116   Circ. 15/52, 31/01/1952. Report on the Conference of the Council of the SI. Brussels, 14-
         16/12/1951. IISG, SI 64.
117   The committee had prepared a first draft at the beginning of February 1952, which was
         sent to a large number of socialist parties, even to parties outside of Europe that were not
         members of the SI. In October 1952, the text was finalized at the Milan Conference. It was
         meant to become 'one of the most significant documents of contemporary Socialism'.

Partido Socialista Popular, which in 1948, under the leadership of Humberto Soto, had torn itself free from Ibañez' party.[118] Both parties were provisionally recognized by the International. A definitive decision was put off, pending "further developments" - a suggestion of Alexander's.[119] To the north, in Peru, Alexander took the side of the Partido Socialista del Peru, which subsequently was not accepted by Braunthal. The party not only had had a tendency to flirt with communism, it was also effectively collaborating with the military regime of Manuel Odría, who in 1948 had seized power in a coup d'état. The APRA, which as an opposition party had been repressed and forced into exile, in the circumstances appeared to be a viable alternative worthy of support.[120] Alexander and Braunthal also saw possibilities in two of Peru's neighbors, Brazil and Ecuador. In Ecuador a relatively small socialist party was already active, although be it with communist sympathies, and it was open to being approached by COMISCO. In Brazil, since the end of Vargas' dictatorship in 1945, a socialist party had also been in forming. The party offered safe haven to both leftist practicing Catholics and died in the wool Marxists. In Mexico Alexander advised Braunthal to establish contact with the Grupos Socialistas de Mexico, which was more a movement than a political party. In Cuba the Federación Socialista seemed a likely potential partner. Braunthal also wrote to the People's National Party of Jamaica.

Not all parties reacted to Braunthal's approaches and even fewer actually took active steps to enter into affiliation with the International.[121] Eventually, only the People's National Party of Jamaica would become a new member in 1952. The limited success of Braunthal's efforts have much to do with the fact that he hardly had the time to follow up on the information he had gathered during his 1950 tour. Shortly after having posted his letters to various Latin American partners Asia began to demand nearly all of his attention.

The International remained therefore more or less blind to the groups that were beginning to take shape in Latin America, and to the regional dynamic which developed there. In 1952, the Partido Socialista Popular de Chile began attempts to form a regional socialist grouping consisting of socialists from Uruguay, Argentina and Ecuador, Apristas from Peru, members of the

---

118   Drake, *Socialism and Populism in Chile*, 283-301.
119   Letter from Alexander to Braunthal, 16/02/1950. IISG, SI 699.
120   Ibidem.
121   Braunthal received answers from Jamaica, Brazil, Cuba and Peru. Letter from Braunthal to Llopis, 21/08/1950. IISG, SI 699. The Brazilians kept in touch; a real accession, however, was impossible, since the internationalization of political parties was forbidden by the Brazilian constitution.

Venezuelan Acción Democrática and from the Labour Movement of Bolivia. The regional grouping held its first congress in 1953 in La Paz, Bolivia. Emilio Frugoni, co-founder and secretary-general of the Uruguayan Socialist Party - which was already a member of the International - informed Braunthal of these developments via his fellow party member Humberto Maiztegui, who at that moment was in London.[122] Frugoni suggested to Braunthal that a regional secretariat be opened immediately in Montevideo as a contact and information center for Latin American socialist groupings.[123] Frugoni's proposal was backed by Alicia Moreau de Justo, the international secretary of the Argentine Partido Socialista and widow of the party's founder. The International's answer left little to the imagination, "in principle" they agreed with the idea as long as it did not entail any costs for the International.[124] The year was 1953, it was a year which saw communism in Asia prepare to go into high gear, a year which saw France slowly loose its grip on Indochina, and a year which saw the International spend more and more energy (and a bit more money) to help establish the Asian Socialist Conference, which is how the regional cooperative association had been dubbed. After receiving this response the Uruguyan socialists temporarily relegated their plan to the back burner.

The Cold War which was manifesting itself so emphatically in Asia, caused hardly a ripple in Latin America. Even in the darkest years of the East-West conflict the South American continent remained firmly in the hands of the United States. After World War II, the hegemony of the United States in the region, in terms of market control, foreign investment, financial and certainly military assistance, was generally accepted, although not always enthusiastically appreciated.[125] Two multilateral agreements, the Inter-American Treaty of Reciprocal Assistance, signed in 1947 (the so-called Rio Pact), and the Charter of the Organization of American States, signed in 1948, together with a whole series of bilateral military agreements kept the hemisphere sternly in Washington's hands. On all important issues (the Korean War, the exclusion of China from the UN, the Afro-Asian neutrality movement) the Latin American elite generally followed the path laid out by their northern bosses.[126]

122   Letter from Frugoni to Maiztegui, 11/03/1953. IISG, SI 705.
123   Circ. 95/53, 28/07/1953. IISG, SI 70.
124   Letter from Braunthal to Frugoni, 30/07/1953. IISG, SI 705.
125   Atkins, *Latin America in the International Political System*.
126   Rabe, *Eisenhower and Latin America*.

Furthermore, the Soviet Union had more or less completely ignored the Western Hemisphere, at least until the Cuban Revolution in 1959. An author such as Pope Atkins posited: "the Soviet view of Latin America and commitment of minimal resources there conformed with earlier Imperial Russian lack of interest".[127] After the Russian Revolution and especially after World War II, the Soviets did begin to show more interest in the region and they attempted to infiltrate local communist parties through their participation in Cominform, yet the Soviets never really saw in these minor efforts a serious attempt to establish a foothold in Latin America. After all, Lenin himself once said that the proximity of the United States seriously limited any real possibility for social revolution in the region. History proved him right. In 1954, there were only three states in the region - Mexico, Argentina and Uruguay - which had diplomatic relations with Moscow. In many Latin American countries the establishing of a communist party had even been made illegal. In the few instances when communists were successful in seating themselves in government and testing Washington's hegemony, their victories were immediately followed by armed intervention putting quick end to communist aspirations, which was the case in Guatemala in 1954 for example.[128] Compared to Latin America, Asia promised much better prospects for the Soviets.

For a different reason, however, the then current international political reality had a dissuasive effect on the International. Not only did it seem that there was not much need in Latin America for the International's anti-communist missionary work, it also became apparent that each intervention in the backyard of the United States was likely to meet with opposition from Washington. Attempts from Europe to support Latin American socialist parties - some of which seriously objected to Washington's support of regional dictators - could not count on receiving much understanding in Washington. Most likely, not all European socialists appreciated this state of affairs, but the situation weighed heavily on the British policy makers who in turn encouraged the International to proceed with restraint in Latin America.[129] This became even more so in the years 1953 and 1954, when it became apparent that the security of the European continent depended more than ever on close ties with the United States.

127   Atkins, *Latin America in the International Political System*, 79; Gouré and Rothenberg, *Soviet Penetration of Latin America*, 1.
128   Gleijeses, *Shattered Hope: the Guatemalan Revolution*.
129   Platt, "British Diplomacy in Latin America", 23-25.

The absence of any particular national agendas with reference to Latin America in combination with the international state of affairs seems to explain the International's relative indifference towards Latin America. When after the Vienna congress of June 1954 a subcommittee was formed to deal with the conceptualization of organizational reform, and particularly the global expansion of the International, it was primarily set up in response to the challenges posed in Asia. Any attention for the socialist movements in Latin America was therefore of a secondary nature.[130] The International did compose a detailed list of socialist movements in Latin America, but there was no talk of any real engagement.[131] Moreover, there were still no funds available for Latin America. An Argentine proposal to set up, for example, a Spanish and Portuguese language version of *Socialist International Information* for the purpose of keeping the Latin American socialists informed was turned down for lack of funds.[132]

A World-Embracing International Tackling the Challenge of Regionalism

The contrast between the International's voluntaristic policy in Asia since the early fifties and its rather passive Latin America policy was remarkable. Shortly after establishing the first contacts with Asian socialist parties, it became apparent, however, that not all of these Asian parties had been waiting impatiently for the International. Confronted with Asia's reticence, the main objective of the International - and especially of chairman Morgan Phillips and secretary-general Julius Braunthal - became to gain the upper hand with the Asian socialists. This was especially so after 1952, when the Asian parties slowly began to integrate in a potentially rival regional association. From that moment on, the two leaders of the International would commit themselves furiously to their task of uniting all socialist parties in one single, worldwide international organization.

It was the Socialist Party of India which played a crucial role in the creation of an Asian socialist network. Despite the ambiguity of the situation, the Indian socialists seemed to be able to combine this regional task effortlessly with

---

130   This Sub-Committee was founded in May 1954 and it met for the first time on 27 and 28 June 1954 in Paris. Circ. 43/54, 30/07/1954. Recommendations of the Sub-Committee on the Work and Organisation of the Socialist International. IISG, SI 74.

131   Circ. B.20/54. Contacts between the Socialist International and Socialist movements in overseas countries. IISG, SI 74.

132   Circ. 51/54, 08/10/1954. IISG, SI 74.

their role as the International's bridgehead in Asia. This latter position entailed that they kept the International regularly informed of developments in other Asian countries. On occasion they even brought London in direct contact with other Asian socialists, as was the case with Japan. The party's other task, that of being the regional pacesetter, they worked out on their own. At their sixth annual party congress, in August 1947, the executive committee of the party charged Shrimati Kamaladevi and Dr. Rammanohar Lohia with the task of warming up similarly oriented parties in neighboring countries to the idea of a regional Asian conference. To support their efforts, a "Foreign Affairs Bureau" was set up, with Madhav Gokhale as secretary.

Gradually socialists from other countries began to get involved. During the visit of Suzuki, chairman of the Japanese SDP, to India in July 1951, the idea of organizing a regional conference of Asian socialist parties was discussed in detail. After Burma, Indonesia and Lebanon had also promised their full participation, it was decided to hold a preparatory meeting in India, in the spring of 1952. This gathering, which eventually took place at the end of March 1952 in Burma, and not in India, was of great practical importance. The crucial outlines for future collaboration were set. In addition, the coopera-tion between India, Indonesia and host country Burma was institutionalized in the form of a "preparatory committee", which was operational as of July 1952. The committee's main task was to encourage socialist parties from all over the Asian continent to come together in a sort of "International". One of the ways they did this was through the publication of the bimonthly bulletin *Socialist Asia,* which not only carried news of the various Asian parties but also laid the groundwork for a regional organization.[133]

The network of Asian socialist parties which began to take shape in the early 1950's did so initially largely outside of the International. The following passage from Braunthal's unanswered letter to the Burmese socialist U Ba Swe illustrates this best. The letter is dated March 1951: "I read with great interest the report on the visit of the Indian Socialist Party's delegation to the Burmese Socialist Party. From the report in *Janata* of 18/2 I learnt that you discussed with our Indian Socialist friends their relations to the Socialist Inter-national and also, a suggestion to convene an Asian Socialist Conference. This question will also be discussed with Dr. Sjharer of the Indonesian Socialist

---

133   The first issue of *Socialist Asia* came out on 16 August 1952. Since then it was published very regularly until halfway 1957. On 1 May 1955, 1956 and 1957 the Asian Socialist Conference and the Socialist International published the bulletin together.

Party, so I learnt from the report."[134] Most probably such conversations, which Braunthal had to discover in the Indian socialist's party publication, stimulated him and chairman Morgan Phillips (and the BLP as a whole) to take an initiative themselves: the special fund for Asian parties, which the International had set up precisely in this period, has already been mentioned. In the same letter in which they informed Mehta of the soon to be established fund, Braunthal and Phillips made him a concrete proposal: "We considered that it might perhaps be useful if the Indian Socialist Party could arrange a conference of Socialist parties of South Asia to consider the setting up of a regional center of Socialist movements in Asia, that is to say, of India, Pakistan, Burma, Indonesia and Ceylon, if there is a Socialist Party."

This is precisely what the Asian socialists were at that moment in the process of planning. Braunthal hoped to take over that initiative or at the very least to become associated with it. To that end the International proposed delegating two members to the first congress of an Asian regional center in order to discuss future collaboration with all the parties present.[135] Shortly thereafter, Mehta updated Braunthal as to all the conversations which he had already had and which were to be continued in the spring of 1952. He promised to keep the International informed and so he did. Regarding the British idea of setting up an "Asian fund", however, Mehta proved rather reticent. The idea was very promising indeed but he thought that Asian socialists should be more involved in its establishment: "My feeling is that the Socialist International should not finalize its plans till the idea has been discussed by the meeting of the representatives of the Socialist Parties in South-East Asia. In such matters hustling sometimes does more harm than good..."[136]

Braunthal's fear was that a parallel network would develop in Asia, independent of the International. This was even more so after an unspecified press agency in Jakarta had reported that Indian and Indonesian socialists were in agreement regarding the establishment of "an Asian Socialist International as a separate body from the International". Moreover, the agency had included a quote from Dr. Lohia, who had taken part in the opening congress of the International in Frankfurt and who had left rather unsatisfied with what he had heard there. Lohia's message was clearly that a new International in Asia might offer an appropriate alternative. The *Manchester Guardian* also carried the report and according to them it had been confirmed by a "prominent

134 Letter from Braunthal to U Ba Swe, 16/03/1951. IISG, SI 491.
135 Letter from Braunthal to Mehta, 17/08/1951. IISG, SI 657.
136 Letter from Mehta to Braunthal, 13/11/1951. IISG, SI 657.

member" of the Labour Party. Braunthal immediately went to the editor of the *Manchester Guardian* to set him straight: "undoubtedly there had been a misunderstanding". Braunthal found the issue important enough to write to the Indian Socialist Party asking for a full explanation. Mehta attempted to assuage the secretary's worries. He assured Braunthal that there had never been any talk of establishing a separate International.[137] Braunthal was not entirely assuaged. A few months later he was to learn from Mehta's fellow party member Gokhale that it was principally the Indonesians and the Burmese who were not interested in closer ties with the International.[138] Braunthal also had other sources of information which pointed in the same direction. The British socialist Bernard, for example, who in the summer of 1952, at the invitation of the Congress of Cultural Freedom, had read a series of lectures in Burma and India, informed Braunthal at length about his contacts with local socialists. The most important conclusion which Bernard drew - "I was surprised to see how deep and how general the anti-Western attitude still is in both India and Burma" - did little to help placate Braunthal's misgivings.[139]

The secretary-general of the Socialist International reacted to these alarming signals by immediately writing a lengthy letter, in an attempt to influence the position of the Burmese and Indonesian parties. His message was unambiguous: "The simple truth is that the Socialist International cannot properly fulfill its task for the common aims of Socialism unless it has a truly universal character. Should the forthcoming congress of the Asian Socialist Parties (...) decide to form an Asian Socialist International, not as a regional organization of the International but independent of it, it would deprive the Socialist International of potential members in regions destined to play a decisive part in world affairs. It would also deprive Asian Socialism of a forum from which it could make its voice heard throughout the world (...) It would, above all, frustrate the ardent hopes of all genuine Socialists, hopes held since the days of Karl Marx, to see the Socialists of all countries united in a universal International".[140]

---

137   Letter from Mehta to Braunthal, 28/11/1951. IISG, SI 657.
138   Report by Gokhale on the Preparatory Meeting in Rangoon, 25-29/03/1952, quoted in Circ. B14/52. IISG, SI 65.
139   Bernard's Report on the Socialist Parties of Burma and India. Circ. B21/52. 04/07/1952. IISG, SI 65.
140   Circ. B15/52. 06/06/1952. Letter to the Asian Socialist Parties. IISG, SI 65.

From this quotation it would appear that Braunthal's apology for a unique, united, and indivisible International was constructed around a double leitmotif. The first argument was that the creation of a separate Asian International would divide social democracy worldwide and therefore also weaken it vis-à-vis the Comintern. Thus, he appealed to the international situation, the Cold War, as the determining factor. In addition, one particular facet of the organizational tradition was to play equally important a role. The International, just like its predecessors, was a centrally oriented inter-party organization with a clear hegemon. It was definitely not so that Marxist inspired internationalism had any commonly shared credibility, rather it had become a myth, a symbol which only here and there was used when convenient. But even without its ideological mantle the organization still had a certain tradition of its own. The attempt of some Asian parties to set up their own regional alliance spurred the International to immediate action, aimed at re-enforcing the model of centralized unity. A decentralized cooperative alliance, at that moment, was not an option. We will see this reflex towards decentralization again, to an even stronger degree, from the mid-fifties on, in the International's relations with Latin America.

The regional Asian structure did come into being. In the spring of 1953, the months of preparatory talks between the various Asian socialist groups finally bore fruit. On January 6, at 9 a.m., roughly 200 representatives gathered in Rangoon City Hall to attend the formal opening of the first Asian Socialist Conference (ASC). The International was also present in Rangoon. Over the course of 1952, for above mentioned reasons, the International had begun to pay considerably more attention to Asia. The presence of an SI delegation in Rangoon was an expression of this tendency. Clement Attlee, Kaj Björk, André Bidet and Saul Rose - in the capacity of Attlee's secretary - were all part of the delegation to Rangoon. Rose would be unable to get Asia out of his system, and later would write a remarkable book about socialism on that continent.[141]

The Burmese chairman of the welcome committee, U Kyaw Nyein, in his introduction immediately set the tone for the gathering: a familiar feeling was to prevail at the conference due to "the general feeling shared by Asian people to understand one another better."[142] Relations between the ASC and the SI

---

141   Rose, *Socialism in Southern Asia*.
142   Opening speech by U Kyaw Nyein. Report of the First Asian Socialist Conference. Rangoon 1953. An Asian Socialist Publication. IISG, SI 513.

were of course a topic of discussion at the conference. On the agenda of a session chaired by the Indian Jayaprakash Narayan, the topic of the relations between the two organizations was listed under the heading "Permanent Machinery of ASC", next to the topics "Principles and Objectives of Socialism" and "Asia and World Peace". Central to the debate was the question of whether the new organization should be linked to the SI and if so, in which way.

The future Israeli prime minister Moshe Sharett, who took the minutes for this session, discerned three tendencies. Some, according to Sharett, saw the socialist movement as having an essential worldwide unity and they therefore strongly defended the idea of eventual fusion as a long-term goal. Opponents of such ideas pointed out the fundamental differences that historically have existed between socialism in "underdeveloped" countries and socialism in the more "advanced" countries. Often they were also very suspicious of socialist parties that had compromised themselves, directly or indirectly, by having taken up colonial attitudes. The last group, to which Sharett attributed chairman Narayan, recognized the historical differences yet still saw one integral ideological identity. This group consisted of socialists who believed that the ASC should certainly maintain its independence as a separate organization, even if only for the time being, yet they also, nonetheless, advocated regular contact with the Socialist International or with its members.[143]

The parties who adhered to the first point of view - socialists from Israel, Malaya, and the right-wing of the Japanese SDP (Japan-R) - were already members of the International. Japan-R considered the ASC as a regional division of the SI and not as a separate organization. They did not deny the difference in background and content between Asian and Western European socialism, nor the assertion that the Western socialists had still not outgrown anachronistic colonial attitudes, yet they still did not believe that those facts needed to result in a separatism which was disadvantageous for Asia: "We sincerely hope that our zeal and enthusiasm in emphasizing the peculiarities of Asia may not carry us too far into committing the mistake of separating ourselves from the West, either structurally or ideologically, with the dangerous possibility of our eventually opposing our socialist comrades in the West. We believe our aim should be integration and unity instead of differentiation."[144] In light of the state of world affairs the Asian socialist

---

143 Report of the First Asian Socialist Conference. Rangoon 1953. An Asian Socialist Publication. IISG, SI 513.
144 Matsuoka in Ibidem.

parties were in "dire need" of that very integration, through membership in the Socialist International. A division between socialism in Europe and socialism in Asia would only play into the hands of the imperialistic designs of the Soviet Union, which already considered Asia its "rearguard base". A similar argument was used by the Nepalese representative B.P. Koirala, although be it less explicitly. Despite seeing the necessity of Asian integration for resolving problems specific to Asia, Koirala realized that socialists from both Asia and Europe would need to work together in order to safeguard democracy (a universal given, according to him) from the very real threat of totalitarianism.[145]

Japan-R was also counting on assistance from the European socialist parties to establish and make operational concrete programs aimed at poverty relief and reduction. "Countries in need of development" were in no position to turn down the capital intended for such development programs, yet they hoped that such assistance would be free of the "imperialistic" designs of the past. The Malayan representative, Mohamed Sopiee, was largely on the same wavelength, and reassured the International that the existence of an Asian Socialist Conference would not hinder the further expansion of international socialist solidarity. On the contrary, through strengthening Asian socialism, Asian aspirations and ideals would be reflected all the more so in the International, especially in issues of colonial politics, an area in which the International did not excel. In other words, the ASC should function as a sort of pressure group within and integral to the International.

The socialist parties from Egypt, Lebanon and Pakistan however were strongly opposed to any potential form of integration with the International. Pakistan went so far as to propose a motion which would forbid all future associations between the Asian Socialist Conference and the Socialist International, as well as ban future double affiliations. Parties which were already members of both associations could stay so, but such dual membership should be avoided in the future. Initially Egypt did not even want to allow continuance of dual affiliation.

The left wing of the Japanese SDP (Japan-L) was somewhat more moderate. For them affiliation with the SI was permissible, but each party would have to decide on that for itself. They also stressed that the ASC did not have to become a mere "regional subdivision" of the International. Full organizational independence, however, did not have to exclude the possibility of close

145   Koirala in Ibidem, 25.

cooperation with the SI. That was also the tenor of the draft of a resolution forwarded by the Indian representative Gokhale, which proposed that the establishment of a "liaison with the SI" should be one of the aims of the ASC.[146] Burma and Indonesia which had always retained a certain distance from the International, went along with this. At the request of the SI, the words "at all levels" were added to the draft which would mean that the secretariat, the bureau, and the conference of the ASC would be expected to stay in contact with their corresponding sectors in the International. After Japan-R, Malaya and Israel received guarantees from chairman Narayan that such a formulation would include the possibility of developing better links with the SI they retracted some of their amendments. Even Egypt and Pakistan acquiesced after an appeal to unity was made, but they let it be known that this in no way meant that they had changed their negative opinion of the SI. The draft was approved without any further obstacle.

The final resolution was therefore a compromise: the Asian Socialist Conference would remain independent and not become part of the Socialist International, yet nor would it obstruct international socialist cooperation. The ASC had no intention of turning into a rival organization, but socialists outside Asia had to realize that the responsibility for solidarity rested not only on Asian shoulders, and that a proactive engagement from the SI was also expected.[147] The cooperation between the two organizations would include everything from sending delegations to important gatherings and the exchange of relevant documents and circulars to the publication of SI articles in *Socialist Asia*, the ASC's journal. The leading Asian parties would enter into relation with the SI to the degree which they deemed "psychologically and politically possible".

According to the SI representatives in Rangoon, at that moment, that was all that could be expected. According to Kaj Björk, who recorded the minutes, the SI delegation in Rangoon limited itself to observation and occasional participation in the discussions within the various sessions. The parties which took part in the organization of the conference had, at any rate, already long before made clear their position regarding the SI. Moreover, the SI delegation was conscious of not giving the impression of imposing their attitudes on the Asians. However, it is clear that the end result was somewhat less than satisfactory for the International, which had assumed that the goals of the

---

146   Circ. B14/52. Preparatory Meeting for the Plenary Congress of the Asian Socialist Parties. IISG, SI 65.
147   Report of the First Asian Socialist Conference. Rangoon, 1953, IISG, SI 51336.

ASC were one and the same with what had been expressed by the council of the International:"the integration of Asian and African Socialism into a world-embracing International."[148]

If the gathering in Rangoon had made one thing clear to the International, it was that if they did not want to see Asia drift away they would have to take a much more proactive stance regarding that continent. That message still rang clearly after the meeting of the council of the International in Paris on 13 April 1953, the first meeting of that body since the Rangoon Conference. The council decided to establish a "Subcommittee on Relations with the ASC", which would deal with the nature of the cooperation between the two organizations in a detailed way. A certain number of concrete measures were needed which would form the basis for a deeper integration of the two organizations, with the end goal of forming one unified International (they just wouldn't give up).[149] Besides representatives from Austria, Germany and Sweden the committee also included representatives from countries with colonial possessions: France, Great Britain and the Netherlands. The recommendations which the subcommittee had come up with were presented to and discussed with the ASC delegation on July 12, in Stockholm, only days before the third congress of the International was to take place in that city. They hoped that together they would be able to come up with a common list of recommendations to present to the conference.[150] A separate meeting on July 13, peripheral to the Stockholm congress, unanimously approved the recommendations. The next day Morgan Phillips presented them to the council and shortly afterwards they were ratified, as a resolution, by the Stockholm congress.

The resolution recognized different components of mutual cooperation. The first component consisted of an exchange of delegations: the SI promised to send delegations, when invited, to the internal meetings and conferences of the ASC and in turn to invite ASC delegations to all SI congresses, general assemblies, internal meetings and expert conferences. Individual members of the ASC and the SI were also encouraged to exchange delegations. This was all partly in recognition of an already existing practice: an SI delegation of three was present at the first ASC Conference (in Rangoon, January

148 Circ. 1/52, 03/01/1952. IISG, SI 64.
149 Circ. 96/53, 28/07/1953. Minutes of the Conference of the Council of the SI. Stockholm 14/7/1953.
150 At the congress representatives were present from countries like Burma, India, Indonesia, Israel, Japan, Malaya and Pakistan. Report of the Third Congress of the Socialist International, Stockholm 1953, Fraternal address of U Tun Win. Circ. 115/53. IISG, SI 71.

1953); the General Assembly of the International (Paris, April 1953) was attended by the secretaries of the ASC, and three months later at the SI congress in Stockholm Asian socialists were represented by Mohd Yusuf Khan, Prem Bhasin, Soerjokoesoemo Wijono and Tun Win. At the last two gatherings the ASC even made a few concrete proposals to expand inter-organizational cooperation, which according to Wijono were accepted by the International in Stockholm.[151]

Soon, however, the financial implications of such intensive collaboration became apparent. The Rangoon Conference, for example, forced the SI to fully review its budget for 1953. The extra costs arising from cooperation with the ASC were estimated to be at about £2,560: £1,400 for the sending of delegations to ASC's internal meetings (two per year) and the ASC conference (one every two years), and £1160 for exchange of information. The total expenses for the year 1953 reached £11,100. Due to the increase, a re-evaluation of member contributions was necessary. The result of which was that it was soon decided not to send a delegation to each and every ASC gathering. The Japanese and the Israeli parties which belonged to both groups could represent the SI just as effectively. In this way "extravagant" costs were eliminated, which gave the SI a little more breathing room and the ability to send a stronger delegation to the plenary congresses of the ASC. Moreover, the SI was able to scale back their representation without embarrassment since the ASC, at a meeting in August 1953, had made a similar decision to henceforth only attend "very important" gatherings of the SI.[152]

A second aspect of the mutual cooperation consisted in holding regular joint conferences at which "urgent problems" which were of interest to both organizations, or the socialist movement at large, would be discussed. Before the year was out, the ASC had tabled a proposal to form a joint conference concerning the review of the UN charter, which in 1954-1955 was a hot issue.

The exchange of information, of the bulletins of both organizations and of the minutes of congresses, expert conferences or general assemblies, was the third component. It was expected that both secretaries would contribute articles concerning important events for European and Asian socialism in *Socialist Asia,* the ASC bulletin, and in *Socialist Information,* the SI bulletin.

---

151   Circ. B19/53, 24/09/1953. Report by Phillips of ASC Bureau Meeting, Hyderabad 10-12/08/1953. IISG, SI 73.
152   Ibidem.

As of September 1953, all members of the International were called upon to subscribe to *Socialist Asia*. The resolution also ordered both organizations to contribute regularly to a joint bulletin.[153] At the ASC's internal meeting in Hyderabad, from August 10 to 12 (at which Morgan Phillips was present), a very similar program of mutual cooperation was accepted.

A fourth aspect of cooperation was the establishment of a Joint Publishing Enterprise, a publishing house for socialist literature destined primarily for the Asian, African and "West Indian" market. Both organizations were invited to study the feasibility of such a project. Along the way, other forms of mutual cooperation popped up, as a result of the initiatives of individual parties. The Swedish socialists, for example, set up a scholarship program in 1954, which gave young Asian students the chance to come and study in Stockholm for half a year.[154]

The above mentioned measures were intended to bring the ASC and the SI into closer organizational harmony. For many Western European social democrats these measures formed, however, only a minimum program. Willi Eichler of the German SPD could count on receiving much support in Stockholm when he complained that the existence of both a Socialist International and an Asian Socialist Conference was "unacceptable". "The Socialist International, to be true to its real meaning, must incorporate all Socialist movements", he argued.[155] In other words, in 1953, the main goal of the International still remained, as Morgan Phillips put it, to be "a single unitary Socialist International in the not too distant future".[156]

153   Circ. 115/53, 05/10/1953. Report of the Third Congress of the Socialist International, 141-142. IISG, SI 71.
154   Circ. 65/54, 30/12/1954. Minutes of the meeting of the Bureau of the SI, Amsterdam, 19/12/1954. IISG, SI 74.
155   Circ. 115/53. Report of the Third Congress of the Socialist International, Stockholm 1953. IISG, SI 71.
156   Circ. 96/53, 28/07/1953. Minutes of the Conference of the Council of the SI. IISG, SI 70.

The Socialist International's Eurocentrism as an Obstacle to Successful Expansion

Asian Objections to a "Colonialist International"

The fact that COMISCO and later the International had an image problem was clear from their very first attempts at expansion. Already in 1948, Western European socialists were confronted with the reluctance of the Indian Congress Socialist Party to become a full member of the International. There were various reasons for that reluctance. After attending their first COMISCO meetings, the Indian representatives could attest that the gatherings were by and large only attended by "functionaries of lesser importance" and that therefore there was no guarantee that the decisions taken during such assemblies would be implemented. They also found that the "Western European vote" carried a disproportionate amount of influence when making decisions. For this reason Rammanohar Lohia, a party member of the Congress Socialist Party, called COMISCO a "post-office and nothing more" in his party's bulletin, *Janata*. Lohia hit the nail on the head when he said: "Can there be a greater condemnation of international Socialism than that its conferences are never attended by front-rank men except of the country where they meet but by second-grade functionaries of the various national parties?"[157]

More important, however, was the nationalistic CSP's ideological and principal objection to the colonial policies of some of the core Western European member parties of the International. The party expressed its dissatisfaction most succinctly in a letter dated July 1948. The CSP remained interested in closer ties with the International but "it feels that there is a basic difference in outlook between a very influential section of European Social Democracy and we Socialists in India and Asia, especially on the colonial question."

The Dutch PvdA, which at that moment was part of a governing coalition which had a particularly bad reputation in Indonesia, had the most to make up for if it wanted to improve its reputation. The Netherlands sat very uneasy with Sukarno's declaration of independence on 17 August 1945. The loss of Indonesia was a trauma and a shock for the Netherlands of which the emotional consequences were more difficult to swallow than the material.

---

157   Letter from Desai to Braunthal, 09/09/1950. IISG, SI 657. Lohia, quoted in a letter from Braunthal to Rohit Dave, editor of Janata, 01/09/1950. IISG, SI 657.

Out of fear of becoming just "a bit of farmland on the shores of the North Sea", or of being "reduced to the rank of Denmark", The Hague strove to bind the independent archipelago to it in a union, in which the "Indonesian Republic would be reduced as much as possible to a member state or even, if necessary, eliminated."[158] To that end, the Dutch had even carried out two military interventions, so-called "police actions" (in July 1947 and December 1948). This aggressive policy against Indonesia was put forward especially by the ministers of the Catholic People's Party, but this did not take away the fact that it was actively supported by their socialist coalition partners. After all, the Dutch prime minister Willem Drees was a socialist.

This solidarity with the government policy produced deep disappointment within the party (after the first "police action" roughly 7000 party members returned their membership cards) yet it was of great tactical importance to the party leadership. Namely, it gave the party the chance to prove that they deserved their difficultly won place among the Dutch political elite, as well as their new image of being worthy of sitting in government.[159] Moreover, they hoped that through the socialist-Christian Democratic coalition they would be able to make important advances in social legislation. These arguments, of course, meant little to Asian socialists.

The criticism of the Indian socialists was also directed against the French SFIO, which until 1951 sat in an equally "imperialistically oriented" coalition government. The French received much criticism for their involvement in Indochina. Finally, the Indians also had a few words for the British Labour Party: "You will excuse me if I tell you that my party is not in agreement with certain aspects of the British Foreign Policy also."[160] Those "certain aspects" were principally related to the British decisions to send troops to both Indochina and Indonesia, which in the region was perceived as support for the French and Dutch in their attempts to maintain control over their respective areas. The criticism was also aimed at the British refusal to discuss India's possible withdrawal from the Commonwealth.

All the same, the British did seem to have a certain degree of credibility, especially in comparison with the Dutch and French socialists (at this point the Belgians received no mention). The myth of a voluntary and fully planned,

---

158 Kuitenbrouwer, *De ontdekking van de Derde Wereld*, 29. See also Wesseling, *Indië verloren, Rampspoed geboren*, 286-288.
159 Orlow, "The Paradoxes of Success. Dutch Social Democracy", 46.
160 Letter from Limaye to BLP, 07/06/1948 in IISG, SI 657.

almost peaceful transfer of power from the British seat of might to the colonial regions was exceptionally strong. The Labour leaders did not neglect to
proudly mention their own involvement in these matters, which according
to them also equally attested to Labour's "anti-colonial" tradition. The British
Labour prime minister Clement Attlee would write in 1960 in a rather self-
satisfied way: "There is only one Empire where, without external pressure
or weariness at the burden of governing, the ruling people has voluntarily
surrendered its hegemony over subject peoples and has given them their
freedom… This unique example is the British Empire."[161] The strength of this
myth can be surmised from the fact that even as late as the 1980's, it was
still being declared in academic studies.[162] Today it is no longer accepted at
face value. Stephen Howe rightly describes Labour policy between 1945 and
1951 as "abortive, incoherent, or merely an ex post facto rationalization for
decisions taken in haste, under pressure, and for quite different reasons from
those publicly presented. And whilst the end of the Empire may have been
a less bloody and traumatic affair for Britain than for France or Portugal, the
record of armed conflict in Ireland, Palestine, Malaya, Kenya, Cyprus and Aden
hardly indicates a smoothly consensual process.[163] Yet in the years 1945 till
1951 pride in the recognition of Indian, Pakistani, Ceylonese and Burmese
independence undoubtedly overshadowed the glaring lack of progress in the
other British colonies.

Other parties of the future Asian Socialist Conference also complained of
the colonialist tendencies in the International. In contrast with the Japanese
party, which was a full member of the Socialist International, and the Indian
Congress Socialist Party which in the end became a consulting member,
contact with Burma was anything but frequent. Braunthal's letter to
U Ba Swe in June 1950, the first attempt to establish contact with Burma,
went unanswered. Braunthal would repeat his efforts two more times, with a
letter to U Kyaw Nyein and U Ba Swe in January 1951, and with a letter to
U Ba Swe in March of the same year. Both attempts went unanswered. Not a
single letter from Burma is to be found in the archives of the International.
The same attitude was also taken up by the very small but well organized
Indonesian Socialist Party. London's attempts to get in touch with the party
via the Netherlands or India remained unsuccessful.

---

161   Attlee, *Empire into Commonwealth*, 1.
162   Cf. the monumental work by Morgan, *The Official History of Colonial Development* and the
      equally impressive *Commonwealth. A History of the British Commonwealth of Nations* by Hall.
163   Howe, *Anticolonialism in British Politics*, 7-8.

It was therefore unimaginable that either the Burmese or the Indonesian party would for the time being enter the International. There was still too much bad blood regarding colonialism. During the preparatory meetings which preceded the Rangoon congress in the spring of 1952, for example, the Burmese and Indonesian socialists lamented vociferously the fact that some European parties still had not lost their "imperialist" outlook.[164] Colonial and occupied Asia couldn't just forget the last two hundred years, and it wasn't only Asia: "There is Africa - the Arabs in the north, the negroes and other natives. Happenings in Tunisia, Algeria or Morocco and South Africa involve the West European Socialists as much as the Asian Socialists. Malaya is as much a concern of the British Socialists as of the Burmese, Indian and Indonesian Socialists. All these factors, whether they belong to the past history or the present are bound to erect a wall between the Socialist movements of Europe and Asia."[165]

The International in a more Forbearing Mood

Gradually, however, a slight shift in the attitude of the Socialist International became noticeable. This was due to two factors. Firstly, both the BLP and the SFIO were out of government as of 1951. For the SFIO their stint in the opposition would last until 1956, while the BLP would remain in the opposition until as late as 1964. The fact that the BLP and the SFIO were able to criticize the colonial policies of their respective governments from the "dugout", so to say, allowed them to be more flexible and critical of colonial policy. The Belgian SP was also in the opposition until 1954, which left the Dutch PvdA as the only party with governmental responsibilities in a country with colonial possessions. With Indonesian independence in 1949, however, those possessions had shrunk dramatically and the colonial policy of the Netherlands was expressed with much more subtlety than during the time of the 1947-1948 "police actions". As a result, the responsibility for the reactionary politics of the Western European countries was no longer entirely laid at the feet of the socialist parties.

Secondly, the outbreak of the Korean War, and with it the Cold War in Asia, began to overshadow the colonial issue. The (according to the International) universal dimension of the East-West opposition impelled the International to strengthen social democracy in a threatened Asia. Experience had shown

---

164   Circ. B14/52. Preparatory Meeting for the Plenary Congress of the Asian Socialist Parties. Rangoon, 25-29 March. IISG, SI 65.

165   Ibidem.

that that was only possible through supporting, advising and when possible even incorporating partner organizations as much as possible. For this, it was necessary to enjoy the Asian socialists' confidence.

The combined effect of both national and international circumstances became immediately apparent within the International after the January 1953 conference of the ASC in Rangoon. In their report of this conference, the delegation from the International deemed the "general appreciation of the world situation and of the remnants of colonialism" as the most significant obstacles to cooperation between socialists in Asia and Europe. Even more so than the Cold War posturing, it was the amount of attention paid to the problems of colonialism which impressed the SI delegation at the Rangoon conference. They stated that that was "[their] most striking observation" at the conference. This conclusion was reworked into a concrete recommendation in their report: "In order to strengthen relations with the Asian socialists, the European socialists should show their active interest in these colonial prob-lems and try to explain their policy towards colonial territories.

As a first step the subject "Socialist Policy towards Colonial Territories" should be made one of the main items on the agenda of the 1953 Stockholm congress of the International."[166] Furthermore, Björk also proposed setting aside more space in the bulletin of the International for discussions on colonial issues, and stimulating study groups to pay more attention to these issues because "European socialists in general had insufficient knowledge of these problems". Already at the congress of Milan, in 1952, socialist policy with regard to the "underdeveloped territories" had been an important topic, but Stockholm had to go much further, according to Björk. The congress had to instigate an awareness campaign on colonial issues, for the benefit of the members of the International who "undoubtedly have insufficient familiarity with these issues." That familiarity could be bolstered through the publication of pamphlets, the printing of more relevant articles in the information bulle-tin of the International, or by organizing special meetings and study groups. Furthermore, in Stockholm there was a general will "to make a friendly gesture" to the ASC. The bureau of the SI therefore decided, one month after the ASC conference in Rangoon, to add the topic "The Socialist Attitude to Colonial Problems" to the agenda of their own congress in Stockholm.

---

166   Circ. 50/53, 19/03/1953. Private and confidential. The Asian Socialist Conference in Rangoon, 6-15/01/1953. Report to the Council of the Socialist International, 12. IISG, SI 68.

The debate on colonialism was the most important topic of the congress. Here too, Stockholm distinguished itself from Milan one year earlier. The discussions took place during the afternoon session of 17 July, and continued during the morning session of 18 July.[167] The majority of the speeches were grouped around themes rejecting colonialism. The search for independence and higher living standards, and the rejection of colonial status and of racial inferiority were challenges which should not be met with any form of repression, in an attempt to secure private interests. Such a reaction would only lead to conflict and chaos and would also add to the bitter enmity already felt between the colonized peoples and Europe. Indo-china, Malaya, Tunisia and Kenya were cited as examples. A "reactionary" and "outdated" policy towards the colonies was considered irreconcilable with the philosophy of social democracy.

Apparently, there was a very clear unanimity of opinion. Morgan Phillips put it succinctly: "As Socialists, believing in the brotherhood of man we are opposed to colonialism and racial discrimination in any form. The problem which faces us is how to achieve their elimination. (...) We have the opportunity of exerting an important influence for practical steps towards the elimination of colonialism. This objective is written in the United Nations Charter [art. 73] to which the countries of the world have subscribed; but it is our special task as Socialists to see that it does not merely remain on paper but is realized in practice as rapidly as possible". Others, such as the Danish socialist Alsing Andersen, confirmed that in the question of colonial issues a grand task was presented to the International: "To democratic Socialists, no matter from what part of the world they may come, there is only one solution to the colonial problem: the colonial system must be abolished. That must be the goal of the SI. We look upon the national movements in Asia and Africa - particularly after the Second World War - as a natural and legitimate development which cannot, and should not, be suppressed by armed force."[168]

The philosophy of social democracy, besides emphasizing solidarity and the "brotherhood of man", was also composed of another element: the strength-ening of liberal democracy, which became all the more imperative in the context of the Cold War. This element was likely to have been noted with chagrin by some Asian socialists present in Stockholm. In his general intro-duction to the debate on colonialism, the British former Colonial Secretary

---

167   The two other important topics were 'the international situation' and the 'European socialist cooperation'. In addition, the relations with the ASC were thoroughly discussed.

168   Circ. 115/53. 05/10/1953. Report of the Third Congres of the SI. IISG, SI 71.

James Griffiths summarized very succinctly the entire issue:"There can be no doubt about what should be our attitude as democratic Socialists. It is our duty to welcome this upsurge of the human spirit. We must work with it, not against it, towards the replacement of colonialism by democratic independence. That is basic and fundamental to our Socialist faith."[169]

The word "democratic" in the above quote is crucial. The end goal was not simply independence in and of itself, but "democratic" independence. Political democracy was the leitmotiv of the BLP and of most of the other Western European representatives in Stockholm.[170] For Griffiths, a successful colonial policy was meant "to guide the people in the dependent territories towards responsible democratic self-government, and in partnership with their peoples, in the first place to seek to establish the economic and social conditions upon which, and upon which alone, democratic self-government can be firmly built and sustained, and secondly to assist in the formation and development of such democratic institutions and forms of government as will enable them to attain independence and full nationhood."

Those democratic conditions, no matter how difficult they were to obtain, formed an important condition for any potential transfer of power, since power could not be transferred to a vacuum. Therefore, it was essential that priority be given to the establishment of strong democratic institutions which might have been able to answer the challenge of communism. Only then, when an "orderly" transfer could be guaranteed, could a date be fixed for "full independence and self-government". Griffiths pleaded therefore for a guided path towards independence, based on the experiences that Europe itself had gained in the establishment of its own democratic institutions. Incidentally, that was also the message which the head of the SI delegation had delivered in Rangoon: the immediate granting of independence might in certain countries lead to a rapid return to feudalism or other forms of autocracy.

Especially some representatives from countries with no colonies advocated for a quicker plan towards the granting of full independence. The debate in the International actually had many similarities with the debates of the same period taking place within the United Nations. In both institutions the camps were divided between those countries with former or current colonial possessions and those countries that had never had them or that had themselves just become independent. However, despite the differences in position vis-

169   Ibidem. James Griffiths (1890-1975) had been a Labour MP since 1936.
170   Ibidem.

à-vis the timing of independence, the great majority of representatives were in agreement with the goal of "conditional", "guided" independence, even the markedly progressive Swedish socialists who were hosting the congress in Stockholm. The ASC representatives therefore heard a more or less coherent social democratic position, and were given ample opportunity to react. In this way the original recommendation for better relations with the ASC - which Kaj Björk had written into his report on the conference in Rangoon - was fulfilled: "to show [our] active interest in these problems and try to explain [our] policy towards colonial territories."

The International had two other friendly gestures in store for the ASC: for the first time representatives from various African "liberation movements" were invited to a congress of the International. Support for the African liberation movements was an important issue for the Asian socialists. This was clearly seen at the gathering of Asian socialists in Rangoon in 1953, where the "liberation movements" from Tunisia, Morocco, Algeria, Kenya and Uganda had all been represented. Next to the Asian speakers, who almost exclusively spoke of their native countries and their own independence struggles, Taieb Slim, representing the Neo-Destour Party of Tunisia had also addressed the assembly. According to the French socialist Mollet, Neo-Destour maintained excellent relations with the French SFIO.[171] Slim's stay in Rangoon was part of a larger Asian tour which he undertook to garner Asian support for Tunisia's struggle for independence. Even though Africa remained in the margins of the Rangoon conference, a show of solidarity featured prominently in the general atmosphere. In a number of resolutions the ASC pronounced its support for the "genuinely democratic and nationalist forces" in Malaya (and thereby explicitly not for the communist insurgents, whose terrorist methods, just like the British administration, were roundly condemned). The ASC also voiced its support for the "legitimate aspirations" of the peoples of Uganda and Kenya, who were fighting for their independence.[172] There was also agreement on establishing a permanent "Anti-colonial Bureau", which when invited would be able to dispatch special research commissions to study the liberation movements and the circumstances surrounding them, and to organize support for such movements.

---

171   According to Mollet, Neo-Destour was not yet a real socialist party; he said it was rather 'in a stage of development when contact with any part of the Socialist International might further its advance towards a democratic Socialist movement'. Circ. 72/52. 28/10/1952. Minutes of the Conference of the Council of the SI. Milan, 17-18/10/1952. IISG, SI 63.

172   Report of the First Asian Socialist Conference. Rangoon, 1953, IISG, SI 513, 56.

At the Stockholm congress as well the ASC promised its support to the liberation movements. U Tun Win, the leader of the ASC delegation, summarized
briefly:"Not only is Asia on the move but so is Africa which has today become
the last refuge of capitalist imperialism and racial oppression. The Socialists of
Asia have pledged to stand by their brethren in Africa in their heroic struggle
against oppression and exploitation. The freedom of all peoples, irrespective
of race, colour and creed, is a fundamental article of faith with Asian Socialists." In their addresses the Asian speakers had only sharp words for colonialism in Africa.

A few non-Asians also mentioned Africa. James Griffiths, a member of the
executive committee of the BLP, called on the International to expand into
that continent:"I speak for every delegate at this congress when I say we look
forward to the day when our Asian comrades will be joined by comrades from
Africa so that within the Socialist International we can find together the road
to the Cooperative Commonwealth of free and equal peoples which has been
and is and will be the goal of our Socialist endeavour."[173] The African contribution itself, however, was limited to a brief address by representatives of the
Tunisian Neo-Destour Party, and of Istiqlal, the party for Moroccan independence. They each received only ten minutes speaking time, yet even this was
a première for the postwar International. Their contributions - of course - had
been checked beforehand by the SFIO. Both parties bristled at the colonial
policy of the French government and had much praise for the SFIO which sat
in the opposition. The representative from the Neo-Destour Party, Salah Ben
Youssef, underlined the merits of European socialism, especially of French
socialism which had always supported his movement "in the long and difficult struggle of the Tunisian people for national independence". His address
was one long eulogy:"I feel it is my duty on this occasion to convey to our
French friends the gratitude felt by the Tunisian people for the constant and
untiring effort made by the French socialists for a just solution of the Franco-
Tunisian problem, a solution which would satisfy our aspirations for national
independence, in complete harmony with the higher interests of France and
the French inhabitants of Tunisia."

The Moroccan representative, Ahmed Bela Iruy, secretary-general of Istiqlal,
also had much praise for the French socialists.[174] In his own speech, André
Bidet, naturally, made use of both testimonies to attest to the anti-colonial
character of the SFIO. He inveighed bitterly against colonial policy, especially

173   Circ. 115/53, 05/10/1953, Report of the Third Congress of the SI. IISG, SI 71.
174   Ibidem.

against the colonial policy of the French government. He spoke forcefully against colonization in all its forms. Bidet certainly enjoyed a measure of credibility since he himself was born in Tunisia. As an opposition party, the colonial issue was certainly of great interest to the SFIO, especially at that moment when France was stuck in the mire in Indochina.[175] This illustrates once again to what extent the national political context reflected upon the transnational level.

For the rank and file of the parties in many countries, especially in France and Great Britain, Stockholm provided much useful propaganda. The Asian socialists, on the other hand, were somewhat less enthusiastic. Despite being satisfied with the promise of self-rule, which the BLP had also made in 1952, the Pan-Malayan Labour Party found Stockholm not far-reaching enough: "It is no use speaking in general terms about giving a people freedom: what matters is how such a promise is implemented. The fixing of a date is important in the case of Malaya, but also in that of other colonies. (...) We are convinced of the BLP's sincerity and we hope that all their proposals and plans will be carried out." The fact that the BLP was then in the opposition was apparently no problem: "Even when in opposition, the Labour Party is in a good position to influence political decisions".[176]

At the first meeting of the ASC after the Stockholm congress, in August 1953 in Hyderabad, the leadership of the ASC openly expressed their disappointment.[177] The fact that the colonial issue had been included on the agenda in Stockholm was a step forward - for the position which had been adopted by the SI one year earlier at the Milan congress had been entirely insufficient - yet the final resolution turned out to be not as clearly nor as forthrightly formulated as the ASC delegation had hoped. [178] "Conditional independence" was what was most difficult to swallow for the Asian representatives. They saw the conditions which the Western European social democrats linked on independence as being little more than paternalistic delay tactics. What they wanted was a concrete date, not vague promises. It was unacceptable to the Indian socialist Prem Bhasin that a government categorically denied full self-rule in the name of "good governance", with arguments such as "for your own best interest" or "true well-being", arguments which according to Bhasin

175   Circ. 115/53, 05/10/1953, Report of the Third Congress of the SI. IISG, SI 71.
176   Ibidem.
177   Circ. B19/53, 24/10/1953. Report by Phillips of ASC Bureau Meeting, Hyderabad 10-
       12/08/1953. IISG, SI 73.
178   Memorandum by Vilfan, Borba Brazilië, 04/08/1953. The Socialist International and Colonialism. IISG, SI 71.

were also used by communism when "liberating" the masses. "The road to hell is often paved with good intentions", observed Bhasin bitterly in Stockholm. His position was clear: "We cannot have two standards - one for judging the communists and another for judging the free world. You may think that good government is better than self-government. But allow me to say frankly that people smarting under the heels of foreign rule prefer self-government. Even Mahatma Gandhi, the great apostle of peace and nonviolence, once felt compelled to say to the British: 'Quit! Leave us in chaos!'"

Bhasin found clear evidence for this double standard in the International's position vis-à-vis the liberation movements. The East Berlin workers' revolt of June 17 against the Russian occupation had been enthusiastically received in Stockholm as an example for all oppressed peoples to overthrow the despotic regimes which held them down. The enthusiasm of the European socialists for the freedom fighters in Tunisia, Kenya and elsewhere was clearly of a lesser degree, according to Bhasin. The French socialists were even of the opinion that terror only led to more repression and that it did the colonized peoples no good at all.[179] For the Asians, Western engagement was all too often limited to well intentioned words, while they themselves saw ample opportunity for real action passed by. The ASC request that the congress make a show of solidarity with the freedom fighters in the colonies and that the governments take up their cause in the UN fell on deaf ears. Even the ASC's suggestion to launch a joint campaign to bring attention to the freedom struggles of the colonized peoples, with among other things a yearly "Dependent Peoples Freedom Day", as a gesture of support for the fighting peoples of Africa and Asia was received rather tepidly by the International.

The articles which appeared after Stockholm in Socialist Asia were clear illustrations: in August 1953, the editors denounced "outmoded concepts" such as "successive stages towards development", "autonomy" and "integration into the French Union", which were still common parlance among French socialists. In one article neocolonial constructions such as the French Union and the British Commonwealth were particularly sharply criticized and that criticism came not only from Asia.[180] Other non-European observers also reacted with disappointment; the Brazilian representative in Stockholm for example aptly exposed the gaps in the final resolution. Her most important criticism was related to the use of the term "self-government" instead of that of "self-determination", a term completely missing from the text: "A promise concerning

179   Circ. 115/53. 05/10/1953. Report of the Third Congress of the SI. IISG, SI 71.
180   'Asia and the New World" in *Socialist Asia*. 2 (1953) 1 August .

self-government without the right to self-determination cannot satisfy the yearnings of the colonial peoples for independence." The terms "self-govern-ment" and "independence" had in the preceding years so often been misused by the colonial powers - often to imply a continuous link with the mother country as was the case with the French Union and the British Common-wealth - that they practically no longer implied the rights of a people to determine their own future. She continued: "It is hard to understand why this resolution in the part in which it speaks of principles, does not mention the Charter of the UN in which three chapters are devoted to the colonial problem. The Charter becomes an ever more powerful weapon in the hands of nations which are fighting for their most basic human right." According to the Charter "self-government" without "self-determination" can only lead to a continuation of the colonial system. In other words the degree to which colo-nialism hindered relations between the Socialist International and the Asian Socialist Conference had only grown more pronounced!

The "Cold War International"

The Cold War was not only a driving factor behind the global expansion of the International, in the sense that it stimulated the recruitment campaign in Asia. It was also an obstacle to that very expansion. Not all potential partners considered it a particularly attractive prospect to become part of the "Cold War International". When in July 1950, one month after the outbreak of the Korean War, the Indian CSP was "requested" once again to consider becoming a full member of the International - this time with more urgency due to "the critical world situation, particularly in the Far East and in Southern Asia"- the CSP asked for a guarantee that (full) members of the International would be allowed "to keep neutral in ideology and practice in a clash between the Atlantic and Soviet camps."[181] From the early 1950's onwards, the largest stumbling block to full membership in the International for the CSP was no longer, in the first place, colonialism but rather "Atlanticism". The party would only consider potential membership on the condition that full members be allowed to remain neutral vis-à-vis the Atlantic and Soviet camps.

In his answer to the Indian socialists Braunthal emphasized that affiliated parties were expected to accept the principles of social democracy, which fundamentally differed from, and often were in opposition to the principles of Russian totalitarian communism. Having started thus, Braunthal, all the

181   Letter from Desai to Braunthal, 09/09/1950. IISG, SI 657.

same, immediately opened the door wide: "Beyond this general attitude, it is, of course, possible that Parties affiliated to COMISCO keep neutral in ideology and practice in a clash between the Atlantic and Soviet camps." He referred to the social democratic parties in Austria, Sweden and Switzerland, which were both members of the International and neutral vis-à-vis NATO. The conclusion that the Indian SP drew from the secretary-general's letter was that each party was free to determine its own position in the East-West conflict. Not until 1953, however, would the party - now known as the Praja Socialist Party - become a "consultative member".[182]

That which held for the Indian socialists, mutatis mutandis, also held for the other Asian socialist parties, such as the Indonesian and Burmese. When these Asian parties met with the Indians in March 1952 to lay the groundwork for future cooperation, one of the described aims was "via an Asian Socialist International to give organized expression to an ideology and a foreign policy of a 'third power', consisting of the Asian bloc, which was aligned with neither the Western nor the Soviet camp."[183] The very first issue of *Socialist Asia*, the bimonthly bulletin of the preparatory committee of the Asian Socialist Conference, described in no uncertain terms the position of "Asian Socialism" regarding the East-West opposition. In the lead article it stated that the newly born Asian socialist parties "refused to become slaves to either Totalitarian Communism or Capitalist Democracies of the West. They had attained the position they occupied in their countries in opposition to and in spite of the Cominform and its agents and were condemned by the latter as traitors and stooges of Anglo-American Imperialism in Asia. Between the Cominformists and these socialists there was therefore no love lost. The Socialist International had no positive repulsion for them, but they felt that it was too much preoccupied with European affairs, was not strong enough in its hostility to the policy of Colonialism pursued by some of their National States and had committed itself in favour of one particular side in the Russo-American conflict, which was threatening to engulf and destroy the entire world."[184]

Before the Rangoon conference of January 1953, Braunthal made one last attempt to redirect the thoughts of the Asian parties. According to him, there was no need to set up a separate Asian Socialist International, because there

---

182   Ibidem; Letter from Braunthal to Desai, 13/09/1950; Letter from Desai to Braunthal, 08/12/1950. IISG, SI 657. A "consultative member" had the right to speak, but not the right to vote, while an "observer" only had the right to attend the meetings.

183   Report by Gokhale on the Preparatory Meeting in Rangoon, 25-29/03/1952, quoted in Circ. B14/52. IISG, SI 65.

184   *Socialist Asia*, 1 (1952) 16 August, 2-3.

was enough room for individual accents within the existing International. He didn't want to deny that the European socialist parties advocated a collective security policy, and by "collective security" only one thing could be meant - the North Atlantic Treaty - but this did not necessarily mean that all members were bound by decisions taken by the majority. The statutes of the International left members free to follow their own policy choices, even if Braunthal emphasized that the coordination of the various policy choices "was of utmost importance".

Perhaps at that moment Braunthal was unable to see just how important the concept of a "third power", or of a "neutral opposition", was going to become in Rangoon. Conference chairman U Ba Swe in his opening address immediately reminded the audience of the importance of neutrality. The conflict between the Western and the Cominform blocs, both of which hoped to win over the neutral countries, brought the threat of a new world war closer to home. According to U Ba Swe, world peace could only be guaranteed through the establishment of a "third power", which would have the "world's masses" behind it. Both the timing and the location of the conference seemed to underline the importance of world peace to the Asian socialists. The conference did take place before Stalin's death on 5 March 1953, at a moment when talks of a cease-fire in Korea were hopelessly bogged down.[185] As far as the location was concerned, the Burmese capital Rangoon, which had been almost completely razed during the Japanese occupation, was a continual reminder of the miseries of war.

Various speakers voiced their agreement with U Ba Swe and the conference succeeded, at least publicly, in arriving at unanimity regarding the interpretation of "neutrality". The interpretation which was arrived at appeared to differ fundamentally from the traditional prewar understanding of the concept.[186] Firstly, it did not refer to an international legal status which was recognized, at least in principle, by all the international players. As soon as the Cold War had reached its apogee the "if-you're-not-with-me-you're-against-me"-principle was put into play, a rule which both superpowers were not adverse to enforcing from time to time. Secondly, the new neutrality, unlike its passive isolationist predecessor, was immersed in an activist voluntaristic discourse. The neutral countries had to "work", "labour" and "toil" for the peace in Asia and the world by playing an arbitrating, mediating role on the international

185   The cease-fire would be signed on 27 July 1953.
186   Willetts, The Non-Aligned Movement, 20 ff.

scene, among other things. They had a "responsibility".[187] The strong emphasis on arbitration underlines the importance that the neutral countries invested in the United Nations. Thirdly, while traditional neutrality referred to the entire foreign policy of a country, the new neutrality related only to the specific conflict between the US and the USSR. In other conflicts, especially those between colonized countries and the colonizers, they did take clear positions. The fact that they thought themselves able to disassociate such conflicts from the conflict between the two superpowers shows that they effectively had a different world view from that of the International, which was only capable of a bipolar vision of the two blocks of power. Only by uniting amongst themselves did they think that they could avoid having a new war thrust upon them by the superpowers.

This idea was expressed most powerfully in Rangoon by the Japanese socialist Suzuki: "In Korea, a war [has] actually [been] going on for more than two years and a half (...). However, the actual war or threats of war in Asia were not created by the Asians themselves, but rather by forces other than Asian. In the two great countries that have ambitions for world domination, an idea is being entertained in some circles of having Asians fight one another. (...). I most ardently hope that our comrades who share my opinion, are determined not to allow the Asian people to shed their blood in furtherance of dollar-inspired policy. In this respect the strengthening of our unity is badly needed."[188]

At the adoption of the draft resolution, Indonesia, Burma and India were in agreement over the need for a policy of "noninvolvement" (later one would speak of a policy of "nonalignment") in the "Cold War", a policy that was described as a policy of the "third power". Not all those present in Rangoon, however, were so enthusiastic about such a policy. Japan-R was in theory willing to accept the principle of a "third power", yet at the same time they made an appeal to common sense, and common sense held that "the aggressive nature of the USSR posed a constant threat to world peace". In such circumstances, according to Komakichi Matsuoka, the Asian parties needed allies, and these were to be found in the Socialist International. If Asian socialism distanced itself from London, there would be dire consequences, he warned: "Under the conditions of the world as it is today it is vital that the Socialist

187   "The responsibility of Asian socialists is clear and in this realisation lies the justification for the Third Force", according to an Indian socialist in Rangoon. Report of the First Asian Socialist Conference. Rangoon, 1953. IISG, SI 513, 48-49.

188   Ibidem. Suzuki belonged to Japan-L.

forces, whether they be in Asia or Europe, be closely integrated. To split the Socialist movement of Western Europe and Asia would be a false and foolish step. It would play into the hands of Soviet Russia and strengthen her imperialist policies, which she is pursuing by trying to drive a wedge between the nations of the free world. It would mean the betrayal of the sincere hopes of workers throughout the world."[189] The "antiquated colonialism" that various Western European social democratic parties still believed in was naturally reprehensible, yet in the given circumstances it would be best to temporarily forget it, an argument which just as well could have come from the International itself. It was no coincidence that Matsuoka's speech was reprinted in *Socialist International Information*. It was, however, a minority position within the ASC.

The difference in orientation vis-à-vis the Cold War between the Asian Socialist Conference and the Socialist International becomes clear when comparing the assembly in Rangoon with that of the third congress of the International in Stockholm, which took place about half a year later, in July 1953. At the moment when the Korean War was running out of steam (the cease-fire would be signed hardly ten days after the end of the conference) and with Stalin's death a few months earlier, the chance of détente between the East and the West seemed more realistic than ever. Yet in Stockholm itself little optimism was to be seen. The fall of the infamous police chief Lavrenti Beria - "an example of the cannibalism in the Kremlin" - and the so-called peace offensive of the new leaders did cause a relative thaw, a thaw which was seen as potentially leading the way out of the current stalemate, as SI chairman Morgan Phillips admitted in his address. Yet he also warned against premature optimism. The attempts at rapprochement coming from the USSR had, to his mind, to do with internal problems within the Soviet Union, and were a sure fruit of the unity and strength of the noncommunist bloc, which absolutely had not to be weakened.[190]

Phillips' address in Stockholm must be placed in the context of the aftermath of the June 1953 uprising in East Germany, an event which was examined in depth at the congress. What began on June 16 as a general strike of limited scope of East Berlin construction workers, by the next day had turned into the first, politically charged rebellion against the Soviet occupation. The East German government called a state of emergency and with the help of Soviet tanks was rather quickly able to restore order. In the weeks following the

189   Report of the First Asian Socialist Conference. Rangoon, 1953. IISG, SI 513, 48-49.
190   Circ. 115/53. 05/10/1953. Report of the Third Congress of the SI. IISG, SI 71.

rebellion East German president Walter Ulbricht strengthened his grip on power with sweeping purges in the Sozialistische Einheits Partei Deutschlands. Seizing upon the events in East Germany the International used them to dedicate the majority of its congress to what it called "new imperialism", or "new colonialism". This was a somewhat insufficient response from the International to the criticism that it had had to swallow in Rangoon for providing shelter to colonialist and imperialistic parties. According to Alsing Andersen, the vice-chairman of the Danish social democratic party, the USSR had developed its own form of political and economic imperialism, which apparently would need to lead to a rethinking of the existing terminology. The image of colonies as overseas territories separated from the mother country by oceans was now outmoded, according to the Dane: "The Soviet Union, which dominates the world's largest colonial area, has rendered that way of thinking out-of-date. Prior to the Second World War, about 800,000,000 people lived under the old type of imperialist rule. After the war 600,000,000 people attained their independence, but at the same time the new communist imperialism enslaved another 600,000,000 people in Asia and Europe. These facts must be kept in mind in discussions on colonialism and imperialism".[191]

When the Western European social democrats were talking of "imperialism" and "colonialism" in Stockholm, they weren't so much talking about capitalist imperialism in the non-European territories. What they really meant was Soviet communist expansionism. According to chairman Phillips, this interpretation was already being used in 1951 in the charter of the International: "In this connection, let me remind you of our Paris declaration [December 1949]. We said: 'Final peace will not be secured until there is an end to imperialism and dictatorship, and nations and peoples everywhere in Europe and throughout the world, enjoy full democratic liberties'. These words recall the 'Aims and Tasks of Democratic Socialism' which we drew up at Frankfurt when the SI was reborn. That document, which is our charter, declares that "democratic Socialism rejects every form of imperialism. It fights the oppression or exploitation of any people". It is our task as democratic socialists to carry on that fight against oppression and exploitation, whether capitalist, fascist or communist".

191   Ibidem.

It is of no great surprise that in Stockholm the Europeans and Asians were often talking at cross purposes. In Stockholm when the Asians used the term "imperialistic", they indeed did so unambiguously referring to the "capitalist" variety. The discourse of the International bothered the secretary of the Indian Praja Socialist Party, Prem Bhasin, excessively. He asked himself why the Western European social democrats were continually talking about "communist imperialism" when the responsibilities of some of their own governments were hardly even mentioned. He could only observe that their attention for themes of utmost importance to the ASC, such as decolonization for example, had to take second place to their "obsession with Russian communist imperialism". Was it a coincidence that the colonial issue was referred to whenever the subject of "socialist action against the expansion of communism in the free world" came up? The obsession with the USSR explains clearly why the International's "friendly gesture" of placing colonial issues on the agenda was doomed to failure.

Even the concept of a "third power", one of the founding principles of the ASC, couldn't count on receiving much support in Stockholm. The anti-communism of the European socialist parties went hand in hand with an unambiguous Atlantic preference. The opening speech, given by the Belgian socialist Victor Larock, aptly illustrated this point: "We owe a debt to the Americans for a decision which perhaps has preserved the peace of Europe since 1949 - the decision to send to Germany a number of divisions which shows the willingness of the USA to react immediately to any act of aggression. The cooperation of the Americans in the work for peace is indispensable to Europe as to the rest of the world and whoever forgets this is guilty of blindness even more than a lack of gratitude".[192] This strong bond with the United States was indeed open to criticism, yet for Larock neutrality in such a context would have been fundamentally wrong: "We are not 'attentists' nor do we favour resignation, and even if some of our countries refuse to join this or that political-military alliance, we are not neutral towards totalitarianism or policies of aggression. We are, all of us, united in the desire for liberty and peace. But precisely because we desire to preserve peace and freedom we are determined never to confuse the defense of our ideal with that of any capitalist regime which supports oppression and a warlike policy. As regards the big Western powers, we always reserve our right to criticism and to that full frankness, which is but an elementary condition of friendship". Larock's choice for the Atlantic alliance, however, in no way implied a choice for capitalism, quite

192   Circ. 115/53. 05/10/1953. Report of the Third Congress of the SI. IISG, SI 71.

the contrary: after communism and fascism, Larock in his opening speech went on to refer to capitalism as an equally dangerous enemy. An "ideological" third way was thus apparently able to hold out in the strictly bipolar international system.

Not all Western social democrats identified with Larock's Atlanticism. According to Walter Bringolf, the chairman of the Swiss social democratic party, the International had fallen too much under the influence of the US. He did indeed recognize the enormous economic contribution that the United States had made to the reconstruction of Europe, yet that was no reason to make oneself dependent upon the US. He entirely disapproved of making socialist pilgrimages to that land.[193] The neutral Asians welcomed this dissident, yet relatively isolated, position.

Conclusion

In general the Asian representatives were seriously disappointed with the Stockholm congress. The criticism of the "Cold War International" was extremly pointed. It was true that the International was a bit more flexible regarding the colonial issue. The BLP and the SFIO, sitting in the opposition, felt less constrained than they had before 1951, when they were both in the government. Yet it was still slightly too early for a fundamental rethinking of the old positions in this matter. Moreover, mentally, the Cold War still held the reins, even if there were small signs of a thaw. The thaw was coming much too slowly, however, to convince the ASC.

Almost imperceptibly intertwined with these two debates, but rarely explicit, was the discussion on the organizational concept of transnational socialism. Sometimes consciously, sometimes not, the representatives of the International attempted to make the global expansion process of their organization fit nicely into the model of a centralized, and somewhat hierarchically structured, interparty organization. They set out from a universalist position which often did not settle well with the feelings of cultural, and therefore also organizational singularity which many Asian socialist parties had discovered on their own. This frustration boiled to the surface at least once. After Stockholm Wijono, the head of the ASC delegation, made clear his dissatisfaction at the broad tendency he had noticed at the congress to consider the ASC as a mere regional movement within the larger International. Stockholm made

---

193   Ibidem.

two things clear to him: "That the time is not yet ripe for us to have a common World Organization of socialists and that if and when this stage comes, the organisational form of this world fraternity of Socialists would be radically different from that of the present International."[194]

194   Circ. B19/53, 24/09/1953. Report by Phillips of ASC Bureau Meeting, Hyderabad 10-12/08/1953. IISG, SI 73.

New Opportunities and Known Limits
Socialist Globalization between 1955 and 1960

East-West Détente as a Window of Opportunity for Globalization

The "Spirit of Geneva" in London

During the first half of the 1950's the Cold War had held Asia firmly in its grip. It was a period "rich in calamity, darkened by war, and torn by insurrection", to use Tacitus' words describing the Roman Empire. After the "loss" of China in 1949 and the clash of arms in Korea, the spotlight fell fully on the conflict in Indochina. From the year 1945 onwards, the year that Ho Chi Minh had declared Vietnam's independence, France was embroiled in a bloody war of independence. After 1950, France received major economic and military support from the United States, an indication of the importance of Indochina in the Cold War. It was in response to the situation in Indochina that the American president Eisenhower came up with his "domino theory".[195]

When in the summer of 1954 the Geneva Agreements put an end to the war in Indochina - to France's disadvantage - the Cold War began to release its grip on that continent. Meanwhile, the consequences of Stalin's death, the end of the Korean War and the explosion of the first Soviet H-bomb (all events from the year 1953), began to have an influence on the international scene. On the European continent as well the Cold War lost some of its grimness.

---

195   It was feared that if Vietnam fell, Cambodia, Laos, Thailand, Maleisia, Indonesia and other countries in the region would follow.

The period of détente, beginning with 1954, definitely saw some setbacks. In May 1955, for example, West Germany was de facto taken into NATO, which drove the USSR to setting up the Warsaw Pact. But in general, the advances were important: in September 1955, the USSR signed a peace agreement with then still occupied Austria, and Adenauer visited Moscow, resulting in mutual recognition by both countries. The high point of détente was the July 1955 meeting of various heads of state in Geneva. The talks between Dwight Eisenhower, Nikolai Bulganin, Anthony Eden and Félix Faure did not lead to immediate results, yet they created an atmosphere of goodwill which was somewhat able to hold the escalation of the Cold War in check, which opened perspectives on the transnational level.

As a result of the Cold War in Asia the Socialist International had found itself in a paradoxical situation. On the one hand they felt obliged to strengthen the position of social democracy in an Asia under threat, while on the other hand, precisely that same anti-communist sentiment made the Asians very nervous of flirting with the Western European social democrats. The international thaw put the International in a position to meet the Asian social democrats half way, which did a great deal to stimulate transnational cooperation between Asian and European socialists. It is remarkable to what degree the International was willing to relativize its position in the East-West conflict during its London congress in July 1955. Under pressure from the Asian Socialist Conference the more biting aspects of the traditional Cold War rhetoric within the International were softened.

At the congress a draft text was presented on the international situation. It had been prepared exclusively by members of the International with no contribution from the ASC. From its opening line the document struck one with its "Cold War-speak": "Through the expansionist policies of the Soviet Union, the world found itself in the era of what came to be called the Cold War. The division of the world into two blocs is to be deplored. But the responsibility rests with the Soviet Union and its policies since the war. Better two blocs than a world which is one bloc under communist dictatorship. On this point Socialists are unanimous."[196] The editors did recognize the fact, however, that not all socialists wished to belong to the Western alliance, and they respected their right not to do so. Those countries had the advantage that they could exercise a "mediating influence" on international politics.

---

196   Circ. 34/55. 20/06/1955. Working paper on the International Situation, submitted by the Drafting Sub-Committee. IISG, SI 78. This Sub-Committee was called into being on 10 March, and consisted of Haakon Lie, Gérard Jacquet, Herbert Wehner and Saul Rose.

Yet all the same, the Atlantic option was considered exceptionally valuable: "The Western alliance provides the counterpoise to communist military strength, without which the free countries, both allied and nonaligned, might be overrun." This basic thought ran as a leitmotif through uncountable addresses, sometimes with a rather fanatical undertone, such as when the Dutchman Evert Vermeer rejected all forms of neutrality which "here and there are sneaking into our party".

In Clement Attlee's speech this was expressed perhaps more subtly but no less directly. He pleaded fiercely for the right to self-determination, a theme dear to the ASC, but which for the International (similarly to the terms "imperialism" and "colonialism") carried first and foremost an anti-communist connotation. "Can we get the application of this principle accepted all over the world? Can we get the Russian communists to allow the Poles, the Ruma-nians, the Hungarians and all the others to have that same right to decide their own future as we in this country gave to the people of India, Pakistan, Ceylon and Burma?", Attlee asked rhetorically. Again, the neutral Swiss and the Austrians were the only ones to go against this discourse.

Madhav Gokhale, the Indian representative of the ASC, also had sharp words for this Atlantic orthodoxy. "We in Asia, and the Socialists in particular, do not accept the division of the world into the free world and the fettered world - the world of democracy and the world of totalitarianism. We believe there is a third world which must keep away from these two and build a 'third force'; and as this area consolidates and extends, the influence of Socialists will extend too". He was particularly irritated by the constant attempts by both the USSR and the Atlantic bloc to try and win Asia over to their sphere of influ-ence. Among other things he complained of the influx of military "assistance" in Asia and the existence of the South East Asian Treaty Organization (SEATO), a treaty of mutual assistance that had been signed one year before between the United States, Australia, New Zealand, Great Britain and France on the one hand and the Philippines, Thailand and Pakistan on the other.[197]

It is remarkable to what degree the ASC was eventually able to influence the final resolution on the international situation. Firstly, the paragraph quoted above where the USSR was explicitly blamed for the Cold War was entirely removed. The final resolution was no one-sided lament against the Soviet

---

197 Report of the Fourth Congress of the Socialist International. London, 12-16/07/1955, 78. IISG, SI 247.

regime, rather it left a small and very cautious opening for reconciliation.[198] This made it possible to avoid emphasizing the differences of opinion between the ASC and the SI.

Secondly, the influence of the ASC was to be seen (this time much more directly) in the paragraph on disarmament. In his address Gokhale expressed criticism for a most ambiguous position which had been included in the draft resolution. On the one hand, the International set as a goal moving towards worldwide elimination of the H-bomb and other weapons of mass destruction, while on the other hand it emphasized that the world would not be made safer by unilaterally eliminating such weapons, leaving the unarmed half of the world undefended against the nuclear superiority of the Soviet bloc. Such a logic effectively excluded the possibility of any such disarmament, according to Gokhale. The position stating that the West had to keep its nuclear arsenal until there was some agreement with the USSR contravened entirely the spirit of socialism. According to Gokhale, the International simply had to state that it was for a complete elimination of nuclear weapons. The topic of nuclear weapons had a very specific significance for the "underdeveloped countries". Gokhale briefly touched upon this in his address: "We have been told at this congress that we live in an atomic era. We in our part of the world do not even live in an era of hand grenades! We consider the atomic weapon as a symbol of inequality, a symbol behind which the powers that possess it are hiding tremendous treasures. We are against nuclear weapons not only because they threaten total destruction, but because those who possess them would want to use them as instruments of frightening the rest of the world into submission." Against the backdrop of the nuclear (im-)balance between the US and the USSR, Gokhale formulated a contrast between the countries with nuclear weapons and those without, or to use a more modern turn of phrase the "haves" and the "have-nots".[199] Gokhale's point of view could be interpreted as supporting unilateral disarmament and was therefore unacceptable to most Western European socialists. In the final resolution the mistrust of the USSR was reinserted. Nevertheless, the tone of reconciliation in the text was notable. In the final version the International contented itself with confirming that the recent Soviet disarmament proposals did come closer to being in agreement with an Anglo-French proposal of 1954, "which provides a practical scheme for general disarmament".

198 'Socialists are glad of the opportunity of a period of peaceful international relations, even if the Soviet Government regards it only as a tactical and temporary device'. Circ. 115/53. 05/10/1953. Report of the Third Congress of the SI. IISG, SI 71.
199 Report of the Fourth Congress of the Socialist International. London, 12-16/07/1955, 79. IISG, SI 247.

There are also other, sometimes smaller, passages to be found in the numerous pages of resolutions adopted at the London congress which attest to the
toning-down of the anti-Soviet rhetoric, especially when compared to that
which came out of the previous congress in Stockholm in 1953. In the resolution on the international situation the government in Beijing was described
as "the effective government" to which a place in the UN had to be offered.
At the same time the resolution was rather critical of the nationalists on
Formosa.[200] With regards to Vietnam, a passage which explicitly expressed
the International's fear of a communist takeover was replaced with a somewhat vaguer text which stressed the need for a democratic government and
strict compliance with the peace agreements. These resolutions attest to the
amount of attention which the International was then paying to Asia. The fact
that Western European and Asian socialists were bridging the gap in their
respective positions vis-à-vis the East-West conflict was clearly related to the
relative thaw in the Cold War. The "spirit of Geneva" was felt as far as London.

The more reserved Atlanticism of the International would not have been
possible if it was not in such perfect concurrence with the positions of the
British Labour Party, which still held strong sway over the International.
To be sure, Denis Healey still exercised a strong influence upon the foreign
and defense policies of the party. By the middle of the decade he had developed into the "éminence grise of the intellectual Cold Warriors", which is how
the left-wing of the party called him. He earned his nickname thanks to his
razor-sharp but at the same time solidly based analyses and pamphlets. In his
multitudinous publications, such as *The New Fabian Essays*, Healey had proved
himself a strong advocate of the power politics approach in international relations. He opposed all forms of "utopianism" or "socialist idealism": "[The party]
has too often fallen victim to Utopianism. In particular, it tends to discount
the power elements in politics, seeing it as a specific evil of the system rather
than a generic characteristic of politics as such (…) Depreciation of the power
factor entails an inadequate understanding of the techniques of power."
Healey's preference for power politics was paired with a rabid anti-communism, which was made apparent in his *The Curtain Falls* (1951), a description
of the installation of the communist regimes in Central and Eastern Europe.
In 1955, the year of the London congress of the International, he published
Neutralism, a strong criticism of the temptations of neutrality in the East-
West conflict.[201] Geneva did not make the slightest impression upon him.
His conviction that the Soviets had not in the least changed the content

200   Ibidem.
201   Healey, *Neutralism*, 19.

of their foreign policy but that it was now only differently packaged he expressed with an image that became the title of an article he authored in *International Affairs*, "When Shrimps Learn to Whistle".[202] Healey could count on the support of the new party leader, Hugh Gaitskell, who in December 1955 succeeded Clement Attlee. The world view of the party leadership seemed to come directly out of the early fifties.

Practical party politics could never be entirely forgotten, however, and the party leaders needed to take the views of its members into account - a great many of whom appeared to have a soft spot for détente initiatives. They also could not entirely ignore their constituents, who expected the BLP, as an opposition party, to differentiate themselves sufficiently from the conservative government. This explains why the party, and even Gaitskell himself, announced initiatives or took up positions meant to alleviate the East-West tensions. In 1957, for example, the BLP accepted a proposal from the USSR making nuclear weapons negotiations dependent upon the stopping of nuclear testing, a position which was not directly in line with the personal convictions of the party leaders and which was mainly suggested for reasons of party politics, namely for the sake of maintaining party unity. After all, it was a relatively harmless proposal for a party not sitting in government.

On the transnational level as well some just as harmless - and just as pragmatic - decisions were made. The International shared in the BLP's zeal for détente. In 1958, Hugh Gaitskell got the International to back his "disengagement plan", a plan which looked quite similar to the better known Rapacki Plan, named after the Polish minister of foreign affairs, Adam Rapacki, who proposed the "denuclearization" of both Germanies, Poland, and Czechoslovakia with the goal in mind of making Central Europe nuclear-free. Gaitskell's plan was, in his own words, "a plan for a zone of controlled disarmament in Central Europe covering as wide as possible an area equal in extent on both sides of the Iron Curtain."[203] The SFIO and the PvdA both wanted to link such a plan to a wider disarmament agreement, but Gaitskell refused to accept that. He saw his plan - which envisioned a neutral reunited Germany - rather as a positive measure which could serve as a first step towards a general disarmament agreement.

---

202   Healey, "When Shrimps Learn to Whistle: Thoughts after Geneva".
203   Circ. 77/60. 18/11/1960. Hugh Gaitskell. Report of the Conference of the Council of the Socialist International. Haifa, 27-29/04/1960. IISG, SI 98.

The fact that the International in the second half of the 1950's evolved beyond being a "Cold War International" into being an International which fully played the hand of détente, was not to be merited solely to the Labour Party. Other parties too had a hand to play in the tempering of the International's Atlanticism, namely the German SPD, which gradually began to carry more weight, and the neutral parties from Sweden, Switzerland and Austria. They no doubt also had the Asian socialists in mind, just like the BLP. This became most apparent during a discussion about SEATO. Within his own party Morgan Phillips was not at all an opponent of this organization, yet in the International he spoke exceedingly cautiously about it. If such an organization was truly necessary in South East Asia then, according to Phillips, the Asians themselves had the right to take the appropriate initiatives.[204] In Asia it must have sounded like music to their ears.

Opportunities in Latin America

During the London congress of the International in July 1955, progress was also made on the Latin American front. The bureau of the International finally decided to set up a "Latin American Secretariat", which institutionally would be part of the International. By doing that, the bureau went along with the two year old request from the Argentine and Uruguayan socialists. That very same week Braunthal sat down with Américo Ghioldi from the Argentine SP, Rodolfo Llopis, the secretary of the Spanish SP in exile and Humberto Maiztegui, the secretary of the Uruguayan SP, who from that moment on would go on to play an ever more important role as go-between between Latin America and London. They quickly agreed to set up a small regional secretariat representing the International in Montevideo for a trial period of one year.

Montevideo was chosen "for reasons of political liberty" and because the Uruguayan Party was the best organized party on the continent. The secretariat, in its capacity as an information center, would publish a Spanish language bulletin with subjects relevant to the continent, and with a selection of contributions from *Socialist International Information*. According to a memorandum approved after the meeting, the main goal of the center was to strengthen socialism in Latin America so that it could resist "Nazism which was spreading over that continent with the aid of the Catholic Church via Spain".

---

204   Circ. 31/54. 14/05/1954. Minutes of the Conference of the Council of the SI, Vienna, 07-08/05/1954. IISG, SI 75.

They also sought to strive against Stalinism, and "capitalist imperialism".[205] The International supported this initiative financially with a contribution of 500 pounds. Maiztegui became the part-time secretary of the secretariat, which besides Uruguayans was also comprised of Chilean and Argentine members. In December 1956, the trial period was extended for another year.

The fact that the International, precisely in the years 1955-1956, began to show more interest in Latin America may seem strange at first glance, especially when one takes into account Guillaume Devin's explanation for the expansion (or lack thereof) of the International into Latin America: "Latin America did not belong to the priorities of the European socialists in the 1950's. The American guardianship over the region was a sufficient guarantee against communist threats".[206] May we then deduce from the above that the United States in 1955 no longer gave sufficient guarantee against communism? Such a position would be difficult to defend. There is not one indication that communism or the USSR in 1955 were able to strengthen their position in Latin America in any way comparable to that which had taken place in Asia between 1950 and 1954. Quite the contrary, if there was one lesson which still reverberated in Latin America it was to be learned from the successful American intervention in Guatemala in 1954. Devin resolved this "difficulty" by simply paying no further attention to the issue between the years 1954 and 1959. He stated that "until 1959-60, the Europeans have not attached any importance to this regional Latin American structure."[207] Only starting with the Cuban revolution in 1959-1960 did the Western Hemisphere truly begin to attract the attention of the International, at a moment when the "patronage of the United States" no longer seemed sufficient to guarantee against "communist trouble making". In other words, at the end of the decade the International set out once again on a crusade against communism.

In this reading of the facts, the International is the victim of its own "Cold War International" image. In reality however, the "Cold War International" once outside its European nest, and in a period of relative détente, seemed to be capable of a surprising amount of flexibility both in its relations with the United States and with respect to the ideological orthodoxy of some potential partner organizations.

---

205   Memorandum The necessity for a regional Secretariat of the Socialist International for Latin America. IISG, SI 507. Supposedly, the author of the memorandum was Ghioldi.
206   Devin, *L'Internationale socialiste*, 96.
207   Ibidem, 101.

With regard to the United States, the International adopted a much less orthodox position at its July 1955 congress than previously was the case. In London the International - together with the Asian Socialist Conference - criticized Washington's policies in Asia. They were doing the same with regard to US Latin American policy. The final resolution, which was based on a draft from the Uruguayan and Argentine SP's, contained a condemnation of dictatorship and despotism and referred to the American responsibility in this regard. The phrasing was of course very cautious. The congress limited its commentary to the *effects* of American economic and military assistance to dictatorships in the region, and emphasized that "the primitive slogans of communism, as the mouthpiece of international Soviet action" were making the situation in Latin America extremely complex. They went on: "It maintains that assistance to dictatorial régimes is violating the principles of democracy and is delaying the rise of freedom in Latin America."[208]

One year later, a year which saw the focus on Latin America steadily increase, the International went a step further. Maiztegui hinted to Bjarne Braatoy (the new secretary-general of the International as of December 1956), that the International would make "a very good impression" and "win much prestige" in Latin America if it were to support certain initiatives undertaken by Latin American parties. Maiztegui would be able to give the necessary publicity to such a show of support.[209] Shortly thereafter, the bureau of the International - following a suggestion from the executive committee of the Latin American Secretariat - was to declare its support for the Venezuelan Acción Democrática (AD). This party, lead by Rómulo Betancourt, had already in 1948 been driven from power. The exceptionally violent dictatorship which then took power in Venezuela, with the support of the United States, became even more violent after 1952, and quickly became the prototype par excellence of the Latin American anti-communist dictatorship. But only in 1957 did the International decide to take up the cause of the AD, despite the fact that their long period of persecution, exile and underground resistance dated from much earlier. Before 1957 the International did not feel urged to meddle in the backyard of the US. In December 1957, after a fraudulent referendum in Venezuela, the International asked its members to protest the usurpation of power in their different countries via their parliaments, the press or directly to the Venezuelan Embassy. The International itself sent a protest telegram to the Venezuelan president.

208   Circ. 115/55, 05/10/1955. Message to the Working People of Latin America. IISG, SI 71.
209   Letter from Maiztegui to Braatoy, 27/12/1956. IISG, SI 493.

In its relations with potential member parties too the International turned out to be surprisingly flexible. This could be gleaned from its relations with the Chilean socialist party, the PSP. In July 1955, the International gave its fiat to closer relations with this party. During the course of 1956, however, the SI received information which brought the PSP in discredit. The International obtained a document via Maiztegui in which the PSP declared as one of its goals the "limiting of the imperialist circles of the North Americans, supporters of the dictatorships".[210] One of the ways of realizing this goal was by the organization of a "congress of democratic parties", an idea which had been circulating since 1953. Such a congress had to result in a broad front of socialist and center or center-left (people's) parties in opposition to the despotic regimes of Latin America. The agenda items which the PSP proposed for such a congress did not leave much to the imagination: "Political and diplomatic relations between the superpowers and Latin America; the question of sovereignty; foreign capital and its impact on political life of each country; economic independence as a general aspiration". Item per item, the agenda was composed of themes all related to the foreign policy of the United States.

Besides Maiztegui, the International also had other important sources of information. By the autumn of 1955 they also had the trusted commentary of the American Robert Alexander, now a privileged advisor of the International. His commentary was not of the sort that would place the PSP in a positive light. According to Alexander, that party was undergoing a radical change in policy by the end of 1955 and the beginning of 1956. It had reversed both its policy of support for President Ibáñez and its opposition to the communist party, now finding itself radically opposed to Ibáñez and in alliance with the communists. At the moment of his writing, the party was busy forming a new alliance composed of various socialist movements and the communist party. In a letter to Maiztegui, Alexander was very pessimistic about the PSP: "The top leadership of the PSP is admittedly and frankly Leninist. They look upon the Titoists, not the democratic Socialists of Western Europe, of Latin America etc. as their closest comrades. They believe in a dictatorship of their party over the nation (…). They are I think misled by the recent events in the Soviet Union to think that the evolution there has gone much further than it really has."

210   PSP, Antecedentes de la proposición del partido Socialista para la convocatoria de un Congreso de Partidos Democráticos de América Latina. IISG, SI 705 (in Maiztegui's correspondence).

Consequently, according to Alexander, it would be a great mistake to take Chile into the Latin American Secretariat, all the more so since various PSP leaders in private conversations with him had made no attempt to hide their disdain for the International.[211] Maiztegui forwarded Alexander's analysis to the secretary-general of the International, Bjarne Braatoy, but attempted to "temper" Alexander's sharp condemnation. He added:"As far as the PSP is concerned, I believe that comrade Alexander is a little pessimistic."[212]

Bjarne Braatoy, however, reacted furiously. On 14 November he suggested that Maiztegui "reconsider" the relationship with the PSP. Yet it appears it was not so much the ideological choices which were worrying the secretary-general of the International. Rather, there was bad blood between the Socialist International and the Chileans, caused by the behavior of the Chilean representative Frederico Klein at the second ASC congress in Bombay, only a few days before Braatoy's angry letter to Maiztegui. Exactly what Klein had said there is difficult to reconstruct, even Maiztegui knew nothing of it until the International had brought him up to date. In their report the SI delegation noted only the "rather hostile and impertinent attitude on communist lines towards the SI", an attitude which was immediately condemned by the Indian delegation, among others. It appeared that the Chilean SP had launched a direct attack on the SFIO, related to the French involvement in the Suez-crisis. This more so than the ideological alignment of the Chilean party was unacceptable for the International.

Maiztegui was obviously concerned about the matter. Re-evaluating relations with the PSP would throw his young organization (it had been in existence for only a year) into a crisis which it would probably not survive. Furthermore, there was no other viable alternative party in Chile which could take the place of the PSP. An accomplished diplomat, Maiztegui attempted to glue things back together. He promised that the Uruguayan and Argentine socialist parties would emphatically resist any attempts at creating an Asian-Latin American front in opposition to the International.

There wasn't much more that he could do, and it appears to have been sufficient. The International finally conceded that they would be able to continue working relations with the Chilean PSP. This appeared to be very much the case in the spring of 1958, when the PSP invited the British socialist Bevan to take part in a conference of the Latin American Secretariat, which took

211   Letter from Alexander to Maiztegui, 09/10/1956. IISG, SI 705.
212   Letter from Maiztegui to Braatoy, 29/10/1956. IISG, SI 705.

place that April in Chile. The presence of Bevan, who was outspokenly leftist in his leanings and who was particularly appreciated in Latin America, was a windfall to the PSP in the run up to the presidential elections which would take place later in the year. The invitation from the party was backed by Albert Carthy, who, in 1957, had succeeded Braatoy as secretary-general of the International. At Maiztegui's written request, Carthy put pressure on the secretary of the Labour Party to have Bevan accept the invitation. In this way the International indirectly lent its support to the alliance of socialists and communists which together with Salvador Allende was striving for the presidency.

The position of the International with regard to the PSP gives some interesting insights into the International's Latin American policy, which actually took shape around 1955-1956, and not in 1959, the year of the Cuban revolution. Parties with pronounced communist sympathies, even parties in alliance with communist parties, could enter into a partnership with the International, especially if those parties were to have sufficient contacts with other potential partners, as was the case with the PSP. In other words, a transnational logic was the determining factor here. The closer Latin America seemed to be to the verge of developing into a dynamic territory for a transnational political organization, the more important it became for the International to have a bridgehead on that continent. At the moment when the International's congress was being held in London, Perón's regime in Argentina was being shaken to its foundations, to collapse a few months later. This was the beginning of what an observer would latter dub the "twilight of the tyrants", a process of democratization which seemed to offer immense potential to the International.[213] Perhaps the International's official explanation for setting up a branch in Latin America - namely that the initiative was part of a larger "fight against Nazism, Stalinism and capitalist imperialism" - should be understood as meaning that they now saw a political opening for social democracy where there had been none during the darkest years of the Cold War.

International events at that moment also gave the International more room to wholeheartedly pursue its role in Latin America. Firstly, it seemed that the Geneva Agreements of 1954 temporarily put an end to four exceptionally turbulent years, during which time all of the International's attention was taken up by the urgency of events in Asia. Secondly, in conjunction with the period of détente, the Western Europeans were gradually able to allow them-

---

213   Szulc, *Twilight of the Tyrants*. One year after the fall of Perón's regime, Odría's dictatorship was overthrown in Peru. In 1957 Rojas Pinilla's government was brought down in Colombia and a year later Pérez Jiménez fell in Venezuela.

selves a greater degree of autonomy from the United States in international relations, and criticism of US foreign policy became to some extent possible. Support for Salvador Allende's alliance in the elections of 1958 fits quite well into this interpretation of events.

Even though the pillars of Atlanticism were never doubted - far from it, there was some tension between the superpower and its 'satellites'. The economic independence of those satellites ensured that their self-confidence only grew.[214] In Europe the United States insisted more and more explicitly on an increase in defense efforts from its European partners, all the more so because its own hands were tied by events in Taiwan, Vietnam, Thailand and Laos, conflicts which the Europeans were decreasingly inclined to support financially. Moreover, the Suez crisis was an "eye-opener" for many Europeans. It appeared that the United States and Europe no longer had the same interests in the Middle East. All the more so as the United States had explicitly distanced itself from the Anglo-French course of action.[215]

The British socialists chose a more independent course of action vis-à-vis the US as well. That was an argument which for example was returned to in the discussions justifying Britain's need for its own H-bomb. In 1960, party chairman Hugh Gaitskell expressed, in a purely Gaullist formulation, his lack of trust in the senior partner: "The real case for our having our own independent nuclear weapons is fear of excessive dependence on the United States. It springs from doubts about the readiness of the United States' government to wish the destruction of their cities on behalf of Europe. It depends also, I think, on fear that an excessive dependence on the United States might force upon us policies with which we did not agree."[216] After the election of J.F. Kennedy, for whom Gaitskell had enormous respect, the BLP would have a much more positive attitude regarding the United States.

In sum, the period of détente after 1955 opened a "window of opportunity". It undoubtedly gave socialist transnationalism greater opportunity for cooperation in both Asia and Latin America. The International itself adopted a very flexible attitude. Only when interests of fundamental importance to the European parties were threatened problems arised. For example, when the Chilean PSP criticized the actions of the French government in Suez (the SFIO had been part of that government since 1956), before the week was out

---

214   Urwin, *Western Europe since 1945*, 182.
215   Hargreaves, *Decolonization in Africa*, 170-171.
216   Quoted in Haseler, *The Gaitskellites*, 181.

the International had already called the "dissident" PSP to order. The fact that a few months earlier, the PSU had expressed very carefully worded criticism of the French Algerian policy was equally not appreciated.[217] Both examples demonstrate that as of 1956, not only new possibilities were presenting themselves, but there were also thunderclouds gathering above the expanding International; thunderclouds full of national interest, which threatened to limit the transnational autonomy of the International.

The Persistence of National Politics: the BLP in the Opposition, the SFIO's Return to Power

The International and the Rise of British Anti-Colonialism

In the period from 1955 until 1960 too, the national political context is of extreme importance to understand the nature and modus operandi of the International as well as their expansion process. The International's increased breathing space caused by the period of détente at the international level was further strengthened by the fact that two of its leading parties were no longer part of the government on the national level. In 1951 the SFIO had left the French government which allowed the International to distance itself from French involvement in Indochina. The five year stint in the opposition however - so it would seem later in retrospect - would hardly bring about any changes in attitude in the party regarding colonial issues. The BLP on the other hand, which had likewise entered the opposition that very same year, did undergo a transformation. It appears that the Britons, unlike the French, had learned their lesson.

The British had been laying the groundwork for these changes since 1950, when Fenner Brockway had been elected to the British Parliament. With his election, until then disparate anti-colonial ideas were brought together and given a concrete reference point, a certain programmatic coherence and a leader of some standing able to defend an anti-colonial program. Brockway's plea for fixed "target dates" for the recognition of full self-rule for the African colonial territories initially received little attention. The colonial paradigm in the party was still too dominant for that. According to the BLP's analysis, colonial policy, despite all of its detriments and irrespective of its sometimes less than noble motives was responsible for a certain number of advances which

217   Letter from Frugoni to the secretary-general of the SI. 06/06/1956.

the territories would not have been able to achieve had they been left to their own devices. Consequently, it was possible and even morally imperative to first lay the basis for the postcolonial progress of the territories in question before giving them full autonomy. Therefore, despite the impatience of the local elites, time was needed.[218] The emphasis was thus placed on "preparing" the colonies. The anti-colonialists in the party, however, considered colonial status itself an obstacle to the economic and social development of the territories; only under the leadership of the local elite would the progress desired by all be made possible. "Transfer of power" was a magic concept to them.

As soon as the BLP landed in the opposition, in 1951, it seemed that the party became a bit more open to the arguments of the anti-colonial group. At the BLP convention of 1952, in Morecambe, "the British Empire" was for the first time the subject of detailed debate. The British author Stephen Howe spoke of "the first real postwar expression of widespread interest (…) in this sphere".[219] A draft resolution calling for the "immediate independence" of all British colonies was shelved, yet it was clear that criticism of the official party line, aimed mainly at the social, economic and political development of the colonial territories was mounting.[220] In the New Statesman of June 1953 for example, Basil Davidson wrote a sharp criticism of the position of the party, which was published shortly before in a new policy document entitled "Challenge to Britain".[221]

However, it was only in the year 1954 that a shift in the colonial thinking of the party was to usher in. The resolutions which were being presented in that period were not only more numerous and more radical than those of the preceding years, they were now also backed by large unions such as the Union of Shop, Distributive and Allied Workers (USDAW). The evolution was largely due to the intense lobbying by the recently founded Movement for Colonial Freedom. It is difficult to overestimate the influence of the organization - which had Brockway as its patron - on the colonial thinking of the BLP. It functioned as the colonial think-tank of the BLP, which through the party's Commonwealth Subcommittee (which consisted of anti-colonialists such as Barbara Castle, Tom Driberg and Anthony Greenwood) was able to weigh in on the decision making process of the party. On top of which further

---

218   Fabian Colonial Bureau. *Labour in the Colonies;* Idem, *Kenya: White Man's Country?;* Idem, *Hunger and Health in the Colonies;* Idem, *Four Colonial Questions;* Idem, *Colonies and International Conscience;* Idem, *Advance to Democracy.*
219   Howe, *Anticolonialism* in British Politics, 219.
220   *Labour Party Annual Conference Report 1952,* 137-139.
221   Davidson. *New Statesman,* 27/06/1953.

wind was added to their sails by a spectacular chain of colonial crises: Kenya, Guyana, Cyprus, Malta, Central Africa and Singapore. The tendency was even further sped up by the nomination of John Hatch, who was claimed by the left-wing of the party, to the position of Commonwealth Officer of the Labour Party. Hatch considered it his mission to radicalize the anti-colonial policy of the party, a calling which soon brought him into conflict with more conservative party bosses such as Morgan Phillips, the International's chairman until 1957.

The evolution on the national level was soon reflected on the transnational level. On colonial issues the difference between the SI congress of 1955 in London and that of 1953 in Stockholm was remarkable. Of course there were remainders of the traditional attitude. In the resolution on Asia and Africa, for example, the message of the previous congress was still to be heard: the International considered it a priority that territories still not independent obtain as soon as possible their freedom "under democratic self-government", and gave their full support to the training of individuals "for the task of self-government under democratic institutions".[222] And in his speech the Frenchman André Bidet proposed an association between France, Morocco and Algeria, as a solution to the colonial problems in those territories. But when the ASC delegation proposed a rather far-reaching "Declaration on Colonialism", it was approved by the International with little or no difficulty. For the first time the term "self-determination" appeared in the International's vocabulary. The right to self-determination was considered as one of the basic principles of a democratically organized society. Self-determination was seen as a right and not a privilege, although be it with two limitations: it should not transgress on others' right of self-determination, and it should not threaten world peace. For the first time there was a printed reference to the UN Charter, which the ASC had already demanded in Stockholm.[223]

Additionally, various Western European social democrats began calling for a concrete timetable for the liquidation of colonialism, and this time they were talking about Africa, not Eastern Europe. The acting chair of the British Labour Party, Edith Summerskill, recognized that Western policy had been in the wrong for years. The West had dragged its feet in its "threadbare colonial policies", it had chosen the side of "reactionary powers such as that of the nationalists on Formosa", and it had propagated the rather unenlightened racial

222 Circ. 52/55. 30/09/1955. Report of the Fourth Congress of the SI. IISG, SI 79.
223 Circ. 52/55. 30/09/1955. Declaration on Colonialism. Report of the Fourth Congress of the SI. IISG, SI 79.

policies in Southern Africa. The French social democrat André Bidet added an extremely harsh criticism of the Dinh Diem government in Vietnam which with American support was carrying out a reign of terror, "a kind of Dolfuss régime". Point by point these were all issues which struck a chord with Asian socialists. In other words the increased freedom of movement of the SFIO and especially of the BLP with regard to national issues strengthened, at the time of the London congress, transnational global cooperation between the social-ist parties.

The French Stronghold on the International

This exceptional situation was, however, not of a lasting nature. Soon enough the International found itself again obliged "from the bottom up", as it were, to adopt certain positions which did not exactly increase its popularity outside of Europe. When the SFIO in 1956 again took up the mantle of government the International found itself confronted with, or at the very least identified with, positions which brought it in discredit in both Africa and the Middle East. The situation also created discord within the International itself, bringing the transnational dynamic of the previous years to a halt.

The fact that the Middle East became a point of debate was relatively new to the International. Despite there having been several attempts to put the "Palestine question" on the agenda during the Zurich congress back in June 1947, Morgan Phillips had adroitly put a stop to it in the name of his party. Such a discussion would have placed the British delegation in a difficult position. Driven by current international politics the 1955 London congress of the International, which took place in July, was the first to pay attention to this region. Edith Summerskill, acting chair of the BLP, provided for the necessary upheaval in her address (for which she alone claimed responsibil-ity) by expressing particularly sharp criticism of Israel. On the one hand she had much admiration for the welfare state which Israel had been able to achieve under exceptionally difficult circumstances, while on the other hand she thought that some of the benefits of that welfare should go to the Arab population as well. According to her, the misery and hopelessness in the Arab refugee camps stood in sharp contrast with the lifestyle of the Israelis and it was high time someone passed that message on to the Israeli government. She ended her address with two concrete proposals. Firstly, it should be ensured that Arabs who had possessions in Israel and who wished to return to them, could do so. All others would need to be compensated. Secondly, the line of demarcation between Israel and the Arab territories needed to be reviewed.

Summerskill was immediately rebuked by the Dutchman Evert Vermeer. He would not stand for the shortcomings of the Israeli government being over-emphasized and he lamented the uncritical attitude of Summerskill with regard to certain "conservative and even feudal" Arab governments. Morgan Phillips reacted as well. He assured the Israeli Mapai delegation that the position of the BLP concerning Mapai and Israel was in no way "cool and critical", quite the contrary: "The attitude of the Labour Party is one of the greatest respect and admiration for the achievements of Israel under the leadership of Mapai, with whom our fraternal solidarity remains, and will remain unshaken."[224]

Historically there was a tight bond between the Zionist lobby in Great Britain and the BLP, and furthermore many British socialists had much admiration for the socialist experiments in the young Israeli state. Other socialists, also from the left, conversely saw Zionism as being a colonialist, imperialistic force and they sympathized with Arab nationalism. The contraposition between Summerskill and Phillips only illustrated the extent of division within the party, and that division did not always follow the left-right fault line. The final resolution of the congress, which sung the praises of Israel, once more underlined this attitude. In the eyes of many social democrats Israel was the incarnation of the new social democratic state, complete with progressive social values, in the middle of reactionary Arab surroundings.

The conference in London was actually nothing more than a warning shot. Only from the spring of 1956 onwards would the Middle East begin to set the agenda of the International. In January the bureau was fraught with worry due to alarming reports of an imminent war against Israel and it immediately launched a campaign "for the preservation of peace in the Middle East". The members of the International were called upon to arouse public opinion and to fully support all national and international actions which would be able to avert the war.[225] The Dutch PvdA in particular made a remarkable show of activism. The party not only held various meetings and organized a poster campaign, they even went so far as to send a delegation to Israel.

---

224   Circ. 52/55. 30/09/1955. Report of the Fourth Congress of the SI. IISG, SI 79; Gorny, The British Labour Movement.
225   Circ. 3/56. 03/02/1956. International Campaign for the Preservation of Peace in the Middle East. IISG, SI 82.

The International hardly concealed the fact that it rushed to the aid of a threatened Israel. One of the suggestions to the members was that they put pressure on their respective governments to speak out "in favour of maintaining the status quo in Israel". Another suggestion was to supply Israel with the necessary weapons to be able to "defend itself".[226] Various factors can help explain the position of the International. In the first place, many socialists considered Israel to be a place where a great socialist experiment was underway, which hopefully would be repeated throughout Asia. Furthermore, it was absolutely to be avoided that Israel should fall into Soviet hands, which would have far-reaching consequences for the West and NATO. And of course, vital economic interests also played an important role in the region. However, it would take us too far to go into any further detail here. It is more relevant to examine one specific example of the Arab-Israeli relationship: the 1956 Suez crisis.

The report of the bureau meeting of the International filed on 1 November 1956, two days after Israeli troops had attacked the Sinai Peninsula, carried no mention of the hostilities. All attention was focused on Hungary and the Soviet crackdown there. The council of the International, which met one month later in Copenhagen, could not avoid the issue, however. Again it was the Dutch PvdA which in a memorandum blatantly attempted to get the International to take up the cause of Israel. It stated that Israel had no other choice than to undertake pre-emptive military action. Under such circumstances one could not speak of an act of aggression, the document concluded.[227]

In the end the PvdA had to satisfy themselves with a compromise which somewhat took Israel out of the storm, but which at the same time placed both the English and French governments at the heart of it. For the BLP, which at the moment found themselves in the opposition, the involvement of the British government supplied sufficient material for criticism. In its draft resolution the party judged the invasion by both France and Great Britain to be "in clear breach of the Charter of the UN and in defiance of the resolutions of the UN Assembly carried by overwhelming majorities", a position which was supported by an overwhelming majority of those who attended the

226   Circ. 14/56. 08/03/1956. Minutes of the meeting of the Bureau of the SI. Zurich, 01/03/1956.
       IISG, SI 82.
227   Circ. 98/56. 01/12/1956. Memorandum on Israel by the Dutch Labour Party. Amsterdam,
       26/11/1956. IISG, SI 84.

congress.[228] The position adopted by the British social democrats was really just the continuation of the process within the BLP which has been described above. The party had remained fundamentally split over the situation in the Middle East up until a few months before the invasion. It was the Movement for Colonial Freedom which from August onwards began to increase protests against a potential British intervention in the region. By the end of October the BLP had almost entirely adopted their point of view. The SFIO (then in the government) on the other hand, found themselves in a difficult position. Pierre Commin, in the name of the French delegation, could not go along with the discussions and announced "the withdrawal of the French from active deliberation on the issues". Four other delegations - the Belgian, Spanish, Israeli and that of the Jewish Labour Union Bund - decided to abstain from voting on the first paragraph, which condemned the invasion.[229]

The position of the International in the Suez Crisis was closely scrutinized, especially by the International's non-European partners. The ASC had already made clear their position a month earlier at their congress in Bombay, which took place from 1 to 10 November. The similarities with the position of the International were remarkable. The bureau of the ASC made a strict distinction between Israel on the one hand and the United Kingdom and France on the other. The strong Israeli delegation to Bombay was able to convince a majority of those present at the congress of their interpretation of events. The very existence of Israel was threatened. Therefore its actions were purely acts of self defense. According to the Israelis their country had nothing to do with the Anglo-French invasion, they hadn't even been informed of the events. At that moment indeed, when the facts of the matter were anything but clear, Israel could undoubtedly enjoy the benefit of the doubt. The Pakistani demand that Israel be sharply criticized was not followed, the position of Israel was only found "regrettable".

There was, however, little understanding for the French and British governments. Their actions were condemned and the BLP received nothing but

---

228 Circ. 99/56. 21/12/1956. Minutes of the meeting of the Council of the SI. Copenhagen, 30/11-02/12/1956. IISG, SI 84.

229 The Bund was founded in 1897. It served as a party, a trade union and a cultural organization of jewish workers and intellectuals in Russia, Lithuania and Poland. After the Russian Revolution only the Polish branch survived. When the Germans invaded Poland, the Bund was forced to become an underground movement, and some of its members went into exile, e.g. to London.

praise for its tenacious opposition to the intervention.[230] The report - in a rather diplomatic way - had no mention at all for the SFIO. The sharpest criticism for that party, which through its participation in government had a share in the responsibility for the attack on Egypt, came from the other side of the world. The Uruguayan Socialist Party submitted a motion to the forthcoming council meeting of the International in which they - "in view of the serious events in the Middle East" - asked for the expulsion of the SFIO from the International.[231] For purely formal reasons - membership was the business of the congress and not of the council - the motion went straight into the wastepaperbasket. All in all the damage was negligible, partly because Israel was able to count on much support both within the International and in the Asian Socialist Conference.

French colonial policy in Africa was even more damaging to the image of the International than the Suez crisis. In the summer of 1956 the Uruguayans had already expressed criticism of the French performance in Algeria. In August the SFIO had to reply to accusations of being involved in "bloody armed interventions" there. According to the SFIO, France was not involved in a struggle against the Algerian people, but in a fight against those who were perpetrating "crimes and murdering women, children and innocent citizens". The French social democrats claimed that the actions of their government were directed at protecting the peaceable majority of Algerians.[232] Such arguments were unable to convince the Uruguayans and the ASC who were extremely sensitive to such issues. The SFIO were condemned in the strongest terms for their involvement in the tragedies in Algeria by the Anti-Colonial Bureau, which met parallel to the ASC Bombay Conference in November of 1956.

The situation in Algeria was also one of the agenda headers at the fifth congress of the International in Vienna in July 1957. The Norwegian socialists had expressly requested that the issue be included on the agenda. The International had ignored the issue long enough, stated Finn Moe. Moreover, the SFIO themselves were finding it more and more difficult to justify the actions in terms of socialist principles (or lack thereof) to their own base and to the public at large. How could socialists explain the brutal violence and even torture used by the French authorities in Algeria? Such practices were

---

230   Circ. 67/56. 23/11/1956. Second Congress of the ASC. Bombay, 01-10/11/1956. Report submitted by the delegation of the SI. IISG, SI 83.
231   Circ. B 47/56. 16/11/1956. Communication from the SP of Uruguay. IISG, SI 85.
232   Letter from the French SFIO to Emilio Frugoni, secretary-general of the Uruguayan SP, August 1956. IISG, SI 83.

strongly condemned when practiced by the USSR. How could the French government and the French social democrats maintain before the United Nations that the Algerian issue was a matter of internal affairs and that therefore the UN should not concern itself any further? Lastly, Finn Moe brought attention to the consequences of the French position on the International: "Socialists and democrats cannot overlook the fact that for the whole so-called underdeveloped world, for Asia and Africa, Algeria is a test case. The unfortunate Suez intervention last year revived the old suspicions of Western imperialism everywhere in Asia and Africa. If Socialism fails to make it clear that we shall liquidate as soon as possible whatever remnants there may be of military, political and economic imperialism, the teeming masses in Asia and Africa will lose their faith in Socialist methods for the liberation of humanity."[233]

Pierre Commin received ample opportunity to explain the French position. Commin defended it using various arguments. Legally, Algeria was not a "colony" but a province of France, with an extremely complex ethnic composition composed of a muslim majority and an important European minority. If France were to withdraw from Algeria the doors would be wide open for Soviet expansion into the area. Independence from France would negate the mission of socialism: to free mankind of all forms of oppression. It would lead to an "economic and social reversal, to a feudal, clerical and totalitarian regime, of the sort which is well-known among arab countries". "Autonomy" or "home rule", with tight bonds between the territory and the mother country was therefore a much more appropriate formula, since it would make practicable an authentic policy of socialist reform politics.[234]

Commin's address caused considerable division. Aneurin Bevan, the BLP representative, tore the French argument to pieces. He thought that it was high time that the demands of individual countries be brought in line with the principles of socialism, and not the other way around, which had usually been the case. The Swede Kaj Björk emphasized that European socialists in general did not have a sense of solidarity with the French Algerian policy. A different tune was heard from the representatives of the two other remaining countries with colonial possessions, especially so since both parties at that moment sat in government in their respective countries. The Belgian representative Joseph Bracops thought that Commin's "far seeing" analysis should be more carefully listened to before passing judgment. Unity within

233   Circ. 70/57. 06/12/1957. Report of the Fifth Congress of the Socialist International, Vienna, 02-06/07/1957. IISG, SI 87.
234   Ibidem.

the International presupposed, moreover, that the other parties would also make an attempt to understand the problems facing the SFIO. Goes van der Naters, speaking on behalf of the Dutch PvdA, went a step further. He accused Bevan of being a hypocrite: the repression of the Mau Mau in Kenya at the hands of his government had been much more gruesome than the actions of the French in Algeria. Moreover the efforts which the British representatives, socialists included, had made at the Council of Europe to keep the question of Cyprus from the agenda was hardly an expression of anti-colonial vigor. Regarding the Algerian question Van der Naters went so far as to ask whether there even was such a thing as the "Algerian people" capable of having their own aspirations.[235] The split between parties that sat in government in countries with colonial possessions and countries with none could hardly be more clearly illustrated.

All the same, even social democrats with a more progressive colonial view knew exactly where to draw the line. A proposal such as the one made by the Uruguayan SP to expel the SFIO from the International was out of the question, even for the Swede Kaj Björk. Such a measure would contravene the basic principles upon which the International was formed. The International could attempt to coordinate the policies of its members, but it could not dictate them. In other words. In the end the International largely agreed with the French reasoning that Algeria was a domestic issue for France. The reasoning which one could deduce therein, namely that the International was not bound by the policy decisions of its members, was in theory equally true, but hardly realistic. The International could go no further than the French (supported by the Belgians and the Dutch) were willing to go and consequently shared the full weight of the damage done to SFIO's image.

The final resolution in Vienna simply stated that the Algerian question was a complex problem which needed to be further studied by sending a "fact-finding mission" to the country. The sending of such a mission was Commin's suggestion; only by means of such a mission could the verity of the French claims of conducting a policy of "reform and reconciliation" be corroborated, and likewise the vicious violence of the Algerian Front for National Liberation, the FLN. In order to guarantee the objective character of the mission, the International turned down the SFIO's offer to cover all travel expenses.[236]

---

235   Until 1958, the PvdA was more or less tied hand and foot by the rigid politics of the Catholic minister for Foreign Affairs Luns, e.g. with regard to Dutch-Guinea. Bosscher, "De Partij van de Arbeid en het buitenlands beleid", 43.

236   Circ. 69/57. 29/11/1957. Fact-finding mission to Algeria. IISG, SI 87.

In this way the Vienna congress was able to bring the parties to a successful compromise. The discussions at the congress, however, were often of a most tiresome and laborious nature and this was not entirely to be blamed on the fact that it took place in a poorly ventilated small hall, in the middle of an exceptional heat wave. It was principally the participation of parties pursuing rather "un-socialist" policies at home which forced the International to tread lightly.

The mission which visited Algeria between 28 November and 12 December 1957, was composed of Jules Bary (Belgium), Sam Watson (Great Britain) and John Sanness (Norway). Initially they also intended to include a representative from the ASC in the delegation. The ASC had chosen Wijono, but in the end he could not disengage himself from affairs at home. A request from the ASC to postpone the mission for two months was rejected. By the following spring the "fact-finding mission" was ready to hand in its report. The International considered it best not to publish the report in its entirety, but rather to prepare a short summary, the reason being that the three members were not able to come to agreement on certain crucial elements. The Frenchman Guy Mollet could not hide his dissatisfaction with that procedure. He feared that the decision would give the wrong impression, but in the end he acquiesced.

His fears were proven right. Soon enough via Reuters excerpts of the report were appearing in the press, which did not exactly put the SFIO in a positive light. *Le Monde*, for example, concluded from the report that French colonial policy had once again "offended the sentiments of many a socialist in the International".[237] Incidentally, it would have been in Mollet's interest to publish the full report, which also contained various passages shedding a positive light on the SFIO. The first paragraph of the report stated that the geographic, economic and cultural relations between France and Algeria were closer than anything they had ever observed elsewhere. If ever a lasting relationship between a European and non-European territory could be possible, then it was between Algeria and France, concluded the commission. Secondly, they laid the responsibility for the problems in Algeria entirely at the feet of past rightist governments. If the SFIO had been listened to earlier such dramatic events would never have come to pass. Thirdly, the group praised the social, economic and educational reforms which the SFIO was attempting to bring about in Algeria. Fourthly, the mission was convinced that if Algeria were to break with France the negative consequences would be enormous: a pure FLN regime would install itself, a massive stream of European and pro-French

237   *Le Monde*, 16-17/02/1958.

Algerian muslim refugees would leave the country, and a bitter enmity against muslims in general would set in in France. Put briefly, it would be a "large set-back for modern civilization". Fifthly, the principles upon which the FLN was formed disqualified it from being a suitable partner for any negotiations.[238]

The Norwegian member of the mission, John Sanness, was in agreement on several points but he still felt it necessary to explain his differences of opinion in an appendix to the report.[239] The final account of the situation in Algeria, which was presented in Brussels in 1958, was somewhat more balanced and therefore more acceptable to many parties. Meanwhile, the "Sakhiet debacle" had taken place. In the beginning of February 1958, France bombarded the settlement of Sakhiet-Sidi-Youssef in order to destroy an FLN base. Sakhiet lay on the Tunisian side of the border with Algeria and a number of Tunisians fell victim to the French attack. Moreover the operation was a flagrant transgression upon Tunisian sovereignty and was widely condemned. By calling for all sides to be willing to discuss all issues in future negotiations, including both potential Algerian integration into France and self-determination, the socialists were able to leave their options open.[240] Of all the European social democrats only the Swedes refused to ratify the resolution.

Another issue illustrates the degree to which the policy options of the SFIO slowed down the transnational workings of the International. The 1955 London congress of the International had decided, in agreement with the ASC, to conduct a joint study looking at "a concrete and time-bound program of the freedom of the colonies", one more example of the closer relations between the SI and the ASC. To prepare that study, the BLP had put together a memorandum, which would serve as a basis for discussion. John Hatch, the progressive Commonwealth Officer of the BLP, was the memorandum's author. Before making the text available for commentary to the ASC, the SFIO and the Belgian BSP were given the opportunity to make their remarks to the secretary-general of the International. The BSP added a few smaller amendments, but the French socialists found every aspect of the text unacceptable. As a consequence, the joint initiative would die a quiet death.

238 Circ. B1/58. 17/01/1958. Report of the fact-finding mission to Algeria. IISG, SI 91.
239 Especially the assumption that negotiating with the FLN was of no use, was unacceptable to him (as he felt that both parties would not budge). Nor did he accept the alleged discrepancy between 'modern civilisation' and the aspirations of nationalist movements. Circ. B13/58. 10/02/1958. Report of the fact-finding mission to Algeria. IISG, SI 91.
240 Circ. 65/58. 21/08/1958. Report of the Meeting of the Council, 12-14/06/1958, Brussels. IISG, SI 90.

Structuring Globalization: the International's Search for the Right Organizational Framework

The colonial image that the International was dragging with it at the end of the 1950's, despite the BLP's change in course, formed an important obstacle to their ambitions of developing into a worldwide transnational organization. In Latin America it was principally the Uruguayan SP which reacted heatedly, but also other socialist parties had their objections. In Asia for example the Asian Socialist Conference were very unhappy with French colonial policy. However, at that moment the ASC were too weak to be able to offer any entrenched opposition. The disadvantages were most strongly felt in Africa, a continent which from 1958 on would increasingly catch the attention of the International.

The International's Unsuccessful First Forays on the African Continent

Before 1953, Africa had come up only a handful of times in discussions in the International, for example when the expansion of the Cold War in 1951 put Africa in the spotlight. At the first meeting of the council, in December 1951 in Brussels, both the Belgian Victor Larock and the former British colonial minister James Griffiths referred to Africa in their addresses. Griffiths stated that Africa was a place "where misery threatens to provoke revolt in many places, with the Communists ever ready to utilize any movement of revolt, be it social or national, for their own ends."[241] Griffiths demonstrated that the existing political parties in Africa were occupied with a radically nationalistic program and that they were at risk of falling victim to the Cominform.

The first impulse to look more deeply at Africa actually came from Asia. Morgan Phillips had attended the bureau meeting of the ASC in Hyderabad in August 1953, and had been impressed by the active policies carried out by the ASC in Africa. On his return he gave a clear warning to the bureau of the International: "I believe that the African continent is one in which the Socialist International should take the initiative and seek to bring them into its ranks, otherwise we are in great danger of the coloured people outside the continent of Asia automatically linking up with the ASC without giving the necessary consideration to joining the SI. This must be avoided if possible

---

241   Circ. 15/52, 31/01/1952. Report of the Conference of the Council of the Socialist International. Brussels, 14-16/12/1951. IISG, SI 64.

although it should be recognized that organizations can, if they so desire, link up with both organizations for the time being." The task of the International lay clearly before it: the bureau urgently needed to take measures to establish contact with democratic parties in Africa.[242] In other words, the International needed to ensure at all costs against allowing the more radical Asian socialists to make too deep an impression on the gradual formation of the political parties in Africa.

Phillips' warning resulted in Braunthal's initiating an information gathering session. At that time, the SI hardly went further than composing an initial, very limited list of potential partner organizations.[243] Braunthal seemed to attach much importance to establishing contact with the Convention People's Party of the Gold Coast, the party of Kwame Nkrumah, but with no forthcoming result. More concrete was the collaboration with the South African Labour Party, which had applied for membership of the International in 1954. Initially, Braunthal had reacted rather reservedly. Officially the party had no racial restrictions, but at the same time it was composed exclusively of white members. The fact that the party, according to their own account, had good relations with both the South African Indian Congress and the African National Congress, which represented the black population, and that they counted 15 members of parliament among their members, no doubt spoke highly in their favour. Moreover, the chairman of the party, Jessie McPherson, was not unknown to the International. He had been present at the Zurich congress of the International in June 1947. The natural result of these contacts was that the party was invited to take part in the March 1955 congress, in the capacity of a "fraternal delegate". In addition, Braunthal had also corresponded with the South Rhodesian Labour Party and with the Action Group of Nigeria, which according to its vice-president was the only progressive party functioning in Nigeria. All in all however, contacts with Africa were limited.

It wouldn't be until 1958 that Africa was once again placed on the agenda of the International. In that year, the first meeting of the All-African People's Conference, an initiative composed of various African parties and anti-imperialist organizations, took place in Ghana's capital Accra, from 5 till 13 December. Bjarne Braatoy began where his predecessor Braunthal had left off:

---

242   Circ. B19/53, 24/09/1953. Report by Morgan Phillips of ASC Bureau Meeting, Hyderabad 10-
        12/08/1953. IISG, SI 73.
243   Circ. 65/54. 30/12/1954. Minutes of the Meeting of the Bureau of the SI, Amsterdam,
        19/12/1954. IISG, SI 75.

with a new information gathering session.[244] Meanwhile the political land-scape in Africa had fundamentally changed, especially in the French colonial territories where in 1956 the socialist Gaston Deferre had introduced the "Loi Cadre". In January 1957 the federations of the SFIO in the African territories were dissolved and "replaced" by the Mouvement Socialiste Africain (MSA), founded that same month in Conakry, Guinea. The MSA functioned as an umbrella organization of various African parties, which often were active in more limited geographical areas under different names. The chairman of the MSA, Lamine Gueye, was present at the fifth congress of the International in Vienna in July 1957. Halfway through 1958 a political shift took place when the MSA, together with a few local parties, formed the Parti de Regroupe-ment Africain (PRA). This new political constellation, headed by Léopold Senghor and Lamine Gueye had its centers of gravity in Senegal, the Sudan, Niger, Upper Volta and Dahomey. The most important rival of the PRA was the Rassemblement Démocratique Africain (RDA), also an "international party", which under the leadership of Houphouet-Boigny existed in and took its support principally from the Ivory Coast, Niger and the Sudan. The SFIO attempted to maintain good relations with both parties, which were "social-istically oriented", irrefutably thanks to the efforts of the SFIO, read a French memorandum.[245] More important, however, was the uncertainty of the future evolution of both parties. As long as it remained unclear which direction the parties would take after decolonialization, which was fast approaching, the International refrained from choosing one over the other.

In the British territories the South African Labour Party was the only party which could pass for a "democratic socialist" party, but it could hardly function as a bridge to the rest of Africa: it was composed principally of Europeans, it no longer held any seats in parliament, and it was scarcely active. The Conven-tion People's Party from Ghana, on the other hand, was worth following. The party sat in government and was proud of its socialist ideas. A British memorandum voiced a concern about certain tendencies within the party which seemed to be in favour of a one party state, but it also stated that "there are certain signs of Socialist interest within the party and it has a basi-cally democratic constitution."[246] Lastly, it seemed that the British were also expecting much to come of the Kenya African National Union and the

244   Braatoy, of Norwegian descent, had succeeded Braunthal on 1 May 1956 (Braunthal had reached retirement age).
245   Circ. B13/59. 19/02/1959. Political parties in the African countries of the 'Community' under French influence. Memorandum submitted by the SP SFIO. IISG, SI 95.
246   Circ. 32/60. 08/04/1960. Memorandum on Political Organisations in British Africa, submitted by the British Labour Party to the Council Conference in Haifa. IISG, SI 97.

Tanganyika African National Union. Those two parties counted certain leading figures among their ranks, such as Tom Mboya and Julius Nyerere, who
were open to socialist ideology. Nyerere in particular, aroused high hopes.

Besides member parties of countries with colonies in Africa, the Israeli party
Mapai also had developed into a well of information on Africa. It was that
party which had brought the International into contact with Nyerere. In his
youth Nyerere had taken part in a Youth Leaders' Seminar in Tel Aviv.
The three month course was an example of the type of cooperation existing
between Asia and Africa, an area in which Mapai was increasingly making its
mark. Representatives from eleven African countries - civil servants, technicians, farmers and union members - all took part in this "Seminar on Cooperation for Asian and African Cooperators", which gave Mapai the chance
of establishing a broad range of contacts. This and many similar initiatives
underlined Israel's interest in the African continent. In the same vein, Golda
Meir, then Israel's foreign minister, made a tour of Africa, and Mapai invited
four party leaders from Ghana to come spend a few months in Israel gaining
political experience. The choice of Haifa for the April 1960 meeting of the
council of the International was in fact in recognition of the important role
Mapai seemed willing and able to play as a bridge to Africa and Asia. This was
the first time that the International had really left the European continent.

The meeting of the council in Haifa, which was organized entirely around
the theme of assistance to the developing countries, was meant as a friendly
gesture to Africa on the part of the International. Such a gesture was necessary given the deep African mistrust of the Western European social democrats. A good illustration of this lack of trust is the fact that at the second
All-African Peoples' Conference in January 1960, in Tunis, the International
was only allowed to watch from the sidelines.

In Tunis one could feel a deep-rooted fear of neocolonialism. The Africans, for
example, had a dislike for NATO, which was letting France conduct "its" war in
Algeria. Kurt Kristiansson, who as secretary-general of the International Union
of Socialist Youth (IUSY) attended the conference in Tunis, brought with him
a list with certain "conditiones sine qua non" for productive cooperation with

socialist movements on the African continent.[247] An absolute condition for the Africans was the unambiguous support for the right of self-determination for all African lands, a right which needed to be enforced as quickly as possible and without any delay manœuvres. Equally important was support for the integration tendencies in Africa. In Tunis one of the themes which held sway was the "United States of Africa", which recognized that Africa was a continent in its own right and not just an extension of Europe. Additionally, Kristiansson mentioned further economic and technical assistance "in forms acceptable to the Africans themselves", by which he meant assistance from the United Nations, which did not come attached with all the conditions of regular bilateral assistance programs. Lastly, he added student scholarships to his list, so that African leaders would be able to go and study the "function of democracy" and the role of parties, unions and feminist and youth organizations.

In January 1960, the International still had not at all met all the criteria on the above list, but it would come a whole lot closer to doing so. The BLP played an important role in this. Anthony Wedgwood Benn, a member of parliament from the Labour Party, who had taken part in the conference in Tunis, had briefed his party in detail. Tunis had made a big impression upon him: "It was impossible to escape the conclusion in Tunis that one was witnessing the beginnings of one of those great movements of history. Pan-Africanism is a bold concept and it will call forth from us an equally bold response. This is far wider than colonial or Commonwealth policy. There is a terrible danger that we may be left behind in these events because we are unwilling or unready to see what is happening."[248] He thought that the BLP needed to be radical when it came to issues of independence. They needed to work hard to ensure that the UN would treat all colonial issues as international issues. They also needed to come up with more proactive actions such as boycott campaigns. A few weeks before the Tunis conference the BLP had decided that for the

---

247   From that moment on, the International Union of Socialist Youth became very important for the International. It provided them with the means to establish contacts with African movements. The relations of major importance which the IUSY maintained with African (and Asian) socialists were a growing source of overtures between the International and the IUSY. Soon after the All-African Peoples' Conference in Tunis, the Bureau decided to set up a Sub-Committee with S. Levenberg and O. Probst to strengthen the ties with the IUSY. They also decided to invite an IUSY representative to the Bureau Meeting once a year. Circ. 13/60. 03/03/1960. Minutes of the Meeting of the Bureau of the Socialist International. London, 25-26/02/1960. IISG, SI 96.

248   Circ. B. 12/60. 18/02/1960. Second all-African Peoples' Conference. Tunis, 25-31/01/1960. Summary of conference decisions and personal observations by Anthony Wedgwood Benn, MP. IISG, SI 99.

entire month of March they would try and set up a boycott of South African products. The campaign was in the spirit of the "Year of Africa" which the party had announced and was also in direct response to a call from the South African National Congress, the South African Indian Congress and the Liberal Party of South Africa. Via the bureau of the International other social democratic parties were warmed up to the initiative, with a certain amount of success.

Such initiatives improved the International's image. The fact that from 1958 onwards, the Belgian socialists, as well as the Dutch for that matter, no longer sat in government was particularly helpful as well. It helped ensure that a second "Algerian fiasco" - this time in either the Belgian Congo or in Dutch Guinea - would not further besmirch the International's reputation. In the beginning of 1959, heavy rioting in Leopoldville in the Belgian Congo brought the area under the scrutiny of the world press. The Belgian social-ist Franz Tielemans delivered a detailed report to the bureau in which he illuminated the position of the BSP.[249] A few months later Jean Luyten, the BSP Party Secretary, submitted a report from the "Belgian Parliamentary Commission on the Recent Events in the Congo". To the BSP, which now sat in the opposition, the Congo was an issue which they could use to attack the "conservative, colonialist" majority, and they were not sparing in their infor-mation. This gave the party the opportunity to present themselves as the anti-colonial standard bearer. Without any doubt, this also reflected positively on the International, which in September 1960 was enthusiastically applaud-ing the admission of the Congo to the United Nations.

There was one party still sitting in government which more and more came to be associated with a colonialist political outlook: the French SFIO. This was reason enough for the BLP to make only limited use of the International when establishing contacts with African parties. A British memorandum, defended by the British at the council meeting of the International in Haifa, left little to the imagination: "The BLP has, for many years, tried to extend and consolidate its personal contacts with African national leaders, and with others in an influ-ential position on the continent. To a large extent it can now be said that the party has succeeded, and is in close touch with each of the newly developing parties (…). It would be unwise at this stage for the SI to make any direct approach to any of these organizations unless there is a profound knowledge of the personalities and organizations involved. Any kind of approach from

---

249   Circ. 7/59. 26/02/1959. Minutes of the meeting of the Bureau of the SI. London, 06/02/1959.
         IISG, SI 92.

the outside can be positively dangerous to the internal political situation of these territories. The Labour Party has been meticulous in refusing at any time to take sides between these different parties, or to take any action which could be used by them to suggest that one was more favourably considered by the Labour Party. (...) Any other outside intervention could well damage this effort and postpone indefinitely its success."[250]

Yet the SFIO gradually began to be reduced in power. When the problems in Algeria were threatening to throw France itself into a civil war, the door was opened for De Gaulle to return to power.[251] The end of the Fourth Republic also meant the end of the SFIO. The party meekly had thrown in its lot with De Gaulle, especially during the referendum of September 1958, and was duly rewarded with a few positions in the government. In 1962 the party received only 13% of the vote, they lost their seats in the government and shortly afterwards completely disappeared from the scene. By 1960 the International was also to see the parceling off of the SFIO's political power. In December 1960 the bureau of the International approved a resolution in which they spoke most earnestly of the urgent need for Algerian self-determination. The resolution was clearly referring directly to De Gaulle himself.[252] Significantly, the SFIO was kept out of the Subcommittee for Developing Nations, established in 1960. This subcommittee was responsible for working out a social democratic development policy. A written request from SFIO-members Georges Brutelle and Josette Pontillon asking to be included in the committee was refused. The International was definitely taking huge steps to improve its reputation. Yet it would still take quite a while before Africa would be convinced that the "Colonial International" was a thing of the past.

To convince the Africans of this, a few robust anti-colonial howls were certainly helpful. In May 1961, for example, the bureau expressed its "deepest concern" about the conflict in Angola, which according to the International was caused by the refusal of the Portuguese government to recognize the right to self-determination in its colonies. They called upon Portugal "in accordance with the resolution of the UN and its obligations to the UN Charter to take immediate steps to accord democratic rights to the people instead of

---

250   Circ. 32/60. 08/04/1960. Memorandum on Political Organisations in British Africa, submitted by the BLP to the Council Conference in Haifa. IISG, SI 97.
251   Vaïsse, La grandeur. Politique étrangère du général De Gaulle, 70 ff.; Cointet, De Gaulle et l'Algérie française.
252   Circ. 85/60. 22/12/1960. Minutes of the Meeting of the Bureau of the SI. London, 02/12/1960. IISG, SI 98.

resorting to violence." In addition, the member parties of the International were requested to put pressure on the Portuguese government.

By the end of 1961, the time seemed ripe for the International to send a mission to Africa in order to establish the necessary contacts there. The departure date was several times postponed, due to "national priorities", but on 28 December 1961 the mission finally set out. It was split into two groups: the "English speaking team" with David Haconen (Israel) and Paul Engstad (Norway) was sent to Ghana, Nigeria, Sierra Leone, Uganda, Kenya, Tanganyika, Madagascar and Mauritius; the "French speaking team" composed of Eugen Stark (Austria) and Günther Markscheffel (Germany) went to Senegal, Mali, the Ivory Coast, Guinea, Togo, Upper Volta, Congo-Brazzaville and Congo-Leopold-ville. The mission returned with a cartload of recommendations which were approved by the bureau of the International. Several of these proposals will be discussed in more detail below.

For the time being no decision was taken regarding the creation of a special secretariat for Africa. Other proposals for expanding contacts were either not very original (European socialist leaders had to make an attempt to meet with African leaders visiting Europe) or not very realistic (the European countries should appoint socialist ambassadors to the various African capitals).[253] The bureau also called upon its members to take part in a conference in Dakar, organized by the Senegalese president Léopold Senghor, in Dakar in the beginning of December 1962. The conference which was organized around the themes "Development policies and the various African roads to Socialism", brought a number of prominent African figures together and was an ideal forum for making acquaintances. Among those present were Guy Mollet, Robert Pontillon, James Callaghan and Moshe Sharett. The International used their presence at the conference mainly in order to drum up interest in their idea to establish training camps for political cadres. James Callaghan, who had talked the idea through with Senghor, was at the end of the day extreme-ly satisfied. Senghor reacted positively to the International's proposition and suggested that a center should be established in Dakar, in collaboration with the local university. In other words, the "development policy" of the International was taking form.

In terms of establishing organizational contacts - one of the principal aims of the mission - little headway was made. There was a list of 13 parties from

---

253   Circ. 57/62. 20/07/1962. Minutes of a Special Meeting on Africa of the Standing Joint Commit-
       tee on Developing Areas. Oslo, 30-31/05/1962. IISG, SI 110.

11 countries to which the International could distribute its English and French publications, but that did not at all mean that these parties would be joining the International. By the end of the 1960's only the Social Democratic Party of Madagascar and the Comoros would have become a member of the International. As an incentive, the International decided to set the contributions from African parties at only £15 per annum. In addition, they would receive *Socialist International Information* free of charge.[254]

In practice, the activities of the International in Africa were actually limited to a few "goodwill campaigns". Between 1960 and 1965, the International was principally preoccupied with Morocco and South Africa. In Morocco, the International cast their lot together with the leaders of the Union Nationale des Forces Populaires (UNFP) who were accused of conspiring against King Hassan II and sentenced to death. According to the International, this was nothing more than a political ruse from the royalist party, the Front pour la Défense des Institutions Constitutionales, which had lost the elections of 17 May 1963, the first elections since independence. Moreover, the International possessed information about confessions which had been obtained by means of coercion and torture. The International asked their members to put pressure on Morocco, via their embassies, to give the UNFP leaders a fair trial.

In South Africa the International's involvement in the anti-Apartheid struggle consisted of a continuation of earlier actions. Via direct appeal to the South African prime minister Hendrik Verwoerd, via resolutions and via political action from its members, the International attempted to bring about observation of the UN resolutions condemning the Apartheid regime. The fact that the International found itself in complete agreement with the work of the UN commission on South Africa was undoubtedly partly due to the fact that the commission was chaired by the Swedish socialist Alva Myrdal, who had already worked closely with the International on several occasions. Such solidarity actions are still one of the main activities of the International today.

254 Circ. 67/61. 06/10/1961. Minutes of the Meeting of the Finance Committee. London, 24/09/1961. IISG, SI 102.

The Collapse of the International's Asian Pillar:
Marginalizing Socialism in Asia

The main threat to the International's concept of a world-embracing, unitary organization initially came from Asia. As soon as the first preparations had been set in motion in 1952 to found a regional Asian Socialist Conference, the leaders of the International resolved to incorporate the ASC into the International. The reserve of many of the constituent parties within the ASC forced Braunthal and Phillips to approach their goal via a circuitous route, namely by collaborating with the ASC on common themes. The themes were rather self-evident. In 1954, for example, when the Dutch socialist Vos worked out a memorandum on "International Investment in Underdeveloped Countries", the International invited the bureau of the ASC to participate in the editing of this document.[255] Both organizations also decided that on appropriate occasions they would publish a joint bulletin. That was the case for the first time on 1 May 1955, May day. However, the International's ambition undoubtedly reached beyond such ad hoc initiatives to include a more institutionalized and more comprehensive collaboration. That ambition is illustrated through the efforts of the SI and the ASC to work together on a theme that from the very beginning had come to top the International's agenda: the United Nations.

The ASC attached much importance to the debate about the revision of the UN Charter, which according to expectations was to be carried out in the UN in 1954 and 1955. Wijono, the secretary-general of the ASC, had proposed Braunthal to hold a joint conference in order to come up with a unified socialist position so as to have more of an impact upon the discussions in the UN. Braunthal submitted the proposal to the bureau of the International, which decided to adopt the theme, "if possible in conjunction with the bureau of the ASC".[256] Not that the entire discussion was of such importance to the International. Finn Moe, who dominated nearly all UN questions within the International, had made it clear that he was not expecting too much from the revision of the Charter. The Charter was indeed far from ideal, but it was good enough, if only the UN members were willing to live up to it. He was anything but an advocate of the strengthening of the UN organs towards something resembling a "world government", by for example abolishing the veto.

---

255   Circ. 31/54. 14/05/1954. Council of the Socialist International in Vienna, 07-08/05/1954. IISG, SI 75.

256   Circ. 118/53. 26/11/1953. Minutes of the Meeting of the Bureau of the Socialist International, London, 19/11/1953. IISG, SI 71.

A majority decision which went against the interests of one of the large states would in any event not be implemented. The only effect would be that one or more of the big powers would turn their back on the UN. Finn Moe therefore warned against "undue insistence on the revision of the terms of the Charter since it might give rise to strife within the organization and thus weaken, rather than strengthen, the UN".[257] Others joined in, including the representatives of the Dutch PvdA. The Dutchman Moser expressed it very clearly: "Hereby, I declare that the Dutch Labour Party is of the opinion that proposals from our Side to revise the UN Charter would come too early."[258]

Nonetheless, to please the ASC, the International spent much energy on the debate. Finn Moe was asked to prepare a memorandum. On the Asian side a six-member study commission was set up with the task of writing up a discussion text of their own. During the months which followed, there was an extensive series of consultations on both of the texts. Opinions were very divided. The ASC deplored the fact that the UN was weakened and misused by the two blocks of power, both of which used the veto and the system of permanent membership on the Security Council to divide the world into big and small states. According to the ASC, the International also exacerbated the situation by placing a one-sided emphasis on themes such as forced labour and human rights in the USSR. Regarding the UN veto and the division of power in the Security Council opinions were also divided. Finn Moe's draft text put it thus: "The International believes that permanent seats as well as veto power correspond to the realities of the world situation today. Thus it will not press for the abolition of veto power nor insist on such limitations of this power, unless they are agreed to by all the permanent members of the Security Council".

Despite these differences in opinion, the positions of various Asian parties were completely taken up in the bulletin of the International and the reactions they received were passed on to the bureaus of both organizations. On several occasions top representatives from both groups had the opportunity to enter into direct debate with each other. At the fourth congress of the International, in London in 1955, a joint commission of SI and ASC members attempted to come up with a definitive text which both organizations would be prepared to endorse.[259] They did not succeed, but this was due principally

---

257 Circ. 32/55. 26/05/1955. Revision of the United Nations Charter. Draft Statement, submitted by Finn Moe to the Fourth Congress of the Socialist International. IISG, SI 74.
258 Letter from Moser to Braunthal, 01/06/1954. IISG, SI 903.
259 Circ. 52/55. 30/09/1955. Report of the Fourth Congress of the SI. IISG, SI 74.

to the fact that the International could not come to internal agreement regarding the necessity of revising the UN Charter, the question of the UN veto, and the position of permanent membership in the UN Security Council. The result of this internal division was that all of these themes were dropped in their entirety from the text. Consequently, the ASC no longer had any interest in co-signing a resolution which only contained some general and vague statements. Nevertheless, this common effort illustrates just how good relations then were between Asian and European socialists.

The seriousness with which the International approached the debate had to convince the Asian socialists that they were being listened to and taken seriously, and further, that the full integration of the ASC into the SI was indeed possible. It was no coincidence that in the middle of this discussion Braunthal submitted a proposal to the ASC to establish a joint commission to lay the groundwork for the complete integration of the ASC into the International. He made this proposal at the bureau meeting of the ASC in Tokyo, in November 1954: "The bureau, the council and indeed the whole Socialist International are most anxious to proceed, as rapidly as possible from the stage of fraternal cooperation, which now exists between our two organizations, to the establishment of organizational unity in a single International".[260] "In the spirit of the tradition of the international Socialist movement", he continued, "the bureau feels that there should be only one International." To show that the International was willing to meet the ASC halfway Braunthal promised some fundamental changes in the structure of the International.

In retrospect the secretary-general of the International was rather satisfied with the discussions which his proposal generated. He felt that "almost all present in Tokyo" (with the exception of Japan-L, Pakistan and Indonesia) were in agreement with the principle of one unified International. Yet still, he returned to Europe empty-handed; the final decision had been put off until the ASC congress of November 1955. Furthermore, not all bureau members of the International welcomed Braunthal's initiative. The fact that he had not kept the bureau informed of his intentions caused bad blood. Kaj Björk, in particular, was critical of Braunthal's method of working, which for him went too fast.

---

260   Report on the Bureau Meeting of the ASC, Tokyo, 15-22/11/1954. Speech Braunthal. Circ.
      60/54. 08/12/1954. IISG, SI 74.

The chairman, on the other hand, completely supported the secretary-general's initiative and proposed reopening the question for a full discussion at the International's 1955 congress, in the presence of the ASC delegation. The fact that Wijono was leading the delegation did not bode well. In his address at the opening of the congress Wijono, speaking on behalf of the ASC, repeated that he did see the need for a worldwide federation of socialist regional experiences, efforts and practices and to that end he proposed strengthening the existing collaboration between the two organizations. There was no room, however, for questions of fusion: "Unity (...) will lead us nowhere", he concluded.[261] At the end of the decade he would still be defending the same position with the same arguments: "The methods of organizing the party and other things according your long experience of Socialism would not be applicable in most of the Asian countries because of the peculiar features in Asian communities, mostly psychologically, which are so different from the European. Socialism in Asia and I believe also in Africa should find out their own methods to develop Socialism in practice."[262]

Wijono's reserve does not diminish the fact that relations between the two organizations were rarely to go so smoothly as in 1955 and 1956. That was also the general sentiment among the delegation of the International which in November 1956 attended the second congress of the Asian Socialist Conference in Bombay. In their report they gave an exceptionally positive evaluation of the congress: "The Asian parties now have more confidence in the SI, as was proved by frequent references to its work and to the extent of its cooperation with the ASC. For instance, special invitations were extended to the SI delegation to attend committee meetings, and they were asked to state their views on all controversial issues. The delegates' reception by the congress chairman and the host party was most cordial. The impression gained by the delegation of the SI is that relations between the two organizations have greatly improved."[263]

Erich Ollenhauer, who was a member of the SI delegation to Bombay and who after the congress spent a month traveling through Asia, came to a similar conclusion in his report for his party, the German SPD. He saw fusion as an impossibility which should not be insisted upon, yet in private conversations leading Asian socialists had let him know that it would be useful if a joint meeting between the SI and the ASC could be arranged sometime in the

261   Report of the Fourth Congress of the Socialist International. Circ. 52/55. 30/09/1955. IISG, SI 79.
262   Letter from Wijono to Carthy, 06/05/1959. IISG, SI 249.
263   Report of the Second Congress of the ASC. Bombay, 01-10/11/1956. Circ. 67/56. IISG, SI 83.

course of the following year.[264] For the International this was undoubtedly a step in the right direction.

The good relations are best illustrated by the contacts which had been established years before between the ASC and Julius Braunthal, who headed the delegation to Bombay, despite the fact that at that moment he was officially already retired. Starting in January 1956, Braunthal had seriously begun lobbying to be included in the delegation. The bureau justly considered him the ideal contact person to strengthen the bonds between the two organizations. Over the years the former secretary-general of the International had become ever more personally interested in the Asian continent. He considered it his task to make European socialism comprehensible to the Asians and Asian socialism comprehensible to the Europeans. His lecture series at various Asian universities and Asian societies and his intention to write a study about the socialist movement in Asia were expressions of this.[265] Most likely Braunthal's presence, along with the presence of a prestigious delegation from Israel, and the progressive policies of the BLP at that moment, explains why the relatively good relations with the ASC were only partly overshadowed by the Suez invasion, which had been launched just before the congress.

The precise impact of the Suez invasion and of the SFIO's return to the French government in 1956 upon the future relations between the SI and the ASC will always remain the subject of speculation. From 1956 onwards the ASC would wither fast. By 1956, there was little left of the enthusiasm and extraordinary expectations which had accompanied the founding of the ASC in 1953. The massive gathering which concluded the founding congress of the ASC on 11 January 1953 had brought together circa 100,000 people in the B.A.A. Stadium in Rangoon. That colorful manifestation was meant to illustrate the growing power of Asian socialism, but hardly three years later, the situation was almost unrecognizable. At the moment of the second ASC conference in Bombay in 1956, not a single Asian party was still in government, except in Ceylon and Burma, where the socialist parties were involved in exceptionally unstable internal situations that devoured all of their energy, leaving little over for any serious politics. Almost all of the Asian parties were rife with internal tensions and even ruptures. In a party landscape where nearly all the large parties claimed to adhere to a "socialist ordering of

---

264   Excerpt from the internal report to the SPD by Ollenhauer. Circ. B.5/57. 15/12/1957. IISG, SI 88.
265   In the third volume of his *Geschichte der Internationale* Braunthal devoted almost 200 pages
         to Socialism in Asia. Braunthal, *Geschichte der Internationale*, 3, 257-439.

society" (Japan and Israel being notorious exceptions) the "true" socialist parties could only with great difficulty maintain their relevance. Moreover, they often suffered from a lack of political experience, and the conversion process from elite to mass party did not go very smoothly either.

Of course, this all reflected upon the workings of the ASC. *Socialist Asia* began to appear less regularly and after 1957 publication stopped entirely. The Asian Socialist Publishing House, founded in 1955, would also never really get off the ground. Braunthal, who after the second ASC congress remained in Asia for a five month lecture tour, burst the illusion of a vigorous and energetic Asian socialism: "In sharp contrast with the great prestige enjoyed by the Asian Socialist Conference is the setup of its organizational machine. The office is run by only one man, U Hla Aung; he had been one of the three Joint Secretaries, and was elected secretary-general in succession to Wijono who became vice-chairman and returned to Indonesia. The other two Joint Secretaries, Madhav Gokhale (India) and Chisato Tatobayashi (Japan) were recalled by their parties. U Hla Aung's only help is from a part-time shorthand-typist and two young men who, it would appear, duplicate stencils, dispatch letters and run errands, but do no true secretarial work".[266]

Out of sheer necessity, the ASC arrived at a similar self-criticism during its bureau meeting in Kathmandu in March 1958. It was to be the last bureau meeting of the ASC, and it took place in the absence of both the chairman and the treasurer. U Ba Swe and U Kyaw Nyein failed to appear "due to urgent national problems".[267] The bureau decided to establish a special committee to work out suggestions for pulling the organization out of its crisis and for strengthening it. That committee was to pay special attention to the training of young party officers, since the lack of trained political personnel was considered one of the principal reasons for the malaise in the socialist parties. But that committee was unable to turn the tide. By 1959, the ASC de facto ceased to exist: the tasks of the secretary were taken on by the vice-chairman Wijono, who kept the ASC artificially alive. He was all too conscious about this. In a letter to Hendrik Vos he wrote: "Nothing can be done (…) as the affiliates (…) are mostly engaged in a dead-struggle to overcome all dangers and difficulties of the home-country today."[268]

266   Circ. B.29/57. 18/04/1957. Report on the Asian Socialist parties. Confidential. IISG, SI 88. Braunthal's lecture tour took him to India, Ceylon, Nepal, Burma, Thailand, Singapore, Indonesia and Israel, in that order.
267   Circ. B.25/58. 28/04/1958. Summary of the Report by Reuven Barkatt of the meeting of the ASC Bureau. Kathmandu, 26-29/03/1958. IISG, SI 91
268   Circ. B.31/58. 01/08/1958. IISG, SI 91.

This development brought about an important reversal in relations between the ASC and the SI. For the Asian socialists the International was now to become their "light in dark days". They counted upon their Western European brethren to breathe new life into socialism in Asia. This is the message which Reuven Barkatt brought back from Kathmandu. The message was actually part of a larger and more detailed wish list which Barkatt had received.[269] While in Nepal, the Israeli had ascertained "a radical change in the attitude of the ASC and its member parties" with regard to the International. Trust in the International had never before been so strong. Barkatt brought the ASC's wish list to the attention of the International. The ASC proposed not less than nine ways in which the International could support declining Asian socialism. The majority of the proposals were already sufficiently known, even if earlier attempts had not amounted to much: the exchange of information, the sending of delegations, organizational support, a jointly published bulletin, an Asian publishing house. The only truly new proposal was the establishment of a "leadership training college", an idea which the bureau of the ASC had launched in Kathmandu. According to Barkatt, the International had an obligation to financially support this and all the other ideas.

The International reacted with an exceptional lack of enthusiasm. At the International's meeting of 4 and 5 November, the members were only called upon to exchange delegations with like-minded parties in Asia and to supply them with printed material.[270] The Hamburg congress in July 1959 was attended by a rather large Asian delegation, but during the congress itself Asia hardly came up in any of the discussions. 'Asia' was reserved for a lunch on 15 July, at the Besenbinderhof, a Hamburg restaurant. At that luncheon the existing forms of collaboration, such as the Dependent Peoples Freedom Day, were reaffirmed. It was also decided to investigate to what extent the Declaration on Colonialism from 1955 was being put into effect, and following the congress, the Asian delegation was invited to visit the offices of the Austrian, British, German and Swedish parties. In other words, the meeting was to produce nothing more than activities which carried with them no promise of financial support. ASC secretary-general U Hla Aung's proposal to send a joint ASC/SI "fact-finding mission" to Africa, for example, was delicately rejected by the International. According to the bureau such a mission would not only be quite a fiasco in terms of organization, but there was also a more funda-

269 Circ. B25/58. 28/04/1958. Summary of the Report by Reuven Barkatt of the meeting of the ASC Bureau. Kathmandu, 26-29/03/1958. IISG, SI 91.
270 Circ. 86/58. 20/11/1958. Minutes of the Meeting of the Bureau of the SI, London, 04-05/11/1958. IISG, SI 90. Circ. 20/59. 01/05/1959. IISG, SI 92.

mental objection:"The bureau believe that such an inquiry should not be undertaken without regard to, or consultation with, African opinion." In other words, it was not for the ASC to undertake such a mission, rather it was more appropriately the task of an African organization. Wijono reacted with disappointment. He accused the International of "not having enough confidence" in Asian socialism which "emotionally has more in common with Africa than Europe" and he hinted that the International was afraid that the ASC would go too far in its conclusions.[271]

There was one bright spot for the ASC. It was invited to participate in a permanent subcommittee which was established in Hamburg with representatives from Germany, Great Britain, Israel, the Netherlands and Sweden. The task of the committee was to work out a program for collaboration with parties from "developing countries".[272] In the near future parties from Latin America and Africa were meant to be involved as well.

The first meeting of this "Standing Joint Committee on Developing Areas" (SJCDA) took place in Haifa, in April 1960, just before the council of the International was to descend upon that Israeli city on the Mediterranean coast. The copious exchange of thoughts which had already taken place in Hamburg regarding possible ways of strengthening the cooperation between parties from "developing" and "developed" countries was thus made concrete by the creation of the SJCDA. This committee would come up with a list of possible forms of tighter ideological, economic, and organizational cooperation between parties, and by extension between countries and continents as well. This list was to become the basis of the development program of the International which will be elucidated below.

The fact that the ASC was invited to be part of the SJCDA had a very specific reason. It was mainly the consequence of the events which were taking place in Africa, a continent which had absorbed the attention of the Asian parties for quite some time. From around 1960 onwards, the attention of the International was no longer so much directed at Asia "an sich", but rather at Africa. Africa was seen as virgin territory ready to be parceled up and conquered. The International was afraid that competitors would come and stake their claims, even if in principle they all belonged to the same team (such as was the case with the ASC). It would all too soon become apparent that Africa's hoped for

271   Correspondence between Carthy and Wijono, 03-04/1959. IISG, SI 249.
272   Circ. 13/60. 03/03/1960. Minutes of the Meeting of the Bureau of the Socialist International. London, 25-26/02/1960. IISG, SI 96.

democratic debut was not to be. Accordingly, from around 1960 on, the activities of the International would focus themselves principally on the Western Hemisphere.

The International, however, did not entirely abandon Asia. Socialists who as members of governmental or parliamentary delegations visited Asia were requested to visit Asian socialists and afterwards to report back to the International.[273] The list of invitees to the 1961 congress of the International in Rome gives a good picture of the existing contacts. The parties or persons who were always sure of an invitation were the Indian Praja Socialist Party, with party chairman Asoka Mehta, the Japanese Social Democratic Party and the Japanese Democratic Socialist Party, and U Ba Swe, who still functioned as the chairman of the ASC. In addition, representatives from Ceylon, Singapore, Iran and Mauritius were also invited despite contributing very little to the congress. Lastly, there was Nepal, the only country which around the end of the decade was sure to receive some attention. In February 1959, the Nepali Congress Party had won an absolute majority in the first general parliamentary elections. Bisheshwar Koirala became the first elected 'socialist' prime minister of the country, which gave him much prestige both in the ASC and in the International. For a moment Nepal, along with Israel, appeared to be the socialist development model par excellence.

After the Nepalese monarch had abolished the centuries old system of hereditary "prime ministers" in 1951, and imported a more modern cabinet system, party politics emerged onto the Nepali political landscape, which was soon dominated by Koirala's Nepali Congress Party. After their electoral victory of 1959, the "socialists" were faced with an immense task. 98% of the population was illiterate, the infant mortality rate was at more than 60% and the average life expectancy was no higher than 35 years. More than 85% of the population was employed in an extremely archaic, feudally organized agricultural system and industrial development was more or less non-existent. Education and healthcare together barely accounted for one percent of government expenditure. It was prime minister Koirala himself who in 1960 received the opportunity to give a detailed account of his country's dire needs before the Central Committee of Mapai. He immediately added certain ambitious, socialist inspired development programs which were to lead Nepal into the modern era.[274] Shortly afterwards, at the instigation of Albert Carthy, who met Koirala returning from the United Nations that October in London, the bureau

273   Circ. 1/61. 06/01/1961. Visit to Socialist parties in Asia. IISG, SI 101.
274   Circ. B.39/60. 06/10/1960. Speech Koirala to the Central Committee of Mapai. IISG, SI 99.

of the International also had an opportunity to examine Koirala's development programs. In other words Nepal was to become a practical example of the more theoretical discussions which had taken place in Haifa.

In any event, Nepal would never become a real engagement of the International. Relations between Koirala and the king of Nepal would soon sour. Hardly two months after Koirala and Carthy's meeting the monarch dismissed and arrested Koirala and his entire government, and reintroduced a system of absolute monarchy banning all political parties. The International quickly shelved its development plans and registered a stern protest against the Nepalese monarchy. The Scandinavian parties in particular were disturbed by the turn of events in Nepal. The head of the Danish delegation to the UN, Per Haekkerup, and the Danish Permanent Representative to the UN brought up the situation in Nepal with the General Assembly of the UN. The International reported all events in *Socialist International Information*. At their congress in Rome the International also approved a strong remonstration of Nepal and wrote several letters of protest to the Nepalese monarch, who in turn thanked the International for their concern.[275] Koirala was to spend the next eight years in prison, followed by another eight years in exile.

The International was to have similar contacts with Korea. In December 1960, the German Willi Eichler had made first contact with two socialist movements there. The forced abdication of president Rhee Syngman in 1960, in the face of violent student protests, had lead to the establishment of a parliamentary system, under which political parties were given more breathing space. Eichler had the Frankfurt declaration translated by a Korean socialist who had studied in Munich, and he then supplied a copy to both socialist groups. In the spring of 1961, the two groups fused into the United Socialist Party of Korea, which immediately applied for membership in the International. Yet here too, political developments were to throw soot on the banquet. The parliamentary system was to lead to great chaos, which Park Chung Hee put an end to with the establishment of a military dictatorship in 1961. The party was banned and the majority of its leaders arrested; three of them, two editors and the publisher of the socialist journal *Minjok Ilbo* (People's Daily) were sentenced to death.

Just as was the case with Nepal, the International now too summoned its members, especially those parties in government, to appeal via the United

---

275   Circ. 13/62. 16/03/1962. Minutes of the Bureau Meeting of the SI. London, 07-08/02/1962. IISG, SI 106; Socialist International Information, 11, nr. 48.

Nations for the release of the Korean party members and the re-establishment of democracy in Korea. Some parties went even further. The Scandinavian parties, for example, made £ 700 available for foodstuffs and medical
aid for socialist political prisoners in Korean prisons. The Dutchman Max
van der Stoel aired his frustrations regarding the political situation in Korea
at the General Assembly of the UN.[276] The choice to work via the UN was a
conscious one since all other requests for intervention either via the US secretary of state, Dean Rusk, or directly to the Korean ruling powers themselves,
had remained unanswered. All these attempts however did not achieve much.
Nonetheless, the International maintained relations with the Koreans as far as
possible, and on occasion things were able to go quite far. On one occasion
the Korean professor Lee Tong Howa, while serving time in a Korean prison,
was able to contribute to a pamphlet working out the distinctions between
socialism and communism.

In August 1963, the International was yet again troubled by the arrests of
U Ba Swe and U Kyaw Nyein, both of whom had worked closely together with
the International. As soon as the information was made public, the International and the British BLP requested an audience with the Burmese Ambassador to London. When the request was turned down due to the Ambassador's
"busy schedule" both groups made public their great disappointment.[277]

Under such circumstances it was, of course, no longer possible for the Asian
Socialist Conference to continue functioning. The International began inves-
tigating alternatives and from their base in London they set up an Asian
Liaison Office, despite the fact that the political reality of the day allowed for
few productive contacts. By 1960, the Asian policy of the International was
clearly defined. Just as was the case with Africa, the International, as a modern
transnational organization, put all its energies behind solidarity actions. These
were aimed at influencing world opinion, via semi-diplomatic channels such
as intergovernmental policy forums or the mass media. The real debates
on organizational matters, however, were to take place around 1960, on the
other side of the world, in Latin America.

---

276   Circ. 9/63. 08/03/1963. Minutes of the Meeting of the Bureau of the SI. London, 24-25/01/1963.
       IISG, SI 112.
277   Circ. 34/63. 16/08/1963. Burma: Arrest of U Ba Swe and U Kyaw Nyein. IISG, SI 112.

Latin America

The Cuban Revolution and the Radicalization of Latin American Socialism

In its relations with Asian socialists the International was guided by their model of a unified, centralized structure. Collaboration on a decentralized basis was not considered an option. A similar modus operandi can again be discerned in the International's contacts with Latin America. Those contacts were just as complex and unsettled as the entire Latin American political situation around the time of the Cuban revolution. They may serve as a perfect example of diplomacy on the transnational level. Furthermore, they were to lead to a discussion in which the centralized organizational structure of the International itself was to be called into question. All this is more than sufficient reason to delve further into the Latin American component of transnational socialist activities around the year 1960.

No matter from what angle one looks at it, the creation of the Latin American Secretariat of the Socialist International (LAS) in 1955 was a compromise. It was a deal between Argentinean and Uruguayan members of the International, and the radical Chilean PSP, which had no interest in such a membership. The Chileans preferred closer ties with other Latin American parties because these could be used as a first step towards founding a broader regional organization of both "true" socialist parties as well as more "bourgeois" people's parties, a project which the PSP had been interested in for quite some time. Frederico Klein, head of the International bureau of the Chilean PSP, was therefore willing to support the creation of the LAS, providing that the setting up of the Secretariat did not go against the Chilean plans. This implied that it would maintain the same level of autonomy vis-à-vis the International as did the Asian Socialist Conference. Klein made his party's engagement conditional upon yet one more important stipulation: PSP membership of the Socialist International was absolutely out of the question.[278] As a sort of compromise a "consultative committee" was set up, as a subsection of the Latin American Secretariat, which unlike the LAS itself, had no direct link with the Socialist International. In this way, the Chilean socialists could become members of this primarily administrative body, the most important task of which was the exchange of information, without needing to become de facto a member of the International.

278   Letter from Klein to Maiztegui, 26/12/1955. IISG, SI 705.

Because of Chile's participation, the consultative committee took up a relatively independent position vis-à-vis the International. In these circumstances
Braunthal's and Phillips' policy was twofold: firstly, they ensured that the
consultative committee would not develop into a true policy organ, capable
of formulating positions independent of the International on themes which
were of importance to the International.[279] Their instructions to Humberto
Maiztegui, secretary of the LAS, were clear: "Declarations and political statements should be made only in cases of emergency, and these should be
submitted to the bureau (or council) of the SI, with a recommendation to
adopt the statement. May I add that political statements issued by the consultative committee of the LAS should concern themselves only with Latin
American aspects, and not with general international affairs. The LAS must
take great care to avoid committing the SI by statements of any kind".[280]

Secondly, Braunthal and Phillips did their best to bind the Latin American
Secretariat itself as strongly as possible to the International, just the converse
of their attitude towards the consultative committee. Consequently, there
existed a strictly hierarchical relationship between the International and
the LAS. On more than one occasion, Maiztegui was to prove his subservi-
ence. His request to the PSP to join the LAS was obviously an assignment
from Braunthal. Braunthal's influence extended even to the level of everyday
practical affairs. He went so far as to give strict orders regarding the type of
letterhead that the LAS was to use: at the top of the page in red, and in the
same font as that used by the International the name "Secretariado Latinoamericano de la Internacional Socialista" had to appear. The Spanish language
bulletin, besides carrying contributions from Latin American socialists or affiliated parties, also carried articles translated from English or Portuguese taken
in their entirety from *Socialist International Information*.[281] Over the course
of the following years, Maiztegui would painstakingly, sometimes on a daily
basis, update the secretary-general of the International or seek his advice
before making a decision. In 1959, at the Hamburg congress of the International, Maiztegui defined the mission and raison d'être of the LAS as follows:
"the dissemination of the thought and action of the SI in the Latin American
sphere where the thoughts and activity and the worldwide importance of our
organization has been almost unknown, except in the Rio de la Plata region

---

279   This again shows how little interest the International had in Latin American political and
      social-economic issues.
280   Letter from Braunthal to Maiztegui, 17/02/1956. IISG, SI 705.
281   When the first issue was published, in 1956, the bulletin had a limited edition of 250 copies.
      One year later, the circulation already reached 3500 copies.

- Argentina and Uruguay - where the socialist parties are members of the SI."[282] The Uruguayan realized all too well where the finances which kept his organization running were coming from. The International was quite pleased: they had managed to foil the schemes of the Chilean socialists to found a sort of "Latin American ASC", while at the same time being able to open a Latin American Secretariat which to a large extent functioned as an extension of the International.

That satisfaction turned out to be premature however. At the end of the 1950's, important changes were underway in the Western Hemisphere. In May 1958, Humberto Maiztegui provided Albert Carthy with a detailed report including certain reactions to the visit of US vice-president Nixon to a number of countries in the region. During Nixon's visit to Lima serious rioting broke out, and in Caracas both Nixon and his wife were physically threatened. The Venezuelan president Betancourt (Acción Democrática) condemned the actions but was unable to block President Eisenhower from immediately sending American troops to Venezuela. However, in the end those troops saw no action.

In both Peru and Venezuela Maiztegui found that there was ample justification for criticism of US policy. In Peru, the criticism had its origin in the aggravated social conditions, which at least in part were attributed to the US, as was made clear by a two month long strike against a North American company. In Venezuela, the hatred of the United States had its origin in the support which the US State Department had given to dictator Pérez Jiménez. The former dictator had been granted asylum in the United States. Despite having distanced himself from the "communist agitators" who played a role in the unrest, Maiztegui, nonetheless, also did have much criticism of his powerful northern neighbor. The US Republicans, "the spokespersons of the private sector", seemed unable to him to understand Latin America. He questioned whether Eisenhower and Nixon would be able to succeed in re-establishing the good relations between the US and Latin America, which had been enjoyed under Roosevelt.

Around the same time Maiztegui also had to inform the International of the break-up of the Argentinean Socialist Party, the PSA. Within the LAS, the PSA was by far the party most loyal to the International, and it was therefore an important pillar of the International's Latin America policy. After the split,

282   Circ. 24/50. 12/06/1959. Report by Humberto Maiztegui on the Latin American Secretariat and Consultative Committee to the Hamburg Congress, April 1958. IISG, SI 93.

a majority group including Moreau de Justo continued as the PSA, while a minority faction led by Ghioldi and Repetto founded the rival Partido Social Democrático de Argentina (PSDA). The "new" PSA, which had no objection to working together with the Argentinean communists, quickly received backing from the majority of the Uruguayan PSU. The Chilean PSP was also overjoyed by the radicalization of Argentine socialism, which previously had been rather moderate. According to Maiztegui, the majority group was "the one which understood best the everyday reality of Latin America".[283] The PSA therefore continued to sit on the consultative committee of the Latin American Secretariat. The International reacted with utmost reserve to the entire affair. Ideologically, the PSDA was more in line with the "social democratic" principles of the International, but the strong position of the LAS left the SI little choice but to accept the membership of the PSA. Maiztegui had also warned the International that any other choice would have "very negative consequences upon the reputation of the International in Latin America."[284]

In the correspondence between Carthy and Maiztegui no connection at all was made between the unrest in Venezuela and Peru surrounding Nixon's visit and the break-up of the Argentinean Socialist Party. Indeed, Maiztegui played the break-up off as if it were merely a conflict between personalities; the consequence of a somewhat childish stubbornness on the part of Ghioldi.[285] Hardly half a year later, however, an event was to take place which would become an important reference point for the entire region. In the wee hours of New Year's Day 1959, the Cuban dictator Batista fled Havana, leaving 32-year old Fidel Castro, the leader of the 26th of July Movement, de facto in control of the island. The Latin American Secretariat described the event as "a great achievement" and depicted Castro as an individual possessed of "great political maturity". He was an anti-communist - "there can be no doubt whatsoever about this" - who would pursue a progressive policy; he would see basic freedoms respected and would put an end to the far-reaching corruption of the Cuban administration. The enthusiasm of the LAS about the fall of yet another dictatorship could hardly have been more exuberant.

"The mood in Latin America after 1958 was clearly one of impatience with the status quo", wrote Thomas Wright in his study of Latin America during the period of the Cuban revolution, and this was noticeable in Latin American

---

283   Letter from Maiztegui to Carthy, 15/09/1958. IISG, SI 707.
284   Ibidem.
285   Ibidem.

socialism as well.[286] Parties which wholeheartedly embraced "fidelismo" and the Cuban revolution, as well as parties which adopted its social program and anti-Americanism without giving to either a communist interpretation, radicalized. The International was directly confronted with this evolution in June 1959, when the Socialist Party of Uruguay submitted a virulently anti-American draft-proposal to the sixth congress of the International. The document denounced Washington's vicious policy of higher tariffs against the underdeveloped countries and the dumping of agricultural surplus at extremely low prices. Both the IMF and the World Bank, "instruments for promoting Wall Street economic policies in Latin America", were severely denounced.[287]

The initiative of the PSU could hardly have come as a surprise to the International. Since as early as 1956, there had been a conflict lying dormant between the PSU and the International. In June of that year PSU secretary-general Frugoni lambasted French policy in Algeria. He regarded the SFIO, being a governing party, as partly responsible for that policy. A few months later, the Suez crisis gave the PSU another reason to sternly condemn the SFIO. In a resolution dated 31 October and approved by the executive committee of the party, the party asked for the SFIO to be excluded from the International, "unless the party withdraws its support from its present leaders."[288] In June 1957, the PSU repeated its request, but the International declared the request inadmissible.

In 1958 and 1959, the PSU furthered its campaign against the French, and the campaign became steadily more personal. On 4 June 1958, for example, Frugoni sent the secretary-general of the International a telegram demanding that the "traitor" Guy Mollet be barred from the International. When at the Hamburg congress in July 1959 Mollet not only had his mandate in the bureau prolonged by two years, but also was re-elected vice-chairman of the International, the PSU had enough of it. At the 32nd party congress of the PSU, which took place in January 1960, the party decided to leave the "revisionist" International. They did however remain on the autonomous consultative committee, where they joined the Chilean PSP. At the same time the PSU chose for complete neutrality, aligning themselves - surprisingly - with the

286   Wright, *Latin America in the Era of the Cuban Revolution*, 55.
287   Circ. 33/59. 19/06/1959. Draft resolution on US Economic Policy, submitted by the SP of Uruguay to the 6th Congress of the SI. IISG, SI 93.
288   Circ. B.47/56. 16/11/1956. Communication from the SP of Uruguay. Resolution adopted by the National Executive Committee, 31/10/1956.

moribund ASC. The resolution in which the PSU made their decision public also contained an aspiration which doubtlessly gave many a nightmare to the leaders of the International: "The fundamental aim is to set up a powerful Latin American Socialist and national-revolutionary organization which shall, throughout the continent, point the way to, and provide the impulse for, the particular revolution which suits each national character; and to develop, as a regional group, relations with all socialist and popular parties and movements in the world, particularly with the ASC and revolutionary movements which are fighting against the subjugation of their countries by one or other of the two great imperialist powers".[289]

That the party began to get more emphatic in its support for "radical social-ists" such as Nenni and Tito, and began to criticize the Israeli Mapai did not go unnoticed by the SI's Latin America expert Robert Alexander. This, however, did not prevent the Uruguayan socialists from continuing to strive for good relations with those members of the International who "had not openly betrayed the elementary principles of Socialism." According to the PSU the SFIO was the party most guilty of such a betrayal. For the PSU it was no longer possible to come to an agreement with them.

Changing Alliances

In 1960, the perspectives for the International in Latin America seemed quite sombre, especially in comparison with 1956. The loyal Argentinean socialists were divided and therefore much weakened, and the just as loyal Uruguayans had turned their back on the International, just as the Chileans had done earlier. Despite all this, Maiztegui - the much tormented secretary of an orga-nization which his own party no longer belonged to - was the "bearer of good tidings". At the meeting of the council of the International in Haifa, he proudly announced that the membership of the consultative committee had been expanded to include the socialist parties of Ecuador, Brazil and Colombia. Besides, there were new contacts with some, what he called, "democratic" or "people's" parties. The second gathering of the LAS for example, in December 1956, in Buenos Aires, had been attended by representatives of the Revolu-tionary Febrerist Party of Paraguay, the Acción Democrática from Venezuela and the Peruvian Apra. At the fourth assembly of the consultative commit-tee, which took place two months before the meeting in Haifa, the National

---

289   Circ. B9/60. Resolution on International Relations, adopted by the SP of Uruguay. Montevideo, January 1960. IISG, SI 99.

Revolutionary Movement of Bolivia, the Acción Democrática and the July-26-Movement had all been represented.[290] The fact that La Paz, Bolivia had been chosen as the meeting place for that assembly illustrated, according to Maiztegui, that the consultative committee was leaving its nest both geographically as well as ideologically. He emphasized this in his report: "There is no doubt that this conference has been the most important so far since it marked a new stage in the consolidation of fraternal relations between the socialist and the popular parties of Latin America." That "consolidation" was institutionalized with the establishment of a coordinating committee headquartered in Montevideo, which had as its goal the preparation of a congress of "Socialist and Peoples' parties".[291]

The meeting which took place at the end of February 1960 in La Paz, was indeed of great importance. It was there that the organization reached out to encompass the largest number of groups and parties thus far. The socialist parties from Argentina, Uruguay, Chile, Ecuador, Brazil and Colombia had all become members, and there were good relations with the Socialist Party of Peru. Besides, there were also constructive relations with Apra, Acción Democrática, the National Revolutionary Movement of Bolivia, the National Liberation Party of Costa Rica and the Revolutionary Febrerist Party from Paraguay. Relations with each of the above parties were based on personal contacts, correspondence, and the exchange of articles for each others' journals.

The meeting in La Paz was also important for another reason. There, in the presence of Morgan Phillips, the basis was laid for a change in tactics of the International, which would come into effect in the early 1960's. Phillips, who in La Paz was directly confronted by the PSU's attack on "his" International, no longer believed in one collective organization which united the small, dogmatic socialist parties and the much more pragmatic people's parties who sat in government (or at least temporarily participated in government). In La Paz, Phillips clearly had made up his mind concerning which parties were to become the future partners of the International. In May 1960, he gave Maiztegui a clear sign to that effect, indicating that it was of great importance that the Latin American Secretariat strengthen its bonds with the Peoples' parties. From the confidential exchange of letters between Maiztegui, Phillips

---

290   Circ. B.51/57. 02/10/1957. Interim Report of the Visit of Comrade Humberto Maiztegui to Latin America. IISG, SI 88.

291   Circ. 26/60. 01/04/1960. Report on the Latin American Secretariat to the Council Conference in Haifa, by Humberto Maiztegui. IISG, SI 97.

and Carthy, it appears that at that moment Maiztegui himself was already thinking of a new initiative - a *Conferencia Democrata-Social de America Latina* or, better yet, a *Conferencia Democrata-Social Americana*. In a letter to Albert Carthy, Maiztegui wrote: "I believe the time has come to establish something new, of course without abandoning that which we already have created."[292]

As his terminology shows, Maiztegui was rather quickly ready to give up the term "socialist". This too was a concession to the people's parties. A few months later he again took up the idea, this time using the term "Conferencia de la Democracia Social Interamericana". He raised the subject with a few representatives of the AD and of the APRA, who apparently reacted positively. Besides Latin American people's parties, such a regional 'conference' would also consist of the Liberal Party of New York, a segment of the Democratic Party of the United States, and perhaps the Canadian Cooperative Common-wealth Federation as well. In this arrangement it would *perhaps* be possible to include a few socialist parties as well. To put it mildly, Maiztegui was playing a double role here. For precisely that reason, he placed much importance on keeping everything as confidential as possible. Moreover, he insisted that such an initiative for a regional organization would come from either the United States or from Europe, thus keeping "his" secretariat out of range.

Maiztegui was all too aware of the risks he was taking. He still had not chosen for one or the other group, and he was involved in a delicate exercise of balance. At the fifth conference of the consultative committee in Montevideo in July 1960, it again became apparent just how much the socialist parties differed from the people's parties. This was clearest in the context of the Cuban Revolution.[293] More than any other topic "The Revolution" was to put much pressure on the relationship between the socialist parties and the people's parties.

In the autumn of 1960, Maiztegui took the time to visit certain socialist and people's parties. He made stops in San José, Caracas and Lima. After his trip he labeled the people's parties "Social Democratic parties, since that is what they really are". The "social democratic" label was strategic: such a label could open the door to closer contacts with the - in reality - "Social Democratic" Interna-

292   Letter from Maiztegui to Carthy, 14/10/1960. IISG, SI 707.
293   At that moment, relations between Cuba and the US were not good at all, and the bene-volent attitude of the Cuban regime towards the communist party was being questioned. Circ. B.31/60. 26/08/1960. Report to the Bureau on the Fifth Conference of the Consultative Committee of the LAS, by Maiztegui. IISG, SI 99.

tional, which Maiztegui advised to invest more time and energy in mutual visits.

Maiztegui himself set a good example. During his visit to Caracas he renewed the ties with the Acción Democrática. At the end of November 1960, for example, he endorsed the publication of the manifesto of the Acción Democrática in the bulletin of the LAS, and he openly declared his support for Betancourt's regime. The international secretary of the AD received the assurance that his party could count on the full support of the LAS and the International.
None of this was truly appreciated by Maiztegui's own party, especially not by the younger party members. Maiztegui found himself more and more often needing to fend off attempts from his own party to weaken the LAS. For this reason Maiztegui attempted from that moment on to keep the bulletin "as neutral as possible" by carefully selecting the material to be published, and explicitly disclaiming any responsibility for the authors' opinions. He hoped that the extremely positive attitude of the socialist parties regarding Cuba - including the attitude of his own party - would gradually change and that the people's parties meanwhile would restrain themselves from expressing overly negative sentiments concerning developments there.

Undoubtedly, Maiztegui realized that the situation could not last long. When he published for example a declaration from a conference of people's parties in the sixth edition of the Bulletin, it immediately provoked a reaction from the socialist parties of Peru, Costa Rica and Venezuela, parties which were at home contending with the APRA, the Partido de Liberación Nacionál and the Acción Democrática. The APRA in particular, at the impetus of the Peruvian SP, received much criticism from Latin American socialists. This put Maiztegui, who harbored much personal sympathy for the APRA, in a very difficult position. He realized that decisions needed to be made, but it seemed that he himself was not ready to make them. He waited for the International to do so.[294]

On 14 April, an ideal opportunity presented itself which could help break the impasse. On that day a force of 1400 Cuban exiles, with the support of the United States, attacked the Bay of Pigs in an attempt to overthrow the Castro regime. In less than two days Castro put an end to the invasion and at the same time wiped out a large swath of the opposition to his regime. Outside of Cuba, the invasion caused a polarization. At the consultative committee meeting of 22 April 1961, in Montevideo, the participants strongly condemned the

294   Letter from Maiztegui to Carthy, 27/02/1961. IISG, SI 710.

invasion and voiced their support to the Cuban Revolution. The Uruguayan socialists launched an appeal to all socialist parties of the world to convince their governments to condemn the invasion.[295] Four months later the Latin American socialists also set themselves against the Pan-American Conference in Punta del Este which was focusing on Kennedy's "Alliance for Progress". The people's parties on the other hand were vocal in their support of that conference.

Unavoidably, the subject of the invasion of Cuba also came up at the bureau meeting of the Socialist International in May 1961. The International's official reaction was rather restrained. The bureau was of the opinion that interventions of both the United States and the Soviet Union constituted a menace to general world peace. Above all the meeting condemned the re-installation of dictatorship on the island. At the same time, however, the bureau created a subcommittee whose task it was to review "certain stipulations" in the statutes of the International. As would later become apparent, the review would pave the way for the subsequent entry of the Latin American people's parties into the International.

The storm finally broke during a meeting of the bureau on September 15, 1961. In the preceding months tensions had risen high. In a letter from June of that year Carthy had expressed himself with exceeding criticism of the continual "wishful thinking" on the part of Latin American socialists regarding Cuba. The letter was also intended to rebuke Maiztegui himself, who had been persisting in the belief that Cuba would not end up within the Soviet sphere of influence, but rather would remain neutral like Yugoslavia.[296] Words were hardly adequate to express Carthy's consternation: "Do you think that, after the enormous shipments of Czechoslovak and Russian arms, and the arrival of hundreds of Soviet technicians and their families, there is any likelihood that Cuba will be able to opt for a Yugoslav solution? (…) We must have no illusions. We all want Cuba's independence, but we do not regard a country as independent where socialists are not allowed to organize and operate freely."[297]

Other European social democrats were also shocked. In particular the declaration made by the LAS shortly after the Bay of Pigs invasion was hard to

---

295   Sixth Conference of the Consultative Committee of the Latin American Secretariat of the SI
      for Support of Cuba. 22/04/1961. IISG, SI 710.
296   Letter from Maiztegui to Carthy, 11/07/1961. IISG, SI 710.
297   Letter from Carthy to Maiztegui, 29/06/1961. IISG, SI 710.

swallow for many. According to the Dutchman Max van der Stoel the position of the LAS was in direct opposition to the convictions of the International.[298] The Italian PSDI took the lead in the protests, under pressure from the many Italian immigrants in Latin America. During the bureau meeting of 15 September 1961, Sigfrido Ciccotti caustically criticized the LAS: "We have nothing against Comrade Maiztegui who, in fact, we do not know. In our opinion, his work must be judged by results, and the results are unfortunately negative. It may be that he lacks the necessary political experience and personal prestige to play a leading part in a sphere as difficult as the Latin American."[299]

According to Ciccotti the LAS needed to be shut down and the International should henceforth take direct contact with the socialist and especially the people's parties in Latin America. His analysis of Latin American socialism was no less sparing. To his mind, socialism had never actually taken root in the majority of Latin America. The idea of social justice, on the other hand, had led to the establishment of popular movements which were "better suited to local needs and circumstances". Haya de la Torre's APRA and the Acción Democrática were two examples of movements which kept alive the struggle against both reactionary dictatorships and communist attempts at infiltration. Ciccotti concluded: "We believe that the International should establish a working relationship with these movements, which combine a strong democratic inspiration with the ideas of economic change and social justice. These relations could in time turn into permanent and organizational links."[300]

In October 1961, the bureau of the International decided for the first time to establish formal contact directly with the people's parties. There was no time to waste, especially since more and more reports kept coming in stating that the Yugoslavian socialists were ready to pounce not only on the socialist parties but on the people's parties as well.[301]

The more contacts between the people's parties and the International increased, the more relations soured between the International and the socialist parties, especially between the International and the Chilean PSP. This was clearly evident from Maiztegui's surprised reaction to a "very warm" invitation to attend the 1961 PSP's conference. The fact that delegates from the Soviet Union and Yugoslavia had been present at the previous congress,

298   Letter from van der Stoel to Carthy, 31/08/1961. IISG, SI 710.
299   Circ. B.25/62. 13/04/1962. Socialism in Latin America, by Ciccotti. IISG, SI 110.
300   Circ. B.25/62. 13/04/1962. Socialism in Latin America, by Ciccotti. IISG, SI 109.
301   Letter from Maiztegui to Carthy, 11/07/1961. IISG, SI 710.

evidently gave him reason to hesitate. Carthy cleared up any doubts Maiztegui might have had: he thought it would not be prudent for Maiztegui to attend the congress. In response Maiztegui, obedient as he was, immediately sent his regrets to the PSP stating that he was much too busy in his TV shop (his real job) to be able to attend the congress.[302] For Carthy the socialist parties were already done for and their position vis-à-vis Cuba was unacceptable:"The socialist parties appear to have deluded themselves over this issue so long, and have shown themselves so basically misguided, that I fear that in a crisis developing, they would reach false judgments (…) When I read in SP writings about 'possible invasion by the US' I ask how they can be ignorant of the actual invasion which has already taken place - by Russians and Czechs - in Cuba."[303] To Carthy, Maiztegui's option of an alliance between socialist and people's parties was hardly tenable at that moment - he himself considered it a pointless venture.[304] In other words, the change in course of the Socialist International was definitively effected.

From then on, the International would spend a lot of time and energy on 'conquering' the people's parties. In 1962 for example, it set up a campaign to support Haya de la Torre, the head of APRA. In that year, after years of forced exile, de la Torre had returned to Peru to participate in the presidential elections. Despite having won a clear majority of the votes, it was insufficient to be directly elected to the presidency. The army, which was extremely hostile to the APRA, proclaimed the elections void, and declared the state of emergency while at the same time calling for new elections. On 3 August 1962 the International called on all its members to protest the actions of the army and to demand free elections.[305]

One year later, in 1963, the International sent a team of three to the region. The mission had been exhaustively prepared. Via Alfred Braunthal, the assistant secretary-general of the ICFTU, the members of the mission were brought in contact with Arturo Jauregui, the secretary-general of the Inter-American Regional Organization of Workers (ORIT). Rita de Bruyn Ouboter, the chair of the Women's Committee of the International, provided useful contacts with Latin American women's groups. Before leaving for Latin America, the team made a stopover in Bonn, where the members met with the

---

302   Letter from Carthy to Maiztegui, 17/11/1961; letter from Maiztegui to the PSP, 21/11/1961. IISG, SI 710.
303   Letter from Carthy to Maiztegui, 09/01/1962. IISG, SI 711.
304   Letter from Carthy to Maiztegui, 10/01/1962. IISG, SI 711.
305   Circ. 63/62. 03/08/1962. IISG, SI 108.

Latin-America experts of the "Weltweite Partnerschaft". The Dutch professor Jan Tinbergen provided the International with a list of names and addresses of prominent Latin American economists whom he had met in Venezuela in the beginning of 1962.[306] With Maiztegui's assistance the core documents of the International were translated into Spanish and distributed throughout Latin America. These are but a few examples which illustrate just how thoroughly the groundwork for the project was laid.

The mission planned on carrying out an impressive number of visits. Remarkably, the delegation also had contact with Chilean Christian Democrats. The Christian Democrats were mentioned in the report of the mission: "The party has a strong Leftist orientation, but is of course a part of the Christian Democratic international movement and no candidate for the Socialist International".[307] At the same time all member parties of the International were urgently requested to make contact with the people's parties, "upon which the political future of Latin America was dependent".[308] In every way possible the International tried to bring the people's parties on board. On the basis of the mission's report the bureau decided to invite as many representatives as possible from Latin American parties to the next congress of the International in Amsterdam. That congress saw the beginning of an expansive recruitment campaign. All invited parties, whether they responded or not, also received an invitation to join the International as observers, a status specially created to accommodate the Latin Americans. Maiztegui's mandate to further maintain the contacts was extended, for which he continued to receive a budget of £ 150 per annum. This was now all the more indispensable to Maiztegui since he had just resigned from the PSU - nothing now linked him with the party, which incidentally was on the verge of splitting up - and he therefore could no longer make use of their premises. Via a press release, the International on 20 August 1963 officially made public the reversal in its Latin American policy. For the people's parties the International had nothing but the most enthusiastic praise: "It was deeply impressed by the clarification which it received of the function which has been, and still is being, performed in the special historical circumstances of Latin America, by Popular Parties in so many of the countries which the Mission visited (…). In many cases, these parties (…) expressed the desire for closer forms of association. This desire is cordially reciprocated by the Socialist International." For the

306   Circ. 10/63. 08/03/1963. Minutes of the Meeting of the Sub-Committee for Developing Areas. London, 23/01/1963. IISG, SI 112.
307   Circ. B24/63. 28/06/1963. Mission to Latin America. IISG, SI 114.
308   Circ. 29/62. 11/05/1962. IISG, SI 106.

socialist parties the International had no kind words: "The bureau was grieved to note that cooperation between Socialist Parties in Latin America has disintegrated. A heavy responsibility in this connection lies with the Socialist Party of Chile, which has used its great influence as a force of disruption, allying itself in spirit and in organization with the totalitarian forces of Communism."[309] Shortly before, Carthy had declared the consultative committee dead, murdered by the hands of the socialist parties themselves.[310]

Not long afterwards, various people's parties eventually took the step that the International had been waiting for. The Partido de Liberación Nacional of Costa Rica let it be known (under the impetus of Luis Alberto Monge, the former secretary of the ORIT), that they wished to join the International as observers.[311] Relations with the influential Acción Democrática were also going smoothly. In March 1964, the Party invited Carthy to attend the official transfer of power from Betancourt to the new president Raul Leoni, of the same party. Carthy was delighted with the reception he received in Caracas: his lodgings in the extremely luxurious Armed Forces Club, a construction dating from the Pérez Jiménez dictatorship, and the fact that he received a limousine and a bodyguard all deeply impressed him. In terms of transnational politics, the meeting which the AD had organized on Friday 13 March with representatives of the people's parties is what made the deepest impression on Carthy's memory. For the AD that was a first step in the direction of a "federation" of Latin American people's parties, which in Carthy unleashed mixed feelings. In a short speech in broken Spanish during the assembly Carthy expressed himself nonetheless positively regarding the establishment of such a formation and he emphasized the readiness of the International to establish relations with any such body. In his report to the bureau, however, he fully expressed his reserves: "My own first impression was that the AD was more interested in the association of a group which shall have some form of group association with the SI, on the lines of the ASC when that was functioning. I hope I am wrong on that last point, and that the AD will pursue its stated aim of taking up observer status as well. AD has an outstanding position of leadership (…) The ideal result would be a dual link, by the individual parties and with the group as a whole."[312]

---

309 Circ. xxxiii/63. 20/08/1963. Press release. IISG, SI 116.
310 Letter from Carthy to Maiztegui, 02/08/1963. IISG, SI 712.
311 Circ. 4/64. 06/03/1964. Minutes of the Meeting of the Bureau of the SI. London, 05-06/02/1964. IISG, SI 117.
312 Circ. 12/64. 20/05/1964. Invitation to Venezuela and visit to other countries, by Carthy. IISG, SI 117.

Carthy could rest assured: in September 1964, Acción Democrática gave the green light to membership as an observer in the International, upon which Carthy, in consultation with the chairman, directly signed into action.

The Costa Rican PLN, the Peruvian APRA, the Paraguayan PRF and the new Chilean PSP followed the example of the AD shortly afterwards.[313] And what became of Maiztegui? He still attempted to fulfil a bridging function. In the autumn of 1964 he emphasized to the International that they shouldn't ignore the socialist parties:"[They] are important by reason of their intellectual core, which in an area like Latin America, which is governed by elites, is very important. (…) We must be a compass to keep them with Social Democracy, or it might be better put, to channel them towards it. Hence my efforts which have been behind the re-sowing of the seeds of Socialist action which is beginning in the Argentine Socialist Party, which is the most important party."[314] The International, however, did not seem to be willing to wait.

Opening the Debate on Regionalization: Towards an 'International Confederation of Socialist Regional Groups'?

The global expansion of the International almost automatically led to a readjustment of the structures of the organization. Both the closer relations with the people's parties in Latin America, as well as the preliminary talks with African kindred spirits caused the bureau to review its statutes. After a joint session of the Standing Joint Committee on Developing Areas with the members of the African Mission, at the end of 1962, David Ennals, acting as the spokesperson for the meeting, proposed that the bureau make allowances in its statutes for "forms of association between the International and political organizations in Asia, Africa and Latin America which are not ready for full membership."[315] The congress of Amsterdam approved the requested revisions in September 1963. From that moment onwards the International was to consist of four recognized categories of members: full members (with both the right to the floor and with voting rights), associate organizations, consultative members (with the right to the floor but with-

313   The new PSP shortly afterwards changed its name into Partido Socialista Democrático de Chile', which was fully supported by Maiztegui. Letter from Maiztegui to Carthy, 14/07/1964. IISG, SI 713.
314   Circ. B.40/64. 06/11/1964. Letter from Maiztegui, 23/10/1964. IISG, SI 119.
315   Circ. 71/62. 19/10/1962. Minutes of the meeting of the Bureau of the SI. Vienna, 24-25/09/1962. IISG, SI 108.

out voting rights), and - with an eye on the developing regions - observing members, who upon receiving the consent of the presidium had the right to the floor but did not have voting rights.

With regard to the associate organizations what was most remarkable was the degree to which relations with the youth organization IUSY and with the ICFTU had strengthened. The IUSY with its extensive network of contacts in developing regions, was a useful source of information for the International. Reacting to a proposal from the BLP, the council in Haifa decided to make full use of that expertise, a decision which seemed to put an end to the inadequate cooperation of the preceding years. Henceforth the youth groups would be invited to the meetings of the Standing Joint Committee on Developing Areas. Cooperation, at the same time, was also a solution to the problems of higher expenditures which accompanied a worldwide engagement. The very same arguments also led the International to establish closer relations with the ICFTU. The worldwide engagement of Omer Bécu, ICFTU secretary-general, did not go unnoticed by the International. At the International's Amsterdam congress, Sven-Erik Beckius stated: "Not the least important in this linking together of Socialist, democratic and progressive forces all over the world is the contribution made by Omer Bécu, the secretary-general of the ICFTU."[316]

Besides these all in all rather minor adjustments, by the middle of the decade a discussion of more fundamental importance was to surface. In September 1963, the Joint Standing Committee on Developing Areas was to get the ball rolling. The committee was of the opinion that "the completely different social structure and economic conditions of these three areas [Africa, Asia and Latin America] make it necessary for the International to work out diverse approaches".[317] In this regard one of the first thoughts was a certain amount of regionalization. The first clear call for the International to regionalize dates actually from three years before. In June 1960, Bruno Pittermann and Otto Probst expressed their dissatisfaction to Alsing Andersen about the way in which socialists were being squeezed out of important positions in the European institutions, in particular in the Council of Europe. The immediate cause of their complaint was the election of the chairman of the Council of Europe's consultative committee, which did not go well for the socialists. According to the Austrian socialists there was a conscious strategy behind their misfortune:

---

316   Circ. B.34/63. 07/11/1963. Problems of Organisation. IISG, SI 115.
317   Circ. 64/63. 25/10/1963. Minutes of the Meeting of the Joint Standing Committee on Developing Areas. Amsterdam, 07/09/1963. IISG, SI 113.

"Conscious actions seem to have been taken to prevent the Socialists from actively participating in the Council of Europe". The socialists needed to better coordinate things on a European level, and that could best be done in a separate meeting of party chairmen and representatives outside of the bureau of the International.

Consequently, in January 1961, the heads of the European socialist parties came together in Salzburg, for what would be the very first *Conference of Party Leaders*. Therefore, when at the International's Amsterdam congress, in September 1963, several speakers proposed possible regionalization, and thus decentralization of the International, that idea was not entirely new. The Austrian Bruno Pittermann, who in 1964 would succeed Erich Ollenhauer as chairman of the International, asked himself whether "regional conferences of parties" would not be a useful thing. His compatriot Karl Czernetz went a step further arguing that in reality "centralized leadership" had no place in the International, due to the fact that the problems on the different continents so sharply differed that it necessitated a decentralized structure. All parties did indeed accept the Declarations of Frankfurt and Oslo, but for specific problems the parties often needed specific solutions. For this reason Czernetz pleaded for the establishment of "regional federations for Europe, Asia, Africa, North America and South America" within the International, which would become a sort of "world federation". A Japanese socialist was in complete agreement with Czernetz: there was a need for inter-regional ties between socialist parties from Africa, Latin America, and Asia, along the same lines as the ties which already existed between EEC parties. The Dutchman Suurhoff recognized the fact that the further the International "globalized" the more regional action and regional organization would become required.
Yet despite this he also saw therein the possible seed of the very disintegration of the International itself. Consequently, he saw a concomitant strengthening of the Secretariat in London as being absolutely essential.[318]

However, it was the French SFIO which went the furthest in its drive to reorganize. The SFIO used the opportunity to launch a frontal assault on the procedural operations of the International as well as on its secretary-general Albert Carthy, in particular on his global ambitions and pretensions. The French - in contrast with their policies of the late forties and early fifties - pleaded for an organization limited in its ambitions, both vertically as well as horizontally. Vertically, it was nonsense to think that all members of the International could come to a common consensus, to say nothing of coming to agree-

318   Circ. B.34/63. 07/11/1963. Problems of Organisation. IISG, SI 115.

ment on binding issues, since "as a Confederation of parties which are thinly scattered over five continents, and which differ from each other in structure and origin, and in the specific conditions which govern their activities, the International is necessarily limited in its objectives. The problems differ. Those of Latin America, Africa and Asia have nothing in common except the criterion of under-development. But in each case the conditions governing political activity take on special forms. The issues with which European social-ist parties or those of the industrially and economically developed countries are concerned are fundamentally different from those of the other countries. (…) As a result, the International cannot promote the adoption of common attitudes".

Horizontally, "universality" did not make much sense: "It [the International] must renounce any claim to universality and must leave it to the parties, which are linked by a common destiny and common problems, to work out common positions among themselves on specific problems. This is especially true in Europe, and particularly so in Continental Europe. There thus appears a need for geographical regrouping which world developments themselves have encouraged during the past decade. The existence of agreements grant-ing mutual privileges between certain nations (…) has made it necessary for the socialist parties concerned to concert their activities, or indeed to create among themselves the machinery for permanent cooperation, such as, for example, the Secretariat shared by the six socialist parties in the EEC."

A similar evolution would also take place in Africa, Asia and Latin America. For the French there was but one solution: the International had to evolve into a confederation of regional socialist groups.[319] Unlike other parties, which did indeed desire a certain amount of regionalization without losing sight of a centralized umbrella organization - Austria for example spoke of a "federation" - the French were in favour of completely eroding the centralized level. The "International Confederation" was to become the "moral authority of socialism worldwide", with a very limited - in practice non-existent - political mission.[320] Its function would be limited to the establishing and maintaining of contacts ('liaisons') between the various regional groups, and the distribu-tion of information. The center of gravity would shift to the regional groups, within the framework of which the policies of the different parties could be harmonized "to the maximum possible degree". Within the regional groups

---

319   Circ. 29/64. 11/09/1964. Proposals for Reorganisation. IISG, SI 118.
320   Ibidem.

the basis for joint actions could be laid and permanent structures could be set up.[321]

The underlying motivations of the SFIO were clear to everyone. Their proposals were nothing more than a somewhat clumsy expression of frustration coming from a party which had lost almost all its political authority at home and which exercised practically no influence within the International. The SFIO's colonialist image prevented the party from playing any meaningful role in an organization which every day was striving more and more to have a global character. No wonder that the French found themselves in opposition to the "universalism" of the International. In a regional (continental European) organization, within which the British socialists - never very pro-European - found themselves at a disadvantage, the French hoped to be able to win back part of their lost prestige and influence. The British succeeded in parrying the French plans by pushing through their proposal to strengthen the bureau of the International and by keeping the seat of the General Secretariat in London. At the behest of the Dutch, the bureau decided to pay more attention to relevant political discussions instead of playing a purely organizational administrative role. In this way, according to the Dutchman Max van der Stoel, the bureau would increase both its importance and influence. In other words, the organization survived is first growing pains, and remained more or less unchanged.

321   Circ. 29/64. 11/09/1964. Proposals for Reorganisation. IISG, SI 118.

The NEI's Reason for Existence
To Realize the European Ideal,
1950-1955

In the course of the 1950's, the Socialist International attempted to reach beyond their hitherto largely Western European biotope. The process of social democratic global expansion which was to unfold in the course of that decade, came predominantly from the center out, having its origin in the London headquarters of the International. London followed everything, guided everything and preferably initiated everything (or at least tried to do so). Julius Braunthal, as secretary-general, made frenetic attempts to rein in and bind the independent-minded Asian Socialist Conference to the International. His personal engagement meshed seamlessly with his personal penchant for Asia. In the second half of the decade SI secretary-general Albert Carthy together with the chairman of the International initiated a similar integration process with Latin American partners. By the end of the decade Africa was also receiving more attention, which in 1961 would lead to the first exploratory mission of the International to the "black continent". The characteristics of the traditional organizational culture of the International - a relatively centralized model with a universal ambition - seemed to be the order of the day in the 1950's, although initially it would not bring the International many successful results.

Unlike the Socialist International, the Nouvelles Équipes Internationales neither wanted to nor could be the motor of a worldwide "International" in the 1950's. Nonetheless, such an "International" would be established in 1961, but in a very different way than had been the case with the social democrats.

The Christian Democratic World Union (rebaptized in October 2000 as the Christian Democrat and people's Parties International), came into existence through the gradual integration of three relatively autonomous, regional organizations: the NEI, composed primarily of Western Europeans, the Latin American ODCA and the CDUCE, a grouping of Central and Eastern European Christian Democratic exiles.[322] From 1950 on, the latter was to put an unmistakable pressure on the globalization process of the NEI. The Western European Christian Democrats, however, were generally able to parry the sometimes exceptionally intensive lobbying of the Central and Eastern European Christian Democrats. The relatively decentralized organizational model of the NEI and their pronounced continental European orientation remained intact. In this chapter, as was the case in the chapter on the Socialist International, the emphasis is placed on the determining factors which drove and at the same time curbed that process of Christian Democratic globalization.

CDUCE's Drive to Globalize: Going Global to the Rhythm of the Cold War

In the Central and Eastern European countries which fell into the hands of the Soviet Union after the war, the Christian Democratic parties were forced underground or into exile. A portion of those exiles, as was mentioned earlier, had joined together in July 1950, forming the Christian Democrat Union of Central Europe (CDUCE). At their founding the CDUCE was composed of members of the Christian Democratic parties of Poland, Hungary and Czechoslovakia, which had been re-established after the Second World War. To the CDUCE also belonged individual members of like-minded parties in Lithuania, Latvia and Slovenia which had not succeeded in re-establishing themselves after the war. Organizationally, the CDUCE was independent from the NEI, but the parties in exile which were active in the CDUCE were also members of the NEI, although be it in a subordinate position. Often the same people were active in both organizations. Konrad Sieniewicz, secretary-general of the CDUCE, for example, had attended the NEI congresses in Chaudfontaine (1947) and in The Hague (1948) just a few years before the establishment of the exile organization.

Sieniewicz was a remarkable person. After the Warsaw Ghetto uprising in April 1943, he was, along with the other Jews who had survived German

---

322   The Christian Democrat and People's Parties International (CDI/IDC) was given its name in October 2000. Until then the organization was called the Christian Democrat International, a name given in 1982. Before that date the organization was called the Christian Democratic World Union, founded in 1964, with preparations for its establishment going on from 1961.

retaliation, deported by the Nazis. Afterwards, he returned to Poland, only to have to leave again in 1945, in the wake of the Soviet occupation. He stayed for some time in Belgium, Paris and London before finally, in 1950, choosing to settle in New York, the home of the CDUCE, of which he would become secretary-general that very same year.[323] In the 1950's he would play a leading role in the globalization process of the Nouvelles Équipes Internationales.

The CDUCE had five representatives in Europe, as well as a youth organization based in Paris. It should come as no great surprise that the motivating factor, and even the raison d'être of the CDUCE was a fervent anti-communism. For this reason the organization could count upon the discreet financial support of the American State Department and the CIA's Free Europe Committee. From 13 to 15 March 1953, one week after the death of their "bête noire", Joseph Stalin, the exiles of the CDUCE were to meet for their first congress, in New York. "The purpose of the Union," it was stated at the opening of the congress, "is to show the free world what everyday life is like in the countries behind the Iron Curtain, to denounce religious persecutions by the communists, to protest against deportations and against all the violations of human rights."

In the charter of the CDUCE the organization set out a few rather ambitious goals for itself, including the liberation of Soviet occupied Eastern and Central Europe and the full integration of that region into a reunited and democratic Europe. It was initially assumed that such goals could be realized in a relatively short period of time. Over the course of the following years, however, the exiles would reconcile themselves to the political reality and their main goal would then become that of warning the West against the false efforts of the Soviet Union towards a détente in the years 1955-1966. Yet, the principal motivating factor of the CDUCE remained the same: to maintain the "intense struggle" against communism, using all means available.[324] One of those means was to put pressure on the NEI meetings and thus attempt to influence their resolutions. Without overestimating the influence of the Eastern European exile group - often their lobbying was explicitly ignored - every now and then it was quite effective, e.g. in the congress resolutions approved in 1950, 1952, 1954, and 1956.[325]

323   Goddeeris, *De verleiding van de legitimiteit. Poolse* Exilpolitik *in België*, 82. In 1957 the CDUCE moved to Paris, five years later to Rome.
324   Christian Democratic World Union. *La Démocratie chrétienne dans le monde*, 556-562.
325   In 1956, e.g., at the insistence of the Central and East Europeans, the phrase 'coexistence with Communism' was deleted from the draft resolutions at the Luxemburg congress. The Belgian representative Van Zeeland had suggested to introduce that phrase. KADOC, ADS 7.2.4.10.

The struggle against communism was necessarily a multifaceted one for the exiles, just as it was for the Socialist International, and it would take on a global dimension, especially after the beginning of the Korean War. This explains the global orientation of the CDUCE, which had as its goal the establishment of as broad as possible an anti-communist network. Right from the beginning the CDUCE tried to bring this global perspective into the NEI. The result of all this was that in the 1950's the CDUCE could be considered the NEI's most important window on the world beyond Western Europe. That window had principally two views: one on the United Nations and one on Latin America.

First and foremost, the Union of Central and Eastern European exiles formed the most important - and at times the only - link between the NEI and the United Nations. In the 1950's, the UN was the preferred action platform of the CDUCE, in sharp contrast with the NEI's relative indifference towards that international body. In May 1949, the NEI had asked for "consultative status" within Ecosoc, a request which was approved on 3 March 1950. That status gave the NEI the right to participate in all public gatherings of Ecosoc and to submit written contributions. However, already at the next Ecosoc meeting, in February 1951, in Santiago, Chile, the NEI failed to show up.[326]

NEI secretary-general Bichet, who was worried about the rather limited degree to which Christian Democratic thinking was represented within the UN, had asked the Belgian van der Straten-Waillet, who was representing the Belgian government at the gathering, to simultaneously represent the NEI. Waillet, however, considered such a double role "out of the question".[327] Henceforth, from 1952 on, Konrad Sieniewicz, who was living in New York, would do the honors for the NEI.

It is not clear if Sieniewicz did this at the request of the NEI, or on his own initiative. The Italian scholar Papini purports that the initiative came from the NEI itself: "In 1951, R. Bichet, secretary-general of the NEI, officially asked K. Sieniewicz, secretary-general of the CDUCE, to represent the whole Christian Democratic movement at the United Nations".[328] It would soon, however, become apparent that the NEI did not place much importance upon their presence in the UN, a conclusion which is not to be found in Papini. Whoever took the initiative, the NEI or Sieniewicz, such a "legitimation" was a gift from

---

326   Procès-Verbal du Comité Exécutif, 24/11/1951. ACDP, IX-002-005/1.
327   Letter from van der Straten-Waillet to Bichet, 12/04/1951. ACDP, IX-002-039.
328   Papini, *The Christian Democrat International*, 79.

heaven for Sieniewicz. He would not miss the chance to fulfill his task according to his own best judgment and in accordance with his own priorities. Case in point, Sieniewicz took advantage of his presence in New York to establish contacts with real or potential Christian Democratic politicians belonging to various UN delegations. Thus during the seventh session of the General Assembly (October 14 - December 22, 1952) he made contact with a dozen or so "Christian Democrats" from Latin America. It is extremely difficult to establish whether these contacts ever led to anything beyond casual acquaintance. Only one of their names would be found again on a list of NEI Latin American contact persons from the year 1958, that of Carlos A. Siri from El Salvador. Perhaps they were only go-betweens, after all they were principally diplomats.

When representing the NEI, Sieniewicz surely had his own priorities. He was exceptionally active on the UN ad hoc committee on forced labor and in the International Labour Organization, where he provided much information about the workers' situation in Eastern Europe. There lay a certain tradition behind that theme. In 1954, Eastern European exiles in New York created an "International Committee for the Abolition of Forced Labor" which worked on an international campaign against forced labor in Eastern Europe. One of the results was that the NEI at its conference in Bruges adopted a resolution sharply critical of forced labor. Another theme which lay close to the Pole's heart was that of religious repression in Eastern Europe and other similar issues dealing with human rights.

On the basis of Sieniewicz's correspondence in the archives of the NEI, it can be inferred that he worked more or less independently.[329] He regularly sent reports of (all?) his interventions to the NEI Secretariat, and kept the NEI informed about what actions he had taken on their behalf, often after he had taken them. Not that the NEI expected more coordination. Sieniewicz's "task" was to do whatever he thought necessary, keeping in mind "the general principles" of the NEI. Schuijt, the deputy secretary-general of the NEI put it very succinctly: "We expect you to study the problems on the spot, always keeping in mind that the NEI's principles (…) may never have another source of philosophical or even theological inspiration than those which are often expressed in statements by the Pope. It goes without saying that it would not be expedient, nor politically prudent to refer directly to pontifical documents. Nonetheless, it would be a good idea to carefully distinguish in those texts

---

329   Letter from Sieniewicz to Bichet, 29/03/1954; Letter from Bichet to Schuijt, 01/04/1954; Letter from Bichet to Sieniwiecz, 01/04/1954. ACDP, IX-002-079/1.

between principles which are considered "in thesi" and principles applied "in hypothesi."" This is the most concrete directive ever given by the NEI to their representative.[330]

A (small) incident at the beginning of 1954 illustrates that at that moment there was no talk of any meaningful involvement on the part of the NEI in the workings of the UN. In June 1953, the Ecosoc Secretariat had decided to evaluate all NGO's which had been given consultative status. The NEI as well was asked to provide an overview of their activities in the context of their membership. Despite a few reminders from Ecosoc, no response was forthcoming. When Sieniewicz warned the NEI, in January 1954, that "the renewal of the NEI's consultative status seems to be improbable", deputy secretary-general Schuijt had to admit that he was unable to find any evidence of involvement with the UN in the organization's records. After intense lobbying by Sieniewicz, the NEI's membership was eventually renewed, allowing the Pole to continue his work, on the behalf of the NEI. On a few more occasions Sieniewicz tried to make good for the NEI's absenteeism. His co-worker Slezynski was therefore undoubtedly correct when he said that in the 1950's the NEI was not directly involved with the UN.[331] Only with the beginning of the next decade, at the impetus of the new secretary-general Seitlinger would the organization begin to show more interest in the UN.

A second area which the CDUCE explored for the NEI was Latin America. The Eastern European exiles sought to establish themselves more explicitly as a link between Latin America and the NEI. By means of his presence in the various UN bodies, Sieniewicz was excellently placed to establish contact with that continent in 1952-1953, the result of which was the appearance of a few Latin Americans at the first and second CDUCE congresses in 1953 and 1955.[332]

Latin America was highly important for the CDUCE. In the span of a very short time Christian Democracy had taken off in that region. Starting in the 1930's, Christian Democratic ideas had been spreading rapidly throughout Latin America, and European Christian Democracy had caught the attention of young Latin American intellectuals - often leaders or members of

---

330   Letter from Schuijt to Sieniewicz, 08/02/1955. ACDP, IX-002-079/1.
331   Letter from Sleszynski to Hogan, head of the United Nations' NGO department, 12/09/1962. ACDP, IX-002-079/1.
332   Papini, *The Christian Democrat International*, 80-81 and 136. In 1953, the CDUCE started a Spanish bulletin, *Información Democrática Cristiana*, and the way was cleared for a Latin American department within the CDUCE.

Catholic student groups - who were inspired by the social doctrines of the Church. Their interest was further stimulated by the numerous seminars and conferences which the Catholic Church organized in Rome in the 1930's.[333] One of these young intellectuals was the future standard bearer of Venezuelan Christian Democracy, Rafael Caldera, who in the 1950's would establish good connections with both the CDUCE and the NEI. In 1932 Caldera had become the secretary of the Juventud de Acción Católica, a function which would allow him to participate the following year in a gathering in Rome, organized by the Acción Católica Universitaria Ibero-Americana. His stay in Rome brought him in contact not only with Don Sturzo's then relatively weak PPI and with the French PDP, but also with other Latin Americans, such as Mario Polar from Peru and Eduardo Frei from Chile.[334] Once back home, just like many of his peers, he applied himself to the task of gradually giving the Church's social teachings an institutional framework, for example, in the form of a student organization. It didn't take long before such organizations were also taking on political issues. This development resulted in the formation of Christian Democratic - or Christian inspired - parties and movements in several Latin American countries shortly after the Second World War.

The spread of Christian Democracy was an essential precondition for the establishment of a regional inter-party organization.[335] In April 1947, the Uruguayan Unión Cívica took the initiative and brought a few like-minded politicians from the region to Montevideo. For the Unión Cívica, which would never play an important political role at home, this conference was the first expression of its international activism which would continue until the 1960's. Representatives from Argentina, Brazil and Chile made an appearance in Montevideo. In those three countries Christian Democracy had its strongest regional base. In Chile, for example, Christian Democratic ideas had especially taken hold in the Falange Nacional, a movement of young intellectuals connected to the Partido Conservador. In 1938, the leaders of the Falange (including Eduardo Frei Montalva) decided to break with the Conservative Party and together with the progressive wing of that party established a new movement: the Movimiento de la Falange Nacional, which in 1947, in Montevideo, was represented by Frei. From this grouping the Partido Demócrata Cristiano would take form in 1957. In Brazil, Alceu Amoroso Lima founded the Partido Demócrata Cristão in 1945. In Argentina, it wasn't until the 1950's that Christian Democracy made an appearance on the political scene.

333   Lynch, *Latin America's Christian Democratic Parties*, 47.
334   Compagnon, "Rafael Caldera, de la Unión Nacional Estudiantil."
335   Bethell and Roxborough, *Latin America*.

The former anti-Peronism of the Christian Democrats brought Argentine Christian Democracy into direct confrontation with the regime, which ultimately put a stop to their activity. Apart from these parties, best wishes were sent to the conference in Montevideo from kindred spirits in Peru and Bolivia, who themselves could not attend.[336]

In sum, Montevideo saw the coming together of a number of politicians who in the years to come would play an important role in Latin American Christian Democracy: the Argentinean Manuel Ordóñez, the Brazilian Alceu Amoroso Lima, the Uruguayan Dardo Regules - who as deputy ambassador to Chile had established contact with Eduardo Frei during the war - and Frei himself. Two years later, in 1949, the same company would meet again in Montevideo.[337] On that occasion the charter of a regional association, the Organización Demócrata Cristiana de América (ODCA), was approved. By 1958, at least 16 countries were represented in the organization, be it often by very small political movements.

Since this study takes the perspective of the Western European NEI as its starting point, it would take us too far to focus in depth on the functioning of the ODCA. It is sufficient to indicate the nature of the relations between the two organizations. On the ideological level it was impossible to miss the influence of the European Christian Democratic thinkers on the ODCA. Eduardo Frei explicitly mentions the Belgian cardinal Mercier, Etienne Gilson, Emmanuel Mounier and in particular Jacques Maritain as his greatest sources of inspiration. In this regard Latin American Christian Democracy was through and through "Eurocentric".

The Western European NEI, however, avoided institutional contacts with the Latin Americans as much as possible. Of course, there were personal contacts between certain European and Latin American Christian Democrats. In September 1947, for example, the executive committee of the NEI took a very close look at a report from Louis-Joseph Lebret, the director of the journal *Économie et Humanisme*, who had just returned from a five-month trip throughout Latin America. Lebret had visited Argentina, Brazil, Chile and Uruguay, the four countries which had been represented at party level in Montevideo, five months earlier.[338] Lebret bore the message that the

---

336   At that time, the Venezuelan COPEI was regarded as 'too conservative', and as a result the party was not invited. It would become a member in 1955, during the third ODCA congress.
337   This time also two Peruvian and one Colombian Christian Democrat were present.
338   Minutes of the meeting of the executive committee in Luxemburg, 28/09/1947. ACDP, IX-002 011/1.

"Montevideo Movement" was interested in establishing contacts with Christian Democrats outside of Latin America. NEI secretary-general Jules Soyeur distributed Lebret's report among the members and the executive committee requested Lebret to "maintain the contacts which he had established". Four months later Lebret was among those invited to the NEI congress in Luxemburg. He thought it best that the NEI should send one or more representatives to the following meeting of the "Montevideo Movement", but his suggestion was not picked up.

At that moment, in contrast with the Socialist International, the NEI paid relatively little attention to events outside of Europe. This is illustrated by an exchange of letters between the Czech Ivo Duchacek's and Jules Soyeur at the end of 1948. At that time Duchacek had already been living in New York for about two months and was temporarily associated with the Institute for International Studies of Yale University. Departing from what he called "the mounting interest of the United States" in all ideas which could help "bring about a true European unity", Duchacek was of the opinion that the time was ripe to involve the United States more deeply in the workings of the NEI.[339] More generally, an expansion of the contacts between the NEI and the United States could also include South America. The executive committee of the NEI had to determine just what form that expansion should take: either by creating national groups (équipes) which would be integrated into the NEI or by means of setting up a regional committee which would be more loosely linked with the NEI. Duchacek realized all too well what it was truly all about: "Are the NEI aiming at becoming a truly international organization, including North and Sourth America, or should we at this early stage limit ourselves to Europe?"[340]

Soyeur carefully spoke out in favour of the former option: the NEI needed to gradually expand itself into a truly global International, with as many branches as possible. This option strongly resembled mutatis mutandis the strategy which the Socialist International aspired to set in place in Latin America, but which had attained a certain amount of success only in Argentina and Uruguay. Others, including Robert Bichet, pleaded for more caution. The executive committee followed Bichet's advice and in the end decided

---

339   Duchacek referred among other things to an article by Almond, an American professor who was also working at Yale University. In November 1948, Almond wrote the article "The Political Ideas of Christian Democracy" in *The Journal of Politics*.

340   Report by Duchacek, 16/12/1948. ACDP, IX-002-002.

for "a cautious expansion".[341] What this rather vague formula comprised was made more clear in a few speeches in the year 1950. During the meeting of the executive committee of February 1950, the duchess d'Atholl expressed her surprise regarding a passage in the NEI literature which posited that for the NEI European integration was only the precursor of global integration. Bichet and De Schryver were just as surprised as the duchess. De Schryver assured her that the passage in question would be omitted when the publication was reprinted.[342] He once again stressed the European perspective of the NEI: to his mind the NEI existed in order to "coordinate the political powers of Western Europe in conjunction with the [Eastern European] exiles".

It was the ambition of the CDUCE to change this strictly European perspective. To that end the NEI was invited to the second international CDUCE congress which took place in New York from 15 to 17 April 1955. The invitation was steeped in the powerful ambitions of the exiles: "We have the intention to make this second congress a gathering of statesmen from all over the world, representatives of political and social movements, all with a Christian Democratic background. This event would be a prime paragon of solidarity among all Christian Democrats and of the unity of the goals that they are all striving for." The struggle between "materialism" on the one hand and "Christianity" on the other was a global struggle, which had to be fought out in Asia and Latin America, as well as in Europe. The conference in New York had a clear aim: "to contribute to the coordination of Christian Democratic activities and efforts to assemble the world's main representatives of Christian Democracy, in spirit or in person, as clear proof of solidarity and unity within the Christian Democratic movement. Our action will be a clear sign of the will and the power of our worldwide members to defend the peoples' right to live by the universal principles of natural law against atheism and communist attacks."[343]

Besides prominent individuals from the NEI and from Latin America, certain distinguished politicians from Vietnam, Lebanon, India, Japan, South Korea and Indonesia also received an invitation. The CDUCE's publications reflected these global tendencies. Every month they published in English the *Christian Democrat Review* and in Spanish the *Información Demócrata Cristiana*, filled with information about Christian Democratic parties and movements in Europe and Latin America. Additionally, members of the CDUCE regularly

341   Procès-verbal du Comité Exécutif, 15-16/01/1949, Paris. ACDP, IX-002-002.
342   Procès-Verbal du Comité Exécutif, 11-12/02/1950, Paris. ACDP, IX-002-005/1.
343   Letter from Sieniewicz to Bichet, 23/02/1955. ACDP, IX-002-067/1.

published circulars in their own languages for their fellow refugees from Eastern Europe. Shortly after the congress Prochazka and Sieniewicz described it as the ultimate proof that Christian Democracy should be taken seriously as "a united, cohesive worldwide force".[344] Now the Eastern Europeans only had to convince the NEI of this.

The NEI's Eurocentrism as an Obstacle to Successful Expansion

There can be no doubt regarding the position of the NEI, or of Western European Christian Democracy in general, vis-à-vis the East-West conflict in the first half of the 1950's. In his report of the 1950 Sorrento congress, the Italian Benvenuti succinctly expressed the repulsion he felt for communism: "Communism is the typical antithesis of our ideas." Totalitarian communism, "which ignores the humanity of the person", in its very totalitarianism presents a "constant threat", was the conclusion drawn in the final resolution of the congress, which later would become known as the "congress of fear".[345] In anti-communist matters, the NEI was initially just as engaged as the CDUCE or the Socialist International, if not more so. An important difference with the two other transnational organizations, however, was that the NEI did *not* give global ambitions to their anti-communism. Of course, the organization had its opinions on the Korean War, but its response to the Soviet threat in that region was defined primarily in terms of European interests.
Shortly after Sorrento, the executive committee of the NEI had come to the conclusion - based on the violence in Korea and Indochina - that "it was now all the more urgent to unite Europe".[346] Motivated by the communist threat, the NEI threw themselves behind the task of European integration, even if certain Christian Democrats insisted that "Europe" primarily had to be envisioned as a positive project, not merely as an anti-communist project.[347] The Socialist International, which was fundamentally divided over the European question, was in much less of a position to do similarly. Things were somewhat different for the NEI.

---

344   Letter from Prochazka and Sieniewicz to Bichet, 19/04/1955. ACDP, IX-002-067/1.
345   NEI. Réunion Internationale à Sorrento, April 1950. KADOC, ADS 7.2.4.4.
346   Procès-verbal du Comité Exécutif, 04/11/1950. ACDP, IX-002-002.
347   Cf. the Dutchman van der Poel. Procès-verbal du Comité Exécutif, 18/04/1953. ACDP, IX-002-005/2.

The pronounced European rather than global orientation of the NEI can be explained by referring to "the old Christian Democratic ideal, dating back to the 19th century, of a common Europe with a peaceful order, free of medieval - to say nothing of reactionary - illusions".[348] Now that Christian Democratic parties held the reins of government in a large number of European countries, that ideal appeared to be within reach for the first time. Wolfram Kaiser, co-author of *Christdemokratie in Europa im 20. Jahrhundert* and also the author of various contributions on the European engagement of the Christian Demo-crats, came to a similar conclusion: "For the Christian Democrats, Europe was not just a political goal; in their eyes the most important goal was to create a Europe with a Christian spirit."[349]

Yet alongside their attachment to an "abendländisch" ideal, national interests - economic, political and security concerns - also played a role in the NEI's preference for continental Europe. This was certainly true of the French MRP, which had become indispensable in the NEI. In Robert Schuman, France had found a minister of foreign affairs who was able to smoothly link France's interests with those of Europe, and effortlessly bring his party in line behind him. The rapid development of the West German economy, in particular its heavy industry, was perceived in France as a threat to their national security and to their own heavy industry.[350] At the same time, the United States (and Great Britain), after the outbreak of the Korean War, candidly began insisting upon the rearmament of West Germany, which only increased the unease in Paris. The Schuman Plan of 9 May, and the Pléven Plan of 24 October 1950, were intended to solve the concerns of both sides. The supranational char-acter which was built into both proposals would allow France to control the pace of both the unavoidable re-industrialization and remilitarization of West Germany. Moreover, the proposals opened perspectives for a political Europe under French leadership, of course "without questioning the importance of France in the entire world, an importance based on the French Empire".[351]

The West German CDU of Konrad Adenauer was also a fierce supporter of a strong, integrated Western Europe. Victor Koutzine, a confidant and fellow party member of Bidault, formulated Adenauer's foreign policy in 1951 with the following words: "Chancellor Adenauer has devoted himself to creating a federal Europe. His whole foreign policy is essentially oriented towards that

348   Papini, *The Christian Democrat International*, 54.
349   Kaiser, "Begegnungen christdemokratischer Politiker", 153.
350   Gillingham, *Coal, steel, and the rebirth of Europe*.
351   Soutou, "Georges Bidault et la Construction européenne."

objective, for he believes that the Franco-German entente - the central idea of his project - is only feasible within the larger framework of Western Europe. Chancellor Adenauer thus deliberately abandons the question of a united Germany."[352]

The political, military and economic integration of a rearmed West Germany in a Europe which would be able to resist Soviet pressure, and not a reunited Germany, was the basis of Adenauer's European engagement. A reunited Germany could only be a neutral Germany, which he feared would only too quickly land within the sphere of influence of the USSR.[353] Two such proposals from the USSR for a neutral Germany (Stalin's memorandum in 1952 and a similar proposal in 1954) Adenauer categorically refused, to the great satisfaction of the MRP. Consequently, it was quite easy for the NEI to arrive at a consensus on this issue. The Socialist International, in contrast, was sharply divided on this issue and in the end was unable to define a common position. The Scandinavian and Belgian socialists and the left wing of the BLP, along with the SPD, reacted positively to Stalin's Memorandum. The PvdA, the SFIO and the right wing of the BLP, however, totally rejected the Soviet initiative.[354] This illustrates yet once more why the NEI chose for a European orientation, while the Socialist International could not do so.

Other Christian Democratic parties also saw their national interests best embodied in the further strengthening of Western Europe. For the Italian Christian Democrats under Alcide De Gasperi, "Europe" could work as a counterbalance in Italy to the presence there of a powerful communist party. Additionally, an integrated Europe would allow Italy to expand its market, by means of which the country could work away its chronic surplus of labor. A combination of political and economic interests also explained the European involvement of the Low Countries, who with their Benelux construction were even able to pave the way for further European integration. The Austrian and Swedish affiliates in the NEI, however, remained outside of the intergovernmental integration dynamic due to their neutral identity (which Austria maintained until 1955). Nevertheless, this was not sufficient to dampen the European discussions in the NEI.[355] Quite the contrary. In confidential communications Austria called again and again for Europe to be strengthened

---

352   La Tactique du Chancelier Adenauer, report (1951) by Koutzine to Bidault. AN, 457 AP 59. Bidault Archives. Notes Koutzine/Nemanoff.

353   Urwin, *A Political History of Western Europe*, 89.

354   Circ. 36/52. 10/04/1952. Minutes of the Council of the Socialist International. London, 03-05/04/1952. IISG, SI 64.

355   Gehler, "Politisch unabhängig", 325.

against the Soviet threat. "Europe" was thus in line with Austrian interests, despite the fact that due to that country's particular situation they were not immediately able to participate in the first European institutions.

National interest, tradition and doctrine explain the almost exclusive attention which the Christian Democrats paid to Europe. This doesn't alter the fact that there were also many socialist parties with a pronounced European orientation. Yet, on the socialist side of the equation the division was undeniably greater. In their parliaments, the Italian and German socialists voted against the Treaty of Paris, while in the six countries of the European Coal and Steel Community (ECSC), all Christian Democratic parties explicitly supported the Treaty.[356] The NEI, moreover, did not have to contend with anything like the British Labour Party, which in the Socialist International continually attempted to marginalize the European agenda. There is no doubt that between 1950 and 1954 the European integration process was a mobilizing and enthusing issue for the Christian Democratic governments, which due to their participation in government were in a position to implement much of their program. It therefore comes as no great surprise that an overview of the topics discussed at the various NEI congresses reveals a remarkable homogeneity: "The Aims of Christian Democracy in Present-Day Europe" (Sorrento, 1950), "Europe and Peace" (Bad Ems, 1951), "Strength and Weakness of Christians in the European Democracies" (Fribourg, 1952) and - even more unambiguous - "Supranational Authority and the Notion of Sovereignty" (Tours, 1953). And in 1954, the NEI congress in Bruges debated "The Economic and Social Policy of Christian Democracy in Tomorrow's Europe".

The almost exclusive attention which the NEI paid to European integration is in sharp contrast with the scant influence which the organization was able to exercise upon that very process. The organization itself did not fail to emphasize its "important contribution" to the construction of a united Europe: "Thanks to the activities of the NEI in the [Consultative] Assembly [of the Council of Europe]", began an NEI report from the end of 1953, "we succeeded in having our proposals adopted by a very nice majority, which stimulated the establishment of a political authority without which there would not have been a European Unity."[357]

---

356   Bellers, *Deutsche Europapolitik und Sozialdemokratie*. This does not mean, though, that all
       Christian Democrats agreed on the European institutional concept - federal or confederal. On
       the contrary: their discord resulted in the NEI only having some very vague views on Europe.
357   Note sur le renforcement du Secrétariat des NEI, December 1953. ACDP, IX-002-91.

Their self-image, however, is highly overblown. Various authors have convincingly shown this to be the case and have correspondingly tempered the enthusiasm of several (engaged) NEI historians.[358] It is not necessary to examine this issue here any further. It is worth mentioning, however, that recent research has led to a revaluation of certain initiatives which took place not in the NEI itself, but in the margins of the NEI. An important one was that of the Geneva Circle, when Christian Democrats - often the same individuals who regularly attended the NEI gatherings - met each other on a "higher" level, in complete secrecy.[359] In the Geneva Circle, besides a small amount of attention paid to the situation in the countries behind the Iron Curtain and the activities of Cominform, meetings were primarily focused on the political organization of Western Europe, built around the French-German axis, and the issue of a divided Germany. It was in this closed forum that the French were able to demonstrate a remarkable openness towards Germany, at a moment when that would have been anything but acceptable to French public opinion. There, the basis was laid for the Schuman declaration of 9 May, which set in motion the process that would end in the ratification of the ECSC Treaty, and the Pléven Plan, which was supposed to lead to a supranational European Army.[360]

Besides these contacts, there were also informal meetings between party chairmen which sometimes took place either before or after a NEI meeting. In July 1950, for example, the Belgian CVP-PSC invited the party chairmen of the future ECSC countries, along with Austria and Switzerland to a brainstorming session on the newly presented Schuman plan, after the gathering of the NEI's executive committtee in Brussels. In a letter to Bichet, De Schryver confirmed that it indeed was his intention to invite "the Christian Democratic parties' chairpersons or their deputies", and not just the chairpersons of the équipes. In an earlier letter De Schryver shed some light on the nature of the intended meeting: "This meeting of the chairpersons (or their deputies) would not have an official character, and should be considered as an opportunity for personal contacts, which - as far as I am concerned - I think would be very useful. Besides, this gathering should not be confused with the ones that took place in Geneva: this time the invitation would have a different, much

358   Hahn, *La Démocratie chrétienne* as well as Papini, *The Christian Democrat International* both overrated the NEI's influence and importance. The same goes for Durand, *L'Europe de la Démocratie chrétienne*. A more critical approach is to be found in Mayeur, *Des Partis catholiques à la Démocratie chrétienne* and in Chenaux, *Une Europe vaticane?*
359   Gehler, "Der 'Genfer Kreis': Christdemokratische Parteienkooperation", 599-625.
360   AN, Bidault Archives, 457 AP 59, Correspondence Koutzine.

more personal character".[361] Owing to the fact that in these ad hoc meetings the party heads were directly involved, the gatherings undoubtedly were much more important than those of the NEI. The often one-sided focus on purely intergovernmental relations in research focusing upon the European integration process has too long ignored this sort of transnational networking.

Certain authors have attempted to show that the European orientation of the NEI was indeed reconcilable with its global calling. Charles Dechert, for example, stated that "the NEI looked toward European political integration as the first step toward world union. It inspired to encourage the leaders and the groups of Christian formation in the British Commonwealth, in the Union Française, and in Latin America toward a great aim: an international political order."[362] Roberto Papini's appreciation that "for all its limits, the NEI had a universal scope", can certainly be seen as valid for the last years of the organization's existence - the early 1960's - but when applied to the first half of the 1950's such a statement would be a gross exaggeration.

Due to the NEI's overloaded European agenda, the question of expanding the geographic scope of the organization was more or less out of the question. In the reports from the committee meetings during the period between 1950 and 1955 the question of expanding the geographic scope of the NEI was to come up a whole of two times. The first time was in Bad Ems, in September 1951 when the NEI decided to make optimal use of the UN meeting in Paris to establish contacts, "particularly with North and South America".[363] During that same meeting, the Dutchman Sassen submitted a proposal to "internationalize" the secretariat of the NEI, by among other things engaging with the "Christian Democratic movements in every country" and by "developing official links with all existing international organizations". At the next NEI gathering in November 1951, the question of possibly expanding the NEI came up for a second time. De Schryver emphasized that "the global orientation of the concept of Christian Democracy (...) should not solely be regarded from a European perspective." The NEI chairman was still of the opinion that, if one could make Christian Democratic ideas appeal to "countries such as America", it would have important consequences.[364] On that occasion Bichet returned

361   Letters from De Schryver to Bichet, 19-20/05/1950. ACDP, IX-002-89.
362   Dechert, "The Christian Democrat International".
363   Procès-Verbal du Comité Exécutif 14-15/09/1951, Bad Ems. ACDP, IX-002/005/1.
364   Procès-Verbal du Comité Exécutif, 24/11/1951, Paris. ACDP, IX-002-005/1. When he said 'America', De Schryver only referred to the United States.

to Sassen's proposal, which was meant to lead to the establishment of "an organization with an international character, capable of ensuring fruitful contacts". It would have to place the NEI in a position to maintain its contacts with the UN. But the discussions in the autumn of 1951, which can largely be seen as a reaction to the reinstitution of the Socialist International (July 1951), were of little or no consequence. Subsequently, the theme of global expansion sunk once more out of the picture and it wouldn't be until the autumn of 1955 that the topic again was placed on the agenda.

The NEI Testing the Waters beyond Europe, 1955-1960

A Regional Organization Tackling the Challenge of Globalization

The First Christian Democratic Intercontinental Conference, Paris 1956

The Nouvelles Équipes Internationales passed the first seven years of their existence in a European cocoon. Though in this period they were not able to exercise any direct influence upon the European integration process itself, indirectly they did contribute to the creation of support for that process. This certainly held true in the six Western European countries of "core Europe", but also, for example, in Austria where from 1955 on, the ÖVP quickly developed into an important pro-European force. The long participation of that party in the NEI discussions on European integration clearly left its mark.[365]

The focus on Europe, however, did not stop such issues as "the loss of China", the Korean War, the problems in French Indochina, or the lack of democratization in Latin America from occasionally being discussed at NEI gatherings. But although for parties which sat in government, these were all important themes, they extremely rarely appeared on the NEI agenda, and were never included in the minutes of the meetings. The representatives of the various parties seemed to leave all non-European concerns at home whenever they came together under the NEI umbrella. The NEI was clearly a club composed of all sorts of Europhiles, but it was no 'International'.

365   Gehler, "Politisch unabhängig", 325.

Starting in 1955, and propelled by the much more globally oriented CDUCE, it seems that the NEI for the first time began to test the waters beyond Europe. It is probable that the CDUCE, with its ambitious meeting in New York in April 1955 - which was intended to show the world that Christian Democracy could be considered as "a united, cohesive world-wide force" - piqued the interest of the Nouvelles Équipes Internationales.[366] Just after that meeting Coste-Floret invited Sieniewicz to the NEI committee meeting in November 1955 in order to present his vision of the "relations between the NEI and the Latin American Christian Democratic parties". Thus Sieniewicz indirectly received his much coveted recognition as go-between between the Western European and the Latin American Christian Democratic parties, a recognition which he undoubtedly deserved. The NEI archives clearly reveal Sieniewicz to have been a "pioneer", playing a bridging function between the NEI and the ODCA. Of course, various personal contacts existed between individual Europeans and Latin Americans. Kwanten, for instance, in his biography of A. E. De Schryver, correctly noted the politician's interest in Latin America.[367] Such contacts, however, do nothing to diminish Sieniewicz's place as a pioneer. He was, for instance, responsible for bringing Coste-Floret in contact with Montoro, the secretary-general of the Brazilian Christian Democrats, which opened the door to further, and fruitful contacts.

Sieniewicz made use of his presence at the committee meeting of the NEI in November to arouse interest among the Western Europeans in a further rapprochement with the ODCA. Sieniewicz thought that the approaching conference of Latin American Christian Democrats in Chile (8-10 December 1955) would be the ideal occasion to give further shape to contacts between Europeans and Latin Americans. He himself considered the conference as a potential new milestone in the evolution towards a global organization.[368] At that moment, Sieniewicz was busy contemplating a new, still to be set up, "coordination bureau" which would consist of four "centers of Christian Democracy". Besides the NEI, the CDUCE and the Latin American Christian Democrats, the Pole was also counting (rather unrealistically) on a future "Asian center" with representatives from Lebanon, Indonesia and the Philippines.

---

366   Letter from Prochazka and Sieniewicz to Bichet, 19/04/1955. ACDP, IX-002-067/1.
367   Kwanten, *August-Edmond De Schryver*, 491-492.
368   Prochazka was elected vice-chairman at the congress, which illustrated the good relations between both regional groups, the CDUCE and the ODCA.

Prochazka and Sleszynski, who represented the CDUCE in Chile, traveled there with the intention of pressuring the Latin American Christian Democrats during the course of the congress to agree in principle to the establishment of Sieniewicz'"coordination bureau" for the various regional groups. As the first step to establishing such a bureau on a permanent basis, a world congress of Christian Democrats had to be called together as soon as possible.[369] The CDUCE could be proud of what it achieved in Chile. The fact that the ODCA gave its secretary-general Tomas Reyes Vicuña the green light for the creation of an intercontinental Christian Democratic network, connecting the ODCA, the CDUCE, and - hopefully - the NEI as well, was music to Sieniewicz's ears. For him that decision marked the beginning of an intensive lobbying campaign to get the Western European Christian Democrats, represented in Chile by the Basque De Aguirre, on board as well.

De Aguirre's report on the gathering in Chile led to a debate in the following committee meeting of the NEI over the direction of future relations with Latin America, a first. Chairman De Schryver, who himself had personal contacts in Latin America, proved to be a supporter of such relations, yet he let it be known that contacts on an institutional level should not go too far. He pleaded two cases: firstly, that the secretary-general expand his contacts with Christian Democratic parties in Latin America and, secondly, that those parties be kept up-to-date on the activities of the European parties. The latter, according to De Schryver, boiled down to Sieniewicz's proposal to create an "intercontinental Christian Democratic network". The network which Sieniewicz had in mind went quite a bit further, though. Sieniewicz preferred tight organizational ties while De Schryver stayed true to his preference for a somewhat looser club of leading Christian Democrats - a preference which in Christian Democracy had a certain tradition, just like the continental European orientation.

During the debate, it was the secretary-general who called to mind this second "point of faith" of the NEI. Coste-Floret remarked that the intercontinental direction in which the activities of the NEI seemed to be going did not tally with the charter of the NEI, which stated that the purpose of the movement was the reconstruction of Europe. Personally, he was not opposed to a worldwide organization, yet he still chose for a cautious approach: "action by stages", as Landaburu formulated it at the same meeting.[370] Both points of view, which in reality were not so far from each other, can be found in the

369   Letter from Sieniewicz to Coste-Floret, 02/12/1955. ACDP, IX-002-067/1.
370   Procès-verbal du Comité Directeur, 28/01/1956. ACDP, IX-002-003.

final decision of the NEI. The chairman asked the secretary-general to take up Reyes Vicuña's proposal to convene a meeting of the three secretaries-general. The équipes represented in the NEI were requested, each via their own political or diplomatic network, to gather information on the actual arrangements of power in the Latin American countries, paying particular attention to the position of the Christian Democrats there. At the same time it was decided that the meeting had to maintain a rather non-binding nature.

On 30 May 1956, the three secretaries-general - Alfred Coste-Floret, Hernán Troncoso (who replaced Tomas Reyes Vicuña) and Konrad Sieniewicz - met, as agreed, at NEI headquarters in Paris. A few days before, Troncoso had represented the ODCA at the NEI congress in Luxemburg. During his address to that congress he had pleaded the case for the founding of a "Global Secretariat", composed of representatives from the ODCA, the CDUCE and the NEI. His proposal also contained a detailed list of possible joint activities, which had to be approved by the gathering of the three secretaries-general.[371]

From the minutes of the meeting on 30 May it can be surmised that, in accordance with the wishes of the NEI, the talks were only exploratory in nature. With respect to the "decisions" taken it was explicitly mentioned that they were "pending definitive approval by the executive committees of the respective organizations".[372] The secretaries-general, who had decided henceforth to work together in a coordination committee, seemed to be in agreement that "due to the recent changes in the international situation and the new responsibilities which had fallen on Christian Democratic shoulders", better cooperation between the three centers was needed.[373] They (conditionally) agreed to exchange information between the various parties or groups and to become familiar with each other's favoured topics. There was also a proposal to start up cultural centers, which would bring together writers, artists and painters of Christian Democratic inspiration. Their task would be to create "a cultural current based on Christian Democratic principles".[374] Finally, the idea of calling together an "intercontinental conference of Christian Democrats" was further elaborated, even if there is no explicit mention of it in the minutes of the meeting. Coste-Floret was particularly elated by the talks. On 6 June, he wrote NEI chairman De Schryver: "I believe that the executive committee and

---

371   Speech by Troncoso in ACDP, IX-002-085/3.
372   Réunion de 30/05/1956, au siège des NEI. ACDP, IX-002-027.
373   Note relative au projet de réunion des dirigeants des partis démocrates chrétiens à l'échelle mondiale. ACDP, IX-002-067/1.
374   Réunion de 30/05/1956, au siège des NEI. ACDP, IX-002-027.

yourself will agree to the decisions which have been taken and which seem to open up new perspectives of interesting collaboration."

After this first meeting, Sieniewicz carried on with his lobbying. On 16 June, he met Fanfani in Rome, and afterwards he held talks with party chairmen in Belgium, the Netherlands and France. At the second meeting of the secretaries-general, on 4 July 1956 in Paris, the program and the speakers for the conference were agreed upon.[375] Initially, Fanfani's proposal to hold the conference in the Italian city of Trento was taken into consideration, but for practical reasons it was eventually held in Paris, on 8 and 9 November 1956. At their committee meeting in the beginning of November the NEI ratified the entire scheme. Shortly afterwards a satisfied Coste-Floret wrote to the secretary-general of the MRP: "We gladly accept the invitation to the World Conference of Christian Democrats on 8 and 9 November in Paris."[376] Between the decision taken on 6 October 1956, to participate in an intercontinental conference and the decision of the NEI executive committee for "a cautious expansion" (in January 1949) lay almost eight years.

For the CDUCE the conference fell at an eventful moment in time. On 29 October, the Hungarian prime minister Nagy announced the end of the one-party system and the withdrawal of the Soviet troops from his country. A few days later he let it be known that his country would soon be pulling out of the Warsaw pact. These expressions of self-determination were unacceptable to the Kremlin. On 4 November, the Soviets attacked Budapest and the Hungarian rebellion was bloodily repressed. The "repression of the Hungarian people" could not but be a subject of discussion at the Intercontinental Conference in Paris, despite certain individuals such as Coste-Floret initially trying to avoid it. Coste-Floret was afraid that the subject would lead to a radical anti-communist position which had to be avoided during the period of détente.[377] Despite the current situation in Europe the accent of the conference was therefore laid on the potential transnational cooperation between Europe and Latin America. The ODCA itself was present in the person of its secretary-general Tomas Reyes Vicuña.[378] At that moment the organization comprised nine members, five of which were represented in Paris: Brazil, Chile, Uruguay,

375   Procès-Verbal de la Réunion du 04/07/1956. ACDP, IX-002-027.
376   Letter from Coste-Floret to Simonnet, 18/10/1956. ACDP, IX-002-067/1.
377   Letter from Coste-Floret to Schuman, 24/10/1956. ACDP, IX-002-027.
378   Apparently not many Western European leaders were charmed by the intercontinental project. The only Western Europeans present were Pflimlin and Golin from France, and Houben, Lefèvre, Tindemans and De Schryver from Belgium.

Venezuela and Peru. The remaining members which were part of the ODCA, namely Argentina, Colombia, Costa Rica and Bolivia, were not represented.[379]

The fact that Western European Christian Democrats were holding a congress together with kindred spirits from Latin America indicates that the NEI had begun to gradually expand their field of activity. At the same time the gathering made it quite clear, however, that the Western European Christian Democrats did not want to go all that far in their collaboration with the Latin Americans, in any case much less so than the Latin Americans themselves wanted to go. Western European representation was in the end somewhat limited. Only the Frenchmen Pfimlin and Golin and the Belgians Houben, Lefèvre, Tindemans and De Schryver were present. Halfway through 1956 NEI-spokesman Coste-Floret deemed the time not yet ripe for an "organization on a global scale" or for an "intercontinental center".

Even before the first "intercontinental conference of Christian Democrats" got off the ground, the NEI was reminding the remaining congress participants to remember the limitations of their engagement. Coste-Floret emphasized over and over again that the gathering was a "conference" and not a "congress". This he did in a letter to various editors-in-chief and agents of the press: "This is not an International congress, but merely a working conference." According to Coste-Floret no conclusions could be reached at the gathering. The only goal was to compare and contrast the positions of the three organizations and where possible to come to some sort of harmonization. The press release of 1 November, however, mainly emphasized the differences between the three organizations: "The Europeans mainly occupy themselves with the question of the European unification, the Christian Democrats from Central and Eastern Europe focus on restoring political liberties in their countries, and the Latin Americans concentrate on social and economic reforms".[380] This emphasis on the distinctiveness of the different regions was in sharp contrast with the discourse of the Western European social democrats in the Social-ist International, who mainly underscored the elements which the different continents had in common.

---

379   Reyes Vicuña referred to the Colombian Testimonio Group, to a Costa Rican Christian Demo-cratic movement led by José Figueres and to a Bolivian Christian Democratic group led by Remo di Natale. Les éléments qui pèsent sur la situation politique de l'Amérique Latine. Conférence Mondiale des Mouvements Démocrates-Chrétiens, 08-09/11/1956. ACDP, IX-002-027.
380   Press communiqué, 01/11/1956. Ibidem.

At the conference in Paris each organization that attended the meeting got time to present itself. Robert Schuman, as chairman of the European Movement, was one of the five introductory speakers, along with Lola Solar of the International Women's Union, Franco Nobili of the Youth Congress of the NEI, and Gaston Tessier who represented the Christian Trade Union International (CTUI). The Chilean Eduardo Frei Montalva was the last introductory speaker. In this summation it is already apparent that the Christian Democrats did not limit themselves to political parties in the strict sense of the term, quite the contrary. From the beginning, during the preparatory meetings, the international umbrella organization of Christian labor unions, the CTUI, was involved in the experiment. August Vanistendael, the secretary-general of the CTUI, sat on the Organizational Committee and CTUI chairman Gaston Tessier was, as already mentioned, one of the introductory speakers.

The NEI did not only want to strengthen their ties with the CTUI because of the transnational network which the trade union international was gradually and successfully enlarging.[381] The fact that Gaston Tessier was very familiar with Latin America was of course a nice side benefit. In the spring of 1951, for instance, Tessier had made a long journey throughout Latin America. He was there on behalf of the French government but he also used the opportunity to establish some interesting contacts for the CTUI. More important perhaps was that the rapprochement between the NEI and the CTUI fit nicely into the primarily Western European strategy of the NEI. In order to be able to exercise more influence upon the European institutions to be created by the Treaty of Rome, it was essential to improve the cooperation between the two organizations. That cooperation was particularly important when it came to nominations within the European institutions. In February 1957, Vanistendael would officially submit the request to the NEI to intensify cooperation between the two organizations. On 24 April 1957, in Arezzo, the leaders of the NEI chose for "active and permanent cooperation" between both organizations, with respect for the autonomy of both movements.

Since the Christian Trade Union International was present in Paris, De Schryver insisted that the international umbrella organization of Catholic employers would also be invited.[382] A similar international umbrella organization for

381   The CTUI's contacts with Latin America are dealt with in Pasture's study *Histoire du Syndicalisme*, 299. Already in 1950 the CTUI had the intention to start a bureau in Bogotá, which would enable them to compete against rival union internationals.
382   From the end of 1958 onwards, the relations between the Uniapac - led by Rik Vermeire, the new secretary-general - and the NEI were strengthened. Procès-Verbal du Comité Directeur, 13/02/1959. ACDP, IX-002-003.

tradespeople was still in formation. The farmers were represented in Paris by the umbrella organization Mijarc. In other words, the Belgian Christian Democrat seemed to transpose the model of his own party onto the transnational level. At the same time this was an illustration of the importance Christian Democracy placed on a balanced representation of the various "intermediary" groups in society, which is difficult to realize through political parties alone. The socialists, on the other hand, due to their Marxist past, placed more importance on the political party as the expression of society's will. This is a good example of how differing organizational styles worked themselves out on a transnational level.

Keeping in mind the diversity of the participants it should be no surprise that little progress was made in Paris towards moving in the direction of a true transnational inter-party organization. The only result was the establishment of a permanent committee consisting of the secretaries-general of the three regional organizations and of the chairman of the youth organization IUYCD, Franco Nobili. That committee was subordinate to yet another "intercontinental committee", also founded in Paris, which was composed of official representatives of all the Christian Democratic parties of the NEI, the ODCA, the CDUCE and the IUYCD.

The Second Christian Democratic Intercontinental Conference, Brussels 1958

The Latin American Christian Democrats who were present in Paris used the opportunity to invite the leaders of the NEI to the following ODCA congress which was to take place in September 1957, in Sao Paolo. It is remarkable just how much importance Christian Democrats from the New World placed on cooperation with their Western European colleagues at that moment in time. This was not very surprising. Above we have already mentioned the enormous influence that the European Christian Democratic thinkers exercised on Latin American youth. At all the NEI gatherings where they were present the Latin Americans never failed to refer with great respect to their European sources of inspiration. During the NEI congress in Luxemburg in 1956, for instance, the Chilean Christian Democrat Hernán Troncoso referred to the dominant influence of Maritain, De Gasperi, Schuman, Adenauer and Van Zeeland.[383] France in particular was an important source of inspiration. The prestige of the European Christian Democrats was further heightened

383   Procès-verbal du Congrès des NEI, Luxembourg, 25-26/05/1956. ACDP, IX-002-085/3.

by the fact that in several Western European countries in the first half of the fifties - and in some countries even later - Christian Democratic parties sat in government. Moreover, they were the principal driving force behind the European integration, which piqued much interest in Latin America. The ODCA congress in Sao Paolo, just like their next congress in Lima, was completely dedicated to developing similar integration schemes for Latin America. Furthermore, many Latin American Christian Democrats were hoping to find in Europe an alternative to the sometimes suffocating dependence on their powerful northern neighbor, the US.

The NEI did not possess the necessary financial means to be able to accept the ODCA's invitation, but a generous gift of $1,350 from Sieniewicz quickly solved that problem.[384] Sieniewicz had also taken care of a good deal of the costs of the previous year's intercontinental conference, which indicates just how important he considered the global expansion of Christian Democracy.[385] Sieniewicz' gift, however, was not the only reason why Coste-Floret decided to travel to Sao Paolo, despite the fact that initially he had very little desire to do so. As the mayor of Luchon, a sleepy holiday makers' village on the French-Spanish border, he felt like he already had more than enough on his plate. Nevertheless, his party, the MRP, via Pflimlin, was able to apply the necessary pressure to make him change his mind:"I consider it extremely advisable to send an MRP delegation to Sao Paolo, since I believe that currently we have to pay attention to the Christian Democratic movement in South America. On the eve of the UN session of the General Assembly, French presence might turn out productive."[386] The fact that all of a sudden the MRP placed so much importance on transnational cooperation, indeed cannot be separated from the debates which at that moment were determining the agenda of the United Nations, and by extension also that of international politics.

Right from the establishment of the UN, successive French governments, just like the other European colonial powers, had stuck to a very narrow interpretation of the UN Charter, which (according to them) gave the General Assembly absolutely no authority regarding the colonial territories or protectorates. From the early 1950's, however, the General Assembly, which was gradually

---

384   Letter from Coste-Floret to Sieniewicz, 28/01/1957. ACDP, IX-002-067/1.
385   According to Coste-Floret the world conference had cost 1,3 million Francs, of which 1 million had been 'arranged' by Sieniewicz. Letter from Coste-Floret to De Schryver, 15/11/1956. ACDP, IX-002-007.
386   Letter from Pflimlin to Coste-Floret, 30/08/1957; Letter from Coste-Floret to Pflimlin, 31/08/1957; Letter from Coste-Floret to De Schryver, 31/08/1957. ACDP, IX-002-028/1.

enlarging with the membership of the newly independent states, became increasingly prepared to discuss the colonial question. It was in the UN where the French attempts to keep decolonialization out of the international forum violently collided with the heightened self-awareness of the Afro-Asian block. In a recent article, Martin Thomas calls the period between 1955 and 1957 the period of the "histrionic rejection of the UN's jurisdictional competence in French colonial affairs".[387] In that period the Afro-Asian block opened the discussion on France's Algeria policy in the UN, and the Algerian resistance movement, the FLN, began to seek official recognition in August 1956. Such events forced the French government to justify its policies and to seek support for its positions. In September 1956, for instance, the French minister of foreign affairs Christian Pineau asked the American State Department to lobby the Afro-Asian states on France's behalf. By 1957, however, France found itself in a particularly weak position. The Suez crisis, the admission of Morocco and Tunisia as independent states to the UN, a strong Afro-Asian group, the foreign policies of the United States and Great Britain, and the reports of French atrocities in Algeria all undermined the French position.

It was in these circumstances that France intensified its lobbying efforts. Among others, Albert Schweitzer and Maurice Papon were set to the task of improving France's image.[388] Schweitzer had to convince President Eisenhower that Algeria fell under French jurisdiction. Maurice Papon, who at that moment was the inspector general of Algeria, was sent in 1957 to the UN to defend France's position. He was an ardent supporter of the use of violence against the FLN. In particular the support of Latin America in the General Assembly was more than welcome. MRP chairman Pflimlin's appeal to Coste-Floret to participate in the Sao Paolo conference should be seen in this context.

In his report of the gathering in Sao Paolo Coste-Floret wrote that his presence had been particularly useful. It was a good thing that a Frenchman had been on the scene, he stated, since this had dampened a motion for complete solidarity with the Afro-Asians just in the nick of time.[389] And this was no one-time occurrence. A detailed study of the diplomatic correspondence of the period will undoubtedly confirm the importance of such lobbying, as can be seen, for instance, in a letter from the French ambassador to Costa Rica to Coste-Floret: "At present, in all those countries, we are making a great

387   Thomas, "France accused: French North Africa before the United Nations", 95.
388   Golsan, «Memory's bombes à retardement: Maurice Papon» 160.
389   Letter from Coste-Floret to Pflimlin, 26/09/1957. ACDP, IX-002-028/1.

effort from an economic point of view, and I think that soon we will reap the rewards of it. You will have noticed that this year, in the diplomatic field, the Latin American countries have shown exemplary behavior towards us in the discussions about the Algerian question."[390] In other words, a policy of French interest served up with an internationalist sauce.

Since the three secretaries-general were present in Sao Paolo, the temptation was apparently great to consider the fourth ODCA conference as "Christian Democracy's second intercontinental conference". The "real" second intercontinental conference, however, was only to take place in July 1958, in Brussels, where at the same time the World's Fair was being held. Again it was Sieniewicz - or the CDUCE - who shouldered the costs of the gathering. The CDUCE paid for the accommodation of 36 invited delegates, the banquet, translation fees and other organizational costs. It was largely thanks to these financial contributions, if we can believe Coste-Floret, that the Eastern European exiles were able to participate in the conference: "As in any kind of business, the one who finances it has the undeniable right to supervision; that is why I had to agree with our friend Sieniewicz to have a representative of the équipes in exile speak with a South American and a European."[391]

From the correspondence it is more than apparent that Sieniewicz was the real inspiration and organizational force behind the conference. It must have been a pleasant surprise for him that the number of participants had greatly increased compared to two years earlier. In addition to the five Latin American countries represented in Paris there were now also representatives from Argentina, Bolivia, Colombia, Ecuador, Guatemala, Panama and El Salvador present, bringing the number of Latin American countries up to twelve. For the first time the report of the conference also mentioned representatives from Africa, even though it was a serious exaggeration when Coste-Floret, on the basis of the one delegate from French Equatorial Africa and the one representative from Kenya, said that "even the African continent was present".[392]

The second intercontinental conference gave the energetic Polish exile a new opportunity to deepen and to institutionalize the collaboration between the CDUCE, the ODCA and the NEI. As far as the exchange of information was concerned, for example, Sieniewicz attempted to bring about an integrated

390   Letter to Coste-Floret, 28/02/1957. ACDP, IX-002-085/3.
391   Letter from Coste-Floret to Sieniewicz, 22/05/1958. ACDP, IX-002-028/2.
392   Coste-Floret. "La Deuxième Conférence Intercontinentale des Démocrates chrétiens."

whole. To that end, even before the gathering he launched the idea of establishing an "intercontinental information center" which would publish its own *Bulletin*. The leaders of the NEI reacted positively but cautiously and created a subcommission consisting of Hahn and Bichet in order to further elaborate this idea.

Nevertheless, relations were soon to sour. The conditions which Hahn and Bichet had attached to the establishment of such a center were unacceptable to Sieniewicz. Moreover, Sieniewicz's decision to nonetheless distribute the first edition of such a bulletin during the second international conference in Brussels made for bad blood between himself and the NEI delegates. During the committee meeting, which took place the very same day, De Schryver made it clear that "the committee of the NEI condemned all such initiatives, considering them entirely unacceptable".[393] In the months to come the NEI would continue to emphasize certain conditions: the NEI would only be able to lend their support to a bulletin if the finances for that bulletin (which likely would again be coming out of Sieniewicz's pocket) and the editing thereof were controlled by the NEI. The initiative was therefore possible, but only "within the framework of the NEI".[394] Moreover, Sieniewicz's idea to put out a bulletin seemed to be more of a private initiative than one coming from the CDUCE. The Lithuanian Turauskas stressed that the possible distribution of a bulletin had never been discussed at a meeting of the CDUCE before the intercontinental conference. Later, Venskus would also emphasize that the exiles had not been informed of all these various "manoeuvres".[395] Such incidents illustrate the mounting disaccord, since the death of Stalin, between the "hard-liners" - the Baltic Christian Democrats, whose countries had been annexed by the Soviets - and the more pragmatic Poles and Czechs, who wished to take advantage of every opportunity to encourage détente.

In 1959, the CDUCE would venture another attempt at institutionalizing the intercontinental collaboration. They had in mind nothing less and nothing more than a fully-fledged International. By the autumn of 1959, they had set on paper the statutes of what they called a *Groupe de Liaison Intercontinental Démocrate Chrétien* (GLIDC), which would be comprised of three bodies. Firstly, an Intercontinental Conference to layout the main policy lines, composed of representatives from each Christian Democratic party which belonged to the ODCA, the NEI or the CDUCE, or to subgroups like the IUYCD

393 Procès-Verbal du Comité Directeur, 09/07/1958, Bruxelles. ACDP, IX-002-003.
394 Procès-Verbal du Comité Directeur, 13/12/1958, Paris. ACDP, IX-002-003.
395 Procès-Verbal du Comité Directeur, 09/07/1958, Bruxelles. ACDP, IX-002-003.

or the CTUI.[396] Secondly, an Intercontinental Committee which would take the actual decisions and would be composed of the chairmen and the secretaries-general of the three member organizations. Lastly, the CDUCE foresaw an Intercontinental Secretariat made up of the three member organizations. The GLIDC received a threefold objective: to study and bring into harmony all Christian Democratic doctrines, to work out Christian Democratic policy on an intercontinental plane, and to coordinate the actions of the various parties.

Sieniewicz's blueprints, however, went just a step too far for the NEI. On 26 November 1959, Coste-Floret in a letter to the Polish exile dropped in passing that "by the way, the executive committee [of 21 November 1959] has not accepted your proposal regarding the articles of association of the GLIDC". The NEI wished to maintain the status quo in its relations with the ODCA and the CDUCE, which consisted of a voluntary exchange of information and a biennial intercontinental conference.[397] At that same meeting, Sieniewicz's proposal was also opposed by Turauskas, who thought that the CDUCE, which at the moment was "in a state of crisis", was not at all a reliable partner. According to him, the organization was rife with unacceptable intrigues and "rather undemocratic and unchristian procedures".[398] Furious, Sieniewicz sent a resolution to the NEI in which the executive committee of the CDUCE, in January 1960, unanimously stated that "there is absolutely no crisis in the UCDEC".[399] Nonetheless, the NEI put the GLIDC draft on ice. Their aversion for all lasting intercontinental ties was still too great for the time being.

The Social-Economic Commission: Sowing the Seeds of Third World Thinking

The fact that in the 1950's the Nouvelles Équipes Internationales felt no need, *on an institutional level*, to go beyond the borders of Europe and expertly withstood all the pressures pushing them in that direction, led to the organization's being labeled through and through "Eurocentric".[400] Such an assessment is justified. However, it would be incorrect to assume that the NEI in the 1950's had absolutely no interest in the (overseas) territories beyond Europe. The interest certainly was there, only it was purely content-based and not institutional. It was mainly dealt with in a specific commission

396   In 1947 a 'youth committee' had been founded, which was named IUYCD in 1951.
397   Letter from Coste-Floret to Sieniewicz, 26/11/1959. ACDP, IX-002-067/1.
398   Letter from Turauskas to Coste-Floret, 12/02/1960. ACDP, IX-002-009.
399   Letter from Sieniewicz to Coste-Floret, 16/01/1960. ACDP, IX-002-009.
400   Gehler, *The 'Geneva Circle' of Western European Christian Democrats.*

- the Social-Economic Commission (SEC) - and only to a much lesser extent in the decision making bodies of the NEI: the congress, the bureau, and the executive committee.

Right from its creation in 1948, the Social-Economic Commission of the NEI was given the relatively broad assignment "to study the economic and social issues to be submitted to the executive committee".[401] In accordance with the interests of the executive committee, and of the NEI as a whole, the entire focus was initially placed on Europe. One of the first activities of the SEC, for instance, was the organization of a three-day study session in March 1949 in Paris in order to further work out the details of the economic resolutions which the NEI had approved a few months earlier, in September 1948 in The Hague. Those resolutions in turn had been inspired by the economic and social activities of the European Congress, which had taken place in May 1948, again in The Hague, organized by the coordination committee of European organizations.

Since the European Congress had paid attention to the "economic ties which at present link the countries of Europe with the Dominions and associated states or overseas dependent territories", the SEC also paid attention to "the economic relations between the European mother countries and their Dominions, their associated states and their dependent overseas territories."[402] The example is somewhat convoluted, yet it illustrates that through the European level, the SEC also paid attention to other continents, especially to Africa. The few paltry sentences which in that period were dedicated to Africa were all concerning Africa's relations with Europe: the "European economic balance" could not be studied separately from the colonial economies which politically were linked with Europe. In other words, it was from the nascent European forum that the theme of the "underdeveloped territories" slowly trickled into the workings of the NEI. That European influence would gain strength in the 1950's.

"Europe" was not the only source of inspiration. The United Nations were also a source of new ideas. At that moment the NEI had very weak institutional links with the UN, but various individual contacts were able to compensate this. SEC chairman and former Belgian minister of foreign trade, van der

401   Commission Économique et Sociale. Règlement Interne, art. 5. ACDP, IX-002-039.
402   Economic and Social Resolution, Point 3, quoted in *Europe Unites: the Hague Congress and After*. London, 1949, 68; Commission Economique et Sociale NEI. Paris, 11-13/03/1949. ACDP, IX-002-039.

Straten-Waillet, for example, as the head of the Belgian delegation, participated in the twelfth Ecosoc session, which took place between 20 February
and 21 March 1951, in Santiago de Chile. He returned from Chile with the
message that the "underdeveloped countries" strongly protested the lack of
means of consumption and of investment and the fixing of prices of certain
raw materials of which the "underdeveloped" countries were the major
producers. The thirteenth session of the Ecosoc, which was entirely dedicated
to the problems of development, also had a large influence upon the NEI, just
as the twelfth session had had. On the basis of a report from the Frenchman
Pierre Abelin the SEC approved a resolution regarding the "underdeveloped"
countries, which was strongly influenced by the discussions in Ecosoc.
The resolution assigned to the Dutch équipe, or more exactly to the Dutch
economist L.H. Janssen, the task to make a comprehensive study of the
problem of development, a topic which the SEC saw as being "a question of
social justice, human development and world peace, especially for Christians".
Janssen was advised to take his inspiration from the activities of the United
Nations, the pope's and the Christian churches' guidelines and from concrete
statistical data.

Janssen was the right person for this job. In 1960, he would receive his doctor-
ate in economics from the Katholieke Economische Hogeschool Tilburg, the
title of his dissertation being *Free Trade, Protectionism and Customs Union:
a quantitative theoretical analysis*. Afterwards, he would become ever more
involved with development issues.[403] From this it appears that the SEC was
able to appeal to the most qualified and interested individuals. Pierre Abelin
himself had defended his doctoral dissertation at the University of Paris,
in 1936, on *La Comparaison internationale des Niveaux de Vie Ouvriers*, and
afterwards went on to specialize in development issues. Between 1974 and
1981, he would occupy the post of minister of development cooperation.
Capable individuals such as the above were, nonetheless, confronted with
organizational problems. In March 1952, chairman van der Straten-Waillet was
named Belgian ambassador to Argentina and a successor was not immediately found. Only in January 1953, when van der Straten-Waillet's compatriot
Raymond Scheyven picked up the torch, it was possible to continue working
again.

The topic was on the agenda whenever the SEC met. At the gathering of 31
October 1953, a long discussion about the "underdeveloped territories" took

---

403   Commission Économique et Sociale. Paris, 23/11/1951. Résolution concernant le développe-
      ment économique des pays sous-développés. ACDP, IX-002-039.

place between Maurice Bye, Jacques Etevenon, Albert Lohest, Schuijt, von Liebermann and chairman Raymond Scheyven. Scheyven gave an update on the state of affairs of the discussions taking place at that moment in the United Nations, including the plans to establish a "Special UN Fund for Economic Development" (SUNFED). This gathering was intended primarily as a preparation for a larger meeting which was to take place in Paris two weeks later. There it became particularly clear that some Christian Democrats preferred a "conservative" solution to the development issue, while others took a more "socialist" approach. Better coordination between Christian Democrats was therefore essential, especially with regards to the second European Economic Conference (EEC) of the European Movement, which was to take place in Westminster, from 29 January to 1 February 1954. The second EEC, just like the first which had also taken place in Westminster, in 1949, placed much emphasis on the overseas territories and was undoubtedly the catalyst for the activities of the SEC. In the SEC the preparations for Westminster were quite thorough. Not only did the commission hold a two-day study session three weeks before "Westminster", in order to tune their instruments, they also dispatched five of the eleven Christian Democrats who had taken part in the gathering in Paris to Great Britain.[404]

The overseas territories would remain an important issue to the SEC. In December 1954, for instance, the commission chose "the attitude towards underdeveloped countries and the connected questions of overpopulation and migration" as one of its five priorities from a potential list of twenty-six.[405] Furthermore, during a meeting at the beginning of February 1955, at which only three members were present, the SEC proposed going so far as to devote the entire congress of 1955 to the "very current and Christian issue of assistance to the underdeveloped territories". At the same time, the commission also submitted a draft resolution on the subject and called for an enormous financial effort on the part of the prosperous countries to make investments in the "underdeveloped areas" possible, even when unprofitable. More specifically, the SEC was vocal in its support of the United Nations' attempts to establish the Special UN Fund for Economic Development.[406] The resolution which clearly carried the stamp of Raymond Scheyven, the specialist in the field, was unanimously approved by the NEI leadership. This was the first time that that topic went all the way up to the top level of the organization.

---

404   *Mouvement Européen. Deuxième Conférence Économique Européenne de Westminster, 29 janvier - 1 février 1954. Compte-Rendu et Résolutions.* Brussels, 1954.
405   Commission Économique et Sociale, 10/12/1954. ACDP, IX-002-040/2.
406   Procès-Verbal du Comité Directeur, 19/02/1955. ACDP, IX-002-003.

Apparently, however, the time was not yet ripe to devote an entire congress to the issue. In the end, NEI chairman De Schryver chose the theme which the Dutchman Sassen had proposed: "The economic integration of Europe".

All this shows that the Social-Economic Commission of the NEI was well prepared when an external stimulus ensured that in the second half of the 1950's development issues remained on the NEI agenda. That external stimulus was the European revival which manifested itself from 1956 onwards.

Such a revival was absolutely essential since the French rejection of the European Defense Community (EDC) had put an abrupt stop to the European integration process. By the spring of 1954, the EDC Treaty had already been ratified by the Low Countries and by West Germany, where the SPD had offered heavy resistance. Italy, where the government was expecting much opposition, decided to wait for French ratification. At that moment, opposition against the EDC Treaty had already mounted in Paris. The left wing of the French political spectrum was - now that Stalin was dead - predominantly in favour of negotiating with the USSR and not so much of the further buildup of European defense. On the right, De Gaulle's RPF was irreconcilably opposed to the supranational character of the treaty. A majority of MRP members of parliament remained behind Schuman, but by the time of the actual vote on 30 August 1954, the MRP was again in the opposition. The EDC Treaty received a not very honorable funeral in the French Assembly with 264 votes for and 319 votes against.[407]

The consequences for the European integration movement were considerable: other projects geared towards sectorial integration - in agriculture, transport and pharmacology for example - were shelved. The ECSC did manage to stay afloat, but the euphoria had drained away only to be replaced by the feeling that the "momentum" of a federal Europe was a thing of the past. At around this same time De Gasperi passed away and in France it seemed as if Schuman's role had played itself out. The NEI, which had come out in favour of the EDC Treaty, was left behind abandoned.

The European depression was of short duration. At the gathering of ECSC ministers in Messina, Sicily, in June 1955, the Benelux presented the other European core countries with a memorandum pleading for the creation of a unified European market. This immediately breathed new life into the Europe-

---

407   Eighty MRP members had voted for, two against, and four had abstained from voting. Berstein and Milza, *Histoire de la France au XXe siècle, 3*, 179.

an ideal. In Messina the ministers set up a commission under the leadership of the Belgian socialist P.H. Spaak, who was to lay the ground work for this new stage. At the end of 1956, negotiations began in the Belgian Hertoginnedal, on the basis of an initial document worked out by the Spaak Commission. This would lead the foreign ministers of the six member countries to sign the EEC Treaty and the Euratom Treaty in Rome in 1957. On 1 January 1958, both of these treaties took effect.

The NEI had followed the revival from close quarters and with much enthusiasm. The NEI congress which took place in Bruges in September 1954, just after the fatal vote on the EDC Treaty, confessed in the so-called "Message of Bruges" its unwavering faith in the further evolution of Europe: "Now, more than ever, the European people need to become conscious of their solidarity, and they need to maintain as well as create supranational institutions with real power, which will make them capable of securing their own future."[408] References to "the highest and most cherished values of Christian civilization" were not missing either, but central to the message were three very concrete objectives: the election of a European assembly by general suffrage, free movement of persons, together with the liberalization of the movement of goods, services and capital, with the harmonization of taxation and social systems. No wonder that shortly after Messina the NEI voiced their complete support for the Benelux initiative.[409] All meetings of the SEC were focused on the topics which had originally come up in the discussions around the European revival: the common market and the integration of atomic energy. The European engagement of the NEI, even after the EDC, showed in other words a remarkable continuity with the Euro-enthusiasm of the early 1950's.

One important difference with the earlier period, however, was that this time the European construction had noticeable consequences for the overseas territories. The congress of The Hague, in May 1948, had only paid a bit of attention to the overseas territories. In the Council of Europe, which had been established in that same year, the overseas territories had been exhaustively discussed, although only in the (relatively powerless) consultative assembly. The much more important and politically more relevant ECSC and EDC, however, were only concerned with European territories. In the early stages of the European revival (Messina and the Spaak report) the overseas territories remained largely outside of the discussions. France, the most important ECSC

408 Le Message de Bruges des NEI in *Europe Unie. Organe du Conseil belge du Mouvement Euro-péen*. 11-12/1954, 29.
409 Procès-Verbal du Comité Directeur, 02/07/1955. ACDP, IX-002-006.

colonial power, initially was rather reserved regarding the Benelux initiative; the EDC debacle was still fresh. The new French government of Guy Mollet, however, with Christian Pineau as minister of foreign affairs and Gaston Deferre as minister of overseas territories, proved to be much more engaged. During the meeting of the ministers of Foreign Affairs in Venice, in May 1956, Pineau fully supported the initiative and asked that the French "outre-mer" be associated with the future European Economic Community. This would not only be advantageous for the French colonial territories themselves, which would receive a position of privileged access to the European market, but it would also benefit France as a whole, so thought Mollet, the prime minister of France. The war in Indochina was an enormous bloodletting financial drain on the French economy. A Europeanization of the "money devouring" developing territories would indeed be very welcome in France.[410] In other words, it was a question of "burden sharing".

By October 1956, French negotiators had convinced Belgium of the importance of such an association. The other countries nevertheless remained skeptical. Some (West Germany, the Netherlands and to a lesser degree Italy) were afraid that privileged treatment of the (ex-) colonial export would interrupt trade relations with Latin America and Asia. In addition they feared that they would have to carry a disproportionate share of the "burden" and would have to cough up too high a contribution to the soon to be established European Development Fund. Finally, they preferred not to be involved in the colonial unrest which was sweeping through French North Africa at that moment. In particular Adenauer was vocal in his fears. He wanted above all to avoid that German funds earmarked for development should end up all together in one pot with French francs and be indirectly associated with the pursuit of the war in Algeria or with colonialism in general. Eventually, at a special gathering of heads of state in Paris, on 18 and 19 February 1957, an agreement was reached over the French proposal. Part IV of the EEC Treaty, which was signed on 25 March 1957, regulated the association accords between the EEC countries and their overseas territories. The "development of the welfare" of the overseas territories became one of the ambitions of the European institutions, so went the preamble.

In the Social-Economic Commission of the NEI, as far as can be gleaned from the often rather superficial reports, the discussions were much less profound than was the case for those on the diplomatic level. The SEC's activities

410   Cosgrove-Twitchett, *Europe and Africa*, 10.

followed the tight schedule of the intergovernmental negotiations. At around the same time that the French were broaching the topic of the overseas territories in the EEC negotiations, the topic was also revived in the SEC, after having been more or less marginalized at the meetings which took place between mid-1955 and mid-1956 - roughly speaking the period between "Messina and Venice". Only in April 1956 did Albert Lohest, the then chair of the SEC gathering, once again shift the focus to "the possible expansion of currently underdeveloped states associated with Europe, an expansion which is closely linked to the creation of the European market."[411] "Europe" was undoubtedly the most important catalyst, but the international scene - which seldom seemed to have a direct effect on the NEI - strengthened the rising interest. NEI chairman August De Schryver, for example, considered the Suez crisis to bear witness to the "emancipation of the native peoples and races of Asia and Africa, and to their needs."[412]

The SEC considered it to be a particularly suitable moment to attempt once again to get the subject on the agenda of the following NEI congress, which would be held in 1957. Efforts to focus the congresses of 1955 and 1956 on the subject had come to nothing. The congress of 1956 for example, which had taken place in Luxemburg, had been dedicated entirely to the themes of European integration and East-West relations in Europe. This time was no different. The proposal from the SEC - "the attitude of Christians towards the underdeveloped territories" - was not heeded. Instead "the solidity of Christian Democracy vis-à-vis the communist crisis" was the topic of discussion in the Italian city of Arezzo in April 1957.

Interest continued to mount, also among certain Belgian Christian Democrats, and on 12 and 13 January 1957, the Belgian équipe organized a study weekend on the "insufficiently developed countries" in Kortenberg Abbey, again at the behest of Albert Lohest.[413] Nevertheless, it would not be until 1960 that the NEI leadership was ready to place development issues on the agenda of a NEI congress. Before the organization got so far, however, a thorough house cleaning seemed to be necessary, which would not only lead to a global expansion in terms of content, but also to the globalization of the institutional framework of the organization itself.

---

411   Commission Économique et Sociale, 14/04/1956. ACDP, IX-002-041.
412   The Suez crisis was merely paid attention to. Apart from the above-cited remark it was also pointed out that the crisis was an "impairment of Europe's prestige and force". Procès-Verbal du Comité Directeur, 06/10/1956. ACDP, IX-002-007.
413   Commission Économique et Sociale. ACDP, IX-002-042.

Global Expansion and the Organizational Culture of Christian Democracy: Incompatible Variables?

In the 1950's only the Social-Economic Commission (SEC) - influenced by the debates in the United Nations and in the still young European institutions - paid some attention to the "underdeveloped world". The commission fruitlessly tried (in 1955, 1956 and 1957) to get the topic discussed in the higher circles of the NEI or to get it on the agenda of a NEI congress. In 1960 they were successful: the Paris congress of that year was entirely dedicated to "Christian Democracy and the Third World". Why were they able to succeed in 1960 and not in all those previous years?

When answering this question we are confronted with two problems. Firstly, there is a danger of being blinded by what was happening on the international scene - 1960 was the year of the great African decolonization wave - and as a result not going any further than a monocausal explanation.
A second problem is that the decision making process for the years 1958 and 1959 is quite difficult to reconstruct. There are serious gaps in the NEI archives for that time: the correspondence from that period, for instance, is relatively limited, and the minutes of the NEI meetings became shorter and shorter, making it difficult to draw accurate conclusions. This is at least partly due to the fact that in this very period the NEI were undergoing a complete reorganization. This reorganization itself is an important explanation of the global expansion process of the NEI. Rather than looking for answers exclusively in the international events of the time, it is at least as important to focus on some transnational evolutions, which have their origins in the period in which the NEI were created.

Giving the NEI a New Impulse: the Long Battle for the NEI's Institutional Renewal

At the founding of the NEI, Italian, Austrian and Swiss Christian Democrats, each for their own reasons, argued in favour of the creation of a truly political inter-party International, which would be able to compete with the Socialist International and the Cominform. Their ambitions, however, as we saw earlier, were shelved mainly by their French and Belgian colleagues. Halfway through 1949, the Italian DCI, the Austrian ÖVP and the Swiss PCPS formed a tripartite commission which again placed the question of forming an International on the agenda. The MRP, in reaction, manoeuvered Robert Bichet into the chair of the secretary-general and decided to enlarge the powers of that position by opening up the post of chairman to an annual renewal. It then proposed that August De Schryver take up the post of chairman. De Schryver had a moderate profile and was furthermore an opponent of an inter-party arrangement.

Later measures seemed principally aimed at consolidating the existing power arrangements. At the meeting of the executive committee of 6 December 1952, the re-election of the bureau was on the agenda. August De Schryver's chairmanship was also at its end. Bichet seized upon the planned restructuring to "exceptionally" extend the mandate of the bureau and the chairman by one year, adjusting the statutes accordingly. Bichet hoped with his proposal, in the first place, to avert a possible shift in power.

In those circumstances, maintaining continuity seemed the most acceptable option to both "factions" within the NEI, even if it wasn't ever put in those terms. The oldest vice-president, the Luxemburg Christian Democrat Schaus, presented the European integration process explicitly as an argument for why not to fiddle with the status quo: "This time, the idea of a united Europe is really gaining ground, and those who started the job need to be present at the moment of its potential realization." De Schryver's candidature, in any regard, had the advantage of being acceptable to everyone. For this reason, even Rosenberg could eventually resign himself to the changes in the statutes. In a letter to Bichet, just before the meeting of the executive committee, Rosenberg had admitted that it would be very difficult to find someone who could fill De Schryver's shoes. Rosenberg thought that insecurity over the leadership of the NEI should be avoided not so much because of European integration, but more because of the coming elections in Austria, Italy and West Germany.

In exchange for his support, the Swiss expected De Schryver to improve the cooperation and coordination between the Christian Democratic parties.[414] Under those conditions, De Schryver's mandate was extended by one year.[415] One month later, he had already laid out the limits within which the potential reform of the NEI could take place: "Actually, a number of political parties may believe that the NEI have to adopt their policy. Some historians think that a NEI representative is always a man with a great mind, a kind of éminence grise sent by his government. We are neither: our organization is a mixed one, which we consider very advantageous. We have to maintain that position and

---

414   Letter from Rosenberg to Bichet, 02/12/1952. ACDP, IX-002-005/2.
415   Procès-verbal du Comité Exécutif, 06/12/1952. ACDP, IX-002-005/2. De Schryver's mandate
       would continue until 1959. Procès-verbal du Comité Directeur, 14/11/1953. ACDP, IX-002-003.

avoid creating an International consisting of parties. Such an organization would not serve the Christian Democratic ideal."[416]

In December 1953 the DCI, the PCPS and the ÖVP, this time accompanied by the CDU, again saw their chance to make their move.[417] The parties submitted a joint memorandum with a number of proposals to reform. The underlying thought was again that the NEI should not remain a "philosophical discussion forum" or a "study center", but that they had to evolve into a political inter-party organization. Rosenberg wanted to reduce what he saw as the pernicious grip that the MRP had on the NEI by setting up a NEI secretariat for the German-speaking world in Bonn. At the same time, the secretariat in Paris had to be strengthened (or partially taken away from the French) via the creation of the position of a deputy secretary-general. In this way, it was hoped that the NEI could redouble their activities in Strasbourg, both in the ECSC group as well as within the European Assembly. At the same time relations with the European movement and its various organizations could be intensified.[418]

An important sentence in the memorandum, which apparently was overlooked, stated that the workings of the NEI should not remain limited to Europe. According to the drafters of the memorandum, Europe was just a stop along the way: "Our European unity is just a step in the direction of a united world. The NEI's universalist mission will have to be supported by the examination of the possibilities to make contact with non-European countries". Canada, Brazil and the United States were named in particular. It is remarkable that alongside the request to strengthen and globalize the organization, the case for a clear "confessional" interpretation of world politics was also pleaded: "A profound study, which would recognize the moral authority of the spiritual leaders of Christianity, and which would examine the moral principles in the encyclicals, in papal statements and in statements by the heads of protestant churches, could help Christians safely define the right direction regarding their temporal deeds".[419] Lastly, the proposal to regularly assemble the secretaries-general of the European Christian Democratic parties came the closest to the setting up of an inter-party organization. On 31 May 1954,

416   Procès-verbal du Comité Exécutif, 31/01/1953. ACDP, IX-002-003.
417   According to Chenaux the immediate cause was the European euphoria at the time. Chenaux, "Les Nouvelles Équipes Internationales," 246.
418   Procès-verbal du Comité Exécutif, 14/11/1953. ACDP, IX-002-003; Procès-verbal du Comité Directeur, 12/6/1954. ACDP, IX-002-003.
419   Mémoire sur le développement de l'activité de l'Union internationale des Démocrates chrétiens (NEI) et sur le renforcement adéquat du secrétariat. Berne, le 26/12/1953. ACDP, IX-002-003.

such a meeting would take place for the first time. In later years this practice was continued.[420] The secretary-general of the NEI was as a "full member" closely involved in the working of this parallel forum.

The Swiss and their allies were deeply disappointed when the MRP (again) blocked the evolution towards an inter-party organization by agreeing to a "technical collaboration between secretaries-general" but to no more than that.[421] The fact that the NEI remained a weak organization was very quickly made clear. On 6 December 1954, the Dutchman W.J. Schuijt, who fulfilled the role of the newly created post of deputy secretary-general, presented his evaluation of the operations of the NEI. In the year 1954, despite repeated appeals, there had not been one new subscription to the *NEI Bulletin,* which had been founded in 1952. Only four prominent members had shown their support for the initiative. Schuijt was severe in his condemnation: "This failure is due to the attitude of the member states of the NEI, who have not lived up to their promises. There is a clear lack of team spirit." At the end of 1955, the new secretary-general Coste-Floret came to a similar conclusion in his own report. The following quote from Josef Klaus illustrates the despondency which was prevalent among the Christian Democrats: "Each time when the Socialist International held one of their well-attended congresses, a certain resignation, mixed with a feeling of irritation filled my heart. There is one thought that always keeps tormenting me: why is it so difficult for us to work together on an international level and, if we gather at all, why does that always go with stiff formality?"[422]

In 1954, the reform plans of the Italians and the German-speaking Christian Democrats were only partly realized. Yet, in that same year three evolutions which a few years later would lead to drastic changes took off. Firstly, after the failure of the EDC Treaty, the MRP had lost a lot of credibility, even among its like-minded parties in the NEI. The fact that shortly before the party had been relegated to the opposition confirmed the downfall of the party, which had actually already begun with the elections of 1951.[423] With the party's downfall an important obstacle to the construction of a more political organization of Christian Democratic parties - the ambition of Amintore Fanfani, the new secretary of the Italian DCI - had disappeared. Fanfani, who was secretary

---

420   In 1955 the secretaries-general met five times: 31/05-01/06 (Bonn), 17/09 (Vienna), 19/10 (Paris), 13/12 (Paris) and 20/12 (Brussels).

421   Compte-rendu de la Conférence des Secrétaires Généraux, Bonn, 31/05/1954. ACDP, IX-002-078/1.

422   Klaus, *Macht und Ohnmacht in Österreich*, 415.

423   Van Kemseke, "The societal position of Christian Democracy," 174-188.

of the DCI from 1954 until 1959, hoped to institutionalize the collaboration between Christian Democratic parties on the transnational level.[424] Coincidence or not, it was an Italian, Franco Nobili, who in April 1957, in the capacity of chairman of the IUYCD, called on Coste-Floret to strengthen the NEI. His argument was a familiar one: the fear of a social democratic Europe: "The executive committee of the IUYCD is shocked at the socialist influence on the European institutions (…) We strongly urge you to do everything to ensure that numerous posts will be assigned to loyal Christian Democrats in all important departments of those new institutions. Besides, we are also amazed at the close collaboration between socialist parties, despite their sometimes big differences of opinion. That is why we also urge you to immediately start examining possible methods of work for us, which, on the one hand, must lead to closer collaboration at the highest level of the six Christian Democratic parties in the Community and, on the other hand, must make sure that a permanent link is established between our parties and the representatives of the European institutions."

The competition with the social democrats - a second factor to stimulate the reform of the NEI - would remain a constant concern for the Christian Democrats. In this vein the Swiss Rosenberg was prepared in 1959 to organize the 1960 NEI congress in Switzerland on the condition that it be a congress on Christian Democratic doctrine: "Just as the socialists recently did, the Christian Democratic parties have to revise their program." Kraske went further than Rosenberg: "We will definitely have to confront our points of view with those of the socialists, not only in the field of economy, but also in the field of ideology, since the socialist parties are making an effort to show that they are also pursuing a Christian policy." And in the spring of 1960, there was a growing consensus to make efforts to have the planned change of chairman take place as smoothly as possible "to give the NEI the impulse that it needs, especially in the light of the activity of the socialists", reported the German Louise Rehling. At that same meeting the Luxemburger Margue pointed out that the Christian Democrats needed to defend themselves against the social democrats: "There is not a single reason why we should receive less from the European Movement than the socialists."[425]

From these quotes a third factor becomes apparent. In 1952, the increased pace of European integration prompted the NEI to thoroughly rethink their

---

424   Mayeur, *Des Partis catholiques*, 186.
425   Letter from Nobili to Coste-Floret, 03/04/1957. ACDP, IX-002-007; Procès-Verbal du Comité Directeur, 21/11/1959. ACDP, IX-002-003; Procès-Verbal du Comité Directeur, 20/02/1960. ACDP, IX-002-004.

organizational style. In the period 1957-1959, with the establishment of the European Economic Community and the Euratom, similar discussions took place. In contrast with the early 1950's, the discussion now actually did lead to a strengthening of the links between the Christian Democratic *parties*. In fact this was nothing more than a reflection of the actual power arrangement, with strong Italian and West German parties and a much weakened French MRP. Some important decisions were taken in February 1959, when the chairmen of the parties from the six ECSC countries met their colleagues from Austria and Switzerland in Bonn. They agreed to institutionalize their collaboration by establishing a permanent organization of which the chairmen of each party would be a member. The composition of this "Chairman's Conference" was soon expanded to include many a Christian Democrat occupying an important post in the European institutions. Strictly speaking this was again a "parallel forum" functioning alongside the NEI.

The gathering in Bonn had consequences for the NEI as well. There was a structural link between the two organizations. The gatherings of the Chairman's Conference, for instance, had to be initiated by the NEI chairman, who could attend the gatherings as well. The NEI also got a silent nod to expand into other regions - Scandinavia and Africa were explicitly named - and were stimulated to strengthen its working methods.[426]

On a more general level, the call to action from the chairmen in Bonn strengthened the exercise which had begun shortly before with a memorandum from the Dutchman W.P. Berghuis to the bureau of the NEI. Berghuis was the chairman of the Anti-revolutionary Party (ARP) and the vice-chairman of the Dutch NEI équipe.[427] Before delivering his memorandum, Berghuis had discussed it carefully with his colleagues in the CHU and the KVP, the two other political parties which belonged to the Dutch équipe. In particular the KVP, which dominated the Dutch équipe, had some enthusiastic and deeply concerned Europeans in the persons of Sassen, Klompé and Schmelzer - not at all unknown in the NEI - who thought it important that the NEI adapt to the new European reality. Berghuis' memorandum must be understood in this context.

---

426   Procès-Verbal du Comité Directeur, 13/02/1959. Paris. ACDP, IX-002-003.
427   Since 1954, apart from representatives of the Catholic People's Party, the Dutch équipe also consisted of representatives of the Protestant Antirevolutionary Party and the Christian Historic Union.

In his memorandum, dated 8 October 1958, Berghuis brought together several ideas concerning the reorganization of the movement. The initial premise of the memorandum was the unfortunate observation that the strength of the NEI was in no way comparable to that of the CTUI or to that of the Socialist International, despite the fact that "large and important political parties" belonged to the NEI. A strengthening of the organizational structure, the decision making process, and the NEI's ability to take action was essential, "on both the European level and on the level of worldwide collaboration".[428] With these words, a new battle over the reorganization of the NEI could begin.

The term battle is undoubtedly befitting, since the opposing camps were still ideologically far afield. Precisely for this reason, the NEI rejected a German proposal to dedicate the next congress of the NEI (their thirteenth congress) to the subject of "the collaboration of the Christian Democrats in Western Europe"."The organization of the Christian Democratic *parties* in Europe" could certainly be discussed in the committee meeting which would take place in the margins of the congress, but not openly in the congress hall. Several NEI members thought it "too dangerous" (to use the Belgian Lohest's words) to discuss such a subject in public.[429]

Lohest's assessment turned out to be correct. Shortly before the congress, the divisions came clearly to the surface during the committee meeting of 13 February 1959, when the above-mentioned "Bonn call to action" and Berghuis' proposals were discussed. At first sight Berghuis' remedy was anything but revolutionary. It was in part the same remedy which had already been proposed during the crisis in the spring of 1951: the affiliated parties should take more interest in the work of the NEI, by for example sending their political leaders to NEI gatherings. The executive committee and the various commissions needed to become more active and to state their intentions more often to the world at large, and the budget needed to be increased. Another proposal was that the office of secretary-general needed to be strengthened and that a deputy secretary-general be appointed:"It is clear that the Secretariat cannot continue to be a minor job; we do need a secretary-general who can devote all his time and attention to the international duties of the Christian Democratic parties".[430] Berghuis proposed raising the

428   Aide-mémoire Berghuis, added to the Procès-Verbal du Comité Directeur, 13/02/1959, Paris. ACDP, IX-002-003.
429   Procès-Verbal du Comité Directeur, 13/02/1958. ACDP, IX-002-003.
430   Aide-mémoire Berghuis, added to Procès-Verbal du Comité Directeur, 13/02/1959, Paris. ACDP, IX-002-003.

budget by 3 million francs, of which 2 million would be earmarked for the creation of a permanent secretariat, and 1 million for travel costs. Berghuis thought that only then the NEI would be ready to expand into Great Britain and Scandinavia, while at the same time strengthening their intercontinental ties. To make a comparison with the Socialist International: the NEI needed to find their own "Julius Braunthal". Braunthal having received his permanent salaried position as secretary-general of the SI almost ten years earlier.

Berghuis' proposal to reform the secretariat was supported by the Swiss, the British, and cautiously by the Germans, but it came up against the total opposition of the French. From the confidential correspondence between Coste-Floret and MRP chairman André Colin, we can glean that the French saw Berghuis' proposal as a new effort to undermine the post of secretary-general, which traditionally rested in French hands. Coste-Floret insisted it be emphasized that the still to be created position of deputy secretary-general would only take over *some* of the tasks of the secretary-general, and that the position first and foremost was an *administrative* one. "Otherwise", he thought, "the Dutch will have succeeded in removing the French from the Secretariat by a cunning trick, which they have been wanting for a long time."[431] Eventually, the entire question of the reorganization of the NEI was passed on to a new still to be founded committee, a tried and tested method in the NEI of indefinitely deferring bothersome subject matters.

This "solution", however, could not prevent the question from being discussed during the congress in March 1959, despite its never explicitly having been placed on the agenda. Several speakers - Italians, Germans and Austrians - used their speaking time to express their dissatisfaction. The Italian Bernassola stated that no one could be satisfied with the current working style of the NEI. "There must be created", he continued, "a union which knows how to direct itself, which raises and follows attentively all the problems which loom on all the people of the world; there must be created a union using all appropriate instruments to constitute a true political force in Europe and in the Christian Democratic world which will have repercussions on the international plane."[432] The contributions of the German Franz Meyers, who called for a "more efficient organism of Christian Democratic groups and parties", and the Austrian Friedrich Weigand-Abendroth were closely connected with the above statement.

---

431   Letter from Coste-Floret to Colin, 11/06/1959. ACDP, IX-002-89.
432   NEI Congress in Fribourg, 28-30/03/1959. ACDP, IX-002-008.

The idea of an inter-party organization could still count on much sympathy in certain corners. Two months after the congress, the executive committee of the NEI approved a resolution whereby all parties were called upon to formulate a collective Christian Democratic doctrine on the basis of which they should jointly develop policy.[433] This call, not incidentally, makes one think back to the efforts of 1952-1953 to develop an ideological program, in conjunction with the attempt to fundamentally reorganize the organization, giving it a more political character.

The call for renewal at the end of 1958 and in the spring of 1959 had smaller as well as larger consequences. The most spectacular of these was undoubtedly the replacement of the leadership of the organization. In July, August De Schryver announced that he wished to step down as chairman. Two weeks earlier he had already informed Coste-Floret of his decision, but to most people it came as a complete surprise. In the notice which the NEI published as a result of De Schryver's resignation, it was explained that he "had been called to take up new and heavy responsibilities", this being a reference to his nomination as the Belgian minister of the Congo, in September 1959.[434] Privately, interim chairman Nicolas Margue gave another explanation. After an engagement of ten years, De Schryver thought it high time to pass the torch to someone from another country. In this way he hoped to give the organizational renewal a chance. Perhaps De Schryver had understood that his vision of the NEI as a non-binding association, a vision which had been much under attack, was no longer tenable. De Schryver was continually warning against too quick an expansion of the NEI. He opposed "proposals which suggest that the NEI be replaced by an organization that would bring all Christian Democratic parties together under one authority. Each party must preserve its autonomy, since its role in domestic politics depends on its position in parliament and in the government."[435]

Secretary-general Coste-Floret was of the same mind and also decided not to stand for re-election. De Schryver's suggestion of immediately passing the leadership on to two new countries was not followed through however. France grabbed the post of secretary-general (the function went to Jean Seitlinger), and as there was no viable candidate forthcoming from any other country for the chairmanship, it again went to Belgium, to the Belgian

---

433 Procès-Verbal du Comité Directeur, 30/05/1959. ACDP, IX-002-008. A subcommittee was set up to that end.
434 Procès-Verbal du Comité Directeur, 21/11/1959. ACDP, IX-002-003.
435 Procès-Verbal du Comité Directeur, 06/10/1956. ACDP, IX-002-003.

Theo Lefèvre. At that same time, the Belgian CVP-PSC decided to join the NEI as a party, which gave the clear signal that the party was behind an inter-party organization. Only the French and the British Christian Democratic équipes resisted joining the NEI at party level. The MRP would join as a party in 1964, at a moment when the party no longer had any real political power.

The NEI entered the 1960's not only under a new leadership, but also with some changes in its organizational structure. On 21 June 1960, the bureau decided to create, or better yet to re-create, the position of deputy secretary-general. Between 1954 and 1957 the Dutchman Schuijt had fulfilled that role until he became a member of the Dutch Parliament in 1956, which barred him from fulfilling his duties in the NEI. The nomination of Schuijt in 1954 had principally been intended to help the NEI maintain and expand its European network, in particular in the newly formed European institutions. In 1960, a different reason was given for the reinstitution of the position of deputy secretary-general. According to the commission which under the chairman-ship of the Italian Nobili had to prepare the reorganization of the NEI, the reorganization needed to lead not only to the organization's expansion into the European countries where Christian Democracy had hardly penetrated, or into Latin America, where collaboration remained limited to the exchanging of documents. It also and especially needed to lead to expansion into Africa, "where, due to the current evolutions, there are great opportunities for Chris-tian Democracy, all of high importance".

The replacement of the leadership of the NEI and the introduction of the position of deputy secretary-general weren't the only visible signs of the restructuring of the organization. The bureau and the executive committee decided to make a thorough evaluation of all the existing commissions. In the NEI, the most important commissions were the Political, Social-Economic and Cultural Commissions, as well as Van Zeeland's East-West Commission, which in May 1958 would be rebaptized the Commission for the Study of Interna-tional Politics. In July 1955, two new commissions had been brought into exis-tence: one which was to focus on "the difficulties in the different parliaments, caused by the proposition of a peaceful coexistence between East and West", and one which was directed at "the most suitable legal possibilities to harmo-nize fiscal and social changes in the six member states of the CECA". In the same year, the executive committee added another commission: one which would "intensify the promotion of European ideas, clarify problems regarding the European unification and promote the collaboration of Christian Democratic forces to help create the European unity".[436]

Any reorganization of these existing commissions would have to make space for the increased attention for Africa in the NEI. The new chairman, Theo Lefèvre, ensured that the transformation happened quickly. For some parties, things went a bit too quickly, but Lefèvre put a direct stop to the discussions which had already been dragging on for years. The Political Commission already for some time had hardly shown a sign of life and was subsequently abolished. In the second half of the 1950's, the Social-Economic Commission (SEC) hauled its own weight, delivering valuable work, yet, nonetheless, it remained extremely weak in terms of its organization. Beginning in 1957, SEC chairman Raymond Scheyven gradually began to find it more and more difficult to combine his political career with his responsibilities to the SEC. The Commission therefore was looking for a new leader. In February 1960, Albert Lohest, who was already functioning as the de facto chairman, was elected to the position.[437] The "reorganized" SEC set two priorities for itself. Besides continuing to follow through with the European integration process, they also decided to pay attention to "Third World issues" (in the NEI they already spoke of "the Third World" and not of "underdeveloped countries" or "insufficiently developed countries"). That topic, as usual, was considered from a European perspective. A new ad hoc subcommission "Christian Democrats and the Third World" - a subcommission of the SEC - with Roger Reynaud as chair would devote itself to that issue.

The most important aspect of the renewal was the approval of Berghuis' proposal to set up a "Study and Documentation Center" in Rome, an idea suggested by the Italian DCI. By November 1960, the "International Christian Democratic Study and Documentation Center" (CIDCED) was up and running. The leadership of the center was entrusted to the Dutchman K.J. Hahn, and its purpose was to study political problems, allowing the parties to work out their doctrine. Additionally it was meant to contribute to the global expansion of Christian Democratic thinking. The Hahn Center, as the CIDCED was usually called, took its globalization mission "with the intention of increasing our influence and our actions in Latin America and Africa" seriously and very soon made a name for itself. At the end of November, for example, the Hahn Center together with the Political Academy of the CDU organized an international conference of development experts, in the German city of Eichholz, near Bonn, in order to work out a Christian Democratic development policy.

436   Procès-Verbal du Comité Directeur, 17/09/1955. ACDP, IX-002-003.

Hahn's (and the Italians') initiatives soon raised the suspicions of the French and the Belgians. The Frenchman Farine pointed out that the Social-Economic Commission of the NEI was more than capable of studying African issues. Moreover, the secretary-general and the executive committee of the NEI were responsible for policy, and therefore also for development policy. The Belgian Degimbe, who sat on the Social-Economic Commission, lamented that certain initiatives - he was referring in particular to the colloquium in Eichholz - were taken up by Hahn without involving the SEC. In his defense Hahn wrote to Seitlinger stating that up until a month before the meeting in Eichholz he had never even heard of the SEC.[438] Secretary-general Seitlinger cleared up the matter: relations with the "Third World" fell under the jurisdiction of the SEC because it was a socio-economic question. If political aspects came along with it, then they would fall under the jurisdiction of the NEI executive committee. At the same time, he insisted that there had to be more coopera-tion with the Hahn Center.

The importance of the meeting in Eichholz was that the Hahn Center, the SEC and its subcommission, experts from mainly the CDU and the DCI and, of course, Sieniewicz' CDUCE (who had been involved with the initiative since the beginning) all came together under one roof. The CDUCE, in the mean time, had been quick in "discovering" Africa, as shown for example by this passage from their correspondence: "For the time being, the CDUCE expects to increase its activity in Latin America and to start contacts with the African Christian Democratic leaders. Our sponsors are interested in a school for younger African Christian Democrats".[439]

On the basis of the cooperation which started in Eichholz, increasing numbers of contacts were made in Africa, starting in the early 1960's. The CDU, to give a very concrete example, maintained contact with the Confédération Chrétienne des Syndicats Malgaches and the Rassemblement Chrétien in Madagascar and they passed these contacts on to Seitlinger and Hahn via CDU chairman Kraske, who was also present in Eichholz.[440] Hahn himself had already taken the initiative, at the end of 1960, to organize a meeting between European Christian Democrats and a number of African parliamentarians who were taking part in the Afro-European meeting of

437   Commission Économique et Sociale, 19/02/1960. ACDP, IX-002-042. The SEC archives, which are rather exhaustive, do not contain documents that make mention of meetings in 1959
438   Letter from Hahn to Seitlinger, 28/10/1961.
439   Letter from Prochazka to Seitlinger, 29/11/1961. ACDP, IX-002-079/1.
440   ACDP, IX-002-094. The "Rassemblement chrétien" (Fivondronana Kristianina Malagasy) was an alliance of eleven small regional parties.

the European Parliamentary Assembly in Strasbourg, in June 1961. In the 1960's, the Hahn Center would play an important role in the global expansion process of the NEI in other ways as well. The center published a bimonthly journal covering worldwide Christian Democratic activities in French, English and Spanish. Additionally, they consistently gathered information on Christian Democratic parties and movements worldwide, and organized courses for young Africans, Latin Americans and Asian political leaders.[441] At the same time the center also functioned as an important contact point for Christian Democrats outside Europe.

The coordination with the NEI at that moment, however, left much to be desired. Among other things, the SEC accused the NEI of not taking action on the resolutions which had been approved by the Paris congress of 1960. Seitlinger admitted as much to Hahn but he also had criticism for the SEC: "The SEC should improve their carrying out the tasks that we assign to them; especially at the recent meeting in Eichholz a clear lack of coherence was shown."[442] Nevertheless, it was clear that the NEI had already begun to work on the structures which would buttress the global expansion of the organization.

Institutional Renewal as a Step in the Direction of Global Expansion

The establishment of the Hahn Center, the creation of the ad hoc subcommission "Christian Democrats and the Third World", and the reinstitution of the position of deputy secretary-general all facilitated the global expansion process of the NEI. That was, as a matter of fact, their main purpose. The re-establishment of the function of deputy secretary-general was even explicitly justified by the need for the NEI to expand into the African continent.

Opening up institutional ties with Africa was a relatively new theme in the NEI. Above it has already been mentioned that 'Africa' entered into the NEI discourse following discussions on Africa in the European institutions. European politics was not the only reason however. The African context itself would become ever more important, especially since the years 1957 and 1958.

---

441   Rapport des Activités du Centre International Démocrate-Chrétien d'Etudes et de Documentation, November 1960. ACDP, IX-002-069.
442   Letter from Seitlinger to Hahn, 29/11/1961. ACDP, IX-002-043.

When in 1957, Macmillan became the prime minister of Great Britain one of his first acts was to order an expense analysis of British colonial policy. This brought to light that the British colonies in general did not bring in all that much more than what they cost to the Treasury.[443] Consequently, British interests were not necessarily served by stubbornly holding on to British colonial control over large tracts of Africa, where at the end of the 1950's the call for independence began to ring ever louder. Macmillan's policy, therefore, was primarily aimed at "guiding" the colonies towards independence, determining the tempo of that process as far as possible and in the end integrating the former colonies into the British Commonwealth.[444]

In France, there was a similar evolution. After "Sakhiet" in February 1958, the indignation over France's Algerian policy rose sharply, both inside and outside the country. In the French government the idea that it was no longer profitable to continue with the colonial system was gradually beginning to take hold. The reasoning went that it was more remunerative to transfer labor-intensive types of production to friendly overseas areas than to invest in maintaining colonial production of raw materials. For some time Algeria would remain a special case - too much had already been invested there - but elsewhere in Africa, De Gaulle, who had become prime minister on 1 June 1958, made quick work of the transfer of power. Via bilateral negotiations, at least twelve French colonies in Africa, including Madagascar, had received their independence by the end of 1960.[445]

In both the French and the British territories decolonialization followed a gradual process whereby internal self-administration was increasingly granted. In other words, a political space came into existence, in which political parties would be able to compete with each other in - one hoped - democratic surroundings. This was also the case in the Belgian Congo. In its "Congo Manifesto" of February 1956, the Belgian CVP-PSC - the party of NEI chairman De Schryver - voiced its support for recognition of a certain amount of "internal independence" in the colony, within the context of a Belgo-Congolese community. This "internal independence" included the holding of local elections, intended to train domestic politicians for a later time when national elections would be held.[446]

443   Morgan, *The Official History of Colonial Development, 5*, 88-100.
444   Goldsworthy, *The Conservative Government, 1951-1957* and in the same series Hyam, *The Conservative Government, 1957-1964*; Murphy, *Party Politics and Decolonization, 1951-1964*.
445   Ageron, *La Décolonisation française.*
446   CVP-Kongomanifest, February 1956. KADOC, CEPESS 7.1.

Almost automatically, this threw up the question of forming or encouraging Christian Democratic parties. De Schryver himself was no advocate of founding a Congolese Christian Democratic party. He thought the political climate in the Congo, and in Africa in general, to be too different from that of Belgium or Western Europe to be able to set up parties there according to the European model. His fellow party member Theo Lefèvre, however, thought a Congolese Christian Democratic party well worth the effort and proposed exploring the potentialities.[447] Here too, it seemed that in 1960, Lefèvre was better suited than De Schryver to the task that the NEI - which were slowly preparing to become an inter-party organization - saw before themselves in Africa: establishing contact with existing or still to be founded African parties.

Decolonialization and the consequent expected creation of a political playing field made Africa not only attractive to Christian Democrats, but also to communists. Until that point the United States had more or less ignored the African continent. In his study of the Cold War in Africa, Fred Marte spoke of a policy of "benign neglect".[448] The US chose to keep the USSR out of the region by keeping themselves out and by supporting their NATO allies who were much more at home in Africa. By the end of the decade, however, things were beginning to change. Krushchev, who had gained control of Soviet diplomacy halfway through 1955, directed Soviet foreign policy increasingly towards Africa. The Twentieth Party Congress, in February 1956, voted to dramatically increase development aid to Africa. The triangle of Ghana, Guinea and Mali would, after they became independent, be able to profit the most from this help. The offensive which the USSR seemed to be launching in the area, called for an effective containment campaign. With this in mind, American vice-president Richard Nixon visited eight African nations in February and March 1957, including Ghana.

The "scramble for Africa", which had to be won from the USSR, was a leitmotif at the NEI congress in Paris in 1960. The idea of the West being involved in a race with the USSR came out of a very concrete proposal which NEI interim chairman Theo Lefèvre launched in Paris. He suggested that the Western European universities reserve a certain number of places for students from developing countries. The possibility of even establishing a European University was discussed, as a possible balance to what already existed in the USSR.[449] The fact that the Cold War was now not only raging in Central

447   CVP Bureau, 09/11/1957. KADOC, CVP 1.2.1.7.; Kwanten, *August-Edmond De Schryver*, 505-506.
448   Marte, *Political Cycles in International Relations*, 74-75.
449   Congrès des NEI, Paris, 22-24/09/1960. ACDP, IX-002-022. Campbell, *Soviet Policy*, 42.

America - read Cuba - but also in Africa - read the Congo - a region that until recently had been solidly in Western hands, came as a shock to many of those present at the congress. Maurice Schumann succinctly summarized the urgency of the situation when he spoke of "Africa which is still doubting, but which will before long make up its mind: accept the offers from the East or sit back and just enjoy its hard-won freedom, realizing that colonialism is almost over."[450] The Polish exile Stefan Glaser went so far as to predict the "death of Europe" if Africa were to fall into the Soviet sphere of influence. Once Africa was controlled, all that was needed was "one small leap over the Mediterranean pond" to have Europe under the Soviet heel. The gauntlet in Hungary which had not been taken up in 1956, "out of respect for Potsdam", now needed to be taken up, and an ideal method of doing so would be to coordinate the development aid of Western Europe and the United States. After all, anti-communism had always been paired with a strong dose of pro-Atlanticism. In this vein the French position in NATO was most explicitly condemned, because it could place in jeopardy the unity of that organization.

While around 1960, the global expansion of the organization was primarily directed at Africa, it was, however, not limited to that continent. To some extent, it also had an impact on relations with Latin America, and with the United Nations.

Under their new secretary-general Seitlinger - who himself for some time had represented France in the UN - the NEI began paying more attention to their contacts with the UN. Sieniewicz fully used that opportunity to increase his role. He regularly, for example, organized a breakfast in the UN banquet hall to which various speakers were invited. In 1960 he invited Moreau de Melen, Belaunde and Kenneth Thompson, the director of the Rockefeller Foundation. In his reports to the NEI, Sieniewicz also explicitly mentioned the presence of William Clancy, John Inman, Miss Frances Grant and Cloyce Houston. It is possible that some of the financial backers of the CDUCE, about whom so little is known, were among those invited. He continued to regret, however, the lack of coordination between the Christian Democratic representatives in the UN, but had high expectations that the NEI would back him in his move to set up a "Christian Democratic group" in the UN, which would lend an institutional context to the receptions and soirées which he and his co-worker Sleszynski organized.[451] Things would only remain in the realm of good inten-

450   Congrès des NEI, Paris, 22-24/09/1960. ACDP, IX-002-022.
451   Rapport sur le Travail de la Représentation des NEI auprès de l'ONU, 1959-1960. ACDP, IX-002-079/1.

tions, however. Seitlinger realized that a financial contribution from the NEI was out of the question, but he did insist that the bureau designate a contact person with the NEI who would closely follow the workings of the UN. The choice fell to K.J. Hahn, the director of the above mentioned "International Christian Democratic Study and Documentation Center". Very quickly an agreement was reached. Seitlinger wrote to the various parties requesting that they insist that their respective governments include sufficient Christian Democratic representation in their UN delegations, and that the names of the representatives be sent to Sieniewicz or Sleszynski.[452] Every year, before the sessions of the UN General Assembly and the Ecosoc, Sleszynski would send a copy of the agendas to Hahn so that his study center could better prepare itself for the UN gatherings.

These sorts of cosmetic measures could, however, hardly hide the lack of enthusiasm for the UN in the NEI. At the congress in Paris, for example, Theo Lefèvre was extremely negative about the United Nations and - a little bit more subtly - about the Afro-Asian countries themselves: "Since the foundation of the UN, the so-called 'colonialist' countries have had to endure numerous attacks of the new member countries, usually Afro-Asiatic, and they have had to incessantly fight a rearguard action against them (…) It seems paradoxical that this anti-colonial bloc is led, or lets itself be led, by the colonial power with the least scruples, the USSR, whose colonial empire extends as far as the Iron Curtain". He lamented that countries such as France, Belgium, Great Britain and Portugal were continually and often unjustifiably being attacked - the French for their involvement in Algeria, the Belgians for their Congo policy. In his capacity as a Belgian politician he also used the opportunity to thank France and Germany, who had supported Belgium in the Security Council. He praised the solidarity among the Western Europeans, which deserved to be encouraged. In his eyes, the UN was all too often used by the forces of anti-colonialism, against "those European countries with a high level of civilization, under whose guardianship insufficient developed regions had been placed".[453] Thankfully not everyone chose for the "East", a reference to Congolese General Mobutu's actions against the Soviet embassy in his country. The congress gave Lefèvre a standing ovation for his address.[454]

452   Letter from Seitlinger to all the secretaries-general of the Christian Democratic parties, 03/07/1961. ACDP, IX-002-079/1.
453   Congrès des NEI, Paris, 22-24/09/1960. ACDP, IX-002-022.
454   Ibidem.

In such circumstances, Sleszynski's and Sieniewicz's proposals to strengthen the ties with the UN didn't stand much of a chance. Sleszynski's suggestion to hold a banquet at the end of November 1961 for all Christian Democratic UN envoys was passed over by Seitlinger: "I will not hide the fact that many of the friends whom I have consulted did not think this is the right time to make a special effort and coordinate our parties at the UN (…) Do believe me that I am by no means conveying the thoughts of the French, whose position is already clear and known, but rather those of our Belgian and German friends."[455]

The NEI were also somewhat ambiguous in their relations with Latin America. In 1959, they had rather abruptly broken off the discussion launched by Latin American Christian Democrats on the creation of a future Christian Democratic world organization. In February 1960, however, the NEI reacted very positively - at least officially - to an invitation from the CDUCE and the ODCA to take part in a third intercontinental (or 'world') conference, which would take place in June 1961, in Santiago de Chile. The departing secretary-general Coste-Floret underlined "the importance of stronger ties with our Latin American friends".[456] The Hahn Center - again - played an important role in these relations. Hahn made contact with various Latin American Christian Democrats and attempted to stimulate exchanges of party programs, pamphlets and similar material.

The Cuban Revolution was undoubtedly largely responsible for the NEI's increased interest. It was all too clear in Europe that Latin America - which had now more democracies than ever before - was particularly vulnerable to the "rising expectations" that Castro's takeover had brought about. During a meeting of the executive committee in February 1960, Arnaldo Ferragni, of the youth organization IUYCD, explicitly referred to the communist threat in Latin America: "Latin America is being terribly threatened by intense communist propaganda." At the same meeting Landaburu presented a report on the Cuban Christian Democratic movement in exile. The events in Cuba stimulated the IUYCD to organize a conference together with Latin American youth organizations. Shortly before, the youth organization had set up a "Global Organization", the executive committee of which consisted of Christian Democrats from Eastern and Western Europe and Latin America.

455 Letter from Seitlinger to Sleszynski, 31/10/1961. ACDP, IX-002-079/1.
456 Procès-Verbal du Comité Directeur, 20/02/1960. ACDP, IX-002-004.

As soon as the NEI had decided to establish ties with Latin America (in February 1960) things moved quickly. In September 1960, the executive committee of the NEI, in Sieniewicz' and Tomas Reyes Vicuña's presence, was suddenly ready to consider a reworked version of the *Groupe de Liaison Intercontinental Démocrate Chrétien* (GLIDC) project. The approval of the statutes at the meeting of the executive committee on 7 April 1961, three months later, resulted in the creation of the International Christian Democratic Union, during the third intercontinental conference (which from that time on would be known as a "world conference"). As a member of the Chilean Christian Democratic Party, which hosted the gathering, Radomiro Tomic, was able to call out: "We are a worldwide force!"[457]

The NEI was part of that "worldwide force", and did not object to being so. At the same time, however, they were limited in their enthusiasm, let alone that they had played a pioneering role. This was once more made apparent in the correspondence of NEI secretary-general Seitlinger. In public the NEI had reacted positively to the Chilean invitation to the third intercontinental conference, but in his correspondence Seitlinger expressed his reserves. The NEI would not even be able to send a delegation, unless all travel and lodging costs were completely covered by the organizers. That is exactly what happened. On 22 July, five representatives of the NEI flew (economy class) to Chile. The more motivated - and better financed - CDU, DCI and the Basque Nationalist Party each sent one representative at their own cost.[458]

Even Hahn, who took relations with Latin America very closely to heart, had reservations. He had been asked to lay out in his speech in Santiago the basic framework for a "Christian Democratic International". In a letter to Seitlinger he expressed that he was not too pleased with the idea: "I do not think it expedient to develop clear ideas about a specific and elaborate international Christian Democratic organization, because that is not yet possible. I will limit myself to stressing the necessity of permanently keeping in close touch with each other, interchanging ideas and experiences."[459] And that is precisely what he did.

To put it briefly, it was with a certain amount of reserve that the NEI ventured beyond Europe. In contrast with the Christian Democratic exiles

457 Speech Tomic. Santiago de Chile, 27-30/07/1961. ACDP, IX-002-029.
458 Letter from Seitlinger to Walker, 14/06/1961; Letter from Reyes to Seitlinger, 15/06/1961. ACDP, IX-002-029.
459 Letter from Hahn to Seitlinger, 13/07/1961. ACDP, IX-002-029.

from Eastern Europe, the NEI did not eye like a hawk every meter of ground that the communists won. In the spring of 1959, for example, Sieniewicz had expressed his concern regarding recent events in Tibet, where "once again spiritual forces lost out to communist aggression". He denounced the "inertia" of the non-communist world in a dossier which he thought was of great importance to the peoples of Asia and Africa. He also asked the NEI to become more involved in the issue: "Our Union is of the opinion that, under the circumstances, the Christian Democrats must make an urgent appeal to form a spiritual global front of politicians, of all religions, against the communist danger in the field of ideology. That appeal should be made by your intercontinental movement." Coste-Floret promised to present his concerns at the meeting of the executive committee, but the minutes of that meeting show no mention of it. In the end Sieniewicz's request was duly filed in the bin.

'We are a Worldwide Force': Defining a Global Strategy on a Regional Basis

In 1960, the NEI had (finally) taken up the repeated offers of the ODCA and the CDUCE and agreed to an institutional association between the three regional groups. Around the same time, the bureau of the NEI had given the green light to expand into Africa and Latin America. It was the "Subcommission on Christian Democrats and the Third World", a subcommission of the Social-Economic Commission, which was asked to work out a strategy for the "construction of a worldwide Christian Democratic network". Not surprisingly, in shaping this global strategy, the subcommission was led by the characteristics of each of the different regions - Africa, Latin America, and Europe.

A 'Pre-Political' Strategy for Africa

Despite the fact that the invitation to the fourteenth NEI congress, in Paris in 1960, explicitly mentioned presentations from representatives from Third World countries on its agenda, attendance by non-Europeans at the congress remained rather limited. There was one representative from Madagascar and there were three delegates from the ODCA, but that was it. Most of the delegates who attended the congress lamented the sorry African showing. When the representative from Madagascar R. Razafimbahyny suggested that the NEI could only truly consider themselves "worthy of being called international" if African parties were also in attendance, he was repeatedly interrupted by loud applause. That same applause was repeated when Fernand Chaussebourg demanded that the Western Europeans in the NEI should all come to the congresses of 1961 and 1962 each of them paired with an African colleague. The advantage which the socialists were thought to have, was often referred to (and blown up). NEI chairman Theo Lefèvre had an explanation for it: "It seems difficult to propagate our movement in Africa because there we are confronted with big problems; socialist parties are rich parties consisting of poor members, our parties are usually poor parties consisting of rich members".[460]

This disadvantage should not, however, prevent the NEI from seriously preparing their contacts with the African countries, added Lefèvre. To that end, the "Subcommission on Christian Democrats and the Third World" was asked to work out a comprehensive strategy. In doing that, the subcommission was inspired by two memoranda, one written by Hahn and another written by the German Walter Molt. The documents were similar in a number of aspects. They both made a fundamental distinction between Africa and Asia on the one hand, where "the traditional and dominant civilization is not Christian", and Latin America on the other hand, where that was not the case and where, moreover, Christian social and political organizations already existed.

In Africa (and Asia) the contacts were necessarily of a "pre-political" or "general political" nature. During his tour in Africa, in June 1962, Molt noticed that there was not much potential for Christian inspired parties.[461] Consequently the NEI had to focus more on social and cultural organizations - volunteer organizations, unions and *perhaps* even churches and missionary organizations - more than on political parties, which more often than not were parties of national unity. In the first phase, direct political action was out of the question. For Hahn this implied that contact would be best established via a "neutral body", independent of the party organizations. In this manner, the Africans and Asians would not have to bind themselves politically and they would be able to maintain a greater degree of autonomy. Hahn realized all too well that European Christian Democracy did not always have a good reputation. In other words, the "Africa experts" in the NEI with their emphasis on "pre-political contacts" defended exactly the same position which their former chairman August De Schryver had defended in his own party, the CVP-

460   Congrès des NEI, Paris, 22-24/09/1960. Speech Theo Lefèvre. ACDP, IX-002-022.
461   Report of Molt's trip to Africa, 22/04-11/06/1962. ACDP, IX-002-094.

PSC, in 1957.[462] The then chairman of the NEI, however, Theo Lefèvre, gave his preference to contacts in a party politics context.

A second aspect which the Africa experts stressed was that the NEI could not allow themselves to be limited to "prominent Christians" but should approach "everyone who in their political and social actions are inspired by spiritual principles and as a consequence are interested in the Christian Democratic movement."[463] As they put it, they were looking for "Christians and non-Christians who are spiritually inspired". It seemed that all were in agreement that every explicit reference to Christian Democracy was undoubtedly an obstacle to expanding the movement in Africa and Asia. In non-Christian regions Christian Democracy - when understood as a religio-philosophical notion - could be seen as a rival religion. Keeping this in mind, the Germans came up with the idea to set up a neutral center, which would be independent of the NEI, but would still draw its inspiration from that organization, and would be able to count on organizational support. In Eichholz all participants had already agreed on the value of a multi-religious starting point. The report of that meeting unambiguously stated: "The Christian Democratic parties have the task to efficiently help the people and groupings in those [African and Asian] countries who share our spiritual and political inspiration. They do not necessarily belong to Christian Democratic parties (…) but they can be any politician of any religious orientation."[464] This text undoubtedly was inspired by August Vanistendael, who was present at the gathering in Eichholz. Perhaps he even held the pen. In his own organization, the CTUI, Vanistendael had fought hard in the previous years for "Christian trade unions action with a spiritual and personalist base" which he thought would open enormous possibilities in Africa and Asia.[465]

At the World Congress of 1963, in Strasbourg, the Christian Democrats took stock of the situation. Africa was still far from being widely represented, but the situation was more promising than it had been in previous years. One of the representatives present was Dombo Thaddé, who at that moment was the chairman of the Parti Démocrate Congolais (PDC), founded in October

---

462 Report of the meeting of the bureau of the CVP, 09/11/1957. KADOC, CVP 1.2.1.7.
463 Aide-mémoire Hahn. Meeting of the enlarged subcommittee 'Christian Democracy and Third World'. San Marino, 28/09/1962. ACDP, IX-002-102/2.
464 Meeting in Eichholz, 27-28/11/1961. ACDP, IX-002-102/2.
465 Pasture, *Histoire du Syndicalisme Chrétien International*, 330. Vanistendael was favourably disposed towards the Hahn center. In his annual report 1962 Hahn mentions that Vanistendael had donated the center 1500 dollars, and that he had promised a second donation of the same amount. CIDCED. Rapport 1962. ACDP, IX-002-069.

1961. This was the party of prime minister Cyrille Adoula and of Joseph Ileo. During a tour in Germany in October 1962, Thaddé had established contact with CDU secretary-general Rasner in an attempt to win moral and financial support from the CDU. Thaddé's trip came only a few months after a CDU representative, Walter Molt from the Institut für Internationale Solidarität in Bonn, had visited the Congo during an exploratory mission to Africa. Molt, who likewise was a member of the "Subcommission on Christian Democrats and the Third World" of the NEI, did not have much positive to say about the political situation in the Congo: "In general, all political groups and organizations more or less only defend their own personal interests." Instead he proposed working together with institutions such as the *Institut Politique Congolais* - an institute for adult education where professors from Lovanium University worked - and the Union of Congolese Workers which was led by the very capable Boboliko. There was but one exception on the political level: Adoula's party. Most likely the necessary contacts where established at that time which led to the eventual participation of Adoula's party in the Strasbourg congress - both Sieniewicz (again!) and the CDU were prepared to stand treat.[466]

Additionally one representative from Basutoland (Lesotho as of 1966) and one from Gabon were present in Strasbourg. Both were brought into contact with the NEI via Molt. The situation in which the Basutoland National Party - the second strongest in the country after the communist Basutoland Congress Party - found itself, presented Seitlinger very directly with another characteristic of the African party landscape. While the communists had six offices, the BNP had but one, which simultaneously served as the bedroom of the secretary-general. The party chairman made sure that a monthly bulletin appeared, which he financed out of his own pocket.[467] The NEI, however, was not willing to risk giving financial support. The only form of support which was available were scholarships for political training.

The African expansion of the NEI, which in 1960 was announced with much bravura, in the end, just like for the socialists, came to no great success. Seitlinger knew very well what was missing: "To succeed, or at least to take a big step forward, we would need to rely on someone whose authority is unquestioned in Africa, and who would be prepared to sacrifice most of his

466   Letters from Thaddé to Seitlinger, 11/12/1962 and 29/01/1963. Letter from Seitlinger to
        Thaddé, 06/06/1963. ACDP, IX-002-094.
467   Letter from Letete to Hahn, 21/11/1962. ACDP, IX-002-049.

time to the creation of an African section of the NEI."[468] A "Maiztegui", who fulfilled that role for the Socialist International in Latin America, was not on hand. According to the NEI leader there was yet another problem: the hoped for political space never manifested in Africa. Africa was dominated by one-party systems and African politicians were "politically immature". They let themselves be influenced by the tribe they belonged to and were interested only in very specific local or regional problems.

This, the NEI had found it to their cost. By the end of 1961, the NEI counted on Henri Effa, who as a representative from Cameroon had participated in the congress in Chile, to set up an African department of the NEI following the model of the ODCA. Soon enough, however, problems had cropped up. Effa complained to Seitlinger about the authoritarian party organization which he - as well as a number of other young party members of the Parti des Démocrates Camerounais (PDC) - threatened to become a victim of: "The whole structure [of the party] leans on just one man, who founded the party and leads it as well. That is one of the reasons why we are trying - using the experience which we gained in several other movements - to enliven the party and to make it look much more sympathetic to the elite, who detest our captain's dictatorship. This is not an easy job, for in Africa, and especially in Cameroon, party leaders easily think that they should behave like traditional chiefs, for whom baiting forms an integral part of their behavior."

In order to enforce his request for support, he pointed out that other parties - the Marxist People's Union of Cameroon and the socialist PSC of Charles Okala - received the support of the Communist and Socialist Internationals. His argument undoubtedly touched a nerve in Paris. The privileged contact between Effa and Seitlinger, however, caused bad blood between Effa and another PDC party leader, André-Marie Mbida. A few months later Effa resigned and joined the governing party, the Union of Cameroon. Three months later the Cameroonian adventure of the NEI had reached its end. In July 1962, the treasurer of the PDC, Pascal Baylon Mvoe, laconically announced: "Democracy has been humiliated". Various leaders such as Mbida, Nana and Okala were arrested. Mvoe attempted via Seitlinger to internationalize what was happening, using among other arguments the argument that Islam was threatening the very existence of Christian civilization in Africa, but Seitlinger remained silent on the issue.[469]

468   Letter from Seitlinger to Chaussebourg, 18/01/1962. ACDP, IX-002-094.
469   Letters from Baylon Mvoe to Seitlinger, 28/08/1962. ACDP, IX-002-049.

Those in the NEI who had built up a certain African expertise realized very well that any transposition of the European "party politics" approach was doomed to failure. Instead the national movements which had "democratic tendencies with a human and societal image anchored in the transcendental" needed to be strengthened. Nyerere's movement was a typical example of this. But this project too was relegated to the back burner. As soon as the restlessness of the years surrounding the wave of African independence subsided, the interest of the NEI in Africa also diminished. Only in 1969 would interest in the continent pick up again. In an internal memo dated 29 April 1969, which the Italian Talentino circulated to the members of the bureau of the European Union of Christian Democrats, the successor of the NEI, he admitted that at the beginning of the decade the time had not yet been ripe for a Christian Democratic presence in Africa.[470]

A Strategy for Latin America:
Discouraging the Emergence of a Third Way

In contrast with Africa, the "Subcommission on Christian Democrats and the Third World" came to the conclusion that in the Western Hemisphere, where references to Christianity posed no problem, the NEI could maintain direct contacts at a party level. According to Hahn, however, Latin America posed another problem: "We may not disregard the fact that the Latin American Christian Democrats find themselves in a political situation which must take into account both national and international issues. As a result, they have developed rather progressive socio-economic programs, and they feel sympathetic towards a third way between the two power blocks. It is gener-ally known that this inclination is nourished by a distrust of the United States. The European Christian Democrats can not avoid the discussion on this topic."[471]

Hahn's analysis touched upon two important and sensitive issues in Latino-European cooperation around 1960: the "advanced socio-economic program" of the Latin American Christian Democrats, and the Cuban Revolution, to which it was inseparably linked. Almost everywhere in Latin America the Revolution had strengthened the call for change. Land reform, for instance, was an issue in the forefront of people's minds. In those countries where the democratic system was strong enough to channel the demands of a large

---

470   Letter from Talentino to the members of the Bureau, 29/04/1969. ACDP, IX-004-052.
471   Aide-mémoire Hahn. Meeting of the enlarged subcommittee 'Christian Democracy and Third World'. Vienna, 22/06/1962. ACDP, IX-002-102/2.

percentage of the population, there was a noteworthy shift to the left. This was for example the case in Chile, where Christian Democracy had reached political maturity. Land reform, along with several other reformist measures, was central to the platform with which the Christian Democrats sent their candidate Frei to the elections of 1964. This program of "comunitarismo", which was also to be found among other parties, largely determined the socio-economic program of the ODCA, but according to Frei the Western European Christian Democrats were not yet ripe for such a program. When the ideologue of the PDC, Castillo, wished to present this "comunitarismo" to the 1961 World Conference in Santiago, Frei called him back: the subject would lead to too much friction with the NEI. This can be linked to what Ricardo Melgar Bao noted in his study of Latin American trade unionism: "The Latin American Christian Democrats defended a third way between capitalism and communism (…) At the beginning of the 1960's, the Christian Democratic governments of Germany (Adenauer), Italy (Gronchi and Segni) and Belgium (Eyskens) were no shining example to the Christian Democrats in Latin America."[472]

At least one Western European Christian Democrat, Hahn, seemed to understand the "far-reaching political formulations". In 1961, the Latin American Christian Democratic parties - except for the Venezuelan *Comité pro Elecciones Independiente* (COPEI) - were all in the opposition, and the socio-economic problems were so serious, "in a few instances even fatal", that liberal or conservative solutions would bring no solace. In a context of leftist-radicalism Christian Democracy could offer a valuable alternative to communism, according to Hahn.[473]

Not only in ideological issues, but in terms of international politics as well, Latin American and Western European Christian Democrats sometimes differed in their views, especially after the Cuban Revolution. At various congresses it became clear that the Latin Americans had a slightly more nuanced position vis-à-vis the Cold War than their compeers in the NEI and - a fortiori - in the CDUCE. The support of the United States allowed regimes which were indeed anti-communist, but nonetheless imperialistic, to maintain their hold on power in Latin America, which was a cause of much dissatisfaction among Latin American Christian Democrats. To give only one example: in a resolution which the National Council of the influential Chilean

---

472   Melgar Bao, *El Movimiento Obrero Latinoamericano*, 376.
473   Third international conference, Santiago de Chile, 27-30/07/1961. Report Hahn. ACDP, IX-002-029.

PDC approved on 9 April 1961 - just five days before the Bay of Pigs' operation - the party spoke out for the "right of self-determination for all states" and for the "principle of non-intervention". The party's criticism surely had its limits. Simultaneously they categorically rejected the totalitarian character of the Cuban regime.[474] In all events, they wished to avoid a break with the United States. The party aligned itself, for instance, explicitly with the Alliance for Progress Program, which Kennedy had announced a month earlier, and which was along similar lines to the party's reformist program.

The position which the Chilean Radomino Tomic defended at the Third World Conference in Santiago de Chile in 1961 was as balanced as his party's position. Of course, he declared himself to be against communism, but he also stressed: "We are not the Anti-Communist World League either!" The US, thanks to Kennedy, received much credit, but when Tomic examined the pros and cons of US policy, he saw the rights and obligations as being too unevenly shared. The large American companies on Latin American soil were causing a lot of friction. Hahn, who had listened to Tomic and a few other Latin American Christian Democrats in Santiago, interpreted this as "a clear tendency to a neutral position between the two blocs." He saw this as nothing truly dramatic. Communism had been sharply condemned and the fact that an American senator, Eugene McCarthy, had been invited to the conference in Santiago was encouraging. Moreover, Hahn was strongly convinced that the Western Europeans would be able to bring their Latin American friends round to their point of view, by means of a well planned information campaign.[475]

Hahn was right. At that time, there could be no doubt regarding the loyalty of the Latin American Christian Democrats to Europe. Tomic's speech was one long eulogy on Western European Christian Democracy. He thought Latin America should be proud of the Western European Christian Democrats: "We consider them our brothers, those who after the Second World War removed the whole Italian colonial system. They are our brothers, those members of the Dutch government who gave Indonesia back its freedom. They are our brothers, those members of the Belgian government who last year gave Congo back its freedom. And our brothers are those who are leading the French government, since they gave or helped giving freedom back to twelve African communities, which now are no French colonies anymore." Even in Algeria, according to him, the Christian Democrats had played a

474   Consejo Plenario del PDC in Politica y Espirity, April 1961, no 259, 49.
475   Third international conference, Santiago de Chile, 27-30/07/1961. Report Hahn. ACDP, IX-002-029.

worthy role: "And let no-one forget that it was one of our brothers - Pierre Pflimlin - who was the prime minister of France at the time when the resurrection of Algeria took place three years ago, and who then made it clear that the Christian Democratic government would not continue the continual suppression of the Algerian people." Tomic emphasized that he was not saying all of that out of pure politeness - what would have been relatively understandable in the circumstances - but rather "because it was the truth". He waxed even more lyrical on the European integration process: never before was there anything "under heaven" more "beautiful, deeper or purer" created than... the ECSC and the EEC.[476]

In 1961, it was clear that relations between the European Christian Democrats with their rich tradition and years of governing experience, and the emergent Latin American parties to whom governing still seemed far away, were still too uneven. Two years later, when a group of thirty young Latin American politicians (or politicians in the making) was invited by the CDU, the Hahn center (CIDCED), the CDUCE and the DCI to take part in a study visit to Europe in September 1963, the situation would hardly be different. Afterwards, the participants complained about the Western European "feeling of superiority, which scares 'those poor Latin Americans'".[477]

In the same period, from 26 to 29 September, Christian Democrats from the ODCA, the CDUCE and the NEI met on the premises of the Council of Europe, in Strasbourg, for their fourth world conference. Latin America was particularly well represented. No less than eighteen different Latin American nationalities were wandering the streets of Strasbourg. Alain Poher, the chairman of the Christian Democratic group from the European Parliament, took advantage of the massive turnout by organizing a study session the day before the congress, so that European parliamentarians and their Latin American colleagues could discuss the relations between the European Community and Latin America.

The large Latin American turnout would not have been possible without Sieniewicz's American financial backers, who once again made a considerable sum available: $ 10,000 for the Latin American participants - which again underlined their dependence - and "a few thousand dollars" for the represen-

---

476   Speech Tomic. Santiago de Chile, 27-30/07/1961. ACDP, IX-002-029.
477   Voyage d'Études en Europe des Jeunes Démocrates Chrétiens, 22/08-19/10/1963. ACDP, IX-002-085/3.

tatives of the CDUCE.[478] An estimated 65% of the organizational costs were covered by the CDUCE.

As in the past, those "donations" again were able to influence the content of the congress. When the bureau of the NEI apparently decided not to leave any space on the agenda for a presentation by CDUCE, Sieniewicz used his "influence" to change that decision. He hoped that Seitlinger was prepared to change the minutes of the bureau meeting, if necessary, so that it would appear in the report that the NEI, at Sieniewicz's request, agreed to a presentation by an official CDUCE representative.[479] That is exactly what happened. Sieniewicz gave a reading on "The Universal Declaration of the Rights of Man and its Application", a theme which offered more than enough opportunity to renew the attack on communist practices. Seitlinger himself paid much attention to the establishment of good contacts with the United States as well. In that vein, he sharply condemned French foreign policy which was driving a wedge in the Atlantic alliance: "Europe cannot be constructed without the United States."[480] Sieniewicz's political friends in New York had reason to be well satisfied.

From the confidential correspondence between Sieniewicz and Seitlinger it appears that those friends expected a clear result from the meeting in Strasbourg. Sieniewicz informed Seitlinger that their donation had been made upon certain conditions: "You know how difficult those 'dollar givers' are, and I am under constant pressure to show them proof of our progress. They want to know how our organizing the 4th World Conference is going on. (…) Please, take that into account and try to arrange a meeting of the Organizing Committee. That will appease the Americans and convince them of the fact that their contributions to the UCDEC are used in a 'productive' manner, which, by the way, is always a conditio sine qua non for any American donation."

Seitlinger answered one week later that he would organize a meeting of the Organizing Committee - the three secretaries-general - at the beginning of September.[481] That meeting cleared the way for the establishment of the

478 Letter from Sieniewicz to Seitlinger, 18/07/1963. ACDP, IX-002-030/2.
479 'It is important for me that the minutes show that I have really made this proposal, in order to appease my political friends.' Letter from Sieniewicz to Seitlinger, 26/03/1963. ACDP, IX-002-030/2.
480 Congrès Mondial à Strasbourg, 26-29/09/1963. ACDP, IX-002-31.
481 Letter from Sieniewicz to Seitlinger, 18/07/1963. ACDP, IX-002-030/2; Letter from Seitlinger to Sieniewicz, 26/07/1963. ACDP, IX-002-030/2.

World Committee, during the conference in Strasbourg. This was the 'clear result' Sieniewicz had asked for. The World Committee, which had its political and administrative secretariat in Rome, was of course a perfect reflection of the inter-regional organizational framework of the Christian Democrats: it was composed of three representatives from the NEI, three from the ODCA and one from the CDUCE. Alongside those members there was also a representative from the youth organization IUYCD, the secretaries-general of the three regional organizations and the secretary-general of the Hahn Center. At a meeting in Caracas, in May 1964, the World Committee approved the charter of the Christian Democrat World Union, which confirmed this regional organizational principle.

For some, this was an important step in the direction of a transnational Christian Democratic organization which could offer an alternative to communism even as far abroad as in Latin America. The fact that, shortly after the Strasbourg meeting, Frei won a decisive victory in the parliamentary elections over Allende, his socialist/communist rival, seemed to illustrate that Christian Democracy could indeed play such a role. The considerable financial support - with or without his conscious knowledge - which Frei's campaign received from various Western European governments, political parties (including the West German CDU) and money lenders from the United States (including the CIA) all helped.[482] This places the Strasbourg congress in a broader perspective.

Neither the NEI nor the Christian Democrat World Union would be able to live up to its ambitions. Frei's electoral victory - the first time a Christian Democrat came to power in Latin America - put an immediate end to the inferiority complex which the Latin American representatives often seemed to suffer from. Moreover, the explicit support of Kennedy's successor Lyndon Johnson for pro-American military regimes in Latin America caused much friction. The Mann Doctrine of March 1964 stated that the recognition of and assistance given to a regime was independent of that regime's origins: democratically elected governments or military dictatorships would both be judged on their merits. The military coup in Brazil in 1964 and the American invasion of the Dominican Republic in 1965 were both covered by the doctrine.

The gap between the Latin American and the Western European Christian Democrats, who strove after strong ties with the United States, was thereby

---

482   Mutchler, *The Church as a political factor in Latin America*; Gross, *The Last, Best Hope: Eduardo Frei*, 110.

made all the wider and finally became unbridgeable during the World Conference in Lima, in 1966. It would take eight years before another worldwide conference was organized. By 1966, the Western European Christian Democrats had again retreated to their European Heimat.

From NEI to EUCD: Europe as a Top Priority

Even in the period when the NEI was flirting with Africa and Latin America the ambition to transform themselves into a strong European transnational organization still topped their priorities. During its meeting in San Marino in September 1962, the bureau asked the Swiss Dr. Rosenberg to work out a proposal for the "intensification of NEI activities".[483] After talks with CDU chairman Kraske, Hahn and the Italian Scaglia - note the continuation of a long-standing coalition - Rosenberg submitted a thirteen page document with proposals three months later. These proposals had to transform the NEI - Rosenberg himself spoke consistently of an International Union of Christian Democrats - into a true "political force". The Rosenberg memorandum paid particular attention to limiting the scope of the new transnational organization's work: "The International Union should regard European politics as its core business (…) though it should not limit itself to European Community politics." He accepted the fact that the "Six" had special relations with each other, but the goal of the International Union had to be broader - specifically "the preparation of a 'rapprochement' between the countries of the European Community and those countries that do not (yet) belong to it, but whose Christian Democratic parties belong to the International Union of Christian Democrats. This is an issue of the utmost importance."[484] In addition, he wanted to strengthen the political character of the bureau. More than ever before that organ needed to become a place where politics was discussed and where real decisions were taken.

On 15 January 1963, the bureau unanimously approved the Rosenberg memorandum and a working group was formed consisting of Rosenberg, Scaglia, Kraske and Seitlinger in order to work out the recommendations in a more concrete way.[485] The Italian Democrazia Cristiana (DCI) fulfilled a prominent role in the reorganization of the NEI, which would be completed only in June 1965, when the committee in Brussels approved the new statutes which the working group had drawn up. In Brussels, Lefèvre was thanked for all his

483   Conference in San Marino, 28-29/09/1962. ACDP, IX-002-030/1.
484   Memorandum-Rosenberg. ACDP, IX-002-010.
485   Procès-Verbal du Comité Directeur. Bruxelles, 15/01/1963. ACDP, IX-002-094.

efforts as chair of the NEI and Mariano Rumor (DCI) was elected as the new chairman of the 'European Union of Christian Democrats', as the new organization was called, for a term of two years. Seitlinger passed the torch of EUCD secretary-general on to the Belgian Leo Tindemans. With this new leadership the seventeenth NEI congress - or rather, the first EUCD congress - took place at the end of 1965, in the Italian city of Taormina. The theme of the congress, "The Democratic Future of Europe", illustrated a thematic continuity with the traditional NEI congresses. After a short world tour, the Western European Christian Democrats had come back home again.

In retrospect the establishment of the EUCD appears to have been a necessary step towards the establishment of a truly "European party". Article 2 of the EUCD charter states clearly that the mission of the EUCD was to work out a common political program: "To promote and coordinate international action by Christian Democratic parties, to develop close and permanent collaboration between the Christian Democrat parties in Europe with a view towards setting in action a common political program for the creation of a federal Europe." Article 2 of the old NEI charter did not go further than just "cooperation between groups and individuals in order to exchange experience and information".

In the EUCD the emphasis was placed unambiguously on "parties", although in the countries where more than one Christian Democratic party existed (the Netherlands, Spain and France), for the time being, the "équipes" stayed in place. The great diversity between the various parties, according to the new chairman Rumor, momentarily kept the formation of a single European Christian Democratic party in the realm of a utopian fantasy, although that still did remain the final goal. In 1971, the EUCD created a "Political Committee", consisting of the Christian Democratic parties from the (at that moment still) six EC-countries and the Christian Democratic group in the European Parliament. The Political Committee - in preparation for the first direct elections to the European Parliament in 1979 - smoothed the way for the founding of the European People's Party (EPP) in 1976. The former prime minister of Belgium and former secretary general of the EUCD, Leo Tindemans, became the first chairman of the EPP and Jean Seitlinger its first secretary-general. The "club" model of the NEI was definitely a thing of the distant past.

The intensive elaboration of a transnational European organization was apparently difficult to reconcile with a process of global expansion. This was perhaps made most apparent at the Bonn bureau meeting of 6 November

1967, which focused extensively on "the global scope of Christian Democratic activity". EUCD chairman Rumor reviewed the previous five years' global activities. What was particularly apparent at the gathering was the degree to which Rumor, together with many other Western European Christian Democrats, attempted to reduce the importance of Christian Democratic cooperation at the global level. Rumor thought that the global level first and foremost had to be a forum in which the existing regional units could come together and exchange information. He did not want to hear of an organization "which systematically imposes unitarian actions on all Christian Democratic parties, which would practically be impossible given the diversity of situations, experiences and national obligations."

In order not to place too much emphasis on the supra-regional level, the EUCD took various measures. Rumor thought it best to organize global congresses only at long intervals - for example every five or six years. What was put into practice, however, exceeded even Rumor's guidelines: the next global conference - the sixth - would only take place nine years later, in November 1975, in Rome. Furthermore, Rumor did not think it necessary for party chairmen or secretaries-general to always be present. He thought that meetings of experts studying concrete problems - the common market in Latin America, for instance (again a typically regional theme) - were at least equally important. In this way, European and Latin American experts could work out "some general guidelines" on appropriate themes. In other words, the pre-political level was the most appropriate forum for the strengthening of Christian Democratic forces active in very different milieus and domains. This also happened to reflect historical reality. The fact that by following this style of interaction the political character of the World Committee was hollowed out was just a convenient side effect.

III
The Discovery
of the Third World,
1960-1965

The Politicized 'Third World' of the 1950's

Conceptual Ambiguity: A 'Third World' Between Politics and Economics

In the course of the 1950's, both the Socialist International and the Nouvelles Équipes Internationales came into contact with the world beyond Europe, be it in very different ways. The process of institutional expansion of both organizations, which was extensively covered in the previous section, went hand in hand with a heightened awareness for the "developing" world outside of Europe. Through their contacts, both transnationals were almost forced to start thinking on development and underdevelopment.

These thoughts on development were influenced in a twofold way by the Zeitgeist. Firstly, the then dominant modernization paradigm unavoidably left its imprint on the development thinking of both the Socialist International and the Nouvelles Équipes Internationales. After the Second World War, an ever increasing number of academics - originally all from an economic background - dedicated themselves to studying development issues. The late 1940's and the early 1950's have often been described as the pioneering years of development theory as an academic discipline in its own right.[486] The second influential factor in the 1950's was colonialism. Since a considerable portion of the underdeveloped world was or had been linked to Europe via colonial ties, this factor almost automatically took an essential place in the development thinking of both transnationals.

486   Hettne, *Development Theory and the Three Worlds*, 5.

It is in this context that both transnationals *discovered* "the Third World". The concept of the "discovery of the Third World" deserves a short explanation. In 1994, the Dutch historian Maarten Kuitenbrouwer published a study entitled *De Ontdekking van de Derde Wereld (The Discovery of the Third World)*, in which he described the conceptualization of the Third World in the Netherlands and the development policy of the Dutch government. Kuitenbrouwer's concept - a sort of "mental' discovery of the Third World - appears extremely attractive. What exactly that "discovery" consisted in, however, remains rather vague. In the conclusion of his otherwise exceedingly clarifying book Kuitenbrouwer wrote: "The discovery of the Third World, which took place in the Netherlands *between 1950 and 1990*, was partly formed by events which took place in those areas of the world."[487] Since Kuitenbrouwer's "discovery" of the Third World seems to be more of a long-term "having-to-do-with" the Third World (forty years, from 1950 until 1990, is a long time) than an actual 'discovery', it is necessary to give a more precise definition to the term. A definition which implies something more than a "having-to-do-with" or "thinking of" development issues.

Not only the word "discovery", but also the entire understanding of the term "Third World" raises conceptual problems. The hybrid character of that understanding was already present in the very first paragraph of the now well-known article, *Trois Mondes, Une Planète* which appeared in *L'Observateur*, in August 1952. In that article the statistician Alfred Sauvy coined the term "Third World": "We like to talk about the two opposing worlds, about their possibly attacking each other, about their coexistence, etc. Too often though, we are forgetting that there is also a third world, which is the most important one, and which is actually the first one chronologically. That world is composed of a large group of countries commonly known - in United Nations language - as the 'underdeveloped countries'."[488] At the end of the article Sauvy wrote: "This Third World - which is ignored, exploited and despised like the Third Estate - also wants to be respected."

The reference to the two existing "worlds" - the West, or the "free world" on the one hand, and the communist East on the other hand - can be misleading. It suggests that the term "Third World" originally developed mainly or only as a consequence of the bipolar division of the international system. According to that logic, where the emphasis is placed on the political dimension, the term refers to the so-called "non- aligned countries", which in terms

487   Kuitenbrouwer, *De ontdekking van de Derde Wereld*, 248.
488   Sauvy, «Trois Mondes, Une Planète», 14.

of international politics desired to maintain an equal distance from both the East and the West. Sauvy himself strengthened the ambiguity when, in the same article, he wrote: "Both worlds really want to conquer the third one, or at least get it on their side." It is no surprise then that that political dimension very soon became an essential component of the concept. In the context of a bitter and particularly dangerous rivalry between two blocks, the term was charged with meaning. In 1955, for example, the term was even used in its political sense by the "Third World" countries themselves at a conference of Afro-Asian countries in Bandung, Indonesia.

Nonetheless, if we interpret Sauvy's article correctly, this was not what he himself had in mind. The statistician/economist was strongly inspired by the pamphlet *Qu'est-ce que le Tiers-Etat?* in which Emmanuel Sieyes in 1789, the year the French revolution broke out, described the "Third Estate" as "all who are chained and oppressed". In his article, Sauvy too stressed the economic dimension of the concept.[489] The Third World was the whole group of socio-economically "underdeveloped" countries, an area where life expectancy was rising and where demographic growth urgently needed to be accompanied by significant investments.[490] The region, which as a sort of original state chronologically came first, as Sauvy already stated in his opening paragraph (we mustn't understand "third" then as an ordinal number), was later left centuries behind by the "Second" and the "First" worlds which in the course of time had 'developed' themselves. From an economic point of view, the First and Second Worlds are not presupposed in the analogy. By situating the Third World chronologically first, as a sort of original state, Sauvy proved himself a good student of the modernization school, which in his time was hardly challenged. The modernization school of development thinking designated a general and rather diverse category of development theories all of which were characterized by considering development as an endogenic, unilinear and irreversible process from tradition to modernity which is inherent in every society and is therefore universal.[491]

When rival schools appeared on the scene in the 1960's, the meaning of the term "Third World" began to change. In his monumental work *Global Rift: The Third World comes of Age* (1981) historian Leften Stavrianos defined the Third World along *dependencia* school lines as: "those countries or regions that participated on unequal terms in what eventually became the global

489   Sieyes and Tulard, *Qu'est-ce que le Tiers Etat?*
490   Sauvy, «Trois Mondes, Une Planète», 14.
491   Hettne, *Development Theory.*

market economy."[492] The Third World in his vision was created as a result of unequal trade relations in the worldwide expansion of capitalism. By the end of the 15th century it included Latin America, and later Eastern Europe and Russia. Eastern Europe could be classified as Third World starting in the 16th century and Russia since the end of the Crimean War, which opened that country to Western capitalism. Lastly, starting with the 19th century, the Middle East, Asia (not including Japan) and Africa could also be considered as belonging to the Third World. When the communist block came into existence, Russia pulled itself and Eastern Europe out of the Third World and - politically speaking - they formed their own (Second) World. With the collapse of that world in 1991, the term Third World had become senseless due to a total absence of its political dimension. The term "Third World" has become a piece of historical jargon, according to Stavrianos.

What Sauvy and Stavrianos, to limit ourselves to these two authors, have in common is that by emphasizing the economic dimension of the term, their "Third World" is conceivable independent of the Cold War. As shown in Sauvy's article, the Cold War is of course extremely important as context, but the emergence and existence of a Third World cannot be derived from it, as it is in the political interpretation. In the 1950's this distinction was hardly - if at all - made and consequently concepts were blurred. The use of the word "Third" made the confusion only greater. Author Shu-Yun in a recent article in the *Third World Quarterly* stated: "It is only through the two-dimensionalisation of the concept of the Third World that the First, Second and Third World were given numeric sense."[493]

If we return to the original meaning of the term in its economic sense, then the "discovery" of the Third World actually presumes a "one-dimensionalization" of the Third World. It is the understanding that the flagrant socio-economic inequalities on a global scale - "the juxtaposition of piling heaps on the one hand and deepening hollows on the other" as Indian sociologist Ashoka Mehta put it at an SI congress in 1961 - exist in their own right, autonomous of the East-West conflict.[494] This autonomy would only become possible if the political dimension, which fed off the ambiguity, was to be weakened.

492   Stavrianos, *Global Rift: The Third World Comes of Age*, 31 -32.
493   Shu-Yun, "Third World studies", 346.
494   Circ. 72/62. 19/10/1962. Report of the Seventh Congress of the Socialist International. Rome, 23-27/10/1961. IISG, SI 252.

More Politics than Economics:
The World Plan for Mutual Aid and SUNFED

I n May 1946, during one of the first postwar gatherings of socialist parties in the English town of Clacton, the finance minister of New Zealand, Walter Nash, referred to the immense differences between his country and India: "We have in New Zealand the lowest death rate and the lowest infant mortality rate in the world, and an expectation of life of 68 years. The Indians have an expectation of 27 years. These two standards cannot exist together in the world without war."[495]

This citation can be recorded as the first reference to the problem of development within the Socialist International (then still COMISCO), although at that time it did not lead to much. If "development" was discussed in COMISCO in the second half of the 1940's, then it was usually in the context of European development, meaning European economic reconstruction. This theme was stimulated by international programs such as the Marshall Plan or the UN Relief and Rehabilitation Administration. In the discussions on European reconstruction the colonies did of course come up. After all, they could make important contributions to the repair of Europe. During the SI congress in Antwerp in 1947, the Belgian socialist Anseele stated: "By supporting the social recovery of the colonies, the European countries would actually provide themselves with substantial aid."[496]

Two years later, during the International Socialist Congress in Baarn (the Netherlands), the overseas territories again were the subject of discussion when the conclusions of a conference of economic experts, which had met shortly before, were debated. That conference was primarily dedicated to the nationalization of primary industries, but related subjects, such as investment policies, were also discussed there. The experts, being the good socialists that they were, presented an investment policy in which governments would play a key role: "We must have a European investment scheme as a basis for our industrialization. Governments must take over. We propose the foundation of a European Investment Bank as an international government institution in public hands, for investments both within Europe and investments abroad. In the latter case it could work like the Truman policy for the development of

---

495   International Socialist Conference. Clacton-on-Sea. 17-20/05/1946. Minutes. IISG, SI 234.
496   Circ. 88/47. International Socialist Conference, Antwerp. 28/11-02/12/1947. Summary of
         Proceedings. IISG, SI 236.

backward areas. The investment bank could make grants and investments in overseas schemes."

The French expert Piette also envisioned a sort of Truman policy for the "backward territories", and for the first time at an international socialist congress he posed the question which would keep the International busy for years to come: "The colonies are a necessary source of wealth, but how are we to reconcile our economic needs with those of the native populations? How can these territories be developed under present conditions?"[497]

The reference to President Truman in the citations mentioned above is important. Four months before the conference in Baarn Truman had, during his inaugural address, laid out the four pillars of American foreign policy. The fourth pillar (the well-known "Point IV") was of historic importance. Point IV - "a bold new program for making the benefits of our scientific advances and industrial progress available for the improvement and growth of underdeveloped areas" - definitively heralded the beginning of the "period of development". Development, however, was first and foremost seen as a new weapon to be used in the Cold War.

The international evolution incited the Socialist International to action. It was at the Seventh Conference of Economic Experts of the International, in Vienna in November 1951, that the British Labour Party proposed to establish a socialist development policy for the underdeveloped regions.[498] The British proposal, which was steeped in Cold War assumptions (Korean War), led one year later to the elaboration of the "World Plan for Mutual Aid" (WPMA), which was approved by the Milan congress of the International in October 1952. The plan was largely based on ideas which had been extensively discussed in Vienna, all based on British documents for development plans in Asia. With the World Plan for Mutual Aid the Socialist International for the first time set down on paper its ideas on development and underdevelopment.

The World Plan for Mutual Aid

The paper on the World Plan for Mutual Aid was through and through a Cold War document. This was made all the more apparent by the document's emphasis on concepts such as freedom and political democracy. In the open-

497   International Socialist Conference. Baarn. 14-16/05/1949. IISG, SI 239.
498   7th Economic Experts Conference. Socialist policy for the under-developed areas of the world. Vienna, 12-16/11/1951. IISG, SI 352.

ing sentence of the document the word "freedom" or etymologically related words (liberation, free, free will) appeared five times, immediately followed by a paragraph on democratic governance and political freedom. Every form of "Capitalist imperialism" - not so much capitalism in and of itself - was condemned, but just that much more attention was placed on condemning "communist imperialism" and the attempts of communists to take advantage of the desperate conditions in the poorer underdeveloped countries.
The WPMA came out of that same atmosphere which had given rise to the Frankfurt Declaration, which was the foundation for the global expansion of the Socialist International. At that time there was little room for a discovery of the Third World.

The document not only reflected the current international climate, but it also mirrored the internal situation for a certain number of European parties and the still fresh expansion of the International into Asia. At the moment when the WPMA was written, anti-colonialism had not yet become a matter of faith in the BLP. Consequently, the draft text contained a few unacceptable passages for the Indian and Japanese socialists, who did have some say in the matter. The theory which had it that the recognition of self-determination could be independent from a modern democratic system or the concept of a partnership between sovereign states and dependent territories - so typical for the early 1950's - could not count on receiving much support among the Asians.[499] The Indian party succeeded in watering down the conscious formulation and even got a passage approved in which the International voiced its sympathy for the liberation movements in the dependent territories. Apart from this small reference, the International's thoughts on development remained very much in the context of colonialism.

The WPMA, besides being steeped in Cold War and colonialist rethoric, was also thoroughly influenced by the modernization paradigm, both in its premises for the causes of underdevelopment and in the solutions which it offered. The main cause of underdevelopment was given to be the various barriers to development - "bottlenecks" in the jargon of the experts - which were situated without exception in all the "underdeveloped territories". Some of these barriers were quite predictable: the primitive agricultural techniques, feudal land divisions, all sorts of legal tricks which concentrated the power in the hands of a limited group, or the outmoded political system which for example was based on a caste hierarchy (this last point being added by the Indian

499   Circ. vii/52. 18/09/1952. Draft Statement on a Socialist Policy for the Underdeveloped Areas of
the World. Amendments by the Indian Socialist Party. IISG, SI 65.

socialists). Another barrier was the "traditional" mentality of the native peoples; this being an excellent illustration of the West's paternalism towards the dependent territories: "too many of the inhabitants of these territories still have an attitude of resignation towards it [their poverty] and, in ignorance, sometimes resist the new ideas and techniques which would raise their living standards."[500] One of the first development theorists who paid attention to such sociological and psychological factors was Arthur W. Lewis, who since the beginning of the 1950's had been a professor of Economics at Manchester University and who himself was born in the West Indies. Later Björne Hettne called him "a true pioneer in development economics".[501] Lewis was not unknown to the International: during the debate on the WPMA the former British colonial minister James Griffiths mentioned Lewis' name, and it was brought up again various other times as well. This once again illustrates the British influence upon the International's development thinking.

Another internal barrier which was mentioned in the text was the quick population growth in many underdeveloped areas. As the figures on population increase began to become known in the early 1950's, development economists began to pay more attention to the phenomenon. One of the pioneers in the field was the economist Harvey Leibenstein, who in 1954 published his study *A theory of economic-demographic development*, at Princeton University. In the International itself, only two years earlier, the topic had been considered to be an exceptionally sensitive one. In the draft text of the WPMA not a word was mentioned on these new demographic theories, which was particularly difficult for the Scandinavian socialists to swallow. For Sweden in particular the issue of population growth was of the utmost importance: "The main weakness of the draft lies in the fact that it does not even mention the population problem. With due regard to the difficulties of some parties, it must be stated that the Socialist International would seriously fall short of its tasks, if it does not deal with this problem in a realistic way."[502]

The Swedes referred to the fact that Nehru had begun a policy of family planning in India and that the World Health Organization was also helping to spread birth control methods. A reference to birth control in the text was "the least" the socialists could do. The Swedish-Norwegian proposal to

500   Socialist Policy for the Underdeveloped Areas of the World. 2nd Congress of the Socialist International, Milan, 17-22/10/1952. IISG, SI 245.
501   Hettne, *Development theory*, 42.
502   Circ. vii/52. 18/09/1952. Swedish Party's comments to Draft Declaration on Socialist Policy for the Underdeveloped Areas. IISG, SI 65.

explicitly refer to the need for birth control campaigns was rejected. The final draft stated only that the problem of population increase needed to be further investigated, not a very daring pronouncement. At the conference of experts in Vienna as well, there was great division regarding the relevance of birth control. One of the counter-arguments which Morgan Phillips employed to justify not paying too much attention to birth control again went back to the Cold War: "We must remember that communist propaganda is at pains to point out that the advocacy of birth control for coloured peoples is part of the armoury of 'Western imperialism'."[503]

Such a divergence of views was in sharp contrast with the unity which was reached on purely economic measures to solving the problem of development. In the early 1950's, development economists referred almost unanimously to the lack of capital and the lack of administrative know-how as the major causes of the "bottlenecks". The International followed them entirely in their conclusions. The answer to both shortages would have to come from "outside" - from the developed countries. The capital or the know-how which could be generated in the underdeveloped countries themselves was far from sufficient. Lewis expressed it as follows: "The central problem in the theory of economic development is to understand the process by which a community which was previously saving and investing 4 or 5 percent of its national income or less, converts itself into an economy where voluntary saving is running at about 12 to 15 per cent of national income or more."[504] Until that conversion had taken place, a "Big Push" or a "Big Spurt" would be necessary - a massive short-term investment of capital and know-how by means of development assistance and financial investments to break the barrier and set the development process in motion. As soon as the process was set in motion, the contributions from the developed countries could be scaled back and the underdeveloped countries would eventually be able to meet their own needs - an optimism which today seems very naive. The WPMA of the International followed this reasoning and directed itself entirely to the build up of capital and assistance. "Technical aid and financial assistance" - via loans with extended reimbursement terms and low interest, and no strings attached grants - were the key concepts, the magic words of the then current thoughts on development in the Socialist International.

---

503   Letter from Phillips to Björk, 12/07/1952. IISG, SI 425.
504   Lewis, "Economic Development with unlimited supplies of labour", 155.

European-Asian Collaboration on SUNFED

The early contacts which the Socialist International developed with like-minded parties from Asia, mainly from 1953 onwards, gradually began to influence socialist thinking on development issues. The first conference of the Asian Socialist Conference, in 1953, had made such an impression that the International, as a sign of goodwill, gave the question of colonialism a central place on the agenda of its following congress in Stockholm. The results achieved in Stockholm, however, were rather limited, as already mentioned above. The congress hardly changed socialist colonial thinking, let alone the bipolar world view of the majority of European socialists. This bothered the Swedish minister of foreign affairs and he made it clear in his final address to the congress: "We, as also the Americans, are accustomed to speak of the West as opposed to the East - this congress is no exception. We attribute to the West certain qualities as regards the political system and spiritual matters, and quite different qualities to the East. This way of thinking is a heritage from a past in which it seemed natural to look at the world from a European - or American - center. But this period belongs really to the past".[505]

Such comments were to be expected from Sweden, a neutral country, and were therefore no indication of a shift in attitude in the International as a whole. Since internal political considerations weighed in heavier on the trans-national level, there was no dismantling, as the Asian socialists would have hoped, of the colonialism nor of the Atlanticism of the International.

In another domain, the collaboration with Asia did, however, deliver results. The joint consultations which had already taken on a rather modest scope with the elaboration of the World Plan for Mutual Aid were further expanded in 1954-1955 when SUNFED - the "Special United Nations Fund for Economic Development" - came to top the agenda of the International.

The creation of SUNFED was a demand from the underdeveloped countries in the United Nations, which considered the existing "UN Expanded Programme of Technical Assistance" (EPTA) as far from sufficient. EPTA was set up by Ecosoc in August 1949, shortly after the announcement of Truman's "Point IV"-program. EPTA defined technical assistance in the broadest terms. It encompassed economic planning, education and training, healthcare, transportation and communication. Nevertheless, the initial capital of EPTA (20 million dollars) was extremely limited in comparison with the development plans

505   Socialist International Information, 3, 1953, 32-33.

intended for Europe through the Marshall Plan, the International Bank for Reconstruction and Development and the International Monetary Fund. Instead of EPTA, the Asian Socialist Conference (ASC) asked for the establishment of a sort of international bank which could make grants or low-cost long-term loans available for capital investment, as a supplement or an alternative to the expensive loans from the World Bank. In a sense the idea was compatible with the World Plan for Mutual Aid of the Socialist International.

The advocate par excellence of SUNFED in the International was the Dutch vice-chairman of the PvdA, Hendrik 'Hein' Vos. The fact that Dutch social democracy played such a prominent role in the debate should not be a surprise. The PvdA sat in a coalition government which included the strongly anti-communist minister of foreign affairs Luns who made multilateral assistance to the underdeveloped areas a policy priority. In May 1954 Vos thus presented the council of the International with a detailed report on the discussions concerning SUNFED which had taken place in the autumn of 1953 in the UN. Vos was in total agreement with the proposal to set up a UN fund, but he found the planned linking of SUNFED to international disarmament unacceptable. He thought there was no point in waiting for the Soviets to approve worldwide disarmament before making sufficient funds available to start up a development fund. On the contrary, he saw developmental assistance as being an ideal instrument of the Cold War: "Socialists have always stressed that if there is to be security we must have both things, and at the same time: a strong system of defense and measures of social progress. Without military strength, freedom and social security would be at the mercy of communist imperialism. Without social progress conditions would favour communist domination from within."[506] Vos' proposal to separate SUNFED from the debate on disarmament and to plead for such a separation in the governments where the socialists were able to exercise some influence was entirely supported by the ASC, even if their motivations for doing so were somewhat different: "Economic development is of sufficient importance to be considered on its own merits."[507]

There was still another - in fact more important - difference between Vos (and the Socialist International as a whole) and the ASC. While the ASC wanted a development fund which fell under the auspices of the UN, Vos more pragmatically did not want to limit it exclusively to that organization.

506   Circ. 31/54. 14/05/1954. Report of the Council, Vienna, 07-08/05/1954. IISG, SI 75.
507   Circ. 59/54. 06/12/1954. Special United Nations Fund for Economic Development (SUNFED), submitted by the Asian Socialist Conference to the Socialist International. IISG, SI 75.

The discussion on the transnational level in fact mirrored the discussion which was taking place on the international level. In the UN the developed countries - led by the United States and Great Britain - were strongly opposed to SUNFED. They preferred to put their money into institutions which they controlled such as the World Bank. In the General Assembly of the UN on the other hand, where each country had one vote, the influence of the under-developed countries soared.

Nevertheless, at the congress of the International in London in July 1955, the SI and the ASC came to a quick agreement on a joint document which preferred the framework of the UN to that of the World Bank.[508] It explicitly mentioned some major limitations of the World Bank: "The International Bank must have regard to business considerations of productivity and, to a certain extent, profitability of the projects it finances as well as the repaying capacity of the borrower. However, to some areas in need of basic development, these considerations of profitability are not applicable, and thus the Bank will not be a suitable institution to meet their requirements." The biggest advantage of SUNFED was that, since it fell under the auspices of the UN, it was safe to assume that it would maintain a democratic character.

In the years which followed - as far as development was concerned - almost all of the Socialist International's attention went into working out proposals to give SUNFED concrete form. Two topics were to dominate the debate. The first topic had to do with the financing of the fund. Already in 1952, the Dutch PvdA had decided to call for the Dutch government to allocate 10 million pounds yearly (1 pound per inhabitant) for the future SUNFED project. If the other European states made a similar effort, that would result in a starting capital of more than 200 million pounds.[509] In a memorandum which Vos wrote for the meeting of the council of the International in Copenhagen in December 1956, he proposed, just as the Labour Party did, setting the contribution at 1% of the net national income.[510] The Scandinavian socialists, however, who sat in government since the end of World War II were completely opposed to very precise financial engagements. Under Kaj Björk's influence the final resolution which was approved in Copenhagen was modified to state "around 1%" of the national income.

508   Circ. 52/55. 30/09/1955. Report of the Fourth Congress of the SI. IISG, SI 79.
509   Ibidem.
510   Circ. 66/56. 23/11/1956. Aid to the Underdeveloped Countries. Memorandum by Hendrik Vos. IISG, SI 83. The BLP assumed that the USSR would never be able to afford the contribution.

Secondly, political questions were continually coming up, in particular the desirability of the USSR's participation in SUNFED. The resolution which was approved in Copenhagen was unambiguous on the subject: "membership of SUNFED must be made possible for each member of the United Nations."[511] Many strategical considerations were hidden behind this short sentence. If the USSR decided to participate in SUNFED - which was not unlikely - they would be obliged to endorse the regulations of SUNFED, which stipulated that they would no longer be able to use their development aid as a political instrument. If, however, the USSR were to decide not to participate in SUNFED, for precisely the above-mentioned reason, they would lose much credit with the developing countries. While in the mid-1950's, a relatively heavy accent was placed on international détente, in the International development aid and anti-communism still went hand in hand. The main explanation is that within the International this theme was dominated by the notoriously anti-communist Dutch PvdA, which enjoyed a monopoly position in all discussions on SUNFED.

In the end, SUNFED would be beached by a lack of will from the donor countries. As a compromise, the General Assembly would establish the "United Nations Special Fund" in December 1958. That fund, which principally was intended to start up projects which in a later phase would be eligible for investments from the World Bank or other sources, had more means at its disposal than EPTA, but significantly less than the World Bank or, from 1960 on, the "International Development Association".

---

511   Circ. 92/56. 01/12/1956. Aid for the Underdeveloped Countries. Resolution of the Council,
       Copenhagen, 01/12/1956. IISG, SI 84.

1959-1960

The Third World in the Spotlight

A t the end of the decade the amount of attention paid to the underdeveloped territories reached an absolute all-time high, both in the
Socialist International and in the Nouvelles Équipes Internationales,
which up until that time had hardly paid any attention to the issue, except in
a separate subcommission.

The Socialists' Quest for the Third World: from Hamburg to Haifa

T he International's congress in the German city of Hamburg in July
1959 and the gathering of the council of the International in the Israeli
port town of Haifa in April 1960 were almost entirely devoted to the
underdeveloped territories. The gathering in Haifa was remarkable. It was the
first time that the International met outside of Europe. At the PvdA's request
the meeting took place in Israel, "at the doorstep of the African continent"
as the gathering's host Moshe Sharett put it.[512] The location was meant to
underline that development issues had become a top priority for the International. Since 1948, under the leadership of socialist premiers, Israel had
known a spectacular socio-economic development. The mayor of Haifa, who
welcomed the international community on 27 April, called Israel an example
of a modern, industrializing nation, built by - and his example illustrates the
importance of the industrial sector in the Israeli development model - "tens
of thousands of seamen and dockworkers, workers in iron and steel foundries,

512 Circ. 77/60. 15/11/1960. Conference of the Council of the Socialist International. Haifa, 27-
29/04/1960. IISG, SI 98.

in oil refineries and chemical factories, metalworkers, quarrymen and build-ers".[513]

Israel served as a model when in Hamburg and Haifa, socialists elaborated their own socialist development model. In Hamburg it became clear that the first pillar of socialist development thinking - the colonial context - was about to collapse, and for various participants it already had done so. As has been discussed in detail above, in the second half of the 1950's anti-colonialism made much progress in the International, particularly under the influence of the British Labour Party. This also influenced the thinking on development in the International. Aneurin Bevan did his party much honor when he sharply criticized the French Algeria policy at the Hamburg congress. His fellow party member Tom Driberg kept his criticism closer to home: "Just as it is natural to Conservatives to seek nostalgically to cling to imperial power, so it is natural to socialists to fight always for the liberation of colonial peoples." He had not a single good word for "the blundering and often brutal colonialism of the British Tory Government in Kenya, in Cyprus and wherever it has been mani-fested."[514] In other words, domestic politics was never far away.

Not everyone, however, was as sharp in their criticism as Bevan and Driberg. Hendrik Vos from the PvdA, in particular, was rather cautious. He was certainly convinced that colonialism had reached its end, but at that moment he - and many of his colleagues - seemed not at all to suspect that within a few months' time, in 1960, one African country after the other would be gaining its independence. Vos was thinking in decades: "It is also to be anticipated that further development will lead to independence. In the coming decades there will undoubtedly be a further movement out of this group [of colonies] into that of the countries which have complete political independence." Therefore, in the development scheme which he presented in Hamburg, an important role for the mother country was built into the development of the colonial territories. This illustrates, in a certain sense, the realism with which Vos approached developmental issues. In many cases the colonial ties were still strong indeed. This did not prevent him, however, from taking up a clear standpoint later in his reasoning: "It must be stressed that where political independence is achieved the responsibility for further national develop-ment, social, economic and political, is the national responsibility of the coun-

---

513   Ibidem.
514   Circ 1/60. 04/01/1960. Report of the Sixth Congress of the Socialist International. Hamburg,
       14-17/07/1959. IISG, SI 249.

try itself. Once colonial status has been thrown off no further guardianship must be exercised."[515]

In contrast with the colonial context, the second pillar of socialist development thinking - the influence of the modernization paradigm - remained solidly standing at the end of the decade. Hendrik Vos, who irrefutably dominated the debate in Hamburg, is again a good guide. His introduction to the subject "Cooperation between Developed and Developing Countries" can serve as a good example of the modernization paradigm. Development was a process which, according to the leading theoretician Walt Rostow, could be divided into various "stages of development". European history served as a contextual framework. According to Rostow's paradigm, on the basis of economic, social and political criteria, one can measure the degree of "backwardness" relative to the developed world. Vos argued that, in the 1950's, the developing countries were situated at about the same place where the European workers had found themselves in the 19th century. In his speech, he painstakingly referred to the similarities in terms of the mortality rate, life expectancy and percentages of the national incomes. Vos shared the great enthusiasm which characterized the modernization theorists:"This much is already certain: absolute and relative impoverishment will come to an end for the people of the underdeveloped areas in an ever more closely knit world, whether results are achieved in a period of ten or more years."[516]

The third pillar of socialist development theory, the influence of the Cold War, was at least as strong as the second pillar. In the second half of the 1950's, the efforts made towards détente had found fertile ground in the International, in particular in the British and German socialist parties. In Haifa, Hugh Gaitskell played his by now well-known tune once more. He worked towards a sort of "neutral" development aid policy:"It is because I think that the granting of aid, in whatever form it may be, should be sterilized from international politics, I think that it should be channelled through the United Nations". He warned against "the danger that on the one hand the Western Powers and on the other hand the Soviet Union treat aid as an instrument of their international policy." Not that he would have chosen for neutrality politically speaking - he lamented the fact that NATO seemed to be growing less cohesive over the last years - but there was clearly more than enough room for a balanced analysis:"I believe that on both sides there are individuals with influence and

515 Circ 1/60.04/01/1960. Report of the Sixth Congress of the Socialist International. Hamburg, 14-17/07/1959. IISG, SI 249.
516 Ibidem.

power in high places who are quite sincerely opposed to any serious negotia-tions; I mean not only the generals in the Pentagon, not only Dr. Adenauer, but also members of the Politbureau itself".[517]

The Belgian Victor Larock was on the same wavelength: "We must beware of neutralism and of national isolation, but it is necessary for us to criticise both sides truthfully and to make positive suggestions in an independent spirit". Of course, it was much easier to manifest such an "independence of spirit" when one was in the opposition and not in the government. Not all social-ists, however, were so nuanced. There were also - as a matter of habit - heavy attacks on the expansionist policies of the USSR from the Dutch PvdA (Max van der Stoel) and from the French SFIO (Guy Mollet).

Mollet's speech in Haifa is a good example of socialist discourse in the early 1950's, with a pronounced, even exclusive emphasis on the "liberal" aspects of socialism. During several minutes, he expounded to his audience what his mentor Bracke - "a world-famous expert in semantics and grammar" - had taught him about the term "democratic socialism". It was a barbarism of "social democracy": etymologically considered, socialism could only be democratic. Communism was not another, un-democratic form of socialism. This had been the essence of the 1951 Frankfurt Declaration. With a similar set of liberal glasses he also looked towards Asia and Africa. Mollet warned that "in Africa (…) where liberty is in jeopardy, where democracy is threatened, the chances of socialism vanish." Van der Stoel applied this position to his development policy: "With respect to the underdeveloped areas, my party has ceaselessly advocated that we ought to channel aid through the United Nations. At the same time, we must realise that Khrushchev has made it clear on several occasions, that he does not want this. He wishes to extend aid via the Soviet-Sino bloc, and if this proves to be a final position, then there is only one other possibility: the free world must itself try and solve the problem."

The Italian Righetti was also looking to Asia: "Our Asian comrades are engaged in a heroic struggle to prevent the whole of Asia from being submerged by the Soviet colossus." In the final resolution In Haifa everything was summed up nicely one last time: "The existence of countries which are poor and inadequately equipped with material resources and technical skill to guarantee the rapid development of their economy represents a threat to the peace of the world. Not only do these countries offer an arena for rival

517   Circ. 77/60. 18/11/1960. Gaitskell. Report of the Conference of the Council of the Socialist International. Haifa, 27-29/04/1960. IISG, SI 98.

propaganda of the Great Powers; they are an easy prey for those powers which have expansionist ideas."[518]

The ongoing competition with communism was a leitmotif throughout the discussions on transnational development policy, which Haifa helped get going. Until then the International had principally been active - via research and to a lesser extent also via lobbying - in discussions on international programs like SUNFED. Now it appeared that the International was willing to act as an engaged participant as well and to work out a concrete development policy. In Haifa the Standing Joint Committee on Developing Areas (SJCDA), which was established in the spring of 1960, met for the first time. The SJCDA was an association between the Socialist International and the Asian Socialist Conference under the chairmanship of the Swede Sven-Erik Beckius, and had as its mission "to examine all questions concerning the developing countries, and to work out proposals for cooperation and the development of contacts." In November 1963, it was decided to include Latin American and African representatives in the committee as well. The purpose of the first meeting was to come up with a number of measures which would help strengthen socialism in the developing countries, a clear example of the politicized character of development aid.[519] Time was of the essence because the International could not afford to wait until African socialist parties came into existence and decided on their own to join the International: "Delay would mean to leave the field in that continent to non-democratic, non-socialist forces."[520] During their first meeting the SJCDA worked out a policy on three levels: an ideological, organizational and economic level.

Fast work was made, in particular, of the first level: ideological cooperation with socialist parties from developing countries. A series of pamphlets was set up for them to illustrate the *"Merits of Social Democracy"* - as the series was called. The International did make a selection: only contributions from 'revisionist' parties which had modernized their program were selected (German, Austrian and British), or from 'successful' parties which had already been in government for some time (Sweden, Norway and Israel). The idea of setting up a socialist library in a number of developing countries, with a set of around 20 reference works was also considered. Various European partners took up

518   Circ. 77/60. 15/11/1960. Resolution on Economic Development. Conference of the Council of the Socialist International. Haifa, 27-29/04/1960. IISG, SI 98.
519   Circ. 14/60. 04/03/1960. Report on Standing Joint Committee of Developing Areas in Report of the Conference of the Council of the Socialist International. Haifa, 27-29/04/1960. IISG, SI 98.
520   Ibidem.

the request from the bureau to provide the ASC with party publications and study materials. That is what the Italian Umberto Righetti called "political cooperation" in Haifa, which he saw as the best way of assisting Asia: "We must define an effective alternative to the Soviet appeal to these countries."

Organizational cooperation was the second level. In order to strengthen democracy, and in particular social democracy, much importance was placed in the transfer of organizational know-how and the training of party leaders and political staff. With this end in mind a seminar took place one year after Haifa in the Indian capital New Delhi. At the invitation of Asoka Mehta's Praja Socialist Party, the delegates also enjoyed a five-week tour of India. On the European side, the seminar was attended by Germans, Austrians, Swiss, Swedes and Israelis. These were the nationalities which, together with the intellectual support of the Dutch, played a leading role in the development policy of the International. The most elaborated idea in organizational coop- eration to come out of Haifa was, however, from a Norwegian. Finn Moe proposed establishing an "International Socialist Employment Agency" which was to supply the parties with trained socialists and which would meet the need for mutual support: "Socialist parties in the less developed countries could draw much-needed technically skilled personnel, provided by their brother parties in the advanced countries." The proposal would be dead in the water - the number of possible partner organizations was in the end rather limited, especially in Africa - but it illustrates once more the role reserved for socialist parties in the working out of development policy.

Another initiative which was meant to strengthen organizational coopera- tion was the awarding of scholarships. This did not happen very smoothly, however. Initially, the International wanted to award three scholarships per year: one for Africa, one for Asia and one for Latin America. In two years time (1961 and 1962) only two socialists - one from Jamaica and one from Tangan- yika - were able to make use of the scholarships. When the advantage to the local organizations turned out to be rather limited, the scholarship program was reduced to just one scholarship per year. Other proposals, such as to send young socialist volunteers abroad, were never realized for lack of funds.

In Haifa, the SJCDA remained rather vague regarding the third level, econom- ic collaboration: a "specifically socialist policy" needed to be worked out and a conference of experts would need to be assembled. In the end it would be precisely this conference which would make an important contribution to the "discovery of the Third World" in socialist thinking.

The NEI on the Lookout for the Third World in Paris

A few months after the gathering of the council of the Socialist International in Haifa, the members of the NEI assembled in Paris for their 14th congress. The congress followed the traditional NEI routine. There was a separate venue planned for the spouses of the delegates - a visit to Versailles and a fashion show - and a sharp distinction was made between the "full-fledged" équipes and the équipes in exile. The latter - the Christian Democrats from Bulgaria, Hungary, Lithuania, Poland, Romania, Czechoslovakia and Yugoslavia - had to be satisfied with just one speaker, who would have to speak in the name of them all. The topic to be discussed in Paris was new, though. The organizational renewal of the NEI went hand in hand with a more global engagement and that reflected on the program of the congress, which was entirely dedicated to development issues and was entitled: "Christian Democracy and the Third World". This was the first time that the NEI paid such a degree of attention to the matter.

In a certain sense the choice of Paris was a symbolic one. Just as France at that moment was trying to bring a close to its colonial rule of Algeria without losing too much face, at their congress the Christian Democrats attempted to bid farewell to their colonial period. The goodbye was apparently a difficult one for some parties. They recognized that all sorts of abuses had been committed, but in contrast with the social democrats, they were also quick to recollect the merits of colonialism. Taviani, in his address, elaborated on those merits in an unambiguous manner: "Although generally only backward peoples were colonized, in the name of colonization, deplorable and terrible mistakes were sometimes made. Nevertheless, thanks to colonization, plenty of those peoples became civilized in a very short time, and reached a degree of civilization comparable to the rest of the world. Thanks to colonization, the majority of African populations without culture, without tradition and without any history became 'peoples', and they learned what the concepts 'society' and 'state' mean. (...) We may not forget that the existence of modern states like Ghana, Cameroon, Togo and Somalia would not have been possible if those territories had never been colonized by the British, the French or the Italians."[521]

The British Member of Parliament A.T. Courtney supported him and added that he was proud to have represented the old colonialism. Fontenau, the deputy secretary of the MRP, referred to "the pain and the suffering which

521   Congrès des NEI, Paris, 22-24/09/1960. ACDP, IX-002-022.

France has to endure due to this dramatic event called the 'Algerian revolution'".They said nothing about the sufferings of the Algerian population. The Belgian Theo Lefèvre thought that the West should not be too masochistic. Not everything that went wrong in the developing countries was the fault of the European countries and churches.They had also done a great deal for the ex-colonies.

Nevertheless, all of those present at the congress were in agreement that whatever help the West was to give to the developing countries it shouldn't *resemble* neo-colonialism. Roger Reynaud, the authoritative introductory speaker at the congress, warned of the mistrust which many African and Asian developing countries felt for the West. Every association with the colonial past would only further drive those countries into the arms of communism.

In this regard Haifa and Paris were closely aligned in their strong emphasis on the competition with Moscow. Not one single speaker in Paris - and there were about 40 speakers - neglected to refer to the purported successes of the communists in Africa and Asia. According to Taviani, Soviet imperialism only fed off of the still extant practices of racism. In Taviani's address almost all of his focus was on "the productivity of the ideal of liberty". Economic prosperity had absolutely no worth without freedom. The winning of the Third World to one's side was as much of a challenge as the conquest of space, a reference to the race which had begun after the launch of Sputnik.[522] For another pioneer of the NEI's global expansion, the Dutchman Hahn, development aid - unfortunately - could not be but an instrument of the Cold War:"Some people think that economic and technical aid can help fight the Cold War. Well, we think that such aid should be an objective in itself, in the interest of the country in question. (…) The only question is how to avoid this dilemma, how to combine those two opposing aspects: on the one hand offer depoliticized aid to a country, and on the other hand see the communists attempt to get the same country in their sphere of influence." A few sentences later he gave an answer to his own dilemma:"It is not only our task to protect those countries from famine, but we must also protect their populations against slavery and against humiliation." In order to achieve this the West needed to form a unified front, even in terms of development aid. Peter Lorenz, a Christian Democrat from Berlin, warned the Africans and Asians against a repeat on their continent of the situation in Berlin, were the African and Asian continents to fall into the hands of the communists.

522   Ibidem.

Not without a touch of bitterness various Christian Democrats indicated that despite the fact that development aid from the Soviet Union was quantitatively considerably less than that from the West, its results were much better. There was almost general agreement on the reasons for this discrepancy. The ideological trimmings of the Soviet aid - "aid from the working class of the USSR", as the German Christian Democrat W. Kunz put it - was significantly more attractive than Western help which came from anonymous, neutral and thus convictionless organizations. That was not what the people of the Third World were waiting for: "The people that we are trying to help are people who are possessed with a profound and very primitive religious philosophy. They like the feeling of being helped by a kind of conviction which could be qualified in a way as religious". The German was therefore making an appeal for development aid with a clearly Christian profile.

The primacy of the ideological also ran through Taviani's address to the Paris congress: "Spiritual and ideological needs in the end will always prevail over economic needs". Accordingly, working together with the Third World had to be done on an ideological and spiritual platform. A spiritual vacuum - or ideological absenteeism - which was present in many Asian countries (a reference to their neutrality) was dangerous in the East-West conflict. Lefèvre explicitly stated that development aid not only was economically essential but that it was also politically urgently necessary. Herein lay the NEI's dilemma: were they to move in the direction of an "inspired" development policy with a political backdrop, or towards a depoliticized collaboration? In Paris the emphasis was placed undeniably on the first option.

The Frenchman Reynaud, the NEI's expert on the Third World, introduced the subject in Paris with a very different tone however. He had sharp criticism for development work which was motivated from pure "fear of political turmoil". He thought that technical assistance should be "as much as possible" extracted from the East-West confrontation. His argument was twofold: on the one hand, the developing countries should not *feel* the amount invested in the East-West conflict - a tactical approach - yet on the other hand, Reynaud emphasized that the rift between the "evolved" economies and the "young" economies had taken on a life of its own. Subsequently, he was one of the few to give a speech which was based on a purely economic analysis. The former French minister and ex-chairman of the Office of Overseas Research, J. Juglas, was another one. Juglas referred to the lack of local capital (the means had to come from the outside) and to the need for economic planning. He advocated industrialization and warned against the downsides of private investment.[523] These were all issues which the socialists were also studying at that moment.

Reynaud himself emphasized two "obstacles" which stood in the way of development. The first negative factor was the ever fluctuating price of raw materials, the only source of income for the developing countries. Reynaud's proposals to try and address this problem were completely in line with the proposals which the socialist economists were forwarding. One of the proposals was to set up an international bureau which would carry on a permanent dialogue between the producers and consumers of raw materials in order to be able to fix prices as much as possible. That bureau would need to have its own financial resources, so that when necessary it would be able to guarantee fixed prices, comparable to the supportive measures which various European countries had accorded to the agricultural sector.

A second obstacle was the rapid population growth in the developing countries, principally in the poorest levels of the population, which was making the gap between the poor and the rich ever larger. Reynaud drew attention to the problem, but the solution he suggested, was rather vague. Shipments of grain, in the fight against hunger, were not going to be enough; what was necessary was a total reform of the economic and agricultural structures in the developing countries. Not a word was said about measures aimed at bringing population growth under control. A subtle observation from the representative of Madagascar, Razafimbahynu, made it clear that family planning was not an option. In order to try and lessen the disparity between population growth and economic growth he postulated that "some techniques" were necessary which did not go against the psychology and mentality of the local population. Christian Democracy could provide them: "For Christian Democrats, the economy is in harmony with a concept of Man. In other words they see human beings in their entirety: not only as economic agents, but also with a mind, a heart and a soul."

The discussion on population growth in the Third World made it clear that there were two contradictory approaches within the NEI. The first approach was represented by Reynaud, who was for a more or less neutral, rational, "depoliticized" development policy, just as was the development economist Tinbergen within the Socialist International. The second approach was formulated by Reynaud's critics, who like most politicians in the International wanted to define a policy which carried a strong ideological stamp. The Swiss

---

523   Congrès des NEI, Paris, 22-24/09/1960. ACDP, IX-002-022.

catholic Bonvin, for instance, the mayor of Sion, referred to the immense work of the missionaries, who had always striven to lay the basis for an economy which took into account human dignity, something which had not even been realized in the Western world.[524] Bonvin had reservations regarding the official developmental aid which Reynaud so strongly defended. He thought that the aid could best be administered by missionaries because that was the only way to tackle things from "the bottom up", from a base of local families. Bonvin received loud applause, but he also met with some opposition. Taviani, for instance, emphatically underlined that not the slightest confusion could be allowed to exist between the activities of the Church (which as the mother of all peoples had a universal calling by definition) and the activities of the political parties which had been represented in Paris and which often had other - European - interests to defend. Taviani too was loudly applauded. André Aumonier, who represented the International Union of Catholic Employers' Associations (UNIAPAC), was also critical of Reynaud. Aumonier mainly had problems with the strong emphasis which Reynaud placed upon the role of states. According to Church doctrine and the thoroughly Christian Democratic principle of subsidiarity, the state was not the only body with an economic function. Room had to be made for private initiative as well. Principles which at the same time were reflective of self-interest: "We have to be careful, for there is a great risk that only governments will develop aid programs, which will not take into account the responsibilities typical of private enterprises." To word it differently, the developing countries needed to remain open to private investment.

Apart from the emphasis on the Christian interpretation of human dignity (for example regarding birth control), and the large amount of attention paid to the intermediary level between the state and the individual - the family, the private sector - Christian Democratic developmental thinking had yet another characteristic. The preference for the regional level, an essential characteristic of Christian Democratic transnationalism, was dominant. In contrast with the social democrats, there was little talk of technical assistance via the United Nations. The emphasis was placed on bilateral (often left over from colonialism) or - even more often - regional European development policy.

It is interesting to note how often the discussion on the developing countries automatically extended to the European integration process. According to Lugiano Dal Falco the influence of individual states was insufficient "against the communists' political and ideological provocation which we are confront-

524   Congrès des NEI, Paris, 22-24/09/1960. ACDP, IX-002-022.

ed with in the Third World ". For Reynaud global solidarity came through regional solidarity, based on "historical ties, human and economic relations - sharing the same language and culture." He let himself be inspired by the ideas of Lemaignen on an agreement between the common market, the most important importer of raw materials, and - in the first instance - the associated African countries. A strengthening of the European Economic Community was seen as one of the basic conditions for the development of the Third World: one could only share what one had.

A similar European regional approach to development issues would at that time have been entirely unthinkable for the socialists. At the SI congress in Hamburg, in 1959, Heinrich Deist spoke out quite sharply against a European development policy:"The key problem of the European Economic Commu-nity is France's attitude towards the struggle for freedom in North Africa (…) We German socialists are extremely sensitive about developments which are not free from certain features of modern colonialism (…) Therefore, at the present time, so we believe, the European Economic Community is not a suit-able instrument for mobilising Europe's support for the underdeveloped countries."[525] Instead he proposed working hand in hand with the UN, through the OECD, in which both the British Commonwealth and the US participated.

The NEI congress in Paris also gave the initial impetus to the NEI's own trans-national development policy, just like Haifa had done for the socialists. At the center of that policy was the founding of a "people's university", again a proposal of Reynaud's. The Frenchman drew his inspiration from an analysis of Paul Hoffman's, the director of the newly founded UN Special Fund. He had calculated that at least 1 million technicians, experts and managers were needed outside of Europe in order to get a development process rolling. They could not possibly all come from the West. It was therefore absolutely necessary to build up local manpower. To that end a people's university was an ideal means. It would create a possibility to compete with communism on a level playing field. The Romanian Cioranescu gave an overview of the schools which the USSR had founded in Eastern Europe for the training of functionaries. There was one in Budapest, one in Warsaw, and there were two in Prague and two in East Germany. Reynaud's proposal was ambitious. Refer-ring to Trotsky - he excused himself if he shocked anyone by dropping that name - Reynaud said that the revolution which was needed in the

---

525   Circ 1/60.04/01/1960. Report of the Sixth Congress of the Socialist International. Hamburg, 14-17/07/1959. IISG, SI 249.

developing countries presumed a "New Man": "We are revolutionary, and we have to show it to those conservatives of all religions who are doing their utmost to obstruct the rise of the New Man in history. (...) The People's University must have the support of this advancement as its essential goal."

Yet the emphasis of his proposal was placed not so much on the training of technicians but rather on the training of the people "who will have to assume responsibilities in politics, administration, social life and education."[526] Reynaud's proposal was unanimously accepted and Hahn was given the assignment of working out the details. Soon enough, however, the proposal bumped into practical problems. In November 1960, Hahn had already written to Seitlinger saying that the founding of a university was far beyond the capacities of the Christian Democrats. A training school for future business directors or a system of scholarships would be much more realistic. In the course of 1961, the idea came up again in the form of an Afro-European institute for social and economic sciences. It would be difficult to more poignantly illustrate the political and anti-communist character of Christian Democratic development policy, and the similarities it shared with the just as embryonic development policy of the Socialist International.

526   Commission Économique et Sociale des NEI. Luzern, 12/10/1961. ACDP, IX-002-042.

Third World *Vistas* Near and Far in the Early 1960's

The World According to the Socialist International

The meeting of the council in Haifa gave an enormous impulse to development thinking within the Socialist International. As a direct result of that meeting, a conference of economic experts was organized in the Austrian city of Baden, in October 1961, entirely devoted to development issues. The five-day conference was attended by 15 European, 15 Asian (from the Far and Middle east) and 15 African experts. Jan Tinbergen introduced the debate. Through him the International came into contact with very current ideas from development experts, such as Professor Rosenstein of the Massachusetts Institute of Technology. Moreover, Tinbergen was very much aware of the discussions about development aid currently taking place on the international level.

One of the most important results of Baden was the establishment of three study groups, which could count on the support of various experts. One study group was focused on "Agricultural Development", under the leadership of Raanan Weitz, the second focused on "International Economic Planning" under the guidance of Jan Tinbergen and the last was focused on "The EEC in relation to developing countries" under the leadership of Alva Myrdal, together with J.J. van der Lee, Director of Relations for Overseas Countries of the European Economic Community.[527] Baden touched upon the basics of the Third World discussions which would take place ten days later at the SI congress in Rome. A large number of the conclusions, analyses and recommendations which had been agreed upon in Baden and Rome were later

---

527   Circ. B.13/62. 30/01/1962. Secretary's Report to Bureau: Activity of Sub-Committee on
       Developing Areas. IISG, SI 111.

- sometimes word for word - taken up in the Oslo Declaration, which was approved in the spring of 1962 by the council of the International. The Oslo Declaration was a "manifesto", a declaration of principles which was meant to bring the 10 year old Frankfurt Declaration up-to-date and to exhibit a "renewed" form of socialism.

One element of that renewal was that the colonial pillar of socialist development thninking had now entirely become a thing of the past. In Hamburg Hendrik Vos still had to take the colonial context into account when developing his development policy. In the development schemes which the International worked out in Oslo (not surprisingly) this was no longer the case. The socialists themselves now asked for decolonialization and they sharply criticized all colonial remnants and neo-colonial practices.[528] The conference in Baden made the socialists realize that there was still a lot of mistrust in the developing countries of the (former) colonial masters. The Moroccan Benbarka and the Tunisian Guen from the Néo-Destour Party objected, for example, to the economic dependence which continued even after political decolonialization was achieved.[529] A representative from Iran feared that as soon as the (British) socialists were back in power, national interests (oil) would again make them forget their anti-colonial stance. The French socialists in particular received much criticism, which was not entirely unjustified. The representative of the SFIO, Julien Junillon, had traveled to Baden in order to elucidate all the advantages of bilateral assistance, according to the French model of aid to French-speaking Africa. Besides advocating bilateral aid he also advocated regional cooperation between Africa and the EEC.[530] Yet France stood all alone in Baden, just as it would later be isolated in Rome. Junillon's address was completely overshadowed by the presentations of the Dutchman Jan Tinbergen and Hillary Marquand from Great Britain, who entirely distanced themselves from the positions of their respective governments. Marquand even lamented the weak performance of the French in Baden.

The definitive "decolonialization" of development thinking, in the short term, hardly had any influence upon the second pillar of the socialist development discourse: the modernization paradigm. In comparison with the discussions which had taken place in the 1950's, it can be observed that certain parties had become somewhat more radical. Birth control - a controversial topic

528   Circ. 50/62. 15/06/1962. The Oslo Declaration. The World Today - The Socialist Perspective. IISG, SI 110.
529   Quote Benbarka. Report on the Economic Experts' Conference. Baden, 14-19/10/1961. Spool 1, side 2. Circ. B.49/61. 08/12/1961. IISG, SI 101.
530   Ibidem.

since long - was no longer a subject in need of further study but was now an essential aspect of any credible development policy. In Baden the Frenchman Julien Junillon had referred to the dramatic consequences of a population increase to 4 billion by 2000 and 6 billion by 2060! The Oslo Declaration also contained a reference to "help to families in planning their growth". A larger engagement was also called for in terms of the amount which the states contributed to development aid. The Oslo Declaration stated that contributions should no longer be "around 1%" of the net national product, but "at least 1%" of the net national product.[531]

The basic elements of the modernization paradigm, however, did not change. The causes of underdevelopment - the "bottlenecks" - were still placed in the developing countries themselves. The idea, for example, that development presupposed a fundamental reorientation in lifestyle and working patterns of the local populations and in the long run also implied a change in mentality, came word for word from Asoka Mehta's addresses in Baden and Rome. The optimism which was so characteristic of modernization was even increased by referring to the potentially emancipating character of technology and science. Hendrik Vos had already referred to this back in Hamburg in 1959, pointing out the contribution science had made to the emancipation of the worker in the 19th century.[532] At the impetus of the PvdA, a paragraph was included in the Oslo Declaration on the quick progression of scientific discoveries, which for the first time in history had made possible the elimination of poverty and hunger.[533] Moreover, the paragraph continued, the developing countries had the advantage of being able to avoid making the same mistakes which the developed countries had made. Lastly, the two principal activities kept their prominent place: financial transfers (the financing of investment projects, as a supplement to what the developing countries were able to invest themselves), and teaching and training, even if the Socialist International tried to give each of them a specifically socialist twist, by stressing planning and the importance of the community over the private sector.

That which was included in the Declaration of Oslo, bore witness to a certain continuity. Even more important was what was not included in the declaration. In her closing address in Baden, Hillary Marquand stated that there was general consensus among the experts regarding the need to stabilize the

531   In Baden Tinbergen had pleaded for a percentage between 1 and 2%.
532   Circ 1/60. 04/01/1960. Report of the Sixth Congress of the Socialist International. Hamburg, 14-17/07/1959. IISG, SI 249.
533   Circ. 50/62. 15/06/1962. The Oslo Declaration. The World Today - The Socialist Perspective. IISG, SI 107.

terms of exchange for the finished products which the West produced and the raw materials provided by the developing countries. "It is the terms of trade between manufactured goods and primary products which must be stabilized and can be stabilized to a greater degree than they have been hitherto."[534] It was a topic that would come up again and again. At the congress of the International in Rome, for example, Asoka Mehta made quite an impression with his ornate plea for trade reform: "While this problem of economic aid is very important, we in our countries have been finding that there is some kind of a Penelope's robe that is being woven. What is woven in the day is undone in the night. What is given to us through economic aid is taken away through the imbalance that has arisen in the terms of trade. We therefore appeal to you to give the highest consideration to the question of stabilization of prices of various agricultural and other commodities."[535]

The Burmese socialist U Kyaw Nyein was more skeptical. He said it was one thing to talk about such a stabilization of prices among economists and intellectuals, but he saw no single government ready to place the topic on its agenda. The few international accords which had been reached on grain, sugar or tin were far from sufficient. In Baden, Asoka Mehta asked that the possibilities of developing countries setting up their own textile industry be looked into. European social democrats could play a role in that: "The socialist movement must help the Trade Union Movement, both in the process of retraining of workers in the rich countries for other occupations and, what is even more important, in creating that atmosphere where this demand of what somebody has called 'one-way free trade' will not be resisted and misunderstood. (…) We, the infant sectors of the world, must be nursed, must be given protection."

Tinbergen in any case wanted to go further. He proposed working out a system to insure against falling export income, an idea which at that moment was being worked on by a group of UN experts. He also proposed introducing a gradual reduction in the external tariff of the European Community and raising the EEC quota for both industrial products from Japan, India and Hong Kong, and for a certain number of agricultural products. The last suggestion was made explicitly on his own behalf: he knew all too well that there would be much political opposition, not the least from "his own" Dutch textile sector.

---

534   Circ. B.49/61. 08/12/1961. Report on the Economic Experts' Conference. Baden, 14-19/10/1961. Spool 12. IISG, SI 104.

535   Circ. 72/62. 19/10/1962. Report of the Seventh Congress of the Socialist International. Rome, 23-27/10/1961. IISG, SI 108.

Tinbergen's assessment proved to be correct. In the chapter on the developing countries in the Oslo Declaration there was no mention of any such structural measure. All attention was focused on the finding of qualified technicians and the accumulating of investment funds, from aid and other sources. The global economy as a whole was only briefly mentioned in the chapter on the industrialized nations, who were called upon to stimulate international trade "unimpeded by high tariff barriers and undisturbed by exchange and currency crises."[536] A stronger global economy would make redistribution, via aid, all the more possible. This was not exactly what Mehta had in mind when he said "trade, not aid". In other words: on the eve of the breakthrough of *dependencia* development theories, the Socialist International was still not paying the least attention to the more structural causes behind underdevelopment, causes which were endemic to the global trade system itself and not necessarily a problem particular to the developing countries themselves.

With regard to the third pillar of socialist development thinking, the Cold War, a considerable evolution took place between the very first draft of the Oslo Declaration in July 1961 and the definitive version in June 1962. The attention which had originally been placed on the Cold War in the first versions was gradually shifted to development issues. The shift was not only in terms of content but it was also visible in the structure of the document. While in the original versions the passages on the communist block headed the document and those on the newly independent countries closed the text, in the final version the order was entirely reversed. An explicit formulation of how these new states constituted easy prey for communist expansion was not included in the final version.

How to explain this shift? A first explanatory factor - on the transnational level - was the conference of experts in Baden, where non-European socialists were particularly vocal. In her report, the British Member of Parliament Hillary Marquand noted that one of the most important conclusions of the gathering was that "they counseled strongly against negative-sounding pronouncements of the Cold War."[537] Marquand undoubtedly had in mind a few of Mehta's outbursts against the French representatives who were of the opinion that development aid could not be entirely separated from ideological considerations. Mehta was categorically opposed to this reasoning: "There

536   Circ. 50/62. 15/06/1962. The Oslo Declaration. The World Today - The Socialist Perspective. IISG, SI 107.
537   Circ. B.49/61. 08/12/1961. Report on the Economic Experts' Conference. Baden, 14-19/10/1961. IISG, SI 104.

are many of us here who feel that the emergent nations must be allowed to pursue their goals, their hopes, their ambitions without being involved, without being sucked into Cold War politics." The Ugandan Nekyon, of the Uganda Peoples' Congress, brought forth various examples, often based on his own experience, demonstrating that anti-communism in Africa was actually one of the largest obstacles to the spreading of socialism; certain individuals were so obsessed with communism that any discussion of improving the lot of the poor was entirely impossible.

The development debate was largely depoliticized not only because many non-European experts were involved in the working out of socialist development policy, but also because of the contributions made by economists. This was made most apparent during Jan Tinbergen's preliminary address in Baden, which to a large extent set the tone for the rest of the debate. Tinbergen emphasized the need for an efficient and pragmatic approach: "If I compare ourselves with both the big partners on the world scene, the communists on the one hand and the Americans on the other hand, then I feel that they are both typically doctrinaire (…) Our idea is I think not to be doctrinaire in this respect but to look for efficiency". Mehta, who also left his impression on the conference, entirely supported Tinbergen: "The formal doctrinaire rigidity has gone; there is today an attitude of understanding of the economic forces that operate in the countries and in the world."[538] According to Mehta this - under certain conditions - made a strong cooperation (a working relationship) with the private sector possible.

The pragmatism of the economists went along well with the pragmatism that had become an essential element of the revisionist trend which had swept over European social democracy since the end of the 1950's. This (internal political) revisionism forms a second - undoubtedly just as important - factor which can help explain the International's discovery of the Third World.

It was this revisionism which made the Socialist International decide to formulate a new manifesto at the beginning of January 1961. In order to wipe the dust off of socialism's reputation, a new declaration of principles seemed just the remedy. Various European parties were aware that if socialism wanted to make a success of it in the ballot box - revisionism was mainly attractive to those parties which seemed to be stuck in opposition - then it was high time that it adapted itself to the new societal reality. In the 1950's, the consumer society and the welfare state - which also served the interests of the working

538   Ibidem, Spool 1, side 1.

class - were in full bloom and capitalism was booking one success after the other. These successes contrasted shrilly with the failures of the socialist recipes such as nationalization schemes.[539] The revisionism of the late 1950's was therefore primarily an attempt to get rid of some of the doctrinal rigidity of the socialist credo which scared off many voters as well as potential Christian Democratic or liberal coalition partners. The revisionists held that capitalism led to continual economic growth and in this it departed from what had long been the end goal of socialism: the abolition of the private ownership of the means of production. Donald Sassoon succinctly summarized the underlying theory of revisionism: "If capitalism can promote growth, then socialism can leave well alone and concentrate on its remaining priority: ensuring an equitable social division of the fruits of growth. In other words, belief in growth justified the greater significance placed by Crosland on the distribution of wealth at the expense of the struggle for the abolition of the private ownership of capital."[540]

This allowed for a stronger emphasis on the ethical dimension of socialism, with values such as the fight against inequality and poverty. These were the goals which henceforth would be emphasized as the essential goals of social democracy. It was indeed mainly a matter of more emphasis. If one compares the program points of the most important revisionist documents with the 1951 Frankfurt Declaration for instance, it immediately becomes apparent that not one single point was actually new. The national context, however, made it necessary to bring all the various points together under one roof, accompanied with lots of publicity. In Great Britain, for example, even a public relations bureau was hired. The firm discovered that the BLP was perceived as an old-fashioned party, obsessed with nationalization, and anchored in a prewar worker's consciousness.

The same held true for the SPD. The revision of the party program which took place in Bad Godesberg was not much more than a run-down of the principles which the party had followed since 1945. It was a question of image building. Besides the British and the German parties, the Austrian SPÖ was also fairly far down that same path. In contrast with the BLP and the SPD, however, the SPÖ was at that moment in power, in a coalition government with the ÖVP. The elections of 1956 widened the gap with the ÖVP though (the SPÖ won 1%, the ÖVP 5%), while the party had hoped to become the bigger of the two. This strengthened the position of the revisionists in the

---

539   Sassoon, *One Hundred Years of Socialism*, 241.
540   Ibidem, 245.

party. In Austria the revisionist change began in 1957, during the party's congress in Salzburg.

On the transnational level, it would take until the beginning of 1961 before the heads of the European parties in the International came together to revise the Frankfurt Declaration of Principles (1951). Right from the beginning the revisionists were able to leave their impression on the working group which had the task of writing down the new declaration of principles. Hugh Gaitskell, the standard bearer of revisionism in the BLP, Bruno Pittermann from the ÖVP and Herbert Wehner from the SPD all participated. The presence of Guy Mollet, the fourth member of the working group, kept things in balance. The SFIO, after all, had no interest in revising the principles of socialism. The presence of the relatively strong Communist Party and of the rather weak Parti Socialiste Autonome (set up by André Philip, who in 1957 had been removed from the SFIO), meant that the SFIO could make no concessions on their Marxist-leftist position.[541] The party did not even want to let go of the concept of "the dictatorship of the proletariat", which made their credibility with the voters sink even further. The SFIO was not alone: both the Belgian SP, which played a very limited role in the ideological discussions in the early 1960's, and the Dutch PvdA, which still carried some weight, were opposed to all forms of revisionism.

The new Declaration of Principles, which was approved in Oslo in June 1962, was therefore a compromise in which the majority of parties - or at least the most important - were to get their way. The text was consequently of a rather hybrid nature. The declaration begun by stating that the International still remained true to the beliefs expressed in the Declaration of Frankfurt, something which the more traditional parties insisted on including. A little further the text stated that history had not confirmed the doctrine of the impoverishment of the proletariat, a victory for the revisionists in the International. The passage which asserted that only a radical restructuring of the former economic and social structures would allow man to reach his full potential - an addition of the PvdA - was actually more radical than most revisionists wanted. The reference to the new class of "managers", which replaced the traditional class of capitalists, was a British addition. At the same time, in the Declaration of Oslo there were more references to a planned economy than in revisionist texts, such as the Bad Godesberg program.[542] And these are but a few examples.

541   Touchard, *La gauche en France*, 303-306.
542   Burnham, *The Managerial Revolution*; Crosland, *The Future of Socialism*, 15; Circ. 50/62. 15/06/1962. The Oslo Declaration. The World Today - The Socialist Perspective. IISG, SI 107.

Despite the fact that the Declaration of Oslo was originally instigated by parties which for reasons of domestic politics had revised their national programs, internal politics were not really central to the document. The passages which were related to domestic topics - the fight against monopolies, planned economies - cover only slightly more than a fourth of the text. The emphasis was placed irrefutably on international politics.[543] Precisely herein lay the added value of the transnational level. The transnational cooperation could only survive by focusing on topics which did not effect the autonomy of the participating members. Development issues lent themselves excellently to this role: they answered perfectly all the demands of the drive towards globalization of the International. It was the combination of these two factors which led to the "discovery of the Third World": revisionism, which was a consequence of domestic political factors, resulted in the belief that capitalism would lead to continual growth. As a consequence, socialists could focus entirely on the equitable distribution of that growth. The transition from an equitable distribution at home to an equitable distribution on the international level was stimulated by the transnational network that bound European and non-European socialists together. It was in these transnational discussions that the Third World came to light.

The World According to the Nouvelles Équipes Internationales

Intensive discussions about the Third World such as those between European and non-European socialists - in Haifa, Baden, Rome and Oslo - did not take place in the NEI. In the 1950's, the NEI had not evolved into a forum which would have stimulated similar debates. Their contacts with Africa, of which initially so much had been expected, rather quickly ended up bearing no fruit, just as had been the case for the social democrats. Asian partners were also missing, which was not the case for the socialists. In the first half of the 1960's, Latin America was the only region outside of Europe with which the NEI had regular contact. Institutionally, however, even these contacts were not very intense. They were of a more ad hoc nature. Except for meeting each other at their congresses, collaboration did not actually amount to much. It

---

543   28,3% of the text relates to domestic policy, 60,9% to foreign policy and international politics. The remaining 10,8% of the document deals with general principles which apply to both policy areas.

did not go smooth either, quite the contrary: the tensions seemed actually to increase when the years passed by, until they eventually led to a long period devoid of any collaboration between Latin America and Europe.

One of the initial sources of tension, which was discussed earlier, was the difference in perception vis-à-vis the Cold War, in particular with regard to the role of the United States in the Cold War. The loyalty of the NEI to the United States varied depending on the particular subject which happened to be discussed at any given moment. At the NEI's Paris congress, for example, the Belgian Christian Democrat de la Vallée Poussin was sharply critical of the "hypocritical" development policy of the United States: "The United States arrive in those underdeveloped countries promising technicians, pretending to be anti-colonialist, but at the same time their businessmen, their companies pursue policies which are ruining the region."

Yet Africa - where Europe had vested interests - was not Latin America. On a continent where communism, ever since the Cuban Revolution, formed a constant threat, the NEI did not question the hegemony of the United States, which was not always appreciated by their Latin American colleagues. This double discourse can best be illustrated by the remarks which the Austrian Herman Witham made at the Third International Conference of the NEI, in Chile, in July 1961. Witham called on the NEI to expand their perspective so that they were not always viewing everything in the light of the East-West conflict. In Vienna, where around 10,000 foreign students from Asia and Africa were completing their studies, the world was observed from a different point of view, namely from a North-South perspective, a concept which otherwise was entirely absent in both the NEI and the Socialist International. But to the Latin American Christian Democrats he said: "Not everywhere changes are caused by communism, but the fact of not having changed a social situation does give rise to communism. We won't win the struggle against communism by just saying 'man can live by bread alone', but we have to provide bread too."[544]

A second source of tension, which likewise has already been discussed, was the difference in socio-economic policy between Latin American and European Christian Democrats. Unavoidably this influenced the discussions on Third World issues which took place during the meetings between Latin Americans and Europeans. At that moment Latin America was exceptionally

---

544   The third international conference, Santiago de Chile, 27-30/07/1961. Report Hahn. ACDP, IX-002-029.

fertile soil for development thinking. At the end of the 1950's, a group of Latin American economists began to work out an original development theory. They questioned the international division of labor on the basis of comparative advantages and replaced that model with a "center/periphery" model. The epicenter of the theoretical renewal was the "Comisión Económica para America Latina" (CEPAL), which was under the leadership of the Argentinean Raul Prebisch. Prebisch would later become the secretary-general of UNCTAD. The "center/periphery" model was primarily a reaction against the neo-classical beliefs that international specialization via free trade would lead to an optimal partition of the world income and to a maximization of the income of all those participating in world trade.[545]

During the International Conference of Christian Democrats in Chile in 1961, Franco Montoro established himself as the voice of this new train of thought. He was extremely critical of all the aid programs which were exclusively focused on the effects of the misery, without taking the system of world trade as a whole into consideration: "For the majority of the underdeveloped countries the most important cause of their underdevelopment and the impossibility to escape it, without any doubt, is the unfair, unstable and insufficient price on the international market for raw materials of agricultural origin or from the mining industry, which are the basis of their economies." Amply armed with UN statistics, he bemoaned two problems in particular: the continual devaluation of raw materials in comparison with the finished products and the price fluctuations. His conclusion was harsh: "the underdeveloped countries are continually being exploited by international commerce". After all, the industrial countries determined the prices and in many instances controlled the markets. Moreover the high salaries of the industrial countries were only possible thanks to the low salaries in the developing countries. He concluded: "Instead of aid programs they want fair prices for their products, since they are convinced that they cannot go on accepting as aid that which, in principle, already belongs to them by right." These problems needed to be discussed in a yet to be called together "global economic conference", a precursor of the foundation of UNCTAD in 1964.[546]

This discourse was rather far from the classical liberal accents which certain Christian Democratic parties emphasized, in particular the German CDU. The Europeans were thoroughly aware that any association with economic

545   Baeck, *Post-War Development Theories and Practice*, 48.
546   The third international conference, Santiago de Chile, 27-30/07/1961. Report Hahn. ACDP, IX-002-029.

classical liberalism was a handicap in their contacts with the Third World. This was a point which was returned to time and again in Paris. The German Hermann Stehle was of the opinion that if capitalism wanted to be a model for the developing countries, then it would have to receive a facelift. An essential element of the new capitalism would be worker participation, a concept which he explained at great length using the example of Volkswagen, which gave its workers the option of becoming shareholders in the company. Albert Coppé, the vice-chairman of the ECSC, was of the same opinion. Christian Democrats had to avoid at all costs being associated with any form of economic classical liberalism, just as they had to avoid being associated with European Catholicism. After all, the developing countries would get the short end of the stick in a classical liberal market economy.

In the end, however, neither the pressure from the Third World - by which Asia and Africa were understood - nor the pressure from the Latin Americans was sufficient either in the NEI or in the CDU to lead to a change in course. In the CDU in particular, trust in classical liberalism was deeply rooted. In the first years after the war, in the American occupied section of Germany, they had become familiar with the policies aimed at the liberalization of the West German economy. In such a climate the classical liberal theories of the German economist Ludwig Erhard, the former director of the *Verwaltung für Wirtschaft des Vereinigten Wirtschaftsgebietes*, flourished. In June 1948, he had placed himself at the disposition of the CDU and he had got the opportunity to entirely rewrite the program of the party.[547] A year later the *Düsseldorfer Leitsätze* were approved, in which classical liberalism had been elevated to a new orthodoxy.[548] From the second half of the 1950's onwards, the influence which the CDU was able to exercise upon the NEI only increased, especially after the withering of the MRP had created a power vacuum. The CDU and its program had become something to be reckoned with, a fact which made relations with Latin America considerably more difficult. Consequently, for the Christian Democrats development issues were not the right theme for building up their transnational network, in contrast with the socialists.

The second factor which in the Socialist International had led to the discovery of the Third World was also missing on the Christian Democratic side. The years in the opposition had forced the social democrats to adapt their programs to the national and the international evolution. Christian Democracy, on the other hand, went through a golden decade in the 1950's.

547   Uertz, *Christentum und Sozialismus*, 197.

The Christian Democratic parties were by and large governing parties, and were more focused on issues of governing than on ideological questions. Status quo parties, as Roberto Papini wrote, were "out of step" with new issues such as development.[549] That lack of renewal would eventually led to a good deal of self criticism by the end of the 1960's, even in the EUCD, the successor of the NEI. EUCD chairman Rumor gave succinct voice to the malaise at the bureau meeting of September 1968: "We have to admit that our parties have not sufficiently renewed themselves; we cannot but observe that everything is on the move (…). We have to admit that we are absorbed in current affairs, and fairly often we are forgetting to take a break in order to reflect on ourselves."[550] The Atlantic Alliance, the market economy and bipolarity: these elements formed the frame of reference for the NEI in the first half of the 1960's.

The lack of a true transnational debate on developmental problems with experts from outside of Europe and the lack of an internal political context which gave rise to ideological renewal explain the lack of a true discovery of the Third World in the NEI in the 1960's. The speeches, documents and activities related to the subject leave no room for doubt. In Eichholz economic analyses were pushed aside by the struggle to work out a religiously inspired development program. The memoranda which the Hahn Center published would make interesting reading for anyone interested in having an understanding of Soviet penetration into Africa: they give a detailed picture of sundry Soviet activities on the African continent. Educational activities, such as the visit of a Latin American youth group to Europe from August till October 1963, contain all sorts of anti-communist propaganda, partly because they were strongly influenced by the CDUCE. In such circumstances the Third World remained on the far horizon.

Let us conclude with an ironical observation: of the two transnational organizations which were studied here, the one which in the early 1960's had yet to discover the Third World - the NEI - was the one to use the term most frequently. In the Socialist International, on the other hand, which very much had the Third World in mind, the term was almost never used. Asian socialists used the term on occasion - mostly, however, they spoke of underdeveloped countries, or from the second half of the 1950's on, of developing countries -

548   Van Kemseke, "From Permission to Prohibition. The Impact of the Changing International Context", 257-258.

549   Papini, *The Christian Democrat International*, 242.

550   Procès-verbal du bureau de l'EUCD. Venice, 12/09/1968. ACDP, IX-004-052.

yet their European colleagues never seemed to pick the term up. Only the Frenchman Christian Pineau used the term "Third World" once in Hamburg in 1959.[551] The "Third World" was after all a term which in the 1950's was firmly anchored in the French-speaking regions, and which would only later break through to the English-speaking world. The use of the term illustrates yet once more the continental orientation of the NEI and the Anglo-Saxon orientation of the Socialist International.

551   Circ 1/60. 04/01/1960. Report of the Sixth Congress of the Socialist International. Hamburg, 14-17/07/1959. IISG, SI 249.

Conclusion

The socialist and Christian Democratic transnational organizations which emerged after the Second World War - the Socialist International (SI) and the Nouvelles Équipes Internationales (NEI) - were different from each other in several respects. The Socialist International was a relatively centralized organization, composed of socialist *parties* and dominated by the British Labour Party (and their foreign policy priorities). The NEI was a rather loosely organized association, largely influenced by the French Mouvement Républicain Populaire (and their foreign policy priorities). It was partly composed of Christian Democratic parties, and partly of Christian Democratic 'équipes' or *groups* which contained party members as well as members of civil society.

In the 1950s, both transnationals would be subject to the influences of globalization at the international level. Before the decade was over they would try to define their position in what the Canadian researcher Marshall McLuhan called "the global village". Between 1945 and 1965 both the SI and the NEI left their Western European home bases to establish contacts - with varying degrees of success - with like-minded socialist and Christian Democratic parties or movements in Asia, Latin America and Africa. Not surprisingly, the globalization process of both organizations evolved rather differently. The more the unitary Socialist International (with their center in London) took on a universalist outlook, the more decentralizing or regionalist tendencies manifested themselves. The globalization process of the Christian Democrats followed another path: regional Christian Democratic organizations gradually expanded contacts with each other, without, however, really reducing the autonomy of the regional level.

National and International Driving Forces of Globalization

The globalization of both Western European ideologies was the result of a broad range of factors at various levels. National interests were a major driving force. It was obvious, for example, that the BLP used the Socialist International to keep the territories which had gained independence from Great Britain in 1947 - India, Pakistan, Burma, Ceylon - within the British sphere of influence. The party, which was then in the government, hoped to see the socialist parties of the British Commonwealth and of Asia united in "a great association of labour and socialist parties of the world", as the BLP expressed it. This explains the early, British-financed expansion of the Socialist International to Asia. International evolutions such as the outbreak of the Korean War in 1950 and the spread of the Cold War to Asia reinforced the necessity to move into Asia. When socialist transnationalism left Europe, the Cold War became its *compagnon de route*. It was, in other words, an expansion to the rhythm of the Cold War. The BLP not only considered the Socialist International a useful instrument in Asia, but also in Europe itself. More than once, the Socialist International was used to make the Atlantic pillar of British foreign policy - as, for example, expressed in the Marshall Plan and NATO - acceptable to more 'ideological' or 'old-fashioned' socialist parties in Europe. The propagation of democratic socialism in the struggle against communism became the International's main function: a function which the British thought worthy of financial support.

A similar combination of national interests and the international evolution determined the Nouvelles Équipes Internationales' globalization process. In this case, it was mainly the Eastern European Christian Democrats in exile - united in the CDUCE - who stimulated their Western European counterparts to expand outside of Europe. With the financial backing from sponsors in the United States, the exiles used every opportunity to stimulate the NEI to fight communism on a global scale. They financed, for example, the 'intercontinental conferences' that brought Christian Democrats together from Europe and Latin America. In 1964, the Eastern European Christian Democrats - and their sponsors - were strengthened in their resolve to turn Latin American Christian Democracy into an anti-communist force by the electoral victory of Eduardo Frei against the socialist/communist Salvador Allende in Chile. The fact that several Western European governments and the US had backed Frei illustrates the complementary role which transnational organizations could play.

The NEI, however, managed to block all efforts towards a more global role for themselves. The NEI's main focus was to strengthen the emerging European institutions, which risked being dominated by the socialists, the NEI thought. Their answer to the Cold War was building a strong Europe, an ambition which was in line with the NEI's long-standing 'abendländisch' ideal, their ideological preference for regionalism and with the national interests of some of their main members, notably France and Germany. Moreover, it was a process which the NEI thought - quite realistically - they could to some extent influence. For the Socialist International, in which the British Labour Party played such a dominant role, European integration was much less a uniting factor, quite the contrary, and thus also quite less attractive.

The UN, a Catalyst of Transnational Globalization

In the globalization process of social democracy and Christian Democracy, a crucial role was played by the United Nations, the forum par excellence where international globalization took shape. In general, the Socialist International paid more attention to their relations with the UN than the NEI did. Several key figures of the socialist movement played an important role both within the UN system and within the International. For example, the International's role in the anti-Apartheid struggle in the early 1960s was directly inspired by the UN Commission on South Africa, chaired by the Swedish socialist Alva Myrdal, who on several occasions had played a prominent role in the International. On the Christian Democratic side, relations with the UN were generally a reserved privilege for some individuals from the CDUCE, e.g. the Polish exile Konrad Sieniewicz. Fiercely anti-communist, Sieniewicz represented the NEI at the UN, and chose his own priorities. He was mainly engaged in human rights issues (especially those violated by the USSR), and was active in the ad hoc committee on forced labour. UN resolutions trickled down through him to NEI deliberations, such as was the case when the 1954 NEI Congress in Bruges adopted a resolution on forced labour. In general, however, the NEI themselves were more indifferent towards the world organization, if not critical. Around 1960, for example, relations were at a low. The UN were mainly considered, as the Belgian NEI President Theo Lefèvre stated at the 1960 Congress in Paris, an organization "used by the forces of anti-colonialism against those European countries with a high level of civilization" - a reference to the Afro-Asian bloc in the General Assembly repeatedly attacking some of the European governments in which Christian Democrats played leading roles.

Despite these reservations, the United Nations played a double role for both the NEI and the Socialist International. Firstly, discussions at the UN stimulated both organizations to pay more attention to other continents. The UN were, in other words, a catalyst of transnational globalization. When Franco, the Spanish Head of State, sought the support of Latin American governments to obtain UN recognition of his regime after the Second World War, the anti-Francoist socialists in exile used the Socialist International to lobby these same governments, through the mediation of Latin American socialists, in order to try to thwart Franco's attempts. When in the second half of the 1950s, France was under fierce criticism in the UN (as a consequence of the admission of Morocco and Tunisia as UN members, and because of reports of French atrocities in Algeria and France's role in the Suez-crisis), the French MRP actively used the NEI to lobby like-minded Latin Americans to support France in the General Assembly. This explained the presence of NEI secretary-general Coste-Floret at the 1957 congress of the Latin American Christian Democratic Organization (ODCA) in Sao Paolo.

Secondly, the UN were also a major source of inspiration for the discussions which took place in both transnational organizations. It became an important agenda point both for the Socialist International and the NEI when the developing countries asked the UN to create a Special United Nations Fund for Economic Development as a supplement or alternative to the World Bank in the early fifties. In other words, the debate on SUNFED to a large extent stimulated development thinking on the transnational level. Often, there was a direct link between the UN agenda and the discussions in the SI and the NEI. In 1952, for example, the chairman of the Social-Economic Commission of the NEI, the Belgian van der Straten-Waillet participated in the 13th session of ECOSOC, where development issues were exhaustively discussed. On his return, and inspired by his report, the NEI asked a Dutch economist to write a "comprehensive report on development" based on statistical data, the guidelines of the Vatican and the Church, and the discussions in the UN. This is a clear indication as to what extent the UN stimulated, or even initiated development thinking at the transnational plane, which would eventually trickle down into the party programs of the national parties which were part of the SI and the NEI.

The Three Pillars of Development Thinking

I n the 1950s and early 1960s, reflections in the SI and the NEI on underdevelopment and development rested on three major pillars. They were first
of all strongly determined by a colonialist framework. Secondly, they were
embedded in the Cold War. And thirdly, they were subject to the so-called
modernization paradigm. Over the course of time, the importance of these
pillars would evolve differently in both transnationals.

In 1952 the Socialist International, the first of the two organizations to set
eyes on the developing world, produced their extensive World Plan for
Mutual Aid, which reflected the BLP's and other socialist parties' colonial way
of thinking; "full independence and self-government" could only be granted
to countries with sufficiently democratic institutions, not to countries in
which there was a political vacuum that risked being filled by communism.
The International's aim was 'to replace colonialism by democratic independence', 'to guide the people in the dependent territories towards responsible
democratic self-government'. At that point in time, the SI could not yet accept
some major demands of the developing countries: the use of the term 'self-
determination' (instead of 'self-government', which still implied a link with
the mother country) and a reference to the UN Charter, which by its call for
respect for the principle of equal rights and self-determination of peoples
had become a powerful weapon in the hands of those countries.

From 1955 onwards this would change. In that year, SI documents included
specific references to the UN Charter as well as to the right to self-determination. The BLP presence in the opposition had gradually strengthened the
position of the anti-colonialist lobby within the party, and consequently
within the International. At the same time, international détente made the
Cold War less omnipresent and dominant. Finally, on the transnational level
there was considerable pressure from the anti-colonialist Asian Socialist
Conference, which let their voice more and more clearly be heard. All these
factors gave the International more flexibility in absorbing new issues and
ideas. The fear of being stuck in the opposition stimulated British, German
and Austrian socialists to thoroughly revise their party programs.
They accepted the capitalist recipe for economic growth, which from that
moment onwards would allow them to focus on the equal distribution of that
growth. The step from equal distribution on the national level to more equality on the international level was facilitated by the existence of a forum where
domestic socialist revisionism and the emerging international issue of devel-

opment could be linked with each other: the Socialist International.

In sum, new ideas flourished in a transnational organization in which the main member parties were in the opposition, rather than in an organization in which the parties' manoeuvring space was limited by government responsibilities.

This explains why on the Christian Democratic side, anti-colonialism made less headway. When the issue of development was put on the international agenda, the NEI was composed of parties that to a large extent made national policy. Immersed in daily decision-making processes, there was little time left to learn new issues. The NEI clearly had more difficulty leaving the colonial framework behind. Several speakers at the 1960 NEI Congress in Paris even expressed their admiration for some of the realizations of colonialism. By that time, the Socialist International had already largely ended that phase, even though the Algerian question would continue to cause problems for some years to come. The colonialist image of the French socialists - which were part of the French government - led to their marginalization within the International, and was one of the reasons why the International preferred not to pay any attention to a ('colonialist') European development policy, the main priority for the NEI. Instead, it focused more on development projects which were elaborated in the UN, which was a forum much less acceptable to the NEI.

The second pillar of the development thinking of socialism and Christian Democracy was the Cold War. In the Socialist International, the lobbying of the neutralist Asian socialists was counterbalanced by the pro-Atlantic Dutch socialists, who succeeded in dominating the discussions on development issues. Reflections on development policies would therefore - throughout the decade - remain imbued with anti-communism, even though in the second half of the fifties the British - and initially also the German - socialists tried to put the International on the way to détente.

The rivalry with the Soviet Union influenced every single issue related to development, even birth control. The availability of statistical data on overpopulation made it become a major issue in the early fifties. In 1952, tackling birth control was still a difficult issue for the International. Morgan Phillips repeatedly reminded his colleagues that according to USSR propaganda 'advocacy of birth control for coloured peoples is part of the armoury of Western imperialism.' In the NEI, other arguments were used against the promotion of birth control policies. Western European Christian Democrats and the few African Christians that participated in NEI congresses (for whom family planning 'went against the psychology and mentality of the local population') opposed them on the grounds of 'human dignity'. This, however, did not mean that the battle against communist infiltration in the developing world did not justify the elaboration of Christian Democratic development aid. Since the launching of the Sputnik, for the Italian Christian Democrat Taviani, the conquest of space and the conquest of the Third World had been two priorities of equal importance. This explains why the contacts which the NEI had established by the end of the decade with Latin America - indeed a very fertile ground for development thinking - did not fundamentally influence Christian Democratic ideology. At that time, just after the Cuban Revolution, Latin America was under the spell of the Cold War, which excluded a depolarisation of the issue. At their congresses, the NEI continued to plead for 'political', and religiously and spiritually-inspired, development aid. The voice of more 'neutral' economists was too weak to influence this preference. On the socialist side, it was very different. There, the debate was largely dominated by leading economists such as Jan Tinbergen and the Myrdals. This facilitated the 'discovery of the Third World': the understanding that the flagrant socio-economic inequalities on a global scale existed in their own right, autonomous of the East-West conflict. It implied that the 'Third World' was beginning to be considered as an economic concept, as a metaphor, rather than as a political concept, and further that the issue of underdevelopment had became an independent topic and no longer only an annex of the Cold War.

Despite the aforementioned differences, the development theories of social democrats and Christian Democrats had one important characteristic in common. Both ideologies were indebted to the modernization paradigm, which in the two decades after the Second World War had hardly been challenged in Western development thinking. Nobody questioned that the main causes of underdevelopment were the various barriers to development situated in the underdeveloped territories themselves: primitive agricultural techniques, feudal land divisions, the concentration of power in the hands of small groups, an outmoded political system, or the 'traditional' mentality of the native peoples. Nobody questioned the optimistic belief that technology and science would soon eliminate poverty and hunger. And nobody questioned that financial transfers, and teaching and training were the main solutions to eradicate underdevelopment.

Of course, in the early sixties, alternative models which stressed the importance of more structural solutions were in the air, influenced or not by the emerging *independencia* school. Economic experts who participated in NEI or SI congresses underlined the need to stabilize the terms of trade between manufactured goods and primary products and intermittently lobbied for trade reform. At a socialist meeting, a representative from the underdeveloped world introduced the powerful image of Penelope's robe: what is woven in the day is undone in the night; what is given to the developing countries through economic aid is taken away through the imbalance that has arisen in the terms of trade. At the same line, the Dutch professor Tinbergen proposed introducing a gradual reduction in the external tariff of the European Community and raising the European Community's quota for industrial products and for a number of agricultural products from developing countries. But such ideas could not yet count on much political support. Structural measures were hardly mentioned in NEI or SI documents of the early sixties. On the eve of the breakthrough of *dependencia* development theories, social democracy and Christian Democracy were still not paying attention to the structural causes behind underdevelopment: causes which were endemic to the global trade system itself and not necessarily a problem particular to the developing countries themselves.

There is a world of difference between global politics in 1945 and global politics in 1965. By 1965, a relatively new era in world politics had set in. An 'era of development' in which theories, strategies and policies to reduce or even eradicate underdevelopment figure prominently on the agenda of international actors (for and foremost the United Nations), transnational players, and various non-governmental and other actors at the level of individual countries. An era in which the distinction between these different levels and actors has become ever less clear. World politics indeed have become a very complex web of interactions, in which transnational relations - too often ignored in a traditional one-sided focus on purely intergovernmental relations - play a crucial role.

Forty years after the 'era of development' set in, the issue of development is still one of the major challenges for the international community. This was once more illustrated when in September 2005 191 Heads of State and government, representatives of international organisations, and transnational entities gathered in New York to evaluate the ambitious UN Millennium Development Goals, which they agreed upon in 2000 and which constitute the current 'paradigm' of development thinking. Although it is clear that development thinking has evolved considerably in the last forty years, many of today's discussions and analyses still sound extremely familiar. In the future, historians will be able to judge whether around 2005 a new era had set in,

Conclusion

an era repeatedly called for by the UN Secretary-General Kofi Annan: an 'era of implementation', in which the analyses, recommendations and policies of the era of development will actually be implemented.

Abbreviations

ACDP   Archiv für Christlich-Demokratische Politik, Bonn
ADS   August De Schrijver, Leuven
AN   Archives Nationales, Paris
IISG   Internationaal Instituut voor Sociale Geschiedenis, Amsterdam
KADOC Documentatie- en Onderzoekscentrum voor Religie, Cultuur en Samenleving, Leuven
SI   Socialist International

Bibliography

ARCHIVES

1. Amsterdam, *Internationaal Instituut voor Sociale Geschiedenis*

- Archief International Union of Socialist Youth
- Archief Socialist International (1945-1965)

2. Leuven, *KADOC*

- Archief A.E. De Schryver
- Archief P.W. Segers
- Archief R. Houben
- Archief T. Lefèvre

3. Manchester, *Labour Party Archives*

- BLP Study Papers
- Files Advisory Committee in International Questions
- Files BLP International Department (correspondance William Gillies)
- Files BLP International Department (Papers Denis Healey)
- Files National Executive Committee (BLP)/ NEC International Sub-Committee
- Papers Morgan Phillips (box 3, 17, 21)

4. Paris, *Archives Nationales*

- 519 AP: Fonds Robert Bichet
- 457 AP: Fonds George Bidault
  457 AP 59: correspondance diplomatique
  457 AP 185: Alfred Coste-Floret
  457 AP 186: Francisque Gay
  457 AP 187: Maurice Schumann
- 350 AP Archives du MRP
  Fonds MRP-National (7-22; 45-60; 71-103)
  Fonds MRP-Seine (9; 32)

5. Paris, *Fondation Nationale des Sciences Politiques*

- *L'Aube* (microfilm)

6. Paris, *Institut Marc Sangnier*

- Archives Marc Sangnier, carton 6: correspondance

7. Sankt-Augustin (Bonn), *Archiv für Christlich-Demokratische Politik*

- Union Mondiale de la Démocratie Chrétienne (IX-009)
- Archief Nouvelles Équipes Internationales (IX-002)
- Archief Union Européenne des Démocrates-Chrétiens (IX-004)

8. The Hague, *Algemeen Rijksarchief*

- Archief J.A. Veraart

WORKS

Abs, Robert. *Histoire du parti socialiste belge de 1885 à 1978.* Brussels: Fondation Louis de Brouckère, 1979.

Acerbi, Antonio. *La Chiesa nel tiempo. Sguardi sui progetti di relazione tra Chiesa e società civile negli ultimi cento anni.* Milan, 1984.

Adler, Friedrich. *Die Besetzung des Ruhrgebietes und die Internationale.* Vienna: Wiener Volksbuch, 1923.

Ageron, Charles-Robert. *La Décolonisation française.* Paris: Colin, 1991.

Ageron, Charles-Robert and Michel, Marc eds. *L'Afrique noire française: l'heure des Indépendances. Actes du colloque "la France et les indépendances des pays d'Afrique noire et Madagascar", organisé par l'Institut d'histoire des pays d'outre-mer et l'Institut d'histoire du temps présent, Aix-en Provence, 26-29 avril 1990.* Paris: CNRS, 1992.

Alamo de Zune, Cecilia. *Síntesis Histórica de Copei.* Caracas: Cuadernos IFEDEC, 1986.

Alba, Victor. "Spanish Diplomacy in Latin America" in: Harold Davis et al. *Latin American Foreign Policies.* Baltimore: Johns Hopkins University Press, 1975.

Allard, Jean-Louis. *L'Humanisme intégral de Jacques Maritain.* Paris-Fribourg: Saint-Paul, 1988.

Almeyda, C. "La democracía cristiana en América Latina". *Nueva Sociedad,* 14 (1986) March-April.

Almond, Gabriel A. and Verba, Sidney, eds. *The civic culture: political attitudes and democracy in five nations.* Boston: Little, Brown & Company, 1965.

Almond, Gabriel A. "The Political Ideas of Christian Democracy." *The Journal of Politics,* 10 (1948) 4, 734-763.

Alphand, Hervé. *L'étonnement d'être. Journal 1939-1973.* Paris: Fayard, 1977.

Alter, Peter. *The German Question and Europe: a history.* London: Arnold, 2000.

Altermatt, Urs. "Die stimmungslage im politischen Katholizismus der Schweiz von 1945: 'Wir lassen uns nicht ausmanövrieren'" in: Victor Conzemius, Martin Greschat et al, eds. *Die Zeit nach 1945 als Thema kirchlicher Zeitgeschichte: Referate der internationalen Tagung in Hüningen/Bern (Schweiz) 1985.* Göttingen: Vandenhoeck und Ruprecht, 1988, 72-97.

Altermatt, Urs. *Le catholicisme au défi de la modernité. L'histoire sociale des catholiques suisses aux XIXe et XXe siècles.* Lausanne: Payot, 1994.

Andras, Charles; Chenaux, Philippe and Durand, Jean-Dominique, eds. *Jacques Maritain en Europe: la réception de sa pensée.* Paris: Beauchesne, 1996. (Bibliothèque Beauchesne: Religions, société, politique, 31).

Andreotti, Giulio. *Vista da vicino.* Milan, 1982.

Arnoulx de Pirey, Elisabeth. *De Gasperi: le père italien de l'Europe.* Paris: Téqui, 1991.

Aron, Raymond. *Paix et guerre entre les nations.* Paris: Calmann-Lévy, 1968.

Atkins, G. Pope. *Latin America in the International Political System.* Boulder: Westview, 1989.

Attlee, Clement Richard. *Empire into Commonwealth. The Chichele lectures delivered at Oxford in May 1960 on Changes in the conception and structure of the British Empire during the last half century.* London: Oxford University Press, 1961.

Attlee, Clement Richard. *The Labour Party in Perspective.* London: Gollancz, 1937.

Bacharan-Gressel, Nicole. "Les organisations et les associations pro-européennes" in: Serge Berstein, Jean-Marie Mayeur and Pierre Milza, eds. *Le MRP et la Construction européenne.* Brussels: Complexe, 1993, 41-66. (Questions au XXe siècle, 57).

Baeck, Louis. *Post-War Development Theories and Practice.* Paris: Unesco, 1993.

Balandier, Georges, ed. *Le tiers monde: sous-développement et développement.* Paris: Presses universitaires de France, 1956. (Institut national d'études démographiques. Travaux et documents, 27).

Bibliography

Balfour, Michael. *Propaganda in War 1939-1945: organisations, policies and publics in Britain and Germany*. London: Routledge and Kegan Paul, 1979.

Balthazar, Herman. "De Socialistische Internationale. De Londense debatten in 1940-1941". *Bijdragen tot de Geschiedenis van de Tweede Wereldoorlog*, 2 (1972) october, 9-28.

Balthazar, Herman. "C. Huysmans en Duitsland 1936-1940" in: in Herman Balthazar, Denise De Weerdt, Wim Geldolf et al. *Bijdragen tot het Camille Huysmansonderzoek*. Antwerpen: Stichting Camille Huysmans, 1971, 171-209.

Bank, Jan. *Opkomst en ondergang van de Nederlandse Volksbeweging (NVB)*. Deventer: Kluwer, 1978.

Bartlett, C.J. *The Special Relationship: a Political History of Anglo-American relations since 1945*. London: Longman, 1992.

Becht, Manfred. *SPD, Ost-West-Konflikt und europäische Sicherheit: Sozialdemokraten und sicherheitspolitische Zusammenarbeit in Westeuropa*. Aachen: Shaker, 1997.

Becker, Winfried and Morsey, Rudolf, eds. *Christliche Demokratie in Europa. Grundlagen und Entwicklungen seit dem 19. Jahrhundert*. Cologne: Böhlau, 1988.

Beerten, Wilfried. *Le rêve travailliste en Belgique. Histoire de l'Union Démocratique Belge, 1944-1947*. Brussels: Vie ouvrière, 1990. (Histoire du mouvement ouvrier en Belgique, 11).

Beerten, Wilfried. *Union Démocratique Belge: een aanzet tot een travaillistische partij 1944-1947*. Diss. Lic., Louvain: KU Leuven, 1984.

Bellers, Jürgen. *Deutsche Europapolitik und Sozialdemokratie in den 50er und 60er Jahren*. Siegen: Universität Siegen, 2000. (Diskussionspapiere des Faches Politikwissenschaft. Rote Reihe, 38).

Bérard, Armand. *Un ambassadeur se souvient*. Paris: Plon, 1979.

Berstein, Serge and Milza, Pierre. *Histoire de la France au XXe siècle. 3: 1945-1958*. Brussels: Complexe, 1991. (Questions au XXe siècle, 23).

Berstein, Serge. *Histoire du parti radical*. 2 vols. Paris: Fondation nationale des sciences politiques, 1980-1982.

Berstein, Serge; Mayeur, Jean-Marie and Milza, Pierre, eds. *Le MRP et la Construction européenne*. Brussels: Complexe, 1993. (Questions au XXe siècle, 57).

Bethell, Leslie and Roxborough, Ian, eds. *Latin America between the Second World War and the Cold War, 1944-1948*. Cambridge: Cambridge University Press, 1992.

Bichet, Robert. *La démocratie chrétienne en France: le Mouvement républicain populaire*. Besançon: Jacques et Demontrond, 1980.

Bloch, Marc. "Pour une histoire comparée des sociétés européennes" in: Marc Bloch. *Mélanges Historiques*. 2 vols. Paris: SEVPEN, 1963.

Blom, J.C.H. and Lamberts, Emiel. *Geschiedenis van de Nederlanden*. Rijswijk: Nijgh en Van Ditmar Universitair, 1993.

Boekenstijn, A.J. "The incantation of a trojan horse, the Dutch government and the Benelux agreements" in: Michel Dumoulin, ed. *Plans des temps de guerre pour l'Europe d'après-guerre 1940-1947. Actes du colloque de Bruxelles 12-14 mai 1993*. Brussels: Bruylant, 1995, 126-152.

Bonacina, C. "Obituary - Barbara Barclay Carter". *People and Freedom,* 124 (1951), 2-3.

Bornewasser, J.A. *Katholieke Volkspartij 1945-1980. 1, Arbeid en groei (tot 1963)*. Nijmegen: Valkhof, 1995. (KDC Bronnen en studies, 26).

Bosscher, D.F.J. "De Partij van de Arbeid en het buitenlands beleid (1945-1973)". *Bijdragen en Mededelingen betreffende de geschiedenis van de Nederlanden,* 101 (1986) 1, 38-51.

Bossuat, Gérard. *L'Europe occidentale à l'heure américaine: le plan Marshall et l'unité européenne, 1945-1952.* Brussels: Complexe, 1992. (Questions au XXe siècle, 51).

Bouquet, Jean-Jacques. *Histoire de la Suisse.* Paris: Presses universitaires de France, 1995. (Que sais-je? 140).

Bowden, Jane Helen. *Development and Control in British Colonial Policy, with reference to Nigeria and the Gold Coast 1935-1948.* PhD Thesis. Birmingham: Birmingham University, 1980.

Braudel, Fernand. *La Méditerrannée et le monde mediterranneen à l'époque de Philippe II.* Paris: Colin, 1966.

Braunthal, Julius. *Geschichte der Internationale.* 3 vols. Berlin: Dietz, 1978. (Internationale Bibliothek, 108-110).

Buhite, Russell D. *Soviet-American Relations in Asia, 1945-1954.* Norman: University of Oklahoma Press, 1981.

Bühl, Walter L. *Transnationale Politik: internat. Beziehungen zwischen Hegemonie und Interdependenz.* Stuttgart: Klett-Cotta, 1978.

Bull, Hedley. *The anarchical society: a study of order in world politics.* London: Macmillan, 1979.

Bullock, Alan. *Ernest Bevin Foreign Secretary, 1945-1951.* 3 vols. London: Heinemann, 1983.

Bunza, Bohumir. *Le Parti Populaire Tchécoslovaque.* Rome: Centre international démocrate chrétien d'information et de documentation, 1971.

Burnham, James. *The Managerial Revolution.* Harmondsworth: Penguin Books, 1945. (Pelican Books, 140).

Buskes, J.J. et al. *Wat bezielt ze?* Amsterdam: Amsterdamsche Boek- en Courantmaatschappij, 1945.

Callot, Emile-François. *Le Mouvement Républicain Populaire: origine, structure, doctrine, programme et action politique.* Paris: Rivière, 1978.

Callot, Emile-François. *Un parti politique de la démocratie chrétienne en France. L'action et l'œuvre du Mouvement Républicain Populaire.* Geneva, 1986.

Calvocoressi, Peter. *World Politics since 1945.* London-New York: Longman, 1996.

Campbell, Kurt M. *Soviet Policy Towards South Africa.* New York: St. Martin's, 1986.

Capalbo, C. "A influencia de Jacques Maritain no pensamento filosófico brasileiro". *Revista bimestral de investigação e cultura.* Mai-June 1978, 281-289.

Carew, Anthony et al, eds. *The International Confederation of Free Trade Unions: A History of the Organisation and its Precursors.* Bern: Lang, 2000. (International and comparative social history, 3).

Carlson, Allan. *The Swedish Experiment in Family Politics: The Myrdals and the Interwar Population Crisis.* New Brunswick: Transaction, 1990.

Carpeaux, Otto Maria. *Alceu Amoroso Lima.* Rio de Janeiro: Graal, 1978.

Cerro, Francisco. *¿Qué es el Partido Demócrata Cristiano en la Argentina?* Buenos Aires: Editorial Sudamericana, 1983.

Bibliography

Chen, Jian. *China's Road to the Korean War: The Making of the Sino-American Confrontation*. New York: Columbia University Press, 1994.

Chenaux, Philippe. "Les Démocrates chrétiens sur le chantier de l'Europe après 1945. Le rôle de la Suisse dans une phase décisive". *Civitas*, 41 (1986), 360-364.

Chenaux, Philippe. "Les Démocrates-Chrétiens au niveau de l'Union Européenne" in: Emiel Lamberts, ed. *Christian Democracy in the European Union. 1945-1995*. Louvain: Universitaire Pers Leuven, 1997, 449-458. (KADOC-Studies, 21).

Chenaux, Philippe. "Les Nouvelles Équipes Internationales" in: Sergio Pistone, ed. *I movimenti per l'unita europea dal 1945 al 1954: atti del Convegno internazionale, Pavia, 19-20-21 ottobre 1989*. Milan: Jaco, 1992, 240-252.

Chenaux, Philippe. *Une Europe vaticane? Entre le plan Marshall et les traites de Rome*. Brussels: Ciaco, 1990.

Christian Democratic World Union. *La Démocratie chrétienne dans le monde: resolutions et déclarations des organisations internationales démocrates chrétiennes de 1947 à 1973*. Rome: Union mondiale démocrate-chrétienne, 1973. (Collection UMDC, 1).

Clark R.L. "Problems of Political Development" in: Philip Warren Thayer and William T. Phillips, eds. *Nationalismus and Progress in Free Asia*. Baltimore: Johns Hopkins Press; London: Oxford University Press, 1956.

Clissold, Stephen, ed. *Soviet relations with Latin America, 1918-1968: A Documentary Survey*. London: Oxford University Press, 1970.

Cohen, Theodore. *Remaking Japan: the American Occupation as a New Deal, 1945-1952*. New York: Free, 1987.

Cointet, Michèle. *De Gaulle et l'Algérie française 1958-1962*. Paris: Perrin, 1995.

Cole, Allan B.; Totten, George O. and Uyehara, Cecil H. *Socialist Parties in post-war Japan*. New Haven: Yale University Press, 1966. (Studies on Japan's social democratic parties, 2).

Cole, George Douglas Howard. *A History of Socialist Thought. 4, Communism and Social-Democracy 1914-1931*. London: Macmillan, 1958.

Cole, George Douglas Howard. *Europe, Russia and the Future*. London: Gollancz, 1941.

Collard, L. "The Future of Socialism". *Le Peuple*, 21/09/1959.

Collette, Christine. *The International Faith: Labour's Attitudes to European Socialism 1918-39*. Aldershot: Ashgate, 1998.

Compagnon, O. "Rafael Caldera, de la Unión Nacional Estudiantil au partido Social-Cristiano Copei: les chemins de la démocratie chrétienne (1936-1948)". *Histoire et Sociétés de l'Amérique latine*, 4 (1996), 55-75.

Connelly, Matthew. *A Diplomatic Revolution: Algeria's Fight for Independence and the Origins of the post Cold-War Era*. Oxford: Oxford University Press, 2002.

Conway, Martin. *Catholic Politics in Europe 1918-1945*. London: Routledge, 1997.

Conzemius, Victor et al, eds. *Die Zeit nach 1945 als Thema kirchlicher Zeitgeschichte: Referate der internationalen Tagung in Hünigen/Bern (Schweiz) 1985*. Göttingen: Vandenhoeck und Ruprecht, 1988.

Coolsaet, Rik. *België en zijn buitenlandse politiek 1830-1990*. Louvain: Van Halewyck, 2001.

Cosgrove-Twitchett, Carol. *Europe and Africa: from association to partnership*. Farnborough: Saxon House, 1979.

Coste-Floret, Alfred "La deuxième Conférence des Démocrates chrétiens". *Le Midi*, 19/07/1958.

Cousté, Pierre Bernard. *L'Association des pays d'outre-mer à la Communauté économique européenne*. Paris: Librairies techniques, 1959.

Cowen, Michael and Shenton, Robert. *Doctrines of Development*. London: Routledge, 1996.

Crosland, Anthony. *The Future of Socialism*. London: Cape, 1956.

Cumings, Bruce. *The Origins of the Korean War. 1, Liberation and the Emergence of Separate Regimes, 1945-1947*. Princeton: Princeton University Press, 1981.

Cumings, Bruce. *The Origins of the Korean War. 2, The Roaring of the Cataract, 1947-1950*. Princeton-Oxford: Princeton University Press, 1990.

Czempiel, Ernst-Otto, ed. *Die anachronistische Souveränität. Zum Verhältens von Innen- und Aussenpolitik*. Cologne-Opladen: Westdeutscher Verlag, 1969. (Politische Vierteljahresschrift Sonderhefte 1).

Daemen, H. "Het begrip politieke cultuur in de politicologie" in: Hans Righart, ed. *De zachte kant van de politiek. Opstellen over politieke cultuur*. The Hague: SDU, 1990, 27-35.

Dahrendorf, G. *Die Zwangsvereinigung der Kommunisten und der Sozialdemokratischen Partei in der russischen Zone*. Hamburg, 1946.

Darwin, John. *Britain and Decolonization: the Retreat from Empire in the Post-war World*. New York: St. Martin's, 1988.

De Geus, Pieter Boudewijn Richard. *De Nieuw-Guinea kwestie. Aspecten van buitenlands beleid en militaire macht*. Leiden: Nijhoff, 1984.

De Jong, L. *Het Koninkrijk der Nederlanden in de Tweede Wereldoorlog. 9, Londen*. The Hague: Staatsuitgeverij, 1979.

De Jonge, Loes. *Links-socialisme in Nederland 1944-1947: ontstaan en ontwikkeling van het eerste sociaal-democratisch centrum in de Partij van de Arbeid*. Diss. Doc., Utrecht: Universiteit Utrecht, 1983.

De Jonghe, Etienne. *Polemologische bespreking van de visie van Pius XII op de publieke opinie als vredesaktor, onderdeel van zijn vredesdenken*. Diss. Lic.,Louvain: KU Leuven, 1971.

de Onaindia, A. *Capitulos de mi vida II: Experiencias del exilio*. Buenos Aires, 1974.

De Preter, Jan. *Het ontwikkelingsdenken binnen de BSP tussen 1945 en 1965*. Diss. Lic., Louvain: KU Leuven, 1999.

De Rosa, Gabriele. *Luigi Sturzo e la democrazia europea*. Rome: Laterza, 1990.

de Senarclens, Pierre. *From Yalta to the Iron Curtain the Great Powers and the origins of the Cold War*. Oxford: Berg, 1995.

De Witte, Ludo. *Crisis in Kongo. De rol van de Verenigde Naties, de regering-Eyskens en het koningshuis in de omverwerping van Lumumba en de opkomst van Mobutu*. Louvain: Van Halewijck, 1996.

Dechert, C.R. "The Christian Democrat International". *Orbis*, 9 (1967) 1, 106-127.

Deighton, Anne, ed. *Britain and the First Cold War*. New York: St. Martin's, 1990.

Deighton, Anne. *Impossible Peace: Britain, the division of Germany and the origins of the Cold War*. Oxford: Clarendon, 1993.

Bibliography

Deighton, Anne. "Towards a 'Western' strategy: The making of British Foreign Policy towards Germany 1945-1946" in: Anne Deighton, ed. *Britain and the First Cold War*. New York: St. Martin's, 1990.

Delbreil, Jean-Claude. *Centrisme et Démocratie-Chrétienne en France. Le Parti Démocrate populaire des origines au MRP 1919-1944*. Paris: Publications de la Sorbonne, 1990. (Université de Paris I. Série France XIX-XXe, 30).

Delbreil, Jean-Claude. *Les catholiques français et les tentatives de rapprochement franco-allemand (1920-1933)*. Metz: Université de Metz: Centre de recherches Relations internationales, 1972. (Publications du Centre de recherches Relations internationales de l'Université de Metz, 2).

Delbreil, Jean-Claude. "Les démocrates d'inspiration chrétienne et les problèmes européens dans l'entre-deux-guerres" in: Serge Berstein, Jean-Marie Mayeur and Pierre Milza, eds. *Le MRP et la Construction européenne*. Brussels: Complexe, 1993, 15-40. (Questions au XXe siècle, 57).

Delwit, Pascal; Kilahci, Erol and Van de Walle, Cédric. *Les fédérations européennes de partis. Organisation et influence*. Sociologie politique. Brussels: Ed. de l'Université de Bruxelles, 2001.

Desai, A.R. *Social Background of Indian Nationalism*. Bombay, 1948.

Devin, Guillaume. *L'Internationale socialiste. Histoire et sociologie du socialisme international (1945-1990)*. Paris: Fondation nationale des sciences politiques, 1993.

Dewachter, Wilfried, ed. *Tussen Staat en Maatschappij, 1945-1995. Christen-democratie in België*. Tielt: Lannoo, 1995.

Di Biagio, A. "The Marshall Plan and the Founding of the Cominform, June-September 1947" in: Francesca Gori and Silvio Pons, eds. *The Soviet Union and Europe in the Cold War, 1943-53*. Basingstoke: Macmillan, 1996.

Di Capua, Giovanni. *Come l'Italia aderi al Patto Atlantico*. Rome: EBE, 1971.

Di Nolfo, Ennio. *Vaticano e Stati Uniti 1939-1952*. Milan: Angeli, 1978.

Divine, Robert A. *Second Chance: the Triumph of Internationalism in America during World War II*. New York: Atheneum, 1967.

Dobbs, Charles M. *The Unwanted Symbol: American Foreign Policy, the Cold War, and Korea, 1945-1950*. Kent: Kent State University Press, 1981.

Dörpinghaus, B. "Die Genfer Sitzungen. Erste Zusammenkünfte führender christlich-demokratischer Politiker in Nachkriegseuropa" in: Dieter Blumenwitz et al, eds. *Konrad Adenauer und seine Zeit: Politik und Persönlichkeit des ersten Bundeskanzlers*. Stuttgart: Deutsche Verlags-Anstalt, 1976.

Dougherty, James E. and Pfaltzgraff, Robert L. jr. *Contending Theories of International Relations*. New York: Harper & Row, 1990.

Drake, Paul W. *Socialism and Populism in Chile, 1932-52*. Urbana: University of Illinois Press, 1978.

Dreyfus, François-Georges. *Histoire des Gauches en France, 1940-1974*. Paris: Grasset, 1975.

Dreyfus, François-Georges. "Les réticences du MRP face à l'Europe 1944-1948" in: Serge Berstein, Jean-Marie Mayeur and Pierre Milza, eds. *Le MRP et la construction européenne*. Brussels: Complexe, 1993, 115-130. (Questions au XXe siècle, 57).

Dumoulin, Michel. *La construction européenne en Belgique (1945-1957)*. Louvain-la-Neuve: Ciaco, 1988.

Durand, Jean-Dominique. *L'Europe de la Démocratie chrétienne*. Brussels: Complexe, 1995. (Questions au XXe siècle, 45).

Duroselle, Jean-Baptiste. *Tout empire périra: une vision théorique des relations internationales*. Paris: Publications de la Sorbonne, 1982. (Série internationale, 16).

Ebersold, Bernd. *Machtverfall und Machtbewußtsein. Britische Friedens- und Konfliktlösungsstrategien 1918-1956*. Munich: Oldenbourg, 1992. (Beitrage zur Militärgeschiche, 31).

Edwards, Ruth Dudley. *Victor Gollancz: a biography*. London: Gollancz, 1987.

Eichler, W. "Socialist International Should Set Example". *The Leeds Weekly Citizen*, 12/06/1942.

Eisenhower, Dwight D. *The White House Years. Waging Peace 1956-1961*. London: Heinemann, 1966.

El Ayouty, Yassin. *The United Nations and decolonization. The role of Afro-Asia*. The Hague: Nijhoff, 1971.

El Khadraoui, Said. *De BSP en de heroprichting van de Socialistische Internationale. De Belgische rol in de internationale socialistische samenwerking (1945-1951)*. Diss. Lic., Louvain: KU Leuven, 1997.

Esping-Andersen, Gosta. *Politics against markets: the social democratic road to power*. Princeton: Princeton University Press, 1988.

Estorick, Eric. *Stafford Cripps: a biography*. London: Heinemann, 1949.

Ewell, J. "Venezuela since 1930" in: Leslie Bethell, ed. *The Cambridge History of Latin America. 8, Latin America since 1930: Spanish South America*. Cambridge: Cambridge University Press, 1991, 747-752.

Eyskens, Gaston and Smits, Jozef. *Gaston Eyskens: de memoires*. Tielt: Lannoo, 1994.

Fabian Colonial Bureau. *Advance to Democracy*. 1952. (Colonial Controversy Series, 8).

Fabian Colonial Bureau. *Colonies and International Conscience*. London: Gollancz, 1945. (Fabian Research Series, 92).

Fabian Colonial Bureau. *Four Colonial Questions*. London: Gollancz, 1944. (Fabian Research Series, 88).

Fabian Colonial Bureau. *Hunger and Health in the Colonies*. London: Gollancz, 1944. (Fabian Research Series, 80).

Fabian Colonial Bureau. *Kenya: White Man's Country?* London: Gollancz, 1944. (Fabian Research Series, 78).

Fabian Colonial Bureau. *Labour in the Colonies*. London: Gollancz, 1942. (Fabian Research Series, 61).

Favez, Jean-Claude ed. *Nouvelle histoire de la Suisse et des Suisses*. Lausanne: Payot, 1982.

Fawcett, Louise L'Estrange. *Iran and the Cold War: The Azerbaijan Crisis of 1946*. Cambridge-New York: Cambridge University Press, 1992.

Feld, Werner J. *Nongovernmental Forces and World Politics, A Study of Business, Labor and Political Groups*. New York: Praeger, 1972.

Filippelli, Ronald L. *American Labor and Postwar Italy, 1943-1953. A Study of Cold War Politics*. Stanford: Stanford University Press, 1989.

Bibliography

Filizzola, Renato. *Amintore Fanfani: quaresime e resurrezioni*. Rome: Editalia, 1988.

Fitzmaurice, John. *The Party Groups in the European Parliament*. Farnborough: Saxon House, 1975.

Fitzsimons, Matthew Anthony. *The Foreign Policy of the British Labour Government, 1945-1951*. Notre Dame: University of Notre Dame Press, 1953.

Fleet, Michael. *The rise and fall of Chilean Christian democracy*. Princeton: Princeton University Press, 1985.

Foote, Geoffrey. *The Labour Party's Political Thought*. London: Croom Helm, 1985.

Forman, Michael. *Nationalism and the International Labor Movement: the idea of the nation in socialist and anarchist theory*. University Park: Pennsylvania State University Press, 1998.

Frei Montalva, Eduardo. *Pensamiento y acción*. Santiago de Chile: Pacífico, 1956.

Freymond, Jacques. *Die Saar 1945-1955*. Munich: Oldenbourg, 1961.

Fulbrook, Mary. *Anatomy of a Dictatorship: Inside the GDR, 1949-1989*. Oxford: Oxford University Press, 1995.

Gaddis, John Lewis. *The Long Peace: Inquiries into the History of the Cold War*. New York-Oxford: Oxford University Press, 1987.

Gaddis, John Lewis. *We Now Know. Rethinking Cold War History*. Oxford: Clarendon, 1997.

Galbraith, John Kenneth. *The affluent society*. Boston: Houghton Mifflin, 1958.

Gallissot, R.; Paris, R. and Weill, C. "L'Internationale et la guerre: le partage d'août 1914". *Le Mouvement Social*, (1989) 147, 3-10.

Gallissot, R. "La patrie des prolétaires". *Le Mouvement Social* (1989) 147, 11-25.

Gardner, Loyd Calvin. *Spheres of Influence: The Great Powers Partition Europe, from Munich to Yalta*. Chicago: Dee, 1993.

Gaus, Helmut, ed. *Politiek biografisch lexicon: Belgische ministers en staatssecretarissen 1960-1980*. Antwerp: Standaard, 1989.

Gazmuri Riveros, Cristián; Arancibia, Patricia. and Góngora, Alvaro. *Eduardo Frei Montalva (1911-1982)*. Santiago de Chili: Fondo de Cultura Económica, 1996.

Gehler, Michael. "Begegnungsort des Kalten Krieges. Der 'Genfer Kreis' und die geheimen Absprachen westeuropäischer Christdemokraten 1947-1955" in: Michael Gehler, Wolfram Kaiser and Helmut Wohnout, eds. *Christdemokratie in Europa im 20. Jahrhundert*. Vienna: Böhlau, 2001. (Historische Forschungen: Veröffentlichungen, 4).

Gehler, Michael. "Der 'Genfer Kreis': Christdemokratische Parteienkooperation und Vertrauensbildung im Zeichen der deutsch-französischen Annäherung 1947-1955". *Zeitschrift für Geschichtswissenschaft*, 49 (2001) 7, 599-625.

Gehler, Michael. "'Politisch unabhängig', aber 'ideologisch eindeutig europäisch'. Die ÖVP, die Vereinigung christlicher Volksparteien (NEI) und die Anfänge der europäischen Integration 1947-1960" in: Michael Gehler and Rolf Steininger, eds. *Österreich und die europäische Integration, 1945-1993: Aspekte einer wechselvollen Entwicklung*. Vienna: Böhlau, 1993. (Historische Forschungen: Veröffentlichungen, 1).

Gehler, Michael. *The 'Geneva Circle' of Western European Christian Democrats*. Paper presented at the KADOC Seminar Religion and Society, Louvain, 06/12/2001.

Gehler, Michael and Steininger, Rolf, eds. *Österreich und die europäische Integration, 1945-1993: Aspekte einer wechselvollen Entwicklung.* Vienna: Böhlau, 1993. (Veröffentlichungen Arbeitskreis Europäische Integration. Historische Forschungen, 1).

Gerschenkron, Alexander. *Economic backwardness in historical perspective: a book of essays.* Cambridge (Mass.): Belknap, 1962.

Ghirardi, Enrique. *La democracía cristiana.* Buenos Aires: Centro Editor de América Latina, 1983. (Biblioteca Política argentina, 5).

Gilbert, Martin. *Winston S. Churchill. 5, 1922-1939.* London: Heinemann, 1976.

Gillingham, John. *Coal, steel, and the rebirth of Europe, 1945-1955: the Germans and French from Ruhr conflict to economic community.* Cambridge: Cambridge University Press, 1991.

Ginsborg, Paul. *A History of Contemporary Italy: Society and Politics, 1943-1988.* Harmondsworth: Penguin, 1990.

Glees, Anthony. *Exile Politics during the Second World War: the German social democrats in Britain.* Oxford: Clarendon, 1982.

Gleijeses, Piero. *Shattered Hope: the Guatemalan Revolution and the United States, 1944-1954.* Princeton: Princeton University Press, 1991.

Goddeeris, Idesbald. *De verleiding van de legitimiteit. Poolse 'Exilpolitik' in België, 1830-1870 en 1945-1980.* Diss. Doc., Louvain: KU Leuven, 2001.

Goldhamer, Herbert. *The Foreign Powers in Latin America.* Princeton: Princeton University Press, 1972.

Goldsworthy, David. *The Conservative Government and the End of Empire 1951-1957.* London: Ashton & Low, 1994.

Golsan, Richard J. "Memory's bombes à retardement: Maurice Papon, crimes against humanity, and 17 October 1961". *Journal of European Studies,* 28 (1998), 153-172.

Goncharov, Sergei N.; Lewis, John W. and Xue, Litai. *Uncertain Partners: Stalin, Mao, and the Korean War.* Stanford: Stanford University Press, 1993.

Gordon, Michael R. *Conflict and Consensus in Labour's Foreign Policy 1914-1965.* Stanford: Stanford Alumni Association, 1969.

Gori, Francesca and Pons, Silvio, eds. *The Soviet Union and Europe in the Cold War, 1943-53.* Basingstoke: Macmillan, 1996.

Gormly, James L. *From Potsdam to the Cold War: Big Three Diplomacy 1945-1947.* Wilmington: Scholary Resources Books, 1990.

Gorny, Joseph. *The British Labour Movement and Zionism, 1917-1948.* London: Frank Cass, 1983.

Gouré, Leon and Rothenberg, Morris. *Soviet Penetration of Latin America.* Miami: Center for Advanced International Studies, University of Miami, 1975.

Greilsammer, Alain. *Les mouvements fédéralistes en France de 1945 à 1947.* Paris: Presses d'Europe, 1975. (Recherches européennes et internationales, 2).

Gresch, Norbert. *Transnationale Parteienzusammenarbeit in der EG.* Baden-Baden: Nomos, 1978.

Grosbois, Thierry. *L'idée Européenne en temps de guerre dans le Benelux (1940-1944).* Louvain-la-Neuve: Academia, 1994. (Pédasup, 28).

Gross, Leonard. *The Last, Best Hope: Eduardo Frei and Chilean Democracy.* New York: Random House, 1967.

Bibliography

Gruner, Erich. *La Suisse depuis 1945: études d'histoire contemporaine.* Bern: Franke, 1971. (Helvetia politica, 6).

Guerrier, Claudine. *La Jeune République: de 1912 à 1945. Thèse pour le Doctorat d'État en Droit.* Grenoble: Service de reproduction des thèses de l'Université des sciences sociales de Grenoble, 1979.

Haas, Ernst B. *The Uniting of Europe: Political, Social and Economic Forces 1950-1957.* London: Stevens, 1958.

Hahn, Karl Josef. *La Démocratie chrétienne en Europe.* Rome: Union européenne démocrate chrétienne, 1979.

Hahn, Karl Josef. *La démocratie chrétienne dans le monde: Résolutions et déclarations des organisations internationales démocrates chrétiennes de 1947 à 1973.* Rome: Union mondiale démocrate-chrétienne, 1973. (Collection UMDC, 1).

Hall, Hessel Duncan. *Commonwealth. A History of the British Commonwealth of Nations.* London: Van Nostrand Reinhold, 1971.

Halle, L.J. "On Teaching International Relations". *The Virginia Quarterly Review*, 40 (1964) 1, 11-22.

Hamilton, Malcolm B. *Democratic Socialism in Britain and in Sweden.* Basingstoke: Macmillan, 1989.

Hanschmidt, A. "Eine christlich-demokratische 'Internationale' zwischen den Weltkriegen" in: Winfried Becker and Rudolf Morsey, eds. *Christliche Demokratie in Europa. Grundlagen und Entwicklungen seit dem 19. Jahrhundert.* Cologne: Böhlau, 1988, 153-188.

Harbutt, Fraser J. *The Iron Curtain Churchill, America and the Origins of the Cold War.* New York: Oxford University Press, 1990.

Hargreaves, John D. *Decolonization in Africa.* London: Longman, 1996.

Hartlyn, J. and Valenzuela, A. "Democracy in Latin America since 1930" in: Leslie Bethell, ed. *The Cambridge History of Latin America. 6, Latin America since 1930: economy, society and politics.* Cambridge: Cambridge University Press, 1994, 99-162.

Haseler, Stephen. *The Gaitskellites. Revisionism in the British Labour Party 1951-1964.* London: Macmillan, 1969.

Haya de la Torre, Victor Raúl. *Treinta Años de Aprismo.* Mexico City: Fondo de Cultura Económica, 1956.

Healey, Denis. *Neutralism.* London: Ampersand, 1955.

Healey, Denis, ed. *The Curtain Falls: the Story of the Socialists in Eastern Europe.* London: Lincolns-Prager, 1951.

Healey, Denis. "The International Socialist Conference 1946-1950". *International Affairs*, 26 (1950), 360-372.

Healey, Denis. *Time of My Life.* London: Joseph, 1989.

Healey, Denis. "When Shrimps Learn to Whistle: Thoughts after Geneva". *International Affairs*, 32 (1956) January, 1-10.

Hebblethwaite, Peter. "Pope Pius XII: Chaplain of the Atlantic Alliance?" in: Christopher Duggan and Christhopher Wagstaff, eds. *Italy in the Cold war: Politics, Culture and Society 1948-1958.* Oxford: Berg, 1995.

Helbling, Hanno et al. *Handbuch der Schweizer Geschichte.* Zurich: Berichthaus, 1980.

Hellema, Duco. *1956. De Nederlandse houding ten aanzien van de Hongaarse crisis en de Suezcrisis.* Amsterdam: Mets, 1990.

Herberichs, Gérard. *Théorie de la paix selon Pie XII*. Paris: Pedone, 1964.

Hetherington, S.J. *Katharine Atholl 1874-1960. Against the Tide*. Aberdeen: Aberdeen University Press, 1989.

Hettne, Bjorn. *Development Theory and the Three Worlds: towards an international and political economy of development*. Harlow: Longman Scientific & Technical, 1995.

Heywood, Andrew. *Key Concepts in Politics*. Basingstoke: Macmillan, 2000.

Hinton, Harold C. et al. *Major Governments of Asia*. Ithaca: Cornell University Press, 1963.

Hörster-Philipps, Ulrike. *Joseph Wirth 1879-1956. Eine politische Biographie*. Paderborn: F. Schöningh, 1998. (Veröffentlichungen der Kommission für Zeitgeschichte, B. Forschungen, 82).

Houben, Robert. "Démocratie Chrétienne: Partis Politiques". *Documents CEPESS*, 19 (1980) 6.

Howe, Stephen. *Anticolonialism in British politics: the left and the end of Empire, 1918-1964*. Oxford: Clarendon; New York: Oxford University Press, 1993.

Hrbek, R. "Transnational Links: The ELD and Liberal Party Group in the European Parliament" in: Emil Joseph. Kirchner, ed. *Liberal Parties in Western Europe*. Cambridge: King, 1915.

Hunin, Jan. *Camille Huysmans 1871-1968*. Diss. Doc., Louvain: KU Leuven, 1998.

Hurrell, Andrew. "The United States and Latin America" in: Ngaire Woods. *Explaining International Relations since 1945*. Oxford: Oxford University Press, 1996, 155-178.

Hustinx, Tim. *De houding van de CVP-jongeren ten aanzien van de ontwikkelingsproblematiek: van bewustwording naar grondige analyse (1951-1965)*. Diss. Lic., Louvain: KU Leuven, 2000.

Hyam, Ronald, ed. *The Labour Government and the End of Empire, 1945-1951*. London: HMSO, 1992. (British Documents on the End of Empire. Series A, 2).

Iatrides, John O. and Wringley, Linda, eds. *Greece at the Crossroads: The Civil War and Its Legacy*. University Park: Pennsylvania State University Press, 1995.

Ike, Nobutaka. "Japan" in: Harold C. Hinton et al. *Major Governments of Asia*. Ithaca: Cornell University Press, 1963, 153-259.

Iriye, Akira. *The Globalizing of America, 1913-1945*. Cambridge: Cambridge University Press, 1993. (The Cambridge History of American foreign relations, 3).

Irving, Robert Eckford Mill. *Christian Democracy in France*. London: Allen & Unwin, 1973.

Irving, Robert Eckford Mill. *The Christian Democratic Parties of Western Europe*. London: Allen & Unwin, 1979.

Jansen van Galen, John. *Ons laatste oorlogje. Nieuw-Guinea: de Pax Neerlandica, de diplomatieke kruistocht en de vervlogen droom van een Papoea-natie*. Weesp: Van Holkema en Warendorf, 1984.

Jansen, Thomas. "The Dilemma for Christian Democracy. Historical Identity and/or Political Expediency: Opening the Door to Conservatism" in: Emiel Lamberts, ed. *Christian Democracy in the European Union 1945/1995*. Louvain: Leuven University Press, 1997, 459-472. (KADOC-Studies, 21).

Jenkins, Roy. *Sir Charles Dilke: a Victorian tragedy*. London: Collins, 1958.

Bibliography

Johansson, K.M. "The Nature of Political Parties in The European Union" in: Georges A. Kourvetaris and Andreas Moschonas. *The Impact of European Integration: political, sociological, and economic changes.* Westport-London: Praeger, 1996, 201-232.

Jones, Goronwy J. *The United Nations and the Domestic Jurisdiction of States: interpretations and applications of the non-intervention principle.* Cardiff: University of Wales, Center for International Affairs, 1979.

Kaden, Albrecht. *Einheit oder Freiheit: Die Wiedergründung der SPD 1945/46.* Hannover: Dietz, 1964.

Kaiser, Karl. "Transnationale Politik, Zu einer Theorie der multinationalen Politik" in: Ernst-Otto Czempiel, ed. *Die anachronistische Souveränität: zum Verhältens von Innen- und Aussenpolitik.* Opladen: Westdeutscher Verlag, 1969, 80-109.

Kaiser, Wolfram. "Begegnungen christdemokratischer Politiker in der Nachkriegszeit" in: Martin Greschat and Wilfried Loth, eds. *Die Christen und die Entstehung der Europäischen Gemeinschaft.* Stuttgart: Kohlhammer, 1994, 139-158. (Konfession und Gesellschaft: Beitrage zur Zeitgeschichte, 5).

Kaiser, Wolfram. "Co-operation of European Catholic Politicians in Exile in Britain and the USA during the Second World War". *Journal of Contemporary History,* 35 (2000) 3, 439-465.

Karnik, V.B. *Indian Trade Unions: A Survey.* Bombay: Labour Education Service, 1960.

Katznelson, Ira and Zolberg, Aristide R, ed. *Working-class Formation. Nineteenth Century Patterns in Western Europe and the United States.* Princeton: Princeton University Press, 1986.

Keohane, Robert O. and Murphy, C.N. "International Institutions" in: Mary Hawkesworth and Maurice Kogan, eds. *Encyclopedia of government and politics.* London: Routledge, 1992, 871-886.

Keohane, Robert O. and Nye, Joseph S. Jr. *Transnational Relations and World Politics.* Cambridge (Mass.): Harvard University Press, 1972.

Khol, A. "Die internationale Parteienzusammenarbeit: Die Beziehungen der Österreichischen Volkspartei zu ihren Schwesterparteien und ihre Mitarbeit in den transnationalen Parteienzusammenschlüssen" in: Robert Kriechbaumer and Franz Schausberger, eds. *Volkspartei - Anspruch und Realität: zur Geschichte der ÖVP seit 1945.* Vienna: Böhlau, 1995, 359-369 (Schriftenreihe des Forschungsinstitutes für Politisch-Historische Studien der Dr. Wilfried Haslauer Bibliothek, 2).

Kimball, Warren F. *The Juggler: Franklin Roosevelt as wartime Statesman.* Princeton: Princeton University Press, 1991.

Klaus, Josef. *Macht und Ohnmacht in Österreich: Konfrontationen und Versuche.* Vienna: Fritz Molden 1971.

Klijn, Annemieke. *Arbeiders- of volkspartij: een vergelijkende studie van het Belgisch en Nederlands socialisme 1933-1946.* Maastricht: Universitaire Pers Maastricht, 1990.

Knipping, Franz and Weisenfeld, Ernst. *Eine ungewönliche Geschichte. Deutschland-Frankreich seit 1870.* Bonn: Europa Union, 1988.

Knopp, Eberhard. *Die Sozialistische Internationale. Herkunft, Aufbau und Ziele einer transnationalen parteienorganisation.* Diss. Doc., Heidelberg: Universität Heidelberg, 1992.

Konrad Adenauer Stiftung, ed. *Konrad Adenauer und die CDU der Britischen Besatzungszone. Dokumente zur Gründungsgeschichte der CDU Deutschlands.* Bonn: Eicholz, 1975.

Kothari, Rajni. *Politics in India.* Boston: Little, Brown & Co., 1970.

Kramer, S.P. "Belgian socialism at the liberation: 1944-1950". *Res Publica*, XX (1978) 1, 115-139.

Kriechbaumer, Robert. *Parteiprogramme im Widerstreit der Interessen. Die Programmdiskussion und die Programme von ÖVP und SPÖ 1945-1986.* Vienna: Geschichte und Politik, 1990. (Österreichisches Jahrbuch für Politik. Sonderband, 3).

Kuitenbrouwer, Maarten. *De ontdekking van de Derde Wereld. Beeldvorming en beleid in Nederland 1950-1990.* The Hague: SDU Koninginnegracht, 1994.

Kuitenbrouwer, Maarten. "Dekolonisatie en revolutie in vergelijkend perspectief: Indonesië, India en Indochina" in: Jurrien Van Goor, ed. *The Indonesian Revolution: papers of the Conference held at Utrecht, 17-20 June 1986.* Utrecht: Instituut voor Geschiedenis, 1986. (Utrechtse historische cahiers, 7.)

Kwanten, Godfried. *August-Edmond De Schryver (1898-1991): Politieke biografie van een gentleman-staatsman.* Louvain: Universitaire Pers Leuven, 2001. (KADOC-Studies, 27).

LaFeber, Walter. *America, Russia and the Cold War 1945-1992.* New York-London: McGraw-Hill, 1993.

Lafon, F. "Structures idéologiques et nécessités pratiques au congrès de la SFIO en 1946". *Revue d'histoire moderne et contemporaine*, 36 (1989), 675-9.

Lagrou, Pieter. *Heroes, Martyrs, victims. A Comparative Social History of the memory of World War II in France, Belgium and the Netherlands, 1945-1965.* Diss. Doc., Louvain: KU Leuven, 1996.

Laïdi, Zaki. *The Superpowers in Africa: the Constraints of a Rivalry, 1960-1990.* Chicago-London: University of Chicago Press, 1990.

Lakhanpal, P.L. *History of the Congress Socialist Party.* Lahore: National Publishers & Stationers, 1946.

Lamberts, Emiel, ed. *The Black International. The Holy See and the Rise of Militant Catholicism in Europe (1870-1878).* Louvain: University Press Leuven, 2002. (KADOC-Studies, 29).

Larock, Victor. "Le nationalisme". *La Grande Cause. Chroniques,* 12/03/1945.

Larock, Victor. "L'Internationale. Lettre ouverte à Morgan Phillips". *Le Peuple*, 05/01/1951.

Larock, Victor. "Une paix juste et durable". *La Grande Cause. Chroniques,* 24/03/1945.

Larson, Deborah Welch. *Origins of Containment: A Psychological Explanation.* Princeton: Princeton University Press, 1985.

Laski, Harold Joseph. *Britain and Russia: The Future.* London, s.d.

Laszlo, Leslie. *Le parti populaire démocrate-chrétien de Hongrie, 1944-1949.* Rome: Centre international démocrate-chrétien d'information et de documentation, 1982. (Cahiers d'études, 25).

Laurent, Pierre-Henri. "Beneluxer economic diplomacy and the creation of little Europe, 1945-1950". *Revue d'intégration européenne*, 10 (1986), 24-37.

Bibliography

Le Dohr, M. *Les démocrates-chrétiens français face à la construction européenne (1944-1957)*. Paris, 1991.

Leffler, Melvyn P. *A Preponderance of Power: National Security, the Truman Administration, and the Cold War*. Stanford: Stanford University Press, 1992.

Leibenstein, Harvey. *A theory of economic-demographic development*. Princeton: Princeton University Press, 1954.

Letamendia, Pierre. *Le Mouvement républicain populaire. Histoire d'un grand parti français*. Paris: Beauchesne 1995.

Lewis, William Arthur. "Economic Development with unlimited supplies of labour". *The Manchester School of Economic and Social Studies*, 22 (1954) 2, 151-162.

Lewis, William Arthur. "Industrialization of the British West Indies". *Caribbean Economic Review*, 2 (1950) 1.

Lewis, William Arthur. *The principles of economic planning: a study prepared for the Fabian Society*. London: Dobson, 1950.

Lewis, William Arthur. *The Theory of Economic Growth*. London: Allen & Unwin, 1955.

Lijphart, Arend. *The Trauma of Decolonization. The Dutch and West New Guinea*. New Haven-London: Yale University Press, 1966. (Yale studies in political science, 17).

Lindberg, Leon N. and Scheingold, Stuart Allen. *Europe's Would-Be Polity: Patterns of Change in the European Community*. Englewoods Cliffs: Prentice-Hall, 1970.

Lipgens, Walter. *Die Anfänge der Europäischen Einigungspolitik 1945-1950*. Stuttgart: Klett, 1977.

Lodge, Juliet and Herman, Valentine. *Direct Elections to the European Parliament: A Community Perspective*. London: Macmillan, 1982.

Loth, Wilfried. *Sozialismus und Internationalismus. Die französischen Sozialisten und die Nachkriegsordnung Europas 1940-1950*. Stuttgart: Deutsche Verlags-Anstalt, 1977.

Loth, Wilfried; Graml, Hermann and Wettig, Gerhard. *Die Stalin-Note vom 10. März 1952: neue Quellen und Analysen*. Munich: Oldenbourg, 2002. (Schriftenreihe der Vierteljahrshefte für Zeitgeschichte, 84).

Louis, William Roger and Bull, Hedley. *The Special Relationship: Anglo-American relations since 1945*. Oxford: Clarendon, 1989.

Louis, William Roger and Owen, Roger, eds. *Suez 1956: The Crisis and its Consequences*. Oxford: Clarendon, 1989.

Luard, Evan. *A History of the United Nations. 2, The Age of Decolonization, 1955-1965*. London: Macmillan, 1989.

Lukes, Igor. "The Czech Road to Communism" in: Norman Naimark and Leonid Gibianskii, eds. *The Establishment of Communist Regimes in Eastern Europe, 1944-1949*. Boulder-Oxford: Westview, 1997, 243-266.

Luque, Guilermo. *De la Acción Católica al partido COPEI, 1933-1946: el proceso de formación de la democracia cristiana en Venezuela*. Caracas: Fondo Editorial de Humanidades y Educación, Universidad Central de Venezuela, 1986.

Lynch, Edward A. *Latin America's Christian Democratic Parties. A Political Economy*. Westport: Praeger, 1993.

Mackenzie, Norman and Mackenzie, Jeanne, eds. *The Diary of Beatrice Webb, 1. Glitter around and darkness within.* London: Virago & London School of Economics and Political Science, 1982.

Maier, Charles S., ed. *The Marshall Plan and Germany. West German Development within the Framework of the European Recovery Plan.* New York-Oxford: Berg, 1991.

Maimann, Helene. *Politik im Wartesaal. Österreichische Exilpolitik in Grossbritannien 1938-1945.* Vienna: Böhlau, 1975. (Veröffentlichungen der Kommission für Neuere Geschichte Österreichs, 62).

Major, Patrick. *The Death of the KPD: communism and anti-communism in West Germany 1945-1956.* Oxford: Clarendon, 1997.

Malycha, Andreas. *Auf dem Weg zur SED: Die Sozialdemokratie und die Bildung einer Einheitspartei in den Ländern der SBZ: eine Quellenedition.* Bonn: Dietz Nachfolger, 1995. (Archiv für Socialgeschichte. Beiheft, 16).

Marchione, Margherita. *Pope Pius XII: architect for peace.* New York: Paulist, 2000.

Marcou, Lilly. *Le Kominform: le communisme de guerre froide.* Paris: Fondation nationale des sciences politiques, 1977.

Marks, Frederick W. "The CIA and Castillo Armas in Guatemala, 1954: New Clues to an Old Puzzle". *Diplomatic History,* 14 (1990) 1, 67-86.

Marseille, Jacques. *Empire colonial et capitalisme français: histoire d'un divorce.* Paris: Albin Michel, 1989. (Points. Histoire, 126).

Marte, Leonard Ferdinand. *Political Cycles in International Relations. The Cold War and Africa, 1945-1990.* Amsterdam: VU University Press, 1994.

Marx, Karl. "The Civil War in France" in: Karl Marx; David Fernbach, ed. *Political Writings. 3. The First International and after.* Harmondsworth: Penguin, 1974.

May, Alex, ed. *Britain, the Commonwealth and Europe: the Commonwealth and Britain's applications to join the European Communities.* Houndmills-Basingstoke-Hampshire: Palgrave, 2001.

May, Alex and Bosco, Andrea, eds. *The round table, the empire/commonwealth, and British foreign policy.* London: Lothian Foundation, 1997.

May, Ernst R., ed *American Cold War Strategy: Interpreting NSC 68.* Boston: St. Martin's, 1993.

Mayeur Jean-Marie. *Des partis catholiques à la Démocratie chrétienne: XIXe-XXe siècles.* Paris: Colin, 1980.

Mayeur, Jean-Marie. "Einige Betrachtungen über die Rolle der Christlichen Demokratie in Frankreich beim Aufbau der Demokratie und Europas nach 1945" in: Winfried Becker and Rudolf Morsey. *Christliche Demokratie in Europa. Grundlagen und Entwicklungen seit dem 19. Jahrhundert.* Cologne: Böhlau, 1988, 225-235.

Mayeur, Jean-Marie. "Pie XII et l'Europe". *Relations Internationales,* 28 (1981), 413-425.

McCullough, David. *Truman.* New York: Simon & Schuster, 1992.

Mélandri, Pierre. "Les Etats-Unis et les indépendances africaines" in: Charles-Robert Ageron and Marc Michel, eds. *L'Afrique noire française: l'heure des Indépendances. Actes du colloque "la France et les indépendances des pays d'Afrique noire et Madagascar", organisé par l'Institut d'histoire des pays d'outre-mer et l'Institut d'histoire du temps présent, Aix-en Provence, 26-29 avril 1990.* Paris: CNRS, 1992, 545-557.

Bibliography

Melgar Bao, Ricardo. *El movimiento obrero latinoamericano: historia de una clase subalterna*. Madrid: Alianza, 1988. (Alianza América, 19).

Menu, Peter. *Congresresoluties van de Vlaamse politieke partijen*. 5 vols. Ghent: Steunpunt Sociopolitiek Systeem, 1994.

Miller, Rory. *Britain and Latin America in the Nineteenth and Twentieth Centuries*. London: Longman, 1993.

Miller, Susanne and Potthoff, Heinrich. *A History of German Social Democracy. From 1848 to the Present*. Leamington: Berg, 1986.

Milward, Alan S. *The Reconstruction of Western Europe, 1945-51*. London: Methuen, 1984.

Misgeld, Klaus. *Die 'Internationale Gruppe demokratischer Sozialisten' in Stockholm 1942-1945. Zur sozialistischen Friedensdiskussion während des Zweiten Weltkrieges*. Stockholm: Almqvist & Wiksell international, 1976. (Studia historica Upsaliensa, 79).

Misgeld, Klaus. *Sozialdemokratie und Aussenpolitik in Schweden: Sozialistische Internationale, Europapolitik und die Deutschlandfrage 1945-1955*. Frankfurt am Main: Campus, 1984. Moraw, Frank. *Die Parole der "Einheit" und die Sozialdemokratie*. Bonn: Dietz, 1990.

Morgan, David John. *The Official History of Colonial Development. 5, Guidance towards self-government in British colonies, 1941-1971*. London: Macmillan, 1980.

Morgan, Patrick M. *Theories and Approaches to International Politics: What are we to think?* New Brunswick: Transaction, 1988.

Morris-Jones, Wyndraeth Humphreys. "Dominance and Dissent. Their Inter-relations in the Indian Party System". *Government and Opposition*, 1 (1966) 3, 451-466.

Morris-Jones, Wyndraeth Humpreys. *The Government and Politics of India*. London: Hutchinson & Co, 1967.

Moulián, Luis. *Eduardo Frei M. (1911-1982): biografía de un estadista utópico*. Santiago de Chile: Editorial Sudamericana, 2000.

Mourin, Maxime. *Les relations Franco-Soviétiques 1917-1967*. Paris: Payot, 1967.

Murphy, Philip. *Party Politics and Decolonization: the Conservative Party and British Colonial Policy in tropical Africa, 1951-1964*. Oxford: Clarendon, 1995.

Mutchler, David E. *The Church as a political factor in Latin America: with particular reference to Colombia and Chile*. New York: Praeger, 1971.

Nagy, Gabriel Francis. *Nouvelles Équipes Internationales and European Unity. A Study of the Organizational Search for Unity of Western European Christian Democrats*. Senior Thesis. Princeton: Princeton University, 1963.

Naimark, Norman M. *The Russians in Germany: A History of the Soviet Zone of Occupation, 1945-1949*. Cambridge (Mass.): Harvard University Press, 1995.

Nakayama, Yohei. *L'Affaiblissement de la SFIO et du MRP et la Troisième Force, 1944-1951. Déclin organisationnel, transformation interne et alliance difficile*. Paris, 1994.

Narayan, Jayaprakash. "Towards a Fuller Democracy". *The Radical Humanist,* 22 (1958) June.

Neumann, Sigmund, ed. *Modern Political Parties: Approaches to Comparative Politics*. Chicago: University of Chicago Press, 1956.

Newman, Michael. *Socialism and European Unity: the dilemma of the left in Britain and France*. London: Junction Books, 1983.

Nicolson, Harold. *Diplomacy*. London: Oxford University Press, 1950. (The home university library of modern knowledge, 192).

Niedermayer, Oskar. *Europäische Parteien? Zur grenzüberschreitenden Interaktion politischer Parteien im Rahmen der Europäischen Gemeinschaft*. Frankfurt-New York: Campus, 1983. (Campus Forschung, 289).

North, Douglass C. *Institutions, institutional change and economic performance*. Cambridge: Cambridge University Press, 1990.

Oman, Charles P. and Wignaraja, Ganeshan. *L'évolution de la pensée économique sur le développement depuis 1945*. Paris: OCDE. Centre de développement, 1991.

Orlow, D. "The Paradoxes of Success. Dutch Social Democracy and its Historiography". *Bijdragen en mededelingen betreffende de geschiedenis der Nederlanden*, 110 (1995) 1, 40-51.

Orren, Karen and Skowronek, Stephen. "Order and Time in Institutional Study: A Brief for the Historical Approach" in: James Farr, John Dryzek and Stephen T. Leonard, eds. *Political Science in History. Research Programs and Political Traditions*. Cambridge-New York: Cambridge University Press, 1995, 296-317.

Packenham, Robert A. *The Dependency Movement: Scholarship and Politics in Development Studies*. Cambridge (Mass.)-London: Harvard University Press, 1992.

Palmer, Norman Dunbar. "Political parties in India" in: Harold C. Hinton et al. *Major Governments of Asia*. Ithaca: Cornell University Press, 1965.

Palmer, Norman Dunbar. *The Indian Political System*. Boston: Houghton Mifflin, 1971.

Papini, Roberto. *Il Coraggio della Democrazia. Sturzo e l'Internazionale popolare tra le due guerre*. Rome: Studium, 1995. (La Cultura, 62).

Papini, Roberto. *L'Internazionale DC: La cooperazione tra i partiti democratici cristiani dal 1925 al 1985*. Milan: Angeli, 1986.

Papini, Roberto. "Les débuts des NEI" in: Hugues Portelli and Thomas Jansen, eds. *La Démocratie chrétienne, force internationale*. Nanterre: Université Paris X, 1986, 31-40. (Recherches de Politique Comparée, 2).

Papini, Roberto. *The Christian Democrat International*. Lanham-Oxford: Rowan & Littlefield, 1997.

Park, Richard L. "Indian Election Results". *Far Eastern Survey.*, 21 (1952) May, 61-70.

Parrish, Scott. "The Marshall Plan, Soviet-American Relations, and the Division of Europe" in: Norman Naimark and Leonid Gibianskii, eds. *The Establishment of Communist Regimes in Eastern Europe, 1944-1949*. Boulder-Oxford: Westview, 1997, 267-290.

Pastorelli, Pietro. "Die Europapolitik von Alcide de Gasperi" in: Martin Greschat and Wilfried Loth, eds. *Die Christen und die Entstehung der Europäischen Gemeinschaft*. Stuttgart: Kohlhammer, 1994, 203-228. (Konfession und Gesellschaft: Beitrage zur Zeitgeschichte, 5).

Pastorelli, Pietro. "La politica europeistica di de Gasperi" in: Pietro Pastorelli. *La politica estera italiana del dopoguerra*. Bologna: Il Mulino, 1987, 723-742.

Pasture, Patrick. "Anti-internationalisme en anti-socialisme in de christelijke arbeidersbeweging: Vlaanderen in internationaal perspectief". *Brood en Rozen*, 2 (1997) 1, 25-40.

Pasture, Patrick. *Histoire du Syndicalisme Chrétien International: la difficile recherche d'une troisième voie*. Paris: L'Harmattan, 1999.

Bibliography

Pasture, Patrick and Verberckmoes, Johan, eds. *Working-class Internationalism and the Appeal of National Identity: historical debates and current perspectives on Western Europe.* Oxford: Berg, 1998.

Pawelka, Peter. "Transnationale Parteiensysteme und Eurokommunismus" in: Hans Georg Wehling and Peter Pawelka. *Eurokommunismus und die Zukunft des Westens.* Heidelberg: von Decker, 1979, 15-28.

Pechatnov, Vladimir O. *The Big Three After World War II: New Documents on Soviet Thinking about Post-War Relations with the United States and Great Britain.* Washington D.C.: Woodrow Wilson International Center for Scholars, 1995. (Working papers Cold War International History Project, 13).

Pedone, Franco. "Il socialismo italiano di questo dopoguerra" in: Franco Pedone. *Il partito socialista italiano nei suoi congressi.* Milan: Avanti, 1968.

Pezet, Ernest. *Chrétiens au service de la Cité: de Léon XIII au Sillon et au M. R. P. 1891-1965.* Paris: Nouvelles éd. latines, 1965.

Pius XII. *Documents pontificaux de sa sainteté Pie XII.* Saint-Maurice: Saint-Augustin; Paris: Labergerie, 1954.

Pius XII and Savignat, Alain, trad. *Relations humaines et société contemporaine: synthèse chrétienne: directives de S. S. Pie XII.* Fribourg: St. Paul, 1956.

Platt, D.C.M. "British Diplomacy in Latin America since the Emancipation". *Intra-American Economic Affairs,* 21 (1967) 3, 18-35.

Poidevin, Raymond. "Die Französische Deutschlandpolitik, 1943-1949" in: Claus Scharf and Hans-Jürgen Schröder, eds. *Die Deutschlandpolitik Frankreichs und die Französische Zone, 1945-1949.* Wiesbaden: Steiner, 1983, 13-38. (Veröffentlichungen des Instituts für Europäische Geschichte Mainz. Universalgeschichte, 14).

Poidevin, Raymond. "France, the Marshall Plan and Germany" in: Charles S. Maier, ed. *The Marshall Plan and Germany. West German Development within the Framework of the European Recovery Plan.* New York-Oxford: Berg, 1991, 331-361.

Poidevin, Raymond. "Frankreich und die Deutsche Frage 1943-1949" in: Josef Becker and Andreas Hillgruber. *Die Deutsche Frage im 19. und 20. Jahrhundert: Referate und Diskussionsbeiträge eines Augsburger Symposions, 23. bis 25. September 1981.* Munich: Vögel. (Schriften der Philosophischen Fakultäten der Universität Augsburg, 24).

Poidevin, Raymond. "La France devant le danger allemand 1944-1952" in: Klaus Hildebrand and Reiner Pommerin. *Deutsche Frage und europäisches Gleichgewicht. Festschrift für Andreas Hillgruber zum 60. Geburtstag.* Cologne: Böhlau, 1985.

Poidevin, Raymond. "La France et le charbon allemand au lendemain de la deuxième guerre mondiale". *Relations internationales,* (1985) 44, 365-377.

Poidevin, Raymond. "La politique allemande de la France en 1945" in: Maurice Vaïsse, ed. *8 Mai 1945, la victoire en Europe: actes du colloque international de Reims, 1985.* Lyon: La Manufacture, 1985.

Poidevin, Raymond. "Plan Marshall et problème allemand: les inquiétudes françaises (1947-1948)" in: René Girault and Maurice Lévy-Leboyer, eds. *Le Plan Marshall et le relèvement économique de l'Europe: colloque tenu à Bercy les 21, 22 et 23 mars 1991.* Paris: Comité pour l'Histoire économique et financière de la France, Ministère de l'économie, de finances et du budget, 1993, 87-98.

Polasky, Janet. *The democratic socialism of Emile Vandervelde: between reform and revolution*. Oxford: Berg, 1995.

Portelli, Hugues. *L'Internationale socialiste*. Paris: Editions Ouvrières, 1983.

Pouthier, J.L. *Les catholiques sociaux et les démocrates chrétiens français devant l'Italie fasciste (1922-1935)*. Paris, s.d.

Power, M. Susan. *Jacques Maritain (1882-1973): christian democrat, and the quest for a new Commonwealth*. Lanham: University Press of America, 1998.

Preston, Peter Wallace. *Development Theory: an introduction*. Oxford: Blackwell, 1996.

Pridham, Geoffrey, ed. *Encouraging Democracy: The International Context of Regime Transition in Southern Europe*. Leicester: Leicester University Press, 1991.

Pridham, Geoffrey; Herring, Eric and Sanford, George, eds. *Building democracy? The international dimension of democratisation in Eastern Europe*. London: Leicester University Press, 1997.

Pridham, Geoffrey and Pridham, Pippa. *Transnational Party Co-operation and European Integration: The Process towards Direct Elections*. London: Allen & Unwin, 1981.

Putnam, Robert D. "Diplomacy and Domestic Politics: The Logic of Two-Level Games". *International Organization*, 42 (1988) Summer, 427-460.

Pye, Lucian. "Party Systems and National Development in Asia" in: Joseph LaPalombara and Myron Weiner, eds. *Political Parties and Political Development*. Princeton: Princeton University Press, 1966. (Studies in political development, 6).

Rabe, Stephen G. *Eisenhower and Latin America: The Foreign Policy of Anticommunism*. Chapel Hill-London: University of North Carolina Press, 1988.

Radkau, Joachim. *Die deutsche Emigration in den USA. Ihr Einfluß auf die amerikanische Europapolitik 1933-1945*. Düsseldorf: Bertelsmann Universitätsverlag, 1971. (Studien zur moderne Geschichte, 2).

Rane M.A., ed. *Festschrift V.M. Tarkunde 90: A Restless Crusader for Human Freedoms*. Mumbai, 1993.

Reid, Escott. *Time of Fear and Hope: the making of the North Atlantic Treaty 1947-1949*. Toronto: McClelland and Stewart, 1977.

Reynolds, David. "Great Britain" in: David Reynolds, ed. *The Origins of the Cold War in Europe*. New Haven-London: Yale University Press, 1994.

Riccardi, Andrea. *Il potere del papa. Da Pio XII a Paolo VI*. Rome: Laterza, 1988.

Riccardi, Andrea. *Pio XII*. Bari: Laterza, 1984.

Righart, Hans, ed. *De zachte kant van de politiek. Opstellen over politieke cultuur*. The Hague: SDU, 1990.

Rimbaud, Christiane. *Maurice Schumann: sa voix, son visage*. Paris: Odile Jacob, 2000.

Rioux, Jean-Pierre. *La France de la Quatrième République*. 2 vols. Paris: Seuil, 1980-1983. (Nouvelle histoire de la France contemporaine, 15-16).

Ritzel, Heinrich Georg. *Kurt Schumacher in Selbstzeugnissen und Bilddokumenten*. Reinbek bei Hamburg: Rowohlt, 1972. (Rowohlts Monographien, 184).

Bibliography

Rivlin, B. "Context and sources of political tensions in French North Africa". *The Annals of the American Academy of Political and Social Science,* 298 (1955) March, 124-143.

Roberts, G. "Moscow and the Marshall Plan: Politics, Ideology, and the Onset of the Cold War, 1947". *Europe-Asia Studies,* 46 (1994), 1371-1386.

Rodríguez Arias Bustamante, Lino. *La democracia cristiana y América Latina:* testimonios de una posición revolucionaria. Lima: Editorial Universitaria, 1961. (Biblioteca de divulgación popular, 5).

Roman, Eric. *Hungary and the Victor Powers, 1945-1950.* New York: St. Martin's, 1996.

Rose, Saul. *Socialism in Southern Asia.* London-New York: Oxford University Press, 1959.

Rosenau, James N., ed. *Linkage Politics: Essays on the Convergence of National and International Systems.* New York: Free; London: Collier-Macmillan, 1969.

Rosenau, James N. *Turbulence in World Politics. A Theory of Change and Continuity.* Princeton: Princeton University Press, 1990.

Rosenstein-Rodan, P.N. "Notes on the theory of the Big Push" in: Howard S. Ellis and Henry C. Wallich, eds. *Economic Development for Latin America: proceedings of a conference held by the International Economic Association.* London: Macmillan, 1961, 57-81.

Rossini, Giuseppe. "I tentativi per un 'Internazionale Popolare'" in: Luigi Sturzo. *Luigi Sturzo: saggi e testimonianze.* Rome: Civitas, 1960, 199-219.

Rossini, Giuseppe. *Il Movimento Cattolico nel periodo fascista: momenti e problemi.* Rome: 5 Lune, 1966.

Rostow, Walt Whitman. *The Stages of Economic Growth: a non-communist manifesto.* New York, 1959.

Rusch, T.A. "Dynamics of Socialist Leadership in India" in: Richard L. Park and Irene Tinker, eds. *Leadership and Political Institutions in India. Seminar on Leadership and Political Institutions in India.* New York: Greenwood, 1969, 204-208.

Rutschke, Gabriele. *Die Mitwirkung der Fraktionen bei der parlementarischen Willensbildung im Europäischen Parlament im Vergleich zu den Parlamenten der Mitgliedstaaten.* Frankfurt am Main: Lang, 1986. (Europäische Hochschulschriften 2. Rechtswissenschaft, 574).

Sainsbury, Diane. *Swedish Social Democratic Ideology and Electoral Politics 1944-1948: a study of the functions of party ideology.* Stockholm: Almqvist & Wiksell International, 1980. (Stockholm studies in politics, 17).

Salemink, Theodorus. *Krisis en konfessie, ideologie en katholiek Nederland 1917-1933.* Zeist: NCSV, 1980.

Sartori, Giovanni. *Parties and Party Systems: A Framework for Analysis.* Cambridge: Cambridge University Press, 1976.

Sassoon, David. *One Hundred Years of Socialism: the West European Left in the twentieth century.* London: Fontana, 1997.

Sauvant, K.P. "Die Institutionalisierung der internationalen Zusammenarbeit" in: Klaus von Beyme et al, eds. *Politikwissenschaft. Eine Grundlegung. 3, Außenpolitik und Internationale Politik.* Stuttgart: Kohlhammer, 1987, 70-97.

Sauvy, A. "Trois Mondes, Une Planète". *L'Observateur,* 14/08/1952, 14-15.

Schaller, Michael. *Douglas MacArthur: The Far Eastern General.* New York-Oxford: Oxford University Press, 1989.

Schaller, Michael. *The American Occupation of Japan: The Origins of the Cold War in Asia*. New York-Oxford: Oxford University Press, 1985.

Schmiermann, Sjef. *Prof. Dr. J.A. Veraart (1886-1955): aspecten van het politieke leven van een recalcitrant katholiek democraat*. Nijmegen: Katholiek Documentatie Centrum, 1990.

Schmiermann, Sjef. "Prof. Dr. J.A. Veraart (1886-1955): een recalcitrant katholiek democraat" in: *Jaarboek van het Katholiek Documentatie Centrum Nijmegen*. Nijmegen, 1990, 119-131.

Schneer, Jonathan. *Labour's Conscience: the Labour left, 1945-1951*. Boston-London: Unwin Hyman, 1988.

Schneider, Burkhart. *Pius XII. Friede, das Werk der Gerechtigkeit*. Göttingen: Musterschmidt, 1968. (Persönlichkeit und Geschichte, 47).

Schonberger, Howard B. *Aftermath of war: Americans and the remaking of Japan, 1945-1952*. Kent-London: Kent State University Press, 1989.

Schreiner, Reinhard. *Bidault, der MRP und die französische Deutschlandpolitik, 1944-1948*. Frankfurt am Main: Lang, 1985. (Europäische Hochschulschriften 3. Geschichte und ihre Hilfswissenschaften, 270).

Schuman, Robert. *Il Piano Schuman: critiche e obiezioni nei Paesi partecipanti*. Rome, 1952. (Quademi di orientamenti, 11).

Schumann, Maurice. "Hésitation au bord de la folie". *L'Aube*, 20/02/1948.

Schumann, Maurice. "L'Exemple belge". *L'Aube*, 16/02/1945.

Schumann, Maurice. "Non! Le monde ne se divise pas en deux blocs". *L'Aube*, 18-19/01/1948.

Schumpeter, Joseph. *Capitalisme, socialisme et démocratie*. Paris: Payot, 1954.

Schuurman, F.J. "Paradigms lost, paradigm regained? Development studies in the twenty-first century". *Third World Quarterly*, 21 (2000) 1, 7-20.

Schwabe, Klaus, ed. *Die Anfänge des Schuman-Plans, 1950/1951: Beiträge des Kolloquiums in Aachen, 28.-30. Mai 1986*. Baden-Baden: Nomos, 1988. (Publications of the European Community Liaison Committee of Historians, 2).

Schwarte, Johannes. *Gustav Gundlach s.j. (1892-1963). Maßgeblicher Repräsentant der katholischen Soziallehre während der Pontifikate Pius' XI und Pius' XII*. Munich: F. Schöningh, 1975. (Abhandlungen zur Socialethik, 9).

Schwartz, Hans-Peter, ed. *Die legende von der verpassten Gelegenheit: die Stalin-Note vom 10. März 1952*. Stuttgart: Belser, 1982. (Rhöndorfer Gespräche, 5).

Schwarzmantel, John. *Socialism and the Idea of the Nation*. London: Harvester Wheatsheaf, 1991.

Shepsle, K.A. "Studying Institutions" in: James Farr, John S. Dryzek and Stephen T. Leonard, eds. *Political Science in history: research programs and political traditions*. Cambridge: Cambridge University Press, 1995, 276-295.

Shu-Yun, M. "Third World studies, development studies and post-communist studies: definitions, distance and dynamism". *Third World Quarterly*, 19 (1998) 3, 339-348.

Sieniewicz, Konrad. *Le parti chrétien du travail polonais*. Rome: Centre international démocrate chrétien d'information et de documentation, 1975.

Sieyes, Emmanuel Joseph and Tulard, Jean. *Qu'est-ce que le Tiers État?* Paris: PUF, 1982. (Quadrige, 30).

Bibliography

Sigmund, P.E. "Christian Democracy in Chile". *Journal of International Affairs,* 20 (1966), 332-342.

Singh, Hari Kishore. *A History of the Praja Socialist Party, 1934-1959.* Lucknow: Prakashan, 1959.

Sinha, Lalan Prasad. *Left Wing in India, 1919-1947.* Muzaffarpur: New, 1965.

Skjelsbaeck, K. "The Growth of International Non-governmental Organization in the Twentieth Century". *International Organization,* 25 (1971), 435-438.

Smets, Paul-F. *Il faut faire l'Europe. Trente ans de la vie et des combats de Paul-Henri Spaak.* Brussels: Fondation Paul-Henri Spaak, 1992.

Smyser, W.R. *From Yalta to Berlin.* New York: St. Martin's, 1999.

Soutou, G. "Georges Bidault et la Construction européenne 1944-1954". *Revue d'histoire diplomatique,* (1997) 111, 267-356.

Staritz, D. "Zur Gründung der SED: Forschungsstand, Kontroversen, offene Fragen" in: Dietrich Staritz. *Was war: Historische Studien zu Geschichte und Politik der DDR; zum 60. Geburtstag des Autors herausgegeben von Günter Braun und Hermann Schwenger.* Berlin: Metropol, 1994, 105-136.

Stavrianos, Leften Stavros. *Global Rift: The Third World Comes of Age.* New York: Morrow, 1981.

Steininger, Rolf. "British Labour". *Internationale wissenschaftliche Korrespondenz zur Geschichte der deutschen Arbeiterbewegung,* 15 (1979), 188-225.

Steininger, Rolf. *Deutschland und die Sozialistische Internationale nach dem Zweiten Weltkrieg. Die deutsche Frage, die Internationale und das Problem der Wiederaufnahme der SPD auf den internationalen sozialistischen Konferenzen bis 1951, unter besonderer Berücksichtigung der Labour Party. Darstellung und Dokumentation.* Bonn: Neue Gesellschaft, 1979. (Archiv für Sozialgeschichte, 7).

Steininger, Rolf. "Die Rhein-Ruhr-Frage im Kontext britischer Deutschlandpolitik 1945/46". *Geschichte und Gesellschaft, Sonderheft,* 5 (1979), 111-166.

Steininger, Rolf. *The German Question: The Stalin-Note of 1952 and the Problem of Reunification.* New York: Columbia University Press, 1990.

Strachey, John. *The End of Empire.* London: Gollancz, 1959. (Principles of democratic socialism, 2).

Stueck, William. *The Korean War: An International History.* Princeton: Princeton University Press, 1995.

Szulc, Tad. *Twilight of the Tyrants.* New York: Henry Holt & Co., 1959.

Theberge, James D. *The Soviet Presence in Latin America.* New York: Crane, Russak, 1974. (Strategy papers National Strategy Information Center, 23).

Thomas, Hugh. *The Suez Affair.* London: Weidenfeld & Nicolson, 1967.

Thomas, Martin. "France accused: French North Africa before the United Nations, 1952-1962". *Contemporary European History,* 10 (2001) March, 94-113.

Thorpe, Andrew. *A History of the British Labour Party.* Basingstoke: Macmillan, 1997.

Tilton, Tom. *The Political Theory of Swedish Social Democracy. Through Welfare State to Socialism.* Oxford: Clarendon, 1990.

Touchard, Jean. *La gauche en France depuis 1900*. Paris: Seuil, 1977. (Collection Points, Histoire, 26).

Tucker, William Rayburn. *The Attitude of the British Labour Party toward European and Collective Security Problems, 1920-1939*. Geneva, 1950.

Uertz, Rudolf. *Christentum und Sozialismus in der frühen CDU: Grundlagen und Wirkungen der christlich-sozialen Ideen in der Union 1945-1949*. Stuttgart: Deutsche Verlags-Anstalt, 1981. (Schriftenreihe der Vierteljahrshefte zür Zeitgeschichte, 43).

United Nations Relief and Rehabilitation Administration. *The Story of UNRRA*. Washington D.C.: UNRRA-Office of Public Information, 1948.

United Nations. *Yearbook of the United Nations 1951*. New York, 1952.

Urwin, Derek W. *A Political History of Western Europe since 1945*. London: Longman, 1997.

Urwin, Derek. *Western Europe since 1945. A short political History*. London: Longman, 1981.

US Department of State. *A Decade of American Foreign Policy, basic Documents 1941-49. Prepared at the Request of the Senate Committee on Foreign Relations by the staff of the Committee and the Department of State*. Washington D.C.: United States Government Printing Office, 1950, 1299-1300. (Document United States. 81st Congres, 1. 1950. Senate, 123).

Vaïsse, Maurice. *La grandeur. Politique étrangère du général de Gaulle 1958-1969*. Paris: Fayard, 1998.

Van de Klashorst, G.O. "Politieke Cultuur: het klassieke begrip en een nieuwe werkdefinitie" in: Hans Righart. *De zachte kant van de politiek. Opstellen over politieke cultuur*. The Hague: SDU, 1990, 51-68.

Van den Doel, H.W. *Afscheid van Indië. De val van het Nederlandse imperium in Azië*. Amsterdam: Prometheus, 2000.

Van der Linden, Marcel. "The National Integration of European Working Classes. Explaining the Causal Configuration". *International Review of Social History*, 33 (1988), 285-311.

Van Dijl, R. *The Stalin-Note: Last Chance for Unification? Paper presented at the conference "The Soviet Union, Germany, and the Cold war, 1945-1962: New Evidence from the Eastern Archives."* Essen-Potsdam, 28/06 - 03/07/1994.

Van Holthoon, Fritz and Van der Linden, Marcel, eds. *Internationalism in the Labour Movement 1830-1940*. Leiden: Brill, 1988.

Van Kemseke, Peter. "From Permission to Prohibition. The Impact of the Changing International Context on Left Catholicism in Europe" in: Gerd-Rainer Horn and Emmanuel Gerard, eds. *Left Catholicism. Catholics and Society in Western Europe at the Point of Liberation 1943-1955*. Louvain: University Press Leuven, 2001, 257-258. (KADOC-Studies, 25).

Van Kemseke, Peter. "The societal position of Christian Democracy in France" in: Emiel Lamberts, ed. *Christian Democracy in the European Union 1945-1995*. Louvain: University Press Leuven, 1997, 174-188. (KADOC-Studies, 21).

Van Oudenhove, Guy. *The Political Parties in the European Parliament: The First Ten Years (September 1952-September 1962)*. Leiden: Sijthoff, 1965. (European aspects, Serie C. Studies on politics, 18).

Bibliography

Vanwelkenhuyzen, Jean. *Les avertissements qui venaient de Berlin. 9 octobre 1939-10 mai 1940*. Brussels, 1979.

Vecchio, Giorgo. *La democrazia cristiana in Europa (1891-1963)*. Milan: Mursia, 1979.

Veraart, J.A. "Internationaal werk in Londen. Fragmenten uit mijn dagboek 1940-1945". *Katholiek Cultureel Tijdschrift,* 76 (1946-1947) 140, 54-68.

Villaça, Antonio Carlos. *O desafio da liberdade: a vida de Alceu Amoroso Lima*. São Paulo: Livraria AGIR, 1983.

Vital, David. *Zionism: the Formative Years*. Oxford: Clarendon, 1982.

Voller, L. "Die europäische Sendung der Alpenländer". *Civitas,* (1945-1946), 286-290.

von Beyme, Klaus. *Parteien in westlichen Demokratien*. Munich: Piper, 1982.

Wahlers, G. "CLAT: Geschichte einer latein-amerikanischen Gewerkschaftsinternationale". *Beiträge zu Wirtschafts- und Sozialwissenschaffen,* 12 (1990), 78-85.

Wall, Irwin M. *France, the United States and the Algerian War*. Berkeley-London: University of California Press, 2001.

Wall, Irwin M. *French Communism in the Era of Stalin. The Quest for Unity and Integration, 1945-1962*. Contributions to European integration. Westport (Conn.)-London: Greenwood, 1983.

Wall, Irwin M. "The United States, Algeria and the Fall of the Fourth French Republic". *Diplomatic History,* 18 (1994), 481-493.

Walling, William English ed. *The Socialists and the War: a documentary statement of the position of the socialists of all countries: with special reference to their peace policy. Including a summary of the revolutionary state socialist measures adopted by the governments at war*. New York: Holt, 1915.

Warner, Isabel. *Steel and sovereignty: the deconcentration of the West German steel industry, 1949-1954*. Mainz: von Zabern, 1996. (Veröffentlichungen des Instituts für Europäische Geschichte Mainz, Abteilung Universalgeschichte, 162)

Warner, Michael, ed. *The CIA under Harry Truman*. Washington DC: Central Intelligence Agency, 1994.

Weathersby, Kathryn. *Soviet arms in Korea and the origins of the Korean War, 1945-1950: New evidence from the Russian Archives*. Washington D.C.: Woodrow Wilson International Center for Scholars, 1993. (Cold War History Project Working Paper, 8.)

Wellens, Karel C., ed. *Resolutions and Statements of the United Nations Security Council (1946-1992). A Thematic Guide*. Dordrecht-London: Nijhoff, 1993.

Wesseling, H. L. *Indië verloren, rampspoed geboren en andere opstellen over de geschiedenis van de Europese expansie*. Amsterdam: Bakker, 1988.

Westad, Odd Arne. *Cold War and Revolution: Soviet-American Rivalry and the Origins of the Chinese Civil War, 1944-1946*. New York: Columbia University Press, 1993.

Wheen, Francis. *Tom Driberg: his life and indiscretions.* London: Chatto & Windus, 1990.

Wiebes, Cornelis and Zeeman, Bert. *Belgium, the Netherlands and alliances, 1940-1949*. Diss. Doct., Leiden: Universiteit Leiden, 1993.

Willetts, Peter. *The Non-Aligned Movement: the Origins of a Third World Alliance*. London: Pinter, 1978.

Wolfers, A. "The Actors in International Politics" in: William Thornton Rickert Fox, ed. *Theoretical Aspects of International Relations*. Notre Dame: University of Notre Dame Press, 1959, 83-106.

Woods, Randall Bennett. *A Changing of the Guard: Anglo-American Relations, 1941-1946*. Chapel Hill: University of North Carolina Press, 1990.

Wright, Thomas C. *Latin America in the Era of the Cuban Revolution*. Westport: Praeger, 1991.

Wrynn, John Francis Patrick. *The Socialist International and the Politics of European Reconstruction 1919-1930*. Diss. Doct., Amsterdam: Vrije Universiteit, 1976.

Yegorova, Natalia I. *The Iran Crisis of 1944-46: A View from the Russian Archives*. Washington D.C.: Woodrow Wilson International Center for Scholars, 1996. (Working Paper Cold War International History Project, 15).

Young, John W. *Britain, France and the Unity of Europe 1945-1951*. Leicester: Leicester University Press, 1984.

Zolberg, Aristide R. "How many Exceptionalisms?" in: Ira Katznelson and Aristide R. Zolberg, ed. *Working-class Formation. Nineteenth Century Patterns in Western Europe and the United States*. Princeton: Princeton University Press, 1986, 397-456.

Zubok, Vladislav and Pleshakov, Constantine. *Inside the Kremlin's Cold War: From Stalin to Khrushchev*. Cambridge (Mass.)-London: Harvard University Press, 1996.

Index

Index

Colophon

Author
Peter Van Kemseke studied history at the K.U.Leuven (Belgium) and the
University of Hull (UK), and obtained a Master of Arts in International
Relations at CSU Los Angeles (US). In 2001, he obtained a PhD degree in
history with a study on "The Cold War and the Discovery of the Third World
in International Socialism and International Christian Democracy".
He currently works as a Belgian diplomat at the Permanent Representation of
Belgium to the United Nations in New York.

The content of this publication solely reflects the personal opinions of the
author and doesn't necessarily represent the official position of the Federal
Public Service Foreign Affairs of Belgium.

Final Editing
Hanne Van Herck
Luc Vints

Translation
Colin Batch

Proofreading
Peter Schoenaerts
Jesse Mintz-Roth

Lay-out
Alexis Vermeylen

Printing Office
Walleyn, Brugge

KADOC
Documentation and Research Centre for Religion, Culture and Society
Vlamingenstraat 39 B - 3000 Leuven
tel. +32 16 32 35 00 fax +32 16 32 35 01
e-mail: postmaster@kadoc.kuleuven.be
website: http://kadoc.kuleuven.be

www.ingramcontent.com/pod-product-compliance
Lightning Source LLC
Chambersburg PA
CBHW080849300326

41935CB00040B/1581